Tokyo

"All you've got to do is decide to go
and the hardest part is over.

So go!"

TONY WHEELER, COFOUNDER – LONELY PLANET

Rebecca Milner, Simon Richmond

Contents

Plan Your Trip 4

Welcome to Tokyo..........4
Tokyo's Top 16 6
What's New....................17
Need to Know 18
Top Itineraries 20

If You Like... 22
Month by Month 24
With Kids 28
Like a Local 29
For Free 31

Eating 32
Drinking &
Nightlife 41
Entertainment 44
Shopping.....................46

Explore Tokyo 50

Neighbourhoods
at a Glance 52
Marunouchi
& Nihombashi............... 54
Ginza & Tsukiji 65
Roppongi, Akasaka &
Around...........................76
Ebisu, Meguro
& Around 87

Shibuya &
Shimo-Kitazawa.......... 95
Harajuku & Aoyama .. 106
West Tokyo 118
Shinjuku &
Northwest Tokyo........125
Kōrakuen &
Akihabara 136

Ueno & Yanesen 147
Asakusa &
Sumida River 159
Odaiba & Tokyo Bay... 171
Day Trips
from Tokyo 177
Sleeping 191

Understand Tokyo 201

Tokyo Today...............202
History.......................204

Pop Culture.................213
Arts & Architecture....218

Onsen 227

Survival Guide 231

Transport 232
Directory A–Z 238

Language 245
Index 255

Tokyo Maps 263

(left) **Koishikawa Kōrakuen p138** Formal strolling garden.

(above) **Akihabara p136** Electronics district.

(right) **Yakitori p36** Chicken skewers.

West Tokyo
p118

Shinjuku & Northwest Tokyo
p125

Ueno & Yanesen
p147

Asakusa & Sumida River
p159

Kōrakuen & Akihabara
p136

Marunouchi & Nihombashi
p54

Harajuku & Aoyama
p106

Roppongi, Akasaka & Around
p76

Ginza & Tsukiji
p65

Shibuya & Shimo-Kitazawa
p95

Ebisu, Meguro & Around
p87

Odaiba & Tokyo Bay
p171

Welcome to Tokyo

Yoking past and future, Tokyo dazzles with its traditional culture and passion for everything new.

Sci-fi Cityscapes

Tokyo's neon-lit streetscapes still look like a sci-fi film set – and that's a vision of the city from the 1980s. Tokyo has been building ever since, pushing the boundaries of what's possible on densely populated, earthquake-prone land, adding ever taller, sleeker structures. Come see the utopian mega-malls, the edgy designer boutiques from Japan's award-winning architects, and the world's tallest tower – Tokyo Sky Tree – a twisting spire that draws on ancient building techniques. Stand atop one of Tokyo's skyscrapers and look out over the city at night to see it blinking like the control panel of a starship, stretching all the way to the horizon.

The Shogun's City

Tokyo may be forever reaching into the future but you can still see traces of the shogun's capital on the kabuki stage, at a sumo tournament or under the cherry blossoms. It's a modern city built on old patterns, and in the shadows of skyscrapers you can find anachronistic wooden shanty bars and quiet alleys, raucous traditional festivals and lantern-lit *yakitori* (grilled chicken) stands. In older neighbourhoods you can shop for handicrafts made just as they have been for centuries, or wander down cobblestone lanes where geisha once trod.

Eat Your Heart Out

Yes, Tokyo has more Michelin stars than any other city. Yes, Japanese cuisine has been added to the Unesco Intangible Cultural Heritage list. But that's not what makes dining in Tokyo such an amazing experience. What really counts is the city's long-standing artisan culture. You can splash out on the best sushi of your life, made by one of the city's legendary chefs using the freshest, seasonal market ingredients. You can also spend ¥800 on a bowl of noodles made with the same care and exacting attention to detail, from a recipe honed through decades of experience.

Fashion & Pop Culture

From giant robots to saucer-eyed schoolgirls to a certain, ubiquitous kitty, Japanese pop culture is a phenomenon that has reached far around the world. Tokyo is the country's pop-culture laboratory, where new trends grow legs. Come see the latest looks bubbling out of the backstreets of Harajuku, the hottest pop stars projected on the giant video screens in Shibuya, or the newest anime and manga flying off the shelves in Akihabara. Gawk at the giant statues of Godzilla; shop for your favourite character goods; or pick up some style inspiration just walking down the street.

Why I Love Tokyo

By Rebecca Milner, Writer

I've lived in Tokyo for 15 years now and am continuously surprised – sometimes on a daily basis – by something new. Such is the joy of living in a city that prides itself on constant renewal and reinvention; it seriously never gets old. Tokyo has everything you can ask of a city, and has it in spades: a rich, cosmopolitan dining scene, more cafes and bars than you could visit in a lifetime, fantastic public transport and grassy parks – plus it's clean and safe. Really, what's not to love?

For more about our writers, see p288

Top: Alley in Shinjuku (p125)

Tokyo's
Top 16

Shinjuku Nightlife (p134)

1 Shinjuku is the biggest, brashest nightlife district in the land of the rising neon sun. There is truly something for everyone here, from the anachronistic shanty bars of Golden Gai, a favourite haunt of writers and artists, to the camp dance bars of Tokyo's gay quarter, Shinjuku-nichōme, and the more risqué cabarets of Kabukichō. There are sky-high lounges, all-night karaoke parlours, jazz dens and *izakaya* (Japanese pub-eateries) stacked several storeys high. The options are dizzying, the lights spellbinding and the whole show continues past dawn.

BELOW LEFT: KABUKICHŌ

Tsukiji Market (p67)

2 Don't mourn Tsukiji yet; while the seafood market may very well move, the lively outer market isn't going anywhere. And it's here that you can wander the stalls snacking on treats from producers that sell *tamago* (rolled omelettes) and *kamaboko* (steamed fish paste) to top Tokyo restaurants; shop for professional quality kitchen tools, such as hand-forged knives and bamboo steamer baskets; listen to the banter of the merchants and their regular customers; and bask in the energy of a storied, old-style, open-air market.

Meiji-jingū *(p108)*

3 Tokyo's largest and most famous Shintō shrine feels a world away from the city. It's reached via a long, rambling forest path marked by towering *torii* (gates). The grounds are vast, enveloping the classic wooden shrine buildings and a landscaped garden in a thick coat of green. Meiji-jingū is a place of worship and a memorial to Emperor Meiji, but it's also a place for traditional festivals and rituals. If you're lucky you may even catch a wedding procession, with the bride and groom in traditional dress.

Dining Out *(p32)*

4 When it comes to Tokyo superlatives, the city's eating scene takes the cake. Wherever you are, you're rarely 500m from a good, if not great, restaurant. It's a scene that careens gracefully between the highs and lows: it's not odd for a top-class sushi restaurant to share the same block as an oil-spattered noodle joint (and the latter might be no less fawned over). Tokyoites love dining out; join them, and delight in the sheer variety of flavours the city has to offer. BOTTOM LEFT: OKONOMI-YAKI (SAVOURY PANCAKES; P37)

Tokyo Cityscape *(p127)*

5 There's nothing quite like gazing out over the Tokyo cityscape from a few hundred metres in the air. From this vantage point, the city is endless, stretching all the way to the horizon (where, if you're lucky, you might spot Mt Fuji). By night, Tokyo appears truly beautiful, as if the sky were inverted, with the glittering stars below. Take in the view from a stylish hotel lounge, atop one of the city's towers or from the (free!) observatories at the Tokyo Metropolitan Government Building.

Shopping in Harajuku (p116)

6 Harajuku is the gathering point for Tokyo's eccentric fashion tribes. The tightly packed pedestrian alley Takeshita-dōri is a beacon for teens in kooky, colourful outfits. Omote-sandō, a broad boulevard with wide pavements and high-end designer boutiques, draws polished divas. The backstreets of Harajuku (known as Ura-Hara) form Tokyo's street fashion laboratory; here's where you'll find the trendsetters, the peacocks and the style photographers who chronicle it all – plus inspiration by the truckload. Simply put: for shopping (and people-watching) there's no better spot in Tokyo than Harajuku.

Roppongi Art Triangle (p77)

7 The opening of three high-profile art museums since 2003 has turned Roppongi, once known exclusively for its bawdy nightlife, into a polished gem. The area nicknamed 'Roppongi Art Triangle' includes the Mori Art Museum, a showcase for contemporary art perched atop a skyscraper; the minimalist Suntory Museum of Art, dedicated to the decorative arts; and the National Art Center Tokyo, which hosts blockbuster shows inside a curving glass structure. Within the triangle there are several smaller museums and galleries too. TOP RIGHT: SUNTORY MUSEUM OF ART (P79)

Sensō-ji *(p161)*

8 The spiritual home of Tokyo's ancestors, this Buddhist temple was founded over one thousand years before the city got its start. Today it retains an alluring, lively atmosphere redolent of Edo (old Tokyo) and the merchant quarters of yesteryear. The colourful Nakamise-dōri arcade approaching the temple complex overflows with vendors selling snacks and souvenirs. The main plaza holds a newly renovated five-storey pagoda and a smoking cauldron of incense. Altogether, Sensō-ji is a heady mix of secular and sacred, and one of Tokyo's most iconic sights.

Sumo in Ryōgoku *(p168)*

9 The purifying salt sails into the air. The two giants leap up and crash into each other. A flurry of slapping and heaving ensues. Who will shove the other out of the sacred ring and move up in the ranks? From the ancient rituals to the thrill of the quick bouts, sumo is a fascinating spectacle. Tournaments take place in Tokyo three times a year; outside of tournament season you can catch an early morning practice session at one of the stables where wrestlers live and train.

Cherry Blossoms in Yoyogi-kōen *(p109)*

10 Come spring, thousands of cherry trees around the city burst into white and pink flowers. If Tokyoites have one moment to let their hair down en masse, this is it. They gather in parks and along river banks for sake-fuelled cherry-blossom-viewing parties called *hanami*. Grassy Yoyogi-kōen, one of the city's largest parks, is where you'll find some of the most spirited and elaborate bacchanals – complete with barbecues and turntables. Many revellers stay long past dark for *yozakura* (night-time cherry blossoms).

Ghibli Museum *(p120)*

11 Even those unfamiliar with the magical world of master animator Miyazaki Hayao – creator of anime (Japanese animation) classics including *Princess Mononoke* and *Spirited Away* – will find this museum enchanting. Fans won't want to leave. Miyazaki designed the space himself and, like his films, it's filled with whirring steampunk-esque machines and fairy-tale structures. And while you won't see staff *cosplaying* (costume playing) any characters, many of the animated characters have been cleverly worked into the designs.

Shibuya Crossing

(p97)

12 This is the Tokyo you've dreamed about and seen in movies: the frenetic pace, the mind-boggling crowds, the twinkling neon lights and the giant video screens beaming larger-than-life celebrities over the streets. At Shibuya's famous 'scramble' crossing, all of this comes together every time the light changes. It's an awesome sight. Come on a Friday or Saturday night and you'll find the whole scene turned up to 11, when fleets of fashionable Tokyoites embark upon a night out on the town.

Tokyo National Museum
(p149)

13 This is the world's largest collection of Japanese art, home to gorgeous silken kimonos, evocative scroll paintings done in charcoal ink, earthy tea-ceremony pottery and haunting examples of samurai armour and swords. Even better: it's totally manageable in a morning and organised into easy-to-grasp, thoughtful exhibitions. The Tokyo National Museum also includes the enchanting Gallery of Hōryū-ji Treasures, a hall filled with dozens of spot-lit Buddha statues dating from the 7th century, as well as art and artefacts that span the Asian continent.

Kabukiza *(p69)*

14 Dramatic, intensely visual kabuki is Japan's most recognised art form. Kabuki developed in Tokyo, then known as Edo, during the 18th and 19th centuries, and an afternoon at the theatre has been a favourite local pastime ever since. Descendants of the great actors of the day still grace Tokyo stages, drawing devoted fans. Established in 1889, Kabukiza Theatre is Tokyo's premier kabuki theatre. Renovated in 2013, the new Kuma Kengo design preserved the showy traditional facade and includes a tower in which you'll find a great teahouse and rooftop garden.

Akihabara Pop Culture *(p213)*

15 Venture into the belly of the pop culture beast that is Akihabara, the centre of Tokyo's *otaku* (geek) subculture. You don't have to obsess about manga or anime to enjoy this quirky neighbourhood: as *otaku* culture gains more and more influence on the culture at large, 'Akiba' is drawing more visitors who don't fit the stereotype. With its neon-bright electronics stores, retro arcades and *cosplay* cafes it's equal parts sensory overload, cultural mind-bender and just plain fun.

Ōedo Onsen Monogatari *(p173)*

16 Don't let Tokyo's slick surface and countless diversions fool you; underneath the city it's pure, bubbling primordial pleasure. Ōedo Onsen Monogatari pumps natural hot-spring water from 1440m below Tokyo Bay into its many bathing pools, which include both indoor and outdoor baths (called *rotemburo*). But it's not just about bathing: Ōedo Onsen Monogatari bills itself as an 'onsen theme park' – a fantastically Japanese concept – and includes a Disneyland-style version of an Edo-era town where guests dressed in *yukata* (light cotton kimonos) can play old-time carnival games.

What's New

Build up to 2020

The countdown to the 2020 Summer Olympics is on as Tokyo prepares for the international spotlight. More and more English is popping up, in the form of navigational signs, apps, menus and brochures; more restaurants and shops are hiring English-speaking staff, too. Free city wi-fi, though still clunky, is improving. Some sights (such as Meiji-jingū) are getting touch-ups; others (such as Tokyo Photographic Art Museum) have recently reopened. (p108)

Ginza Reboot

Roppongi, Marunouchi and Nihombashi have all had makeovers in the last decade, and now it's Ginza's turn. In spring 2017, the neighbourhood will welcome its newest shopping centre, Ginza Six (p74). Also new: Ginza Sony Park, Ginza Place and Tōkyū Plaza Ginza.

Go-Karting

The latest Tokyo craze is racing around the city streets in go-karts – dressed like your favourite video-game character. Operators include Akiba Kart (p146) and Maricar (p175).

Artsy East Tokyo

Kuramae, near Asakusa, is shaping up to be a hot spot for contemporary artisan studios and boutiques. (p169)

Sumida Hokusai Museum

In 2016, east Tokyo neighbourhood Ryōgoku got a striking new museum devoted to hometown artist – and woodblock print master – Hokusai. (p164)

More Activities

There's lots to do in Tokyo, including new cooking classes and crafts workshops in English. (p39)

Tsukiji Update

The fate of Tsukiji Market is up in the air again, moving at the earliest (if at all) in 2017. Either way, the fantastic Outer Market, now with even more tours and activities taking place, will remain. (p67)

Tennōzu Isle Art & Architecture

All of a sudden things are happening in this warehouse district on Tokyo Bay, with recent openings including the fantastic architecture model storage gallery Archi-Depot (p174), the arts supply store Pigment (p175) and a gallery complex (p174).

Guesthouses Galore

The stylish hostels and guesthouses just keep coming and, with new openings in neighbourhoods near Marunouchi and Roppongi, they're no longer confined to the east side of town.

Cafes, Cafes, Cafes

The coffee third wave has shown no signs yet of cresting in Tokyo. There's a new cafe belt forming in Kiyosumi, to rival the one established in the Shibuya-Harajuku-Yoyogi corridor.

For more recommendations and reviews, see **lonelyplanet.com/japan/tokyo**

Need to Know

For more information, see Survival Guide (p231)

Currency
Japanese yen (¥)

Language
Japanese

Visas
Visas are generally not required for stays of up to 90 days.

Money
Post offices and most convenience stores have international ATMs. Credit cards are accepted at major establishments, though it's best to keep cash on hand.

Mobile Phones
Purchase prepaid data-only SIM cards (for unlocked smartphones only) online or at airport kiosks or electronics stores. For voice calls, rent a pay-as-you-go mobile.

Time
Japan Standard Time (GMT/UTC plus nine hours)

Tourist Information
Tokyo Metropolitan Government Building Tourist Information Center (Map p280; ☎03-5321-3077; 1st fl, Tokyo Metropolitan Government bldg 1, 2-8-1 Nishi-Shinjuku, Shinjuku-ku; ⏰9.30am-6.30pm; [S]Ōedo line to Tochōmae, exit A4) offers English-language information and publications. Other branches in Keisei Ueno Station, Haneda Airport and Shinjuku Bus Terminal.

Daily Costs

Budget: less than ¥8000
- Dorm bed: ¥3000
- Free sights such as temples and markets
- Bowl of noodles: ¥750
- Happy-hour drink: ¥500
- 24-hour subway pass: ¥600

Midrange: ¥8000–20,000
- Double room at a business hotel: ¥14,000
- Museum entry: ¥1000
- Dinner for two at an *izakaya* (Japanese pub-eatery): ¥6000
- Live music show: ¥3000

Top End: more than ¥20,000
- Double room in a four-star hotel: ¥35,000
- Sushi-tasting menu: ¥15,000
- Box seat for kabuki: ¥21,000
- Taxi ride back to the hotel: ¥3000

Advance Planning

Three months before Purchase tickets for the Ghibli Museum; book a table at your top splurge restaurant.

One month before Book any tickets for sumo, kabuki and Giants games online, and a spot on the Imperial Palace tour; scan web listings for festivals, events and exhibitions.

As soon as you arrive Look for free copies of *Time Out Tokyo* and *Metropolis* magazines at airports and hotels.

Useful Websites

Go Tokyo (www.gotokyo.org) The city's official website includes information on sights, events and suggested itineraries.

Lonely Planet (www.lonelyplanet.com/tokyo) Destination information, hotel bookings, traveller forum and more.

Time Out Tokyo (www.timeout.jp) Arts and entertainment listings.

Tokyo Food Page (www.bento.com) City-wide restaurant coverage.

Tokyo Cheapo (https://tokyocheapo.com) Hints on how to do Tokyo on the cheap.

WHEN TO GO

Spring and autumn are the best times to visit. Mid-June to mid-July is the rainy season; August is hot and humid, but is also the month for summer festivals.

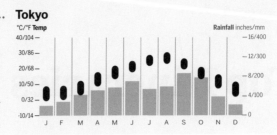

Tokyo

°C/°F **Temp**   **Rainfall** inches/mm

40/104 — 30/86 — 20/68 — 10/50 — 0/32 — -10/14 —

—16/400 —12/300 —8/200 —4/100 —0

J F M A M J J A S O N D

Arriving in Tokyo

Narita Airport An express train or highway bus to central Tokyo costs around ¥3000 (one to two hours). Both run frequently from 6am to 10.30pm; pick up tickets at kiosks inside the arrivals hall (no advance reservations required). Taxis start at ¥20,000.

Haneda Airport Frequent trains and buses (¥400 to ¥1200, 30 to 45 minutes) to central Tokyo run frequently from 5.30am to midnight; times and costs depend on your destination in the city. There are only a couple of night buses. For a taxi, budget between ¥5000 and ¥8000.

Tokyo Station Connect from the *shinkansen* (bullet train) terminal here to the JR Yamanote line or the Marunouchi subway to destinations around central Tokyo.

For much more on **arrival** see p232

Getting Around

Subway The quickest and easiest way to get around central Tokyo. Runs 5am to midnight.

➡ **Train** Japan Rail (JR) Yamanote (loop) and Chūō-Sōbu (central) lines service major stations. Runs from 5am to midnight.

➡ **Taxi** The only transport option that runs all night; unless you're stuck, taxis only make economical sense for groups of four.

➡ **Cycling** A fun way to get around, though traffic can be intense. Rentals available; some hostels and ryokan lend bicycles.

➡ **Walking** Subway stations are close in the city centre; save cash by walking if you only need to go one stop.

For much more on **getting around** see p234

Sleeping

Tokyo's accommodation is expensive, though more attractive budget and mid-range options are popping up all the time. Business hotels are an economic option and ryokan (traditional inns with Japanese-style bedding) fill the need for small, character-filled sleeping spaces. The best deals are on the east side of town, in neighbourhoods such as Ueno and Asakusa. Standards of cleanliness and service are generally high everywhere.

Useful Websites

➡ **Jalan** (www.jalan.net/en/japan_hotels_ryokan) Japanese discount accommodation site.

➡ **Japanican** (www.japanican.com) Accommodation site for foreign travellers, run by Japan's largest travel agency.

➡ **Lonely Planet** (www.lonelyplanet.com/japan/tokyo/hotels) Compare prices, check availability and book accommodations.

For much more on **sleeping** see p191

WHAT TO PACK

➡ Tokyo hotels can be tiny, so bring as small a suitcase as possible.

➡ You may be taking your shoes on and off a lot, so it helps to have ones that don't need lacing up.

Top Itineraries

Day One

Harajuku & Aoyama (p106)

 Start with a visit to **Meiji-jingū**, Tokyo's signature Shintō shrine. Then walk down **Omote-sandō** to check out the jaw-dropping contemporary architecture along this stylish boulevard. Work (and shop) your way back through the side streets of **Ura-Hara**, and then up **Takeshita-dōri**, the famous teen fashion bazaar.

> **Lunch** Stop for dumplings at local fave Harajuku Gyōza-rō (p111).

Shibuya & Shimo-Kitazawa (p95)

Head down to Shibuya (you can walk) and continue your schooling in Tokyo pop culture by wandering the lanes of this youthful neighbourhood. Don't miss **Shibuya Center-gai**, the main drag, and the mural, **Myth of Tomorrow**, in the train station. Stick around Shibuya until dusk to see **Shibuya Crossing** all lit up.

> **Dinner** Classic *izakaya* Donjaca (p132) or *yakitori* in Omoide-yokochō (p130).

Shinjuku & Northwest Tokyo (p125)

 Take the train to Shinjuku and immerse yourself in the swarming crowds and neon lights of this notorious nightlife district. The **Tokyo Metropolitan Government Building** observatories stay open until 11pm for free night views. Freshen up at urban onsen **Thermae-yu**. From around 9pm the shanty bars of **Golden Gai** come to life; take your pick from the quirky offerings and finish up with a time-honoured Tokyo tradition: a late-night bowl of noodles at **Nagi**.

Day Two

Ginza & Tsukiji (p65)

 Skip breakfast and head to **Tsukiji Outer Market**, where you can cobble together a morning meal from the food vendors here. There are also stalls selling kitchen tools, tea and more. From Tsukiji it's an easy walk to the landscape garden **Hama-rikyū Onshi-teien**, where you can stop for tea in the teahouse **Nakajima no Ochaya**. Then walk (or take a taxi) to **Ginza**, home to department stores, art galleries and luxury boutiques.

> **Lunch** Go for broke at sushi counter Kyūbey (p70); book ahead.

Ginza & Tsukiji (p65)

Continue exploring Ginza, walking as far as Hibiya, to see the edge of the **Imperial Palace**, with its moats and keeps. Then hop on the subway and ride back to **Kabukiza** (in Higashi-Ginza), to see a single act of kabuki (check the schedule online beforehand).

> **Dinner** Night-time noodles at Kagari (p69).

Marunouchi & Nihombashi (p54)

 Walk up Namiki-dōri, home to high-end hostess bars, and pretty, tree-lined Naka-dōri to Marunouchi. In nearby Yūrakuchō, you can stop for sake, beer and small plates of food under the elevated train tracks at **Manpuku Shokudō**. Or go upscale with cocktails at Peter atop the Peninsula Hotel.

Day Three

Ueno & Yanesen (p147)

 Spend the morning exploring the many attractions of **Ueno-kōen**, home to the **Tokyo National Museum**, centuries-old temples and shrines, and Tokyo's biggest zoo. Then take a stroll through the old-fashioned, open-air market, **Ameya-yokochō**, and the historical neighbourhood of **Yanaka**; in the latter you'll find art galleries and studios.

 Lunch Get a course of seasonal skewers at historic Hantei (p157).

Asakusa & Sumida River (p159)

Catch the subway for Asakusa to visit the temple complex **Sensō-ji**, the shrine **Asakusa-jinja** and the maze of old-world alleys that surround these sights. There are lots of shops selling traditional crafts and foodstuffs around here, too. Don't miss the temple complex all lit up from dusk.

Dinner Fill up on steaming *oden* at 100-year-old Otafuku (p167).

Asakusa & Sumida River (p159)

Asakusa has some fun, low-key nightlife, from the historic beer hall **Kamiya Bar** to the modern **Asahi Sky Room** (where the view of the illuminated Tokyo Sky Tree and the snaking Sumidagawa is excellent); you can also catch folk-music shows at **Oiwake**. Or just take the subway to Ryōgoku for more beer: **Popeye** boasts Tokyo's largest selection of Japanese craft brews.

Day Four

West Tokyo (p118)

 Take the train west to the magical **Ghibli Museum** (reservations necessary; we recommend getting in early at 10am). Afterwards walk through woodsy **Inokashira-kōen**, stopping at **Inokashira Benzaiten**, to Kichijōji, home to the old market, **Harmonica-yokochō**.

Lunch Skewers at Tetchan (p122) or *wagyū* steak at Satou (p123).

Kōrakuen & Akihabara (p136)

After lunch, work your way east on the Sōbu line: your final goal is pop culture centre **Akihabara**. (But if you get distracted by the vintage clothing shops of **Kōenji** or the more underground *otaku* scene in **Nakano**, that's OK too.) In Akiba you can play retro video games at **Super Potato Retro-kan** and ride go-karts – while dressed as video-game characters – through the streets with Akiba Kart (reserve ahead; international driving licence necessary).

Dinner Get the *izakaya* experience at Jōmon (p84) or Gonpachi (p81).

Roppongi, Akasaka & Around (p76)

Hop on the Hibiya line for Roppongi to check out **Roppongi Hills**, the first of Tokyo's new breed of live-work-and-play megamalls. On the top floor of a tower here is the excellent **Mori Art Museum**, which stays open until 10pm. Then head out into the wilds of Roppongi's infamous nightlife. Make sure to get in a round of karaoke.

If You Like...

Shintō Shrines

Meiji-jingū Tokyo's grandest Shintō shrine, set in a wooded grove. (p108)

Ueno Tōshō-gū Recently restored, gilded homage to warlord Tokugawa Ieyasu. (p153)

Inokashira Benzaiten Ancient sanctuary of the sea goddess, Benzaiten. (p121)

Akagi-jinja Centuries-old shrine updated with modern style. (p143)

Buddhist Temples

Sensō-ji Tokyo's oldest and most famous Buddhist temple and the epicentre of old-world Asakusa. (p161)

Fukagawa Fudō-dō An active temple of the esoteric Shingon sect, which performs regular fire rituals. (p164)

Sengaku-ji This Sōtō Zen temple is the final resting place of the famous 47 *rōnin* (masterless samurai). (p90)

Zōjō-ji The very rare main gate of this Pure Land Buddhist temple dates to 1605. (p81)

Museums

Tokyo National Museum Home to the world's largest collection of Japanese art. (p149)

Intermediatheque Experimental museum drawing on the holdings of the University of Tokyo. (p57)

Nezu Museum Asian antiques in a striking contemporary building. (p111)

Tokyo at dusk

Sumida Hokusai Museum New museum dedicated to woodblock artist Hokusai. (p164)

Contemporary Art & Design

Mori Art Museum Sky-high galleries that host travelling shows by top Japanese and foreign artists. (p78)

21_21 Design Sight Museum devoted entirely to contemporary design. (p79)

Archi-Depot Repository for architecture models by famous names. (p174)

Complex 665 New destination housing three leading galleries. (p79)

Crafts

Japan Folk Crafts Museum Exhibitions highlighting the beauty of everyday objects. (p99)

Crafts Gallery Ceramics, lacquerware and more from Japan's 'living national treasures'. (p57)

Suntory Museum of Art Modern setting for changing displays of decorative works. (p79)

History

Edo-Tokyo Museum Tells the story of how a fishing village evolved into a sprawling, modern metropolis. (p164)

National Shōwa Memorial Museum Learn what life was like for ordinary Tokyoites during WWII. (p138)

Shitamachi Museum Recreation of a wooden, Edo-era tenement neighbourhood. (p153)

Traditional Gardens

Rikugi-en Tokyo's most beautiful landscape garden, evoking scenes from classical literature. (p152)

Hama-rikyū Onshi-teien An ancient shogunate hunting ground, now a vast green space with a traditional teahouse. (p68)

Kiyosumi-teien A former villa pleasure garden with sculptural stones from around Japan. (p164)

Koishikawa Kōrakuen Built by the Tokugawa clan, a fine example of traditional Japanese garden design. (p138)

Parks

Ueno-kōen Tokyo's oldest park with museums, temples, woodsy paths and water lilies. (p153)

Shinjuku-gyoen Home to 1500 cherry trees, vast lawns and a tropical greenhouse. (p127)

Yoyogi-kōen A big grassy expanse and a popular weekend gathering spot. (p109)

Inokashira-kōen Wooded strolling paths, performance artists and pedal boats. (p121)

People Watching

Akihabara See *cosplay* (costume play) kids on Sundays along Chūō-dōri, or anytime riding go-karts through the neighbourhood. (p136)

Yoyogi-kōen With people living in tight quarters, dancers and musicians head to the park to practise. (p109)

Omote-sandō The city's de facto catwalk draws fashionistas from all over the world. (p110)

For more top Tokyo spots, see the following:

➡ Eating (p32)

➡ Drinking & Nightlife (p41)

➡ Entertainment (p44)

➡ Shopping (p46)

Ginza Head out in the twilight hours and catch high-end hostesses in kimonos and elaborate up-dos. (p65)

City Views

Tokyo Sky Tree Dizzying views from the lookouts on this 634m tower, the world's tallest. (p163)

Tokyo Metropolitan Government Building The 45th-floor observation decks in this marvel by Tange Kenzō are free. (p127)

New York Bar One of many luxury hotel cocktail bars with stunning night views. (p133)

Tokyo Bay Take a night cruise and see the shoreline from the bay. (p175)

Markets

Tsukiji Outer Market A warren of stalls selling kitchen tools and foodstuffs to chefs and home cooks alike. (p67)

Ameya-yokochō Tokyo's last open-air market dates to the tumultuous days after WWII. (p158)

Harmonica-yokochō Classic low-ceiling, lantern-lit covered market. (p121)

Ōedo Antique Market Hunt for undiscovered antique treasures at this twice-monthly gathering. (p64)

Month By Month

TOP EVENTS

Hatsu-mōde, January

Cherry Blossoms, April

Sanja Matsuri, May

Sumida-gawa Fireworks, July

Kōenji Awa Odori, August

January

Tokyo comes to a halt for O-shōgatsu, the first three days of the new year set aside for family and rest; most places close and many residents return to their home towns.

Hatsu-mōde

Hatsu-mōde, the first shrine visit of the new year, starts just after midnight on 1 January and continues through O-shōgatsu. Meiji-jingū (p108) is the most popular spot in Tokyo; it can get very, very crowded, but that's part of the experience.

Coming of Age Day

The second Monday of January is *seijin-no-hi*, the collective birthday for all who have turned 20 (the age of majority) in the past year; young women don gorgeous kimonos for ceremonies at Shintō shrines.

February

February is the coldest month, though it rarely snows. Winter days are crisp and clear – the best time of year to spot Mt Fuji in the distance.

Setsubun

The first day of spring is 3 February in the traditional lunar calendar, a shift once believed to bode evil. As a precaution, people visit Buddhist temples, toss roasted beans and shout, '*Oni wa soto! Fuku wa uchi!*' ('Devil out! Fortune in!').

Shimo-Kitazawa Tengu Matsuri

On the weekend nearest to Setsubun (p24; late January or early February), Shimo-Kitazawa hosts a parade with revellers dressed in *tengu* (devil) costumes.

Plum Blossoms

Plum *(ume)* blossoms, which appear towards the end of the month, are the first sign that winter is ending. Popular viewing spots include Koishikawa Kōrakuen (p138) and Yushima Tenjin (p154).

March

Hina Matsuri

On and around 3 March (also known as Girls' Day), public spaces and homes are decorated with *o-hina-sama* (princess) dolls in traditional royal dress.

Anime Japan

In late March, Anime Japan (www.anime-japan.jp) has events and exhibitions for industry insiders and fans alike, at Tokyo Big Sight.

April

Warmer weather and blooming cherry trees make this quite simply the best month to be in Tokyo.

Cherry Blossoms

From the end of March through the beginning of April, the city's parks and riversides turn pink and Tokyoites toast spring in spirited parties, called *hanami*, beneath the blossoms. Ueno-kōen (p153) is the most famous spot, but grassy Yoyogi-kōen (p109) and Shinjuku-gyoen (p127) are more conducive to picnicking.

May

There's a string of national holidays at the beginning of May, known as Golden Week, when much of the country makes travel plans. Festivals and warm days make this an excellent time to visit.

Children's Day

On 5 May, also known as *otoko-no-hi* (Boys' Day), families fly *koinobori* (colourful banners in the shape of a carp), a symbol of strength and courage.

Tokyo Rainbow Pride

In May, Japan's LGBT community comes together for the country's biggest pride event (http://tokyorainbowpride.com), in some years followed by a parade. It's not London or Sydney, but a spirited affair just the same.

Kanda Matsuri

This is one of Tokyo's big three festivals, with a parade of *mikoshi* (portable shrines) around Kanda Myōjin (p138). It's held on the weekend closest to 15 May on odd-numbered years (next up 2019).

Design Festa

Weekend-long Design Festa (www.designfesta.com), held at Tokyo Big Sight in mid-May, is Asia's largest art festival, featuring performances and thousands of exhibitors.

Sanja Matsuri

Arguably the grandest Tokyo *matsuri* (festival) of all, this three-day event, held over the third weekend of May, attracts around 1.5 million spectators to Asaku-sa-jinja (p162). The highlight is the rowdy parade of *mikoshi* carried by men and women in traditional dress.

June

Early June is lovely, though by the end of the month *tsuyu* (the rainy season) sets in.

Sannō Matsuri

For a week in mid-June Hie-jinja (p81) puts on this major festival, with music, dancing and a procession of *mikoshi*. The parade takes place in even-numbered years.

July

When the rainy season passes in mid- to late July, suddenly it's summer – the season for lively street fairs and *hanabi taikai* (fireworks shows).

Tanabata

On 7 July, the stars Vega and Altar (stand-ins for a princess and cowherd who are in love) meet across the Milky Way. Children tie strips of coloured paper bearing wishes around bamboo branches; look for decorations at youthful hang-outs such as Hara-juku and Shibuya.

Mitama Matsuri

Yasukuni-jinja (p138) celebrates O-Bon early: from 13 to 16 July, the shrine holds a festival of remembrance for the dead with 30,000 illuminated *bonbori* (paper lanterns).

Ueno Summer Festival

From mid-July to mid-August various events, including markets and music performances, take place in Ueno-kōen (p153).

Lantern Festivals

Toro nagashi is a photogenic summer tradition, connected to O-Bon, where candle-lit paper lanterns are floated down rivers. It takes place from mid-July to mid-August; two big ones happen at Chidori-ga-fuchi, along the Imperial Palace moat, and at Sumida-kōen in Asakusa.

Sumida-gawa Fireworks

The grandest of the summer fireworks shows, held the last Saturday in July, features 20,000 pyrotechnic wonders. Head to Asakusa early in the day to score a good seat. Check events listings for other fireworks displays around town.

August

This is the height of Japan's sticky, hot summer; school holidays mean sights may be crowded.

Asagaya Tanabata

Asagaya holds a Tanabata festival over the first weekend of August, with colourful lanterns strung up in its *shōtengai* (shopping arcade), Pearl Centre (p124).

O-Bon

Three days in mid-August are set aside to honour the dead, when their spirits are said to return to the earth. Graves are swept, offerings are made and *bon-odori* (folk dances) take place. Many Tokyo residents return to their home towns; some shops may close too.

✿ Fukagawa Hachiman Matsuri

During this spirited festival at Tomioka Hachiman-gū (p165), spectators throw water over the *mikoshi* carriers along the route. It's held in a big way only every three years; next up in 2020.

✿ Asakusa Samba Carnival

On the last Saturday in August, Tokyo's Nikkei Brazilian community and local samba clubs turn Kaminarimon-dōri into one big party for the Asakusa Samba Carnival (www.asakusa-samba.org).

✿ Kōenji Awa Odori

Kōenji Awa Odori (www.koenji-awaodori.com) is Tokyo's biggest *awa odori* (dance festival for O-Bon) with 12,000 participants in traditional costumes dancing their way through the streets over the last weekend of August.

September

Days are still warm, hot even – though the odd typhoon rolls through this time of year.

◉ Moon Viewing

Full moons in September and October call for *tsukimi*, moon-viewing gatherings. People eat *tsukimi dango* – *mochi* (pounded rice) dumplings round like the moon.

☆ Tokyo Game Show

Get your geek on when the Computer Entertainment Suppliers Association hosts Tokyo Game Show (http://

(Top) Fukagawa Hachiman Matsuri (p26)
(Bottom) Koishikawa Kōrakuen (p138) in autumn

SAETHAPOENG TRIECHORB / SHUTTERSTOCK ©

MAGICFLUTE002 / GETTY IMAGES ©

tgs.cesa.or.jp), a massive expo at Makuhari Messe in late September.

☉ Tokyo Grand Tea Ceremony

Held in late September or early October, at Hama-rikyū Onshi-teien (p68) and Edo-Tokyo Open Air Architecture Museum (p121), this is a big outdoor tea party (http://tokyo-grand-tea-ceremony.jp/eng/index.html), with traditional tea ceremonies held in various styles, usually including one with English translation.

October

Pleasantly warm days and cool evenings make this an excellent time to be in Tokyo.

☉ Roppongi Art Night

Held in mid- to late October, this weekend-long (literally, as venues stay open all night) arts event (www.roppongiartnight.com) sees large-scale installations and performances taking over the streets of Roppongi.

🎎 Tokyo International Film Festival

During the last week in October, the Tokyo International Film Festival (p77) screens works from Japanese and international directors, with English subtitles.

☉ Halloween

Tokyo has gone mad for Halloween with thousands of costumed revellers converging on Shibuya Crossing (p97). Shinjuku

Ni-chōme and Roppongi see action, too.

🎎 Chrysanthemum Festivals

Chrysanthemums are the flower of the season (and the royal family), and dazzling displays are put on from late October to mid-November in Hibiya-kōen (in Ginza) and at shrines including Meiji-jingū (p108) and Yasukuni-jinja (p138).

November

🎎 Design Festa

Round two for Design Festa (www.designfesta.com) takes place in early November.

🎎 Tori-no-ichi

On 'rooster' days in November, 'O-tori' shrines such as Hanazono-jinja (p127) hold fairs called Tori-no-ichi (*tori* means 'rooster'); the day is set according to the old calendar, which marks days by the zodiac. Vendors hawk *kumade* – rakes that literally symbolise 'raking in the wealth'.

🎎 Shichi-go-san

This adorable festival in mid-November sees parents dress girls aged seven (*shichi*) and three (*san*) and boys aged five (*go*) in wee kimonos and head to Shintō shrines for blessings.

☉ International Robot Exhibition

The world's largest robot expo (www.nikkan.co.jp/eve/irex/english) takes place every other year at Tokyo Big Sight (www.bigsight.jp).

☆ Tokyo Filmex

Tokyo Filmex (http://filmex.net), which kicks off in late November, focuses on emerging directors in Asia and screens many films with English subtitles.

☉ Autumn Leaves

The city's trees undergo magnificent seasonal transformations during *kōyō* (autumn foliage season); Rikugi-en (p152) and Koishikawa Kōrakuen (p138) have spectacular displays.

December

Restaurants and bars are filled with Tokyoites hosting *bōnenkai* (end-of-the-year parties). Commercial strips are decorated with seasonal illuminations.

🎎 Gishi-sai

On 14 December, Sengaku-ji (p90) hosts a memorial service honouring the 47 *rōnin* (masterless samurai) who famously avenged their fallen master; locals dressed as the loyal retainers parade through nearby streets.

🍴 Toshikoshi Soba

Eating buckwheat noodles on New Year's Eve, a tradition called *toshikoshi soba*, is said to bring luck and longevity – the latter symbolised by the length of the noodles.

Joya-no-kane

Temple bells around Japan ring 108 times at midnight on 31 December, a purifying ritual called *joya-no-kane*. Sensō-ji (p161) draws the biggest crowds in Tokyo.

With Kids

In many ways, Tokyo is a parent's dream: hyperclean, safe and with every mod con. The downside is that many of the top attractions aren't as appealing to younger ones. Older kids and teens, however, should get a kick out of Tokyo's pop culture and neon streetscapes.

Hang out in Odaiba

Local families love Odaiba. At the National Museum of Emerging Science & Innovation (Miraikan) (p173) meet humanoid robot ASIMO, see a planetarium show and interact with hands-on exhibits.

At 'onsen theme park' Ōedo Onsen Monogatari (p173), kids wear *yukata* (lightweight kimonos) and play old-fashioned carnival games. There's also virtual-reality arcade Tokyo Joypolis (p176), and one of the world's tallest Ferris wheels. Restaurants are family-friendly.

Explore Ueno

Sprawling park Ueno-kōen (p153) has a zoo (with pandas) and the fascinating National Museum of Nature & Science (p153). See swords and armour at Tokyo National Museum (p149).

Spot Trains

Japanese kids love trains, and chances are yours will too. A platform ticket to see the *shinkansen* (bullet train) costs ¥140. Another popular train-spotting location is Shinjuku Station's southern terrace, overlooking the multiple tracks that feed the world's busiest train station.

Fun & Games

Amusement Parks

Head to Tokyo Dome City (p146) for thrill rides, play areas and baseball at Tokyo Dome. Or brave the long lines at Tokyo Disney Resort (p176), Asia's most visited amusement park.

Anime City

Explore the magical world of famed animator Miyazaki Hayao (Ponyo, Spirited Away) at Ghibli Museum (p120). Shop for their favourite character goods at Pokemon Center Mega Tokyo (p135), Sanrioworld Ginza (p75) and KiddyLand (p117).

Photo Ops

Get up close to the giant Godzilla statue atop the Hotel Gracery Shinjuku (p198). Snap (and decorate) family photos at high-tech photo booths at Purikura no Mecca (p105).

Karaoke

Spend a rainy day at a karaoke parlour such as Shidax Village (p104).

Arts & Crafts

Learn the Japanese art of paper craft at Origami Kaikan (p138).

Fishing

Here's something they won't expect: fishing in the middle of the city at Ichigaya Fish Centre (p146).

For more ways to explore Tokyo's exciting pop culture, see p213.

Like a Local

Tokyo is far more liveable than you may think. Get beyond the skyscrapers, the omnipresent neon and the crowds and you'll find a city that's more like a patchwork of towns, each with its own character and characters.

mbōchō bookstore (p145)

Local Hang-outs

Spend an afternoon in one of these neighbourhoods loved by locals.

Shimo-Kitazawa (p100) A bastion of bohemia for decades, with snaking alleys, secondhand stores, coffee shops, hole-in-the-wall bars and live-music halls.

Yanaka (p156) Long-time artists' neighbourhood, with studios, galleries, art supply shops and cafes – many of which are in old wooden buildings.

Naka-Meguro (p92) Few tall buildings and a leafy canal flanked by small shops and restaurants give this artsy district a small-town vibe.

Kichijōji (p121) Popular with students for its woodsy park, funky cafes and casual restaurants, and oft-voted among the best places to live in Tokyo.

Jimbōchō (p145) A favourite destination for local bibliophiles with more than 100 secondhand bookshops. As you'd expect, there are lots of cafes here.

Nakano (p121) Tokyo's underground *otaku* (anime and manga fans) haunt, without the flash and bang of Akihabara.

Tomigaya (p104) Hipster 'hood with cafes, bistros and indie shops, right down the street from Shibuya.

Kagurazaka (p142) Cobblestone streets give this district a romantic feel; good for dates and for snapping photos with friends.

Kōenji (p124) Punk-rock clubs, grungy bars and secondhand shops are the hallmarks of Tokyo's counter-culture den.

Kuramae (p169) A growing scene of young artisans drawn by cheap rent on the east side of town.

Top Local Experiences

➡ Queuing up for the latest trendy ramen shop.

➡ Signing up for a *nomi-hōdai* (all-you-can-drink) plan at a karaoke parlour and singing until the first train starts running in the morning.

➡ Riding the Chūō line at rush hour – if you dare.

➡ Spending a sunny weekend afternoon at Yoyogi-kōen (p109) or Inokashira-kōen (p121).

➡ Finding everything you need (from sundries to slippers to lunch) on a *shōtengai*, a typical shopping street.

➡ Getting a *conbini* (convenience store) *bentō* (boxed meal) for dinner.

OGIYOSHISAN / GETTY IMAGES ©

Get to Know the Old City

Literally the 'low city', Shitamachi was where merchants and artisans lived during the Edo period. The city is no longer carved up so neatly; however, many of the old patterns remain. On the east side of the city, former Shitamachi neighbourhoods remain a tangle of alleys and tightly packed quarters, with traditional architecture, artisan workshops and small businesses.

The term 'Shitamachi' is still used to describe neighbourhoods that retain this old-Tokyo vibe, such as Asakusa and Fukagawa. Not everyone in Tokyo is enamoured with the city's forward push; the Shitamachi lifestyle has its staunch defenders. Spend an afternoon strolling through one of these districts and you'll see a whole other side to the city – one that is utterly down-to-earth and unpretentious.

Join the Celebrations

Hanami, the spirited parties that occur every spring under the boughs of the cherry trees, is Tokyo's most famous celebration, but festivals happen year-round. This is especially true during the summer months, when every neighbourhood has its own festival – a custom that goes back centuries. These riotous spectacles usually include a parade of *mikoshi* (portable shrines) by locals in traditional garb (which sometimes means only loincloths and short coats on the men).

Street fairs and *hanabi taikai* (fireworks displays) draw crowds dressed in colourful *yukata* (light cotton kimonos). And where there are festivals there are stalls selling food and beer. Don't be shy: by all means join in the merry-making (though we recommend stepping back from the heavy *mikoshi* so you don't get jostled).

Websites such as **Go Tokyo** (www.gotokyo.org/en/index.html) and **Time Out Tokyo** (www.timeout.jp/en/tokyo) have listings.

Eat Like a Local

Think Seasonally

They may live in concrete boxes but Tokyoites are still attuned to the rhythms of nature – at least when it comes to food. Share their excitement over the first *takenoko* (young bamboo shoots) in spring or *sanma* (mackerel pike) in autumn. Even fast-food restaurants and convenience stores offer seasonal treats, luring customers in for the taste of the month.

Look Up

If you're accustomed to scanning the street at ground level, you stand to miss out on a lot in Tokyo. In downtown areas restaurants are stacked on top of each other, creating multiple storeys of competing vertical neon signs. Most department stores, and even some office buildings, have food courts on the top floors with restaurants that are often surprisingly good.

Party Like a Local

With small apartments and thin walls, most Tokyoites do their entertaining outside the home. A *nomikai* is literally a 'meet up to drink', and they typically take place in restaurants or *izakaya* (Japanese pub-eateries). A 'party plan' (パーティプラン; *pāti puran*) is arranged, consisting of a course of food and a couple of hours of *nomi-hōdai* (飲み放題; all-you-can-drink booze, a good word to know). Never mind the stereotype about Japanese people being quiet and reserved – *nomikai* are loud and animated. There's no worry about disturbing the neighbours – or cleaning up.

While large groups require advance reservations, a group of around four can usually ask for a party plan when ordering – as long as you're not picky, this also simplifies the ordering process!

Bathe Like a Local

Public bathhouses *(sentō)* have a centuries' old tradition in Tokyo. Though their numbers are dwindling, most communities still have one. Serious devotees come to take advantage of extras such as saunas, to gossip with neighbours or just to revel in soaking longer than would be fair at home (with others clamouring for a turn). Custom calls for a beer afterwards.

To learn more about *sentō,* see p229.

For Free

Tokyo consistently lands near the top of the list of the world's most expensive cities. Yet many of the city's top sights cost nothing and free festivals take place year-round. Of course, the best way to enjoy Tokyo is to simply wander its colourful neighbourhoods – which doesn't cost a thing.

Free Sights

Shrines & Temples
Shintō shrines are usually free in Tokyo and most Buddhist temples charge only to enter their *honden* (main hall) – meaning that two of the city's top sights, Meiji-jingū (p108) and Sensō-ji (p161) are free.

Museums
Tokyo has many free niche museums. Often no bigger than a room, they offer a succinct look at the more plebeian aspects of the city, such as its artisan craft culture (p163) or the history of beer production (p89).

Markets
Tsukiji (p68) is the most famous of Tokyo's many markets. There's also the old-fashioned open-air market Ameya-yokochō (p158) and a weekend farmers market (p109) in Aoyama.

City Views
Some skyscrapers, like the Tokyo Metropolitan Government Building (p127), have free observatories on the upper floors.

Architecture
Tokyo has some fascinating buildings, such as the designer boutiques lining Omotesandō (p110) in Harajuku, designed by many of the big names in Japanese architecture.

Galleries
Take the pulse of the city's art scene in its free galleries; you'll find clusters of them around Ginza, Roppongi and Harajuku.

Parks & Gardens
Spend an afternoon people-watching in one of Tokyo's excellent public parks, perhaps Yoyogi-kōen (p109) or Inokashira-kōen (p121). Grab a *bentō* (boxed meal) from a convenience store for a cheap and easy picnic. Or set aside time to explore the secret (and free!) gardens of Akasaka (p80).

Money-Saving Ideas

Cheap Sleeps
All-night *manga kissa* (cafes for reading comic books) and spas double as ultra-discount lodgings. You probably wouldn't want to spend many nights like this, but one or two would save you some yen.

Cheap Eats
Restaurants that charge several thousand yen per person for dinner often serve lunch for just ¥1000. In the evenings, grocery stores, bakeries and department-store food halls slash prices on *bentō*, baked goods and sushi.

Convenience Stores
The best friend to all budget travellers, convenience stores stock sandwiches, rice balls, hot dishes and beer, all of which you can assemble into a very affordable (if not exactly healthy) meal.

Resources
Expat-run **Tokyo Cheapo** (http://tokyo-cheapo.com) is full of tips on how to enjoy Tokyo on the cheap. See **Go Tokyo** (www.gotokyo.org) for a list of festivals.

Omoide Yokocho (p130), Shinjuku

Eating

As visitors to Tokyo quickly discover, the people here are absolutely obsessed with food. The city has a vibrant and cosmopolitan dining scene and a strong culture of eating out – popular restaurants are packed most nights of the week. Best of all, you can get superlative meals on any budget.

Yakitori (grilled chicken skewers; p36)

Tokyo Food Scene

Tokyo foodies take pride in what they like to think of as their 'boutique' dining scene. Rather than offer long menus of elaborate dishes, many of the best restaurants make just a few things – and sometimes even just one! Sushi shops make sushi; tempura shops make tempura. A restaurant that does too much might be suspect: how can it compare to a speciality shop that has been honing its craft for three generations?

It's easy to make a connection between Tokyo's deep-rooted artisan culture – born of its early days as a castle town – and this preponderance of small restaurants hell-bent on perfecting a single dish, be it *tonkatsu* (deep-fried pork cutlets) or hamburgers.

Yes, hamburgers: Tokyoites love novelty and are eager consumers of the world's myriad cuisines. The perfectionist streak applies here, too: local chefs love deconstructing, coaxing and reassembling dishes from different traditions. The result might not always look and taste like what you're used to, but odds are it'll be good.

Top Tokyo Dining Experiences

➡ Noshing on *yakitori* (chicken skewers) and knocking back beers with Tokyo's workday warriors under the train tracks in Yūrakuchō.

➡ Gazing upon (and sampling) all the glorious delights to be found in a department-store food hall.

➡ Making a pilgrimmage to Tsukiji's Outer Market (p67) for street food (such as grilled oysters) and professional tools (such as chef's knives).

NEED TO KNOW

Price Range

The following price ranges represent the cost of a meal for one person.

¥ less than ¥2000

¥¥ ¥2000 to ¥5000

¥¥¥ more than ¥5000

Opening Hours

Most restaurants open roughly 11.30am to 2.30pm for lunch and 6pm to 10pm for dinner. Chains usually stay open through the afternoon. *Izakaya* open around 5pm and run until 11pm or later. Last order is usually 30 minutes before closing.

Reservations

Reservations are recommended for high-end places or for groups of five or more; popular places fill up quickly.

Paying

➡ If a bill hasn't already been placed on your table, ask for it by catching your server's eye and making a cross in the air with your index fingers.

➡ Payment is usually settled at the counter. Traditional or smaller restaurants may not accept credit cards.

Tipping

Tipping is not customary, though most high-end restaurants will add a 10% service charge to the bill.

Etiquette

➡ Don't stick your chopsticks upright in your rice or pass food from one pair of chopsticks to another – both are reminiscent of funereal rites.

➡ The Japanese frown upon eating in public places; festivals and parks are two big exceptions.

Useful Websites

Tokyo Food Page (www.bento.com) Listings and review site edited by a *Japan Times*' dining columnist.

Food Sake Tokyo (https://foodsaketokyo.com) Blog penned by a local food writer with excellent recommendations.

Tabelog (https://tabelog.com/en) English version of Japan's most popular customer-review website.

Above: Traditional Japanese kitchen knives for sale at Tsukiji market (p68)

Left: Sushi

- Visiting a traditional festival and getting *yaki-soba* (fried noodles) or *okonomiyaki* (savoury pancakes) hot off the grill.
- Grabbing late-night noodles after a rousing round of karaoke.
- Splurging on an *omakase* (chef's tasting menu) at a top-class sushi restaurant.

The Basics

When you enter a restaurant in Japan, the staff will likely all greet you with a hearty '*Irasshai!*' (Welcome!). In all but the most casual places, where you seat yourself, the waitstaff will next ask you '*Nan-mei sama?*' (How many people?). Indicate the answer with your fingers, which is what the Japanese do. You may also be asked if you would like to sit at a *zashiki* (low table on the tatami), at a *tēburu* (table) or the *kauntā* (counter). Once seated you will be given an *o-shibori* (hot towel), a cup of tea or water (this is free) and a menu.

When your food arrives, it's the custom to say '*Itadakimasu*' (literally 'I will receive' but closer to 'bon appétit' in meaning) before digging in. All but the most extreme type-A chefs will say they'd rather have foreign visitors enjoy their meal than agonise over getting the etiquette right. Still, there's nothing that makes a Japanese chef grimace more than out-of-towners who over-season their food – a little soy sauce and wasabi go a long way (and heaven forbid, don't pour soy sauce all over your rice; it makes it much harder to eat with chopsticks).

On your way out, it's polite to say '*Gochisō-sama deshita*' (literally 'It was a feast'; a respectful way of saying you enjoyed the meal) to the staff.

What to Eat

SUSHI

Sushi (寿司 or 鮨; raw fish and rice seasoned with vinegar) comes in many forms; however, the most well-known, *nigiri-zushi* – the bite-sized slivers of fish placed on pedestals of rice – is a Tokyo speciality. It's also called 'Edo-mae', meaning in the style of Edo, after the old name for Tokyo. Sushi was originally a way to make fish last longer; the vinegar in the rice was a preserving agent and older forms of sushi, more common in western Japan, taste much more of vinegar. Edo-mae sushi was developed in the 19th century as a snack for busy merchants to eat on the spot. There was less need for preservation because Tokyo Bay could provide a steady stream of fresh fish.

If you visit one of Tokyo's top sushi counters, most likely you'll be served a belly-busting set course of seasonal *nigiri-zushi*. At sushi restaurants, ordering a set or a course is almost always more economical than ordering à la carte. However, you don't have to pay through the nose for sushi that's leagues better than what you can get back home. For a more casual experience, try a *kaiten-zushi* (回転寿司), where ready-made plates of sushi are sent around the restaurant on a conveyor belt. The best thing about these restaurants is that you

A FOODIE'S DAY IN TOKYO

Start with a trip to **Tsukiji Outer Market** (p67) to rummage up breakfast among the street stalls. The *ebi-katsu sando* (deep-fried prawn sandwiches) at **Kimagure-ya** (気まぐれ屋; Map p268; 6-21-6 Tsukiji, Chūō-ku; sandwiches from ¥140; 🕒5am-10am; [S]Hibiya line to Tsukiji, exit 1) are a good choice; you can get coffee here, too. This is also the place to hunt for professional-grade cooking tools; **Tsukiji Hitachiya** (p67) sells hand-forged chef's knives.

Work off breakfast with a walk to Ginza (15 minutes). Have a wander through the basement food hall at **Mitsukoshi** (p75). Nearby **Akomeya** (p74) is a beautiful foodstuffs boutique that stocks packaged foods from around Japan. All are fantastic for gifts.

Hungry again yet? Head to **Kagari** (p69), one of Tokyo's hottest ramen shops (you might have to queue). After lunch, visit tea parlour **Cha Ginza** (p71), where you can sit and enjoy *matcha* (powdered green tea) and traditional sweets on the roof and shop for tea on the ground floor.

In the late afternoon take the subway to Ueno. Here you can stroll through the old-fashioned outdoor market, **Ameya-yokochō** (p158), on your way to **Shinsuke** (p155), one of Tokyo's best *izakaya*. Order dishes one or two at a time, paired with Shinsuke's excellent sake. If you have energy to make it back across town, end with a nightcap at **Zoetrope** (p133), which stocks the world's best selection of Japanese whiskies.

don't have to worry about ordering: just grab whatever looks good as it goes by.

RAMEN

Ramen originated in China, but its popularity in Japan is epic. Your basic ramen is a big bowl of crinkly egg noodles in broth, served with toppings such as *chāshū* (sliced roast pork), *moyashi* (bean sprouts) and *negi* (leeks). The broth can be made from pork or chicken bones or dried seafood; usually it's a top-secret combination of some or all of the above. It's typically seasoned with *shio* (salt), *shōyu* (soy sauce) or hearty miso – though at less orthodox places, anything goes. Tokyo's classic style is a *shōyu*-flavoured broth with a subtle bitter smokiness that comes from *niboshi* (dried young sardines). Another popular style is *tsukemen*, noodles that come with a dipping sauce (like a really condensed broth) on the side.

Given the option, most diners get their noodles *katame* (literally 'hard' but more like al dente). Ramen should be eaten at whip speed, before the noodles get soggy; that's why you'll hear diners slurping, sucking in air to cool their mouths. If you're really hungry, ask for *kaedama* (another serving of noodles), usually only a couple of hundred yen more.

TOKYO CLASSICS

Tokyo has restaurants specialising in every facet of Japanese cuisine. There are a few dishes, though, that have a special place in the city's collective, er, stomach.

Curry Rice (カレーライス) Curry entered Japan through the British and became a beloved dish; here it's hardly spicy at all (unless you request it), but rather a bit sweet and thick, served over sticky rice (and sometimes with *tonkatsu*, deep-fried pork cutlets). In Tokyo, the neighbourhood of Jimbōchō is known for its curry shops. It's also a popular haunt for book lovers, who will tell you that curry is the perfect dish: as it's eaten with a spoon, you've got one hand free to hold a book.

Monja-yaki (もんじゃ焼き) This Tokyo speciality is similar to the classic dish *okonomiyaki* (a thick savoury pancake stuffed with meat, seafood and cabbage), but the batter is runnier, making for a thin crêpe that crisps at the edges. Tsukishima is the birthplace of the dish and has a whole strip of specialists.

Soba (蕎麦) Western Japan eats more udon (thick wheat noodles); eastern Japan (which includes Tokyo) eats more soba (buckwheat noodles) – though most shops sell both. Connoisseurs order their soba noodles cold (since hot soup quickly

Monja-yaki

turns al dente noodles to mush), served with a dipping broth on the side. Better soba restaurants serve *to-wari* (十割; 100% buckwheat) noodles; otherwise they're made of a blend of buckwheat and wheat. Cheaper *tachigui* (立ち食い; stand-and-eat) noodle bars can be found all over the city.

Tempura (天ぷら) Tokyo has been enjoying this dish of seafood and vegetables deep-fried in a fluffy, light batter for centuries; Asakusa is especially known for the dish. Be sure to try *ebi-tendon* (えび天丼), tempura prawns over rice.

Yakitori (焼き鳥) Come evening, alleys all over the city are lit with the signature red lanterns that hang over the entrances to stands and restaurants serving *yakitori* (nominally grilled chicken skewers, but in practice a huge variety of meat, seafood and veg salted or sauced and set to grill over hot coals).

Where to Eat

SHOKUDŌ

Dining trends may come and go but *shokudō* (食堂; inexpensive, all-round eateries) remain. The city's workers take a significant number of their meals at these casual joints; you'll find them around every train station and in tourist areas. Meals typically cost ¥800 to ¥1500 per person.

Most serve *teishoku* (定食; set-course meals), which include a main dish of meat or fish, a bowl of rice, miso soup, a small salad and some *tsukemono* (pickles). Usually on the menu are various *donburi* (どんぶり or 丼; meat or seafood on a bowl of rice) and comfort food dishes, like *tonkatsu* (deep-fried pork cutlets) and *ebi-katsu* (breaded and fried prawns).

IZAKAYA

Izakaya (居酒屋) translates as 'drinking house' – the Japanese equivalent of a pub. Here food – a mix of raw, grilled, steamed and fried dishes – is ordered for the table a few dishes at a time and washed down with plenty of beer, sake or *shōchū* (a strong distilled alcohol often made from potatoes). If you don't want alcohol, it's fine to order a soft drink instead, but it would be strange to not order a drink.

There are orthodox *izakaya*, ones that incorporate pub-style dishes (like chips) and chef-driven ones with creative menus. While the vibe is lively and social, it's perfectly acceptable to go by yourself and sit at the counter.

If you're unsure what to order, you can say '*Omakase de onegaishimas[u]*' (I'll leave it up to you). It's probably a good idea to set a price cap, like: '*Hitori de san-zen-en*' (one person for ¥3000). Depending on how much you drink, a typical bill runs to about ¥2500 to ¥5000 per person.

STREET FOOD

Street-food stands, called *yatai* (屋台), don't have the same ubiquitous presence in Tokyo as they do in other Asian cities; however, you can find them in markets, including Tsukiji Outer Market (p67) or Ameya-yokochō (p158), heavily touristed areas, such as Asakusa and Ueno-kōen (p153), and always at festivals. Typical *yatai* food includes *okonomiyaki* (お好み焼き; savoury pancakes), *yaki-soba* (焼きそば; stir-fried noodles) and *tai-yaki* (たい焼き; fish-shaped cakes stuffed with bean paste).

Food trucks are popular with the downtown office crowd, gathering daily around the Tokyo International Forum (p58) at lunchtime; they also make the weekend rounds of farmers markets. And keep an eye out for Tokyo's original food trucks: the *yaki-imo* (roasted whole sweet potato) carts that rove the city from October to March crooning '*yaki-imohhhhh…!*'.

amen

KISSATEN

Most restaurants (that aren't chains or fast food) in Tokyo only open for lunch and/or dinner. The exception are *kissaten* (喫茶店) – coffee shops. Many serve 'morning sets' (モーニングセット; *mōningu setto*) from 8am until around 11am that include thick, buttery toast, a hard-boiled egg and a cup of coffee, for about the same price as a cup of coffee (around ¥500).

Food to Go

CONVENIENCE STORES

Konbini (コンビニ; convenience stores) are a way of life for many Tokyoites. Indeed, there seems to be a Lawson, 7-Eleven or Family Mart on just about every corner. In addition to *bentō* (boxed meals) and sandwiches, other *konbini* staples include *onigiri* (おにぎり), a triangle of rice and *nori* enveloping something savoury (tuna salad or marinated kelp, for example); *niku-man* (肉まん), steamed buns filled with pork, curry and more; and, in winter, *oden,* a dish of fish cakes, hard-boiled egg and vegetables in *dashi* (fish stock) broth.

DEPARTMENT STORE FOOD HALLS

The below-ground floors of Tokyo's department stores hold fantastic food halls called *depachika* (literally 'department store basement'). Dozens of vendors offer a staggering array of foodstuffs of the highest order; most are branches of famous restaurants, producers and confectioners. You can find prepared food, such as sushi and salads to take away, as well as sweets, *sembei* (rice crackers), tea and sake gorgeously packaged for presentation as gifts. Two *depachika* to try are Isetan (p135) in Shinjuku and Mitsukoshi (p64) in Nihombashi.

FARMERS MARKETS

On weekends, farmers markets take place around the city and are a good place to get fresh fruit and bread, plus packaged goods (such as miso and pickles) to take home. Some regular favourites:

Farmer's Market @UNU (p109) Tokyo's largest, every weekend in Aoyama.

Taiyō no Marché (www.facebook.com/taiyou nomarche) Second weekend of every month in Kachidoki (near Tsukiji), with a new theme each time.

Yebisu Marché (www.marche-japon.org) Every Sunday from 11am to 5pm at Yebisu Garden Place (p89).

Top: Cold soba noodles
Middle: *Ebi-tendon* (tempura prawns over rice)
Bottom: Curry rice with *tonkatsu* (deep-fried pork cutlets)

Check out the blog **Japan Farmers Markets** (www.japanfarmersmarkets.com) to see what else is happening where.

Cooking Courses & Food Tours

Buddha Bellies (p146) Small chef-led courses on sushi and *bentō*-making.

Tokyo Cook (p86) Learn to make *shōjin ryōri*, vegetarian temple food.

Tokyo Cooking Studio (p75) Soba-making lessons from a seasoned pro.

Tokyo Kitchen (p170) Japanese standards; can do vegetarian and gluten-free.

Tokyo Sushi Academy (p75) Crash course in sushi-making.

Special Diets

Vegetarians & Vegans Tokyo has a few vegetarian restaurants and many can accommodate the request *'Bejitarian dekimasu ka'* (Can you do vegetarian?); see Happy Cow (www.happycow.net/asia/japan/tokyo) for a list. One note of caution: often dishes that look vegetarian are not (miso soup, for example) because they are prepared with *dashi* (fish stock).

Allergies & Gluten-Free Many chain restaurants and deli counters label their dishes with icons indicating potential allergens (such as dairy, eggs, peanuts, wheat and shellfish). Gluten free is hard: many kitchen staples, such as soy sauce, contain wheat and even restaurant staff may not be aware of this. The Gluten-Free Expats Japan Facebook group is a good resource.

Halal Tokyo now has more halal options than it used to have. See Halal Gourmet Japan (www.halalgourmet.jp) for a list of restaurants that can accomodate halal (and vegetarian) diners.

Eating by Neighbourhood

➡ **Marunouchi & Nihombashi** Midrange options for the local office crowd in Marunouchi; classic Japanese in Nihombashi.

➡ **Roppongi, Akasaka & Around** Both break-the-bank and midrange options, with a good selection of international cuisines.

➡ **Ginza & Tsukiji** Upscale restaurants and the best sushi in the city.

➡ **Ebisu, Meguro & Around** Cosmopolitan and hip, with excellent dining options in all price ranges.

➡ **Shibuya & Shimo-Kitazawa** Lively, inexpensive restaurants that cater to a young crowd in Shibuya; good *izakaya* in Shimo-Kitazawa.

➡ **Harajuku & Aoyama** Fashionable midrange restaurants and excellent lunch options aimed at shoppers.

➡ **Shinjuku & Northwest Tokyo** High-end restaurants, under-the-tracks dives and everything in-between; ramen in northwest Tokyo.

➡ **West Tokyo** Nothing fancy, but lots of local faves doing Japanese classics.

➡ **Akihabara, Kagurazaka & Kōrakuen** Famous for historic eateries in Kanda, comfort food in Akihabara.

➡ **Ueno, Yanesen & Komagome** Classic Japanese restaurants, mostly midrange and budget.

➡ **Asakusa & Sumida River** Unpretentious Japanese fare, old-school charm and modest prices.

➡ **Odaiba & Tokyo Bay** Restaurants popular with teens and families; lots of big chains.

MATT MUNRO / LONELY PLANET ©

Sushi restaurant

Lonely Planet's Top Choices

Kyūbey (p70) Rarefied Ginza sushi at its finest.

Shinsuke (p155) Cult noodles shop.

Kikunoi (p84) Centuries-old *izakaya* adored by sake aficionados.

Tonki (p93) *Tonkatsu* raised to an art.

Tensuke (p122) *Tamago* (egg) tempura to die for.

Kagari (p69) Ramen shop.

Best by Budget

¥

Onigiri Yadoroku (p165) Expert *onigiri* (rice balls) from the city's oldest specialist.

Harajuku Gyōza-rō (p111) Addictive dumplings served all night.

Maisen (p111) Delectable *tonkatsu* (deep-fried pork cutlets) in a former bathhouse.

d47 Shokudō (p98) Regional specialities from around Japan.

¥¥

Kado (p139) Classic home-cooking in an old house.

Innsyoutei (p155) Lovely place to eat *kaiseki*-style in Ueno-kōen.

Steak House Satou (p123) The most reasonably priced *wagyū* (Japanese beef) steaks in town.

Apollo (p69) Modern Greek (and views over Ginza) in the new Tōkyū Plaza building.

¥¥¥

Kozue (p132) Exquisite Japanese dishes and stunning night views over Shinjuku.

Tofuya-Ukai (p85) Handmade tofu becomes haute cuisine.

Matsukiya (p99) Melt-in-your-mouth *sukiyaki*.

Best by Cuisine

Tokyo Classics

Monja Kondō (p74) Tokyo's oldest *monja-yaki* restaurant, in Tsukishima, where it all started.

Kappō Yoshiba (p168) *Chanko-nabe*, the protein-rich stew that fattens up sumo wrestlers, served in an old sumo stable.

Ethiopia (p139) A classic Jimbōchō curry shop.

Daikokuya (p167) Down-home tempura in Asakusa.

Yūrakuchō Sanchoku Inshoku-gai (p70) Lantern-lit alleyway brimming with *yakitori* stalls (and diners).

Kanda Yabu Soba (p143) Venerable Kanda shop making soba since 1880.

Sushi & Seafood

Yanmo (p112) Extravagant spreads of seafood, raw and grilled.

Numazukō (p132) Tokyo's best conveyor-belt sushi restaurant.

Trattoria Tsukiji Paradiso! (p70) Linguine and clams instead of sushi at Tsukiji Market.

Ramen

Gogyō (p81) Taste the *kogashi* (burnt) ramen at this popular late-night haunt.

Harukiya (p122) The definitive Tokyo ramen.

Kikanbō (p139) A match made in heaven for fans of ramen and spice.

Rokurinsha (p165) Find out why Tokyoites can't get enough of *tsukemen* (noodles with dipping sauce on the side).

Best for Old Tokyo Atmosphere

Hantei (p157) Deep-fried skewers in a century-old heritage house.

Otafuku (p167) Charming 100-year-old *oden* restaurant.

Omoide-yokochō (p130) Atmospheric *yakitori* stalls near the train tracks.

Komagata Dozeu (p165) Landmark restaurant serving *dojō-nabe* (loach hotpot) for 200 years.

Izakaya

Shirube (p100) Loud, lively and hip, serving creative fusion dishes.

Donjaca (p132) An *izakaya* straight out of the Shōwa era (1926–89).

Okajōki (p122) Sit at the counter around the huge hearth and watch the chefs work their magic.

Vegetarian

Sougo (p84) Buddhist temple cuisine.

Mominoki House (p112) Gourmet macrobiotic fare.

Nagi Shokudō (p99) Hip vegan hang-out.

Street Food

Yamachō (p67) The perfect breakfast: rolled omelette on a stick at Tsukiji Outer Market.

Commune 246 (p109) Hipster food-truck park.

Nezu no Taiyaki (p157) Popular vendor for fish-shaped bean-paste cakes.

Drinking & Nightlife

Make like Lady Gaga in a karaoke box; sip sake with an increasingly rosy salaryman in a tiny postwar bar; or dance under the rays of the rising sun at an enormous bayside club: that's nightlife, Tokyo-style. The city's drinking culture embraces everything from refined teahouses and indie coffee shops to craft-beer pubs and maid cafes.

Tokyo's Drinking Culture

Drinking in all its forms is a social lubricant in Japan. If alcohol is not your bag, fear not, as the city is as packed with cafes and teahouses as it is bars and clubs. Cafes are also where you'll tap into Tokyo's fads and fashions, such as *cosplay* (costume play) at maid cafes or rent-by-the-hour pets at a wide variety of animal cafes.

Where to Drink

Roppongi has the lion's share of foreigner-friendly bars, while Shinjuku offers the retro warren Golden Gai and the gay-bar district Ni-chōme.

Other top party districts include youthful Shibuya and Harajuku; Shimbashi and Yūrakuchō, which teem with salarymen; and Ebisu and nearby Daikanyama, both of which have some excellent bars. Asakusa's Hoppy-dōri (p165) is a fun, retro-style hang-out.

BARS & IZAKAYA

Places selling alcohol run the gamut from *tachinomi-ya* (standing-only bars) to ritzy cocktail lounges. A staple is the humble *nomiya,* patronised by businesspeople and regular customers. Some will demur at serving foreigners who don't speak or read Japanese.

Izakaya can be cheap places for beer and food in a casual atmosphere resembling that of a pub; more upmarket ones are wonderful places to sample premium sake and the distilled spirit *shōchū.*

In summer, beer gardens open up on department-store roofs, and in hotel grounds and gardens. Many of these places offer all-you-can-eat-and-drink specials for around ¥4000 per person.

KARAOKE & CLUBS

If you've never tried a karaoke box (a small room rented by you and a few of your friends), it's definitely less embarrassing than singing in a bar in front of strangers. With booze and food brought directly to your room, it can easily become a guilty pleasure; rooms generally cost around ¥700 per person per hour.

Tokyo holds its own with London and New York when it comes to top dance venues. Top international DJs and domestic artists do regular sets at venues with body-shaking sound systems. Most clubs kick off after 10pm or so, when the volume increases and the floor fills, and continue until dawn (or later).

CAFES & TEAHOUSES

Chain cafes such as Doutor, Tully's and Starbucks (a nonsmoking oasis with free wi-fi) are common. But don't miss the opportunity to explore Tokyo's vast range of *kissa* (short for *kissaten,* nonchain cafes) and tearooms – many are gems of retro or contemporary design, sport art galleries or are showcases for a proprietor's beloved collection, such as vintage jazz records or model trains.

NEED TO KNOW

Cheers

Don't forget to say (or yell, depending on the venue) *'Kampai!'* when toasting your drinking buddies.

Prices

To avoid a nasty shock when the bill comes, check prices and cover charges before sitting down. If you are served a small snack (*o-tsumami*) with your first round, you'll usually be paying a cover charge of a few hundred yen or more.

Smoking

Tokyo remains a smokers' paradise, but there's a small but growing number of nonsmoking bars and cafes.

Etiquette & Tipping

It's customary to pour for others and wait for them to refill your glass. At smaller bars, male bartenders are often called 'master' and their female counterparts are 'mama-san'. There's no need to tip in bars.

Opening Hours

Tokyo's nightspots stay open from 5pm well into the wee hours.

Beware

Avoid *sunakku* (snack bars), cheap hostess bars that charge hefty sums, and *kyabakura* (cabaret clubs), exorbitant hostess clubs that are often fronts for prostitution. These are concentrated in Shinjuku's Kabukichō and Roppongi.

Useful Websites

Beer in Japan (http://beerinjapan.com/bij) The microbrewery scene.

Tokyo Beer Drinker (http://tokyobeerdrinker.blogspot.co.uk) Reviews of craft-beer bars across the city.

Nonjatta (www.nonjatta.com) Comprehensive source on Japanese whisky.

Sake-world.com (http://sake-world.com) Site of leading non-Japanese sake authority John Gauntner.

25Cafes.com (www.25cafes.com) Reviews smoke-free cafes across Tokyo.

Tokyo Cheapo (http://tokyocheapo.com) Where to drink if you're short on cash.

What to Drink

SAKE & SHŌCHŪ

Japan's national beverage is sake, aka *nihonshū* (酒 or 日本酒). Made from rice it comes in a wide variety of grades, flavours and regions of origin. According to personal preference, sake can be served hot (*atsu-kan*), but premium ones are normally served well chilled (*reishu*) in a small jug (*tokkuri*) and poured into tiny cups known as *o-choko* or *sakazuki*.

More popular than sake, the clear spirit *shōchū* (焼酎) is made from a variety of raw materials including potato and barley. Because of its potency (alcohol content of around 30%), *shōchū* is usually served diluted with hot water (*oyu-wari*) or in a *chūhai* cocktail with soft drinks or tea.

BEER

Biiru (beer; ビール) is by far Japan's favourite tipple. Lager reigns supreme, although several breweries also offer darker beers, including the top four – Kirin, Asahi, Sapporo and Suntory. The craft-beer scene, however, is booming and at specialist pubs and microbreweries such as Yanaka Beer Hall (p157) and Baird Brewery's Harajuku Taproom (p113), you can happily work your way through a range of ales from across Japan.

In bars you can order either *nama biiru* (draught beer) or *bin biiru* (bottled beer) in many varieties. Hoppy, a cheap, low-alcohol mix of carbonated malt and hops that debuted in 1948, is also found on the menus of some retro *izakaya* (Japanese pub-eateries) and bars.

WHISKY

Japan produces some of the finest whiskies in the world and Tokyo now has a growing number of dedicated whisky and scotch bars where travellers can sample the best of the major makers Suntory and Nikka, as well as products from several other active single-malt distilleries in Japan and abroad.

COFFEE & TEA

Cafes where passionate baristas coax the best from roasted coffee beans are increasingly common. It's the varieties of local tea that you may not be so familiar with. Green tea is the default, coming in a variety of forms. *Matcha,* powdered green tea, features in the traditional tea ceremony and has a high caffeine kick. *Sencha* is medium-grade green tea, while *o-cha* and the brownish *bancha* are the regular stuff. You may also come across *mugicha* (roasted barley tea) and *hōjicha* (roasted green tea).

Lonely Planet's Top Choices

Golden Gai (p134) Travel back in time and wander this postwar maze of intimate bars.

Popeye (p168) Get very merry working your way through the most beers on tap in Tokyo.

BenFiddich (p132) Original cocktails made using freshly ground spices and herbs.

SuperDeluxe (p85) Tokyo's most interesting club with an eclectic line-up of events.

Jugetsudo (p71) All kinds of Japanese tea at the Kabuki-za branch of this venerable tea merchant.

Best Bars with a View

New York Bar (p133) Make like Bill Murray in the Park Hyatt's starry jazz bar.

Two Rooms (p113) Cool views and a cool crowd, plus an outdoor terrace.

Jicoo the Floating Bar (p175) See Tokyo illuminated as you cruise the bay.

Bistro Marx (p71) Gaze across to Ginza's iconic Wako department store.

Best Clubs

Womb (p100) Four levels of lasers and strobes at this Shibuya club fixture.

Contact (p100) Sign up online to get into Tokyo's coolest members-only club.

Ageha (p175) One of Asia's largest clubs, set on Tokyo Bay.

Best Indie Coffee Shops

Cafe de l'Ambre (p71) Ginza institution specialising in aged beans from around the world.

Turret Coffee (p71) Ideal for an early morning espresso en route to or from Tsukiji.

Blue Sky Coffee (p123) Tiny wooden cottage concealing a shiny, state-of-the-art coffee roaster.

Best Teahouses

Cha Ginza (p71) Stylish contemporary version of a teahouse in the heart of Ginza.

Uni Stand (p123) Sample single-origin teas and carefully crafted *matcha* lattes.

Mujyōan (p89) Rustic traditional teahouse in the beautiful garden Happō-en.

Imasa (p143) Sip tea in a lovely old wooden house and protected cultural property.

Best for Craft Beer

Craft Beer Market (p63) With several outlets and a good food menu.

Good Beer Faucets (p99) Fine choice of ales in Shibuya.

Harajuku Taproom (p113) Serves the beers of Baird Brewing.

Yanaka Beer Hall (p157) Microbrew ales in a charming complex of old wooden buildings.

Best Gay & Lesbian Venues

Aiiro Cafe (p133) Start your Ni-chōme night at this popular corner bar.

Bar Goldfinger (p133) Friendly vibe at this lesbian bar designed to look like a '70s motel.

Town House Tokyo (p71) Spacious Shimbashi gay bar attracting salarymen and others.

Arty Farty (p134) Rub shoulders (and other body parts) on this bar's packed dance floor.

Best for Karaoke

'Cuzn Homeground (p168) Offering a wild night of warbling in Asakusa.

Shidax Village (p104) Sing your heart out in a deluxe karaoke box.

Best for Cocktails & Spirits

Zoetrope (p133) Sample premium whiskies at this Shinjuku hole-in-the-wall.

Bar Trench (p93) Ebisu-based pioneer in Tokyo's new cocktail scene.

Fuglen Tokyo (p104) Aeropress coffee by day and creative cocktails by night.

Bar Martha (p94) Moodily lit bar with top whisky list and record collection.

Best Quirky Places

N3331 (p144) Ultimate trainspotters' cafe occupying a former train platform.

Samurai (p133) Classic jazz at this *kissa* stacked with 2500 *maneki-neko* (praying cats).

Nakame Takkyū Lounge (p93) Hang with ping-pong-playing hipsters in Naka-meguro.

Ren (p134) Wear sunglasses, as the decor at the Robot Restaurant's sister establishment will dazzle.

Entertainment

Tokyo's range of entertainment is impressive. Take your pick from smoky jazz bars, grand theatres, rockin' live houses, comedy shows and major sports events. And don't be afraid to sample the traditional performing arts: the major venues that stage these shows will offer earphones or subtitles with an English translation of the plots and dramatic dialogue.

Traditional Performing Arts

Little can prepare the uninitiated for the lavish costumes, sets, make up and acting of a classic kabuki play. This highly dramatic, visually arresting form of theatre, with all male performers, is the best known of Japan's traditional performing arts, but there are other forms you can readily view in Tokyo, too, including the stately, slow moving drama of *nō*, and bunraku plays with large puppets expertly manipulated by up to three black-robed puppeteers.

Contemporary Theatre

Language can be a barrier to the contemporary theatre scene, as nearly all productions are in Japanese. Sometimes, though, a show's visual creativity compensates, such as with the camp, colourful musical review shows of Takarazuka (p71) or the *Sakura – Japan in the Box* production at Meiji-za (p63). The long-running Tokyo International Players (www.tokyoplayers.org) regularly performs English-language theatre, as does Black Stripe Theater (http://blackstripetheater.com). You can also catch English and other language shows at Festival/Tokyo (フェスティバル/トーキョー, F/T; http://www.festival-tokyo.jp), usually held each November.

Dance

While Tokyo has Western dance performances, including shows by Tokyo Ballet (http://thetokyoballet.com), it's the home-grown forms of movement that are likely to be of more interest. Keep an eye out for special dance shows in Asakusa and elsewhere by Tokyo's dwindling communities of geisha.

Top troupes specialising in the avant-garde genre *butō*, in which dancers use their naked or seminaked bodies to express the most elemental human emotions, include Sankai Juku (www.sankaijuku.com) and Dairakudakan Kochūten (www.dairakudakan.com), based in Kichijōji. Tokyo Dolores (http://tokyodolores.com) blends elements of Japanese pop culture, folklore and acrobatic dance.

Live Music

All kinds of live music, including rock, blues, jazz, classical and electronica, can be seen performed live in Tokyo. Big international acts often appear at major venues such as Nippon Budōkan (p63) or Tokyo Dome (p144). There are also many good small live houses for intimate shows.

Sports

Sports fans are well served with baseball matches held at Tokyo Dome (p144) and Jingū Baseball Stadium (p113) during the April to October season. Even if you're not in town for one of the year's big sumo tournaments (in January, May and September), it's still possible to watch wrestlers training daily at their stables.

Lonely Planet's Top Choices

National Theatre (p86) Top-notch *nō*, bunraku and other drama in a grand setting.

Kabukiza Theatre (p69) A visual and dramatic feast of traditional theatre awaits inside and out.

Setagaya Public Theatre (p104) Renowned for contemporary drama and dance.

Ryōgoku Kokugikan (p168) Clash of sumo titans at the city's three big tournaments.

Unit (p94) Offering both live gigs and DJs to a stylish crowd.

Best for Live Music

Shinjuku Pit Inn (p134) Tokyo jazz-scene institution for serious devotees.

Liquid Room (p94) A great place to catch big-name acts in an intimate setting.

Club Quattro (p105) Slick venue with an emphasis on rock and roll and world music.

WWW (p104) Great views of the stage for all at this happening Shibuya live house.

Cotton Club (p63) Centrally located venue for high-pedigree performers.

Ni Man Den Atsu (p124) Connect with the underground scene at this notorious punk venue.

Best for Traditional Arts

National Nō Theatre (p116) Watch dramas unfold slowly on an elegant cypress stage.

Asakusa Engei Hall (p169) Best venue for traditional *rakugo* (comedic monologue).

Oiwake (p160) Listen to indigenous tunes at this rare *minyō izakaya* (pub where traditional folk music is performed).

Best for Contemporary Theatre

Setagaya Public Theatre (p104) Leading noncommercial theatre.

Tokyo Takarazuka Theatre (p71) Glitzy, all-female musical revues and plays.

Meiji-za (p63) Venue for the anime-meets-traditional-Japanese dance-and-music spectacular Sakura – Japan in the Box.

Best for Spectator Sports

Ryōgoku Kokugikan (p168) Location of the three annual Tokyo sumo *bashō*.

Tokyo Dome (p144) Home to the Yomiuri Giants, Japan's top baseball team.

Jingū Baseball Stadium (p113) The base of Tokyo underdogs Yakult Swallows.

Best Classical Music Venues

Tokyo International Forum (p58) Location for the La Folle Journee au Japon classical-music festival.

Tokyo Bunka Kaikan (p157) Great acoustics and interiors at this Ueno-kōen venue.

Tokyo Opera City Concert Hall (p134) With legendary acoustics, this halls hosts the Tokyo Philharmonic Orchestra and other famed ensembles.

PLAN YOUR TRIP ENTERTAINMENT

NEED TO KNOW

Tickets

The easiest way to get tickets for many live shows and events is at one of the **Ticket Pia** (http://t.pia.jp; ☎0570-02-9111; ⊙10am-8pm) kiosks scattered across Tokyo. Its online booking site is in Japanese only.

Cinemas

The best time to go to the movies in Tokyo is Cinema Day (generally the first day of the month) when all tickets cost ¥1100 instead of the regular price of ¥1800.

Useful Websites

Tokyo Time Out (http://www.timeout.com/tokyo) Sign up for regular bulletins on what's happening.

Kabuki Web (www.kabuki-bito.jp/eng/top.html) Book tickets online for Shochiku's theatres, including Kabukiza (p69).

Japan Times (www.japantimes.co.jp/events) Listings from the daily English-language newspaper.

Creativeman (http://creativeman.co.jp) Tickets for some theatre and music shows.

Tokyo Dross (http://tokyodross.blogspot.co.uk) Listings for live music and other events.

Tokyo Jazz (http://tokyojazzsite.com) Low-down on the jazz scene.

The Kappabashi area (p167) of Asakusa

Shopping

Since the Edo era, when courtesans set the day's trends in towering geta (traditional wooden sandals), Tokyoites have lusted after both the novel and the outstanding. The city remains the trendsetter for the rest of Japan, and its residents shop – economy be damned – with an infectious enthusiasm. Join them in the hunt for the cutest fashions, the latest gadgets or the perfect teacup.

Crafts

Trendy Tokyo still has a strong artisan tradition. Older neighbourhoods on the east side of town such as Asakusa and Ningyochō have shops that sell woven bamboo boxes, hog's hair brushes and indigo-dyed *noren* (cloths hung as a sunshade, typically carrying the name of the shop or premises) – much like they did 100 (or more) years ago.

There's also a new generation of craftspeople who are no less devoted to *monozukuri* (the art of making things), but who are channelling more contemporary needs

and tastes. They too are drawn to east Tokyo (largely by cheap rent) and are breathing new life into districts formerly known for small-scale manufacturing, turning old warehouses into ateliers, shops and galleries. Some areas to explore include Kuramae (p169), Bakurochō (p59) and 2k540 Aki-Oka Artisan (p144) mall under the elevated tracks between Akihabara and Okachi-machi.

Kimonos

New kimonos are prohibitively expensive – a full set can easily cost a million yen; used kimonos, on the other hand, can be found

for as little as ¥1000 – though one in good
shape will cost more like ¥10,000. It takes
a lot of practice to get down the art of tying
an *obi* (sash) properly, so it's a good idea to
get shop staff to help you (though there's
no reason you can't just wear one like a
dressing gown and forgo the sash entirely).
Another option is a *yukata,* a lightweight,
cotton kimono that's easier to wear. During
the summer you can find these at department stores and even Uniqlo new for less
than ¥10,000. Used kimono and *yukata*
can also be found year-round for bargain
prices at flea markets.

Antique Fairs & Flea Markets

Flea markets and antique fairs pop up
regularly around Tokyo; odds are there will
be at least one on when you visit. Many
take place on the grounds of Shintō shrines,
which adds an extra dimension to the experience of trolling for ceramics, costume
jewellery, old prints and the like. Though
bargaining is permitted, remember that it
is considered bad form to drive too hard a
bargain. Note that sometimes shrine events
(or weather) interfere with markets. Hipster
flea market Raw Tokyo (p109) is held on the
first weekend of the month. For an updated
schedule of all the city's flea markets, see
www.frma.jp (in Japanese).

Electronics

So well known for its electronics shops is
Akihabara that it is nicknamed 'Denki-gai' –
literally 'Electric Town'. However, the big
chain shops such as Yodobashi Camera, Bic
Camera and Laox can be found in major
hubs including Shinjuku, Shibuya, Ueno
and Ikebukuro. Despite the 'camera' in the
name, these shops sell all sorts of things,
including computers, household appliances
and various electronic beauty gadgets (the
latter include items you might not find at
home). You can shop duty-free, but these
days it's unlikely that you'll land much of a
bargain. Make sure anything you purchase
will work in your region.

Top Shopping Experiences

➡ Strolling the boutique-lined backstreets of
Ura-Hara (p116).

➡ Window-shopping and people-watching on
Chūō-dōri, fashionable Ginza's main drag.

➡ Making a trip to the original **Mandarake**
(p124) in Nakano.

NEED TO KNOW

Opening Hours

➡ Department stores: 10am to 8pm

➡ Electronics stores: 10am to 10pm

➡ Boutiques: noon to 8pm

Service

Service is attentive, increasingly so at
more expensive stores, where sales staff
will carry your purchase to the door and
send you off with a bow. If you're feeling
a little claustrophobic, you can put both
yourself and the clerk at ease with '*Mit-
teiru dake desu*' ('I'm just looking').

Paying

Traditional and smaller stores may not
accept credit cards.

Duty-Free

Major department stores and electronics
stores offer duty-free shopping; increasingly, so do smaller shops. Look for stick-
ers in windows that say 'tax-free shop'. To
qualify, you must show your passport and
spend more than ¥5000 in any one shop.
For details, see http://enjoy.taxfree.jp.
Otherwise, sales tax is 8%.

Sizes

All sorts of sizing systems are used and
often you'll find only a 'medium' that's
meant to fit everyone (but is smaller than
a 'medium' in a Western country). To ask
if you can try something on say '*Kore o
shichaku dekimasu ka?*'.

Sales

Clothing sales happen, sadly, just twice a
year in Japan: at the beginning of January
(after the New Year's holiday) and again at
the beginning of July.

Useful Websites

Tokyo Fashion (http://tokyofashion.
com) Info on the latest trends, brands and
boutiques.

Spoon & Tamago (www.spoon-tamago.
com) Blog covering Japanese design, with
shopping recommendations.

Style from Tokyo (http://reishito.com)
Blog from influential Japanese fashion
photographer.

PLAN YOUR TRIP SHOPPING

Shopping by Neighbourhood

Ueno & Yanesen
An old-time
open-air market (p158)

Shinjuku & Northwest Tokyo
Major shopping hub
with everything (p135)

Kōrakuen & Akihabara
Electronics, manga and
contemporary crafts (p144)

West Tokyo
Homewares,
secondhand clothes
and collectables (p124)

Asakusa & Sumida River
Traditional crafts and
artisan workshops (p169)

Imperial
Palace

Marunouchi & Nihombashi
Classic department
stores and fashionable
new malls (p64)

Harajuku & Aoyama
Quirky street fashion
and designer labels (p116)

Roppongi, Akasaka & Around
Designer wares and
ultramodern malls (p86)

Ginza & Tsukiji
Department stores,
luxury boutiques and
foodstuffs (p74)

Shibuya & Shimo-Kitazawa
Trendy youth fashion
and vintage
shops (p105)

Ebisu, Meguro & Around
Stylish clothes and
interior goods (p94)

Odaiba & Tokyo Bay
Mostly malls, but
a few odd finds (p175)

Tokyo Bay

➡ Stocking up on the basics at **Uniqlo**.

➡ Visiting one of Tokyo's grand old *depāto* (department stores), such as **Mitsukoshi** (p64).

➡ Browsing the secondhand shops in Kōenji.

➡ Taking the pulse of youth fashion in Shibuya.

➡ Shopping for traditional crafts on Asakusa's side streets.

Where to Shop

➡ **Boutiques** These are the style arbiters in Tokyo, serving up a carefully edited selection of domestic and international brands. Concentrated in neighbourhoods on the west side of town, such as Shibuya, Harajuku, Aoyama and Daikanyama.

➡ **Department Stores** The city's *depāto* (department stores) are good for accessories on the ground floor, gourmet food items in the basements and Japanese-style homewares on upper floors.

➡ **Malls** Tokyo's many malls pull together popular national and international chains and branches of trend-setting boutiques, plus homewares shops. Spend more time shopping and less time looking for shops.

➡ **Secondhand Stores** Harajuku, Shimo-Kitazawa and Kōenji are neighbourhoods known for having lots of secondhand and vintage clothing shops. You'll find merchandise to be expensive but of excellent quality.

➡ **Variety Stores** Called *zakka-ten* (literally 'miscellaneous stores'), these are a local speciality, carrying an offbeat selection of beauty goods, clever kitchen gadgets and other quirky sundries in attractive packaging – all intended to add a little colour, ease or joy to daily life. Excellent for souvenir hunting.

➡ **¥100 Stores** Stationery, homewares, accessories and snack foods, all priced at ¥100. Need we say more? You'll find these all over the city.

Lonely Planet's Top Choices

Tokyu Hands (p105) Fascinating emporium of miscellaneous oddities.

2k540 Aki-Oka Artisan (p144) Modern artisan bazaar under the train tracks.

Tsukiji Outer Market (p67) Professional-quality kitchen tools.

Dover Street Market Ginza (p74) Comme des Garçons and other avant-garde labels.

Akomeya (p74) Beautifully packaged, traditional gourmet foodstuffs.

Isetan (p135) Trendy Japanese fashion labels and a great basement food hall.

Best for Fashion

Laforet (p116) Harajuku department store stocked with quirky and cutting-edge brands.

Fake Tokyo (p105) A hotbed of up-and-coming Japanese fashion designers.

Kapital (p94) Denim woven on vintage looms and lush, hand-dyed textiles.

Sou-Sou (p116) Traditional Japanese clothing with contemporary panache.

Best for Traditional Crafts

Takumi (p74) One-stop shop for earthy traditional crafts from all over Japan.

Japan Traditional Crafts Aoyama Square (p86) Collection of high-end Japanese artisan work.

Sumida City Point (p164) Showroom for local Tokyo-made products.

Musubi (p116) Versatile patterned cloths in classic and contemporary designs.

Best for Food & Kitchen

Marugoto Nippon (p169) Showcase of food products from around Japan.

Tsukiji Hitachiya (p67) Hand-forged knives and other kitchen tools.

Kappabashi-dōri (p167) Tokyo's kitchenware shopping strip, favoured by pros.

Best for Homewares

Yanaka Matsunoya (p158) Handmade household staples, such as brooms and baskets.

Muji (p64) Minimalist, utilitarian and utterly indispensable homewares at reasonable prices.

Starnet (p59) Beautiful pottery and wooden bowls.

Best for Stationery & Art Supplies

Itōya (p74) Ginza institution for stationery and art supplies.

Pigment (p175) Gorgeous traditional pigments and brushes.

Kakimori (p169) Custom notebooks and pens galore.

Kurodaya (p170) The 150-year-old *washi* (Japanese paper) specialist.

Best for Anime, Manga & Character Goods

Mandarake Complex (p145) Home sweet home for anime and manga fans.

KiddyLand (p117) Toy emporium stocked with character goods.

Sanrioworld Ginza (p75) For all your Hello Kitty needs.

Pokemon Center Mega Tokyo (p135) The gang's all here.

Best for Antiques & Vintage

Ōedo Antique Market (p64) Quality vendors twice a month at Tokyo International Forum.

Tokyo Hotarudo (p169) Treasure trove of early-20th-century accessories and homewares.

Dog (p116) Outré vintage clothes favoured by club kids.

Gallery Kawano (p117) Vintage kimonos in good condition.

Chicago (p117) Bargain bins of secondhand kimonos and yukata.

Best Malls

mAAch ecute (p145) Craft and food stores in a former train station.

Coredo Muromachi (p64) Top-class made-in-Japan fashion and food items.

Ginza Six (p74) Tokyo's newest high-fashion mall.

Shibuya Hikarie (p105) Full of popular fashion boutiques loved by trendy Tokyoites.

Best for Books

Daikanyama T-Site (p92) Designer digs for art and travel tomes.

Jimbōchō Bookstores (p145) Concentrated collection of more than 100 secondhand bookshops.

Kinokuniya (p135) The city's best selection of books on Japan in English.

Explore Tokyo

Marunouchi & Nihombashi **54**
Top Sights .... .56
Sights .... .57
Eating .... .58
Drinking & Nightlife ...... .63
Entertainment .... .63
Shopping .... .64
Sports & Activities .... .64

Ginza & Tsukiji **65**
Top Sights .... .67
Sights .... .68
Eating .... .69
Drinking & Nightlife ...... .71
Entertainment .... .71
Shopping .... .74
Sports & Activities .... .75

Roppongi, Akasaka & Around **76**
Top Sights .... .78
Sights .... .79
Eating .... .81
Drinking & Nightlife ...... .85
Entertainment .... .86
Shopping .... .86
Sports & Activities .... .86

Ebisu, Meguro & Around **87**
Sights .... .89
Eating .... .90
Drinking & Nightlife ...... .93
Entertainment .... .94
Shopping .... .94

Shibuya & Shimo-Kitazawa **95**
Top Sights .... .97
Sights .... .98
Eating .... .98
Drinking & Nightlife ...... .99
Entertainment .... .104
Shopping .... .105
Sports & Activities .... .105

Harajuku & Aoyama .. **106**
Top Sights .... .108
Sights .... .109
Eating .... .111
Drinking & Nightlife ...... .113
Entertainment .... .113
Shopping .... .116
Sports & Activities .... .117

West Tokyo **118**
Top Sights .... .120
Sights .... .121
Eating .... .122
Drinking & Nightlife ...... .123
Entertainment .... .124
Shopping .... .124

Shinjuku & Northwest Tokyo **125**
Sights .... .127
Eating .... .130
Drinking & Nightlife ...... .132
Entertainment .... .134
Shopping .... .135
Sports & Activities .... .135

Kōrakuen & Akihabara **136**
Sights .... .138
Eating .... .139
Drinking & Nightlife ...... .143
Entertainment .... .144
Shopping .... .144
Sports & Activities .... .146

Ueno & Yanesen **147**
Top Sights .... .149
Sights .... .153
Eating .... .155
Drinking & Nightlife ...... .157
Entertainment .... .157
Shopping .... .158
Activities .... .158

Asakusa & Sumida River **159**
Top Sights .... .161
Sights .... .163
Eating .... .165
Drinking & Nightlife ...... .168
Entertainment .... .168
Shopping .... .169
Activities .... .170

Odaiba & Tokyo Bay .. **171**
Sights .... .173
Eating .... .174
Drinking & Nightlife ...... .175
Shopping .... .175
Sports & Activities .... .175

Day Trips from Tokyo .. **177**

Sleeping **191**

TOKYO'S
TOP SIGHTS

Imperial Palace.................56

Tsukiji Outer Market 67

Roppongi Hills 78

Shibuya Crossing.............97

Meiji-jingū
(Meiji Shrine)...................108

Studio Ghibli....................120

Tokyo National
Museum...........................149

Rikugi-en.........................152

Sensō-ji 161

Neighbourhoods at a Glance

① Marunouchi & Nihombashi p54

Marunouchi is a high-powered business district. Its top draw is the Imperial Palace, Tokyo's symbolic centre. Neighbouring Nihombashi is the city's geographic centre, a historic neighbourhood with shops and restaurants that date to the era of the shogun.

② Ginza & Tsukiji p65

Ginza is Tokyo's most polished neighbourhood, a fashion centre resplendent with department stores, art galleries and the city's principal kabuki theatre. A short walk away is a commercial centre of a different kind: Tsukiji's Outer Market.

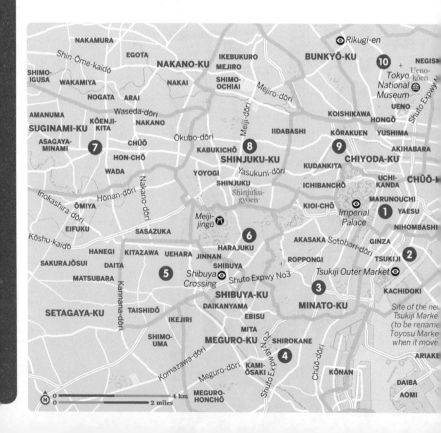

❸ Roppongi, Akasaka & Around p76

Legendary for its nightlife, Roppongi has reinvented itself in the last decade via art and architecture. Nearby Akasaka has a palace, gardens and an upmarket cachet.

❹ Ebisu, Meguro & Around p87

This broad collection of hip neighbourhoods has excellent art and crafts museums, fashionable boutiques, (relatively) quiet streets and few tourists by day.

❺ Shibuya & Shimo-Kitazawa p95

Shibuya is the heart of Tokyo's youth culture and is striking with its continuous flow of people, glowing video screens and the tangible buzz. A short train ride away, Shimo-Kitazawa is a beloved, bohemian haunt.

❻ Harajuku & Aoyama p106

Harajuku is one of Tokyo's biggest draws, thanks to its grand shrine, Meiji-jingū, outré street fashion, contemporary architecture and art museums. Aoyama is a shopping and dining district for the city's elite.

❼ West Tokyo p118

Locals love neighbourhoods Nakano, Kōenji, Ogikubo and Kichijōji for their vintage mid-20th-century look and bohemian spirit.

❽ Shinjuku & Northwest Tokyo p125

Shinjuku is a whole city within the city. To the west is a planned district of soaring skyscrapers; to the east, the city's largest entertainment district. To the north are diverse communities and popular student haunts.

❾ Kōrakuen & Akihabara p136

This swathe of Tokyo runs alongside the former outer moat of Edo Castle, and the Kanda-gawa, from the dazzling traditional garden Koishikawa Kōrakuen to the electronic and pop-culture emporiums of Akihabara.

❿ Ueno & Yanesen p147

Ueno is the cultural heart of Tokyo, with the city's highest concentration of museums. Neighbouring Yanesen is a charming part of Tokyo that feels like time stopped several decades ago.

⓫ Asakusa & Sumida River p159

These districts on the banks of the Sumida-gawa have an old-Tokyo (*shitamachi*) feel, with venerable temples, shrines and gardens, traditional restaurants and artisan shops.

⓬ Odaiba & Tokyo Bay p171

Odaiba, a collection of islands on Tokyo Bay, is a family-oriented leisure district, with shopping malls, galleries and the onsen theme park Ōedo Onsen Monogatari.

NEIGHBOURHOODS AT A GLANCE

Marunouchi & Nihombashi

IMPERIAL PALACE & KITANOMARU-KŌEN | MARUNOUCHI | NIHOMBASHI

Neighbourhood Top Five

❶ Imperial Palace (p56) Strolling through the manicured gardens that were once only for the emperor and his family, and climbing the base of the keep that was at the centre of Edo Castle.

❷ Intermediatheque (p57) Being blown away by the beautiful displays at this fascinating museum crafted from the eclectic collection of Tokyo University.

❸ Tokyo International Forum (p58) Gazing up at the vast atrium of this convention and arts centre, which also hosts a great antiques market twice a month.

❹ National Museum of Modern Art (MOMAT) (p57) Browsing the impressive collection of artworks by both Japanese and international artists and enjoying a panoramic view across the Imperial Palace East Garden.

❺ Nihombashi (p58) Eyeballing the sculpted dragons on Tokyo's most famous bridge, then sailing underneath it on a river cruise.

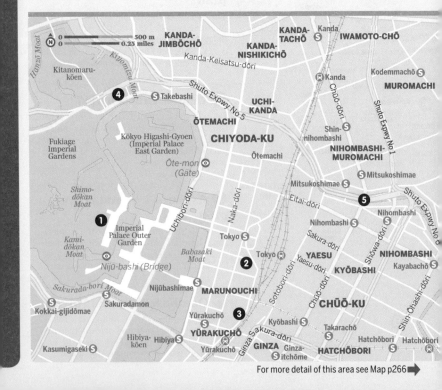

For more detail of this area see Map p266 ➡

Explore Marunouchi & Nihombashi

Tokyo's geographical centre is the Imperial Palace, home of Japan's emperor. Little is open to the public, though it is possible to tour some areas and to visit the Imperial Palace East Garden (p56), where you can admire the remains of the mammoth stone walls that once constituted Edo-jō, the largest fortress in the world. Kitanomaru-kōen, north of the main palace area, is renowned for the springtime cherry blossoms by its northern gate, and contains a trio of arts and science museums.

Immediately east of the palace, the once drab business stronghold of Marunouchi has blossomed in recent years with a slew of new and revamped buildings including high-end hotels, shops and restaurants. Tree-lined Naka-dōri has morphed into one of Tokyo's most pleasant thoroughfares, the ideal way to saunter from Tokyo Station's (p58) handsomely reappointed red-brick entrance to Yūrakuchō.

Also having undergone a recent architectural facelift is Nihombashi (also spelled Nihonbashi), northeast of Tokyo Station. Joining the elegant department stores Mitsukoshi (p64) and Takashimaya (p64) here is the Coredo Muromachi (p64) shopping, dining and entertainment complex. Further east towards the Sumida-gawa, the old *shitamachi* (downtown) areas of Ningyōchō and Bakurochō are worth browsing for traditional shops, smalls shrines and contemporary galleries.

Local Life

➡**Market** At Tokyo International Forum's twice monthly Ōedo Antique Market (p64), shop for unusual and unique souvenirs and gifts.

➡**Shopping** Browse high-end boutiques along Marunouchi's Naka-dōri or craft and gourmet-food stores on Ningyōchō's Amazake Yokochō (p59).

➡**Exercise** Jog or cycle around the Imperial Palace (p56), or get a gentle workout from the rental pedal boats in the north section of the moat.

Getting There & Away

➡**Train** The Yamanote and other JR lines, including the Narita Express and *shinkansen* (bullet train) services, stop at Tokyo Station. Yūrakuchō Station, one stop south, is also convenient for the area.

➡**Subway** The Marunouchi line connects with Tokyo Station. The Mita, Chiyoda and Hanzōmon lines also have stops nearby. The Ginza line is handy for Kyōbashi and Nihombashi.

Lonely Planet's Top Tip

At the foot of Nihombashi is a landing from which you can board boats run by **Tokyo Bay Cruise** (www.ss3.jp; 1 Nihombashi, Chūō-ku; %03-5679-7311; 45/60min cruises ¥1500/2000) for a unique perspective of the city. Lasting either 45 minutes or an hour, the cruises proceed along the Nihombashi-gawa, under the historic bridges and the expressway built above the river, out to the Sumida-gawa, or make a loop around Nihombashi-gawa to Kanda-gawa.

Best Places to Eat

➡ Hōnen Manpuku (p59)
➡ Taimeiken (p58)
➡ Dhaba India (p58)
➡ Tamahide (p59)

For reviews, see p58.➡

Best Places to Drink

➡ Manpuku Shokudō (p63)
➡ Peter: the Bar (p63)
➡ Nihombashi Toyama (p63)
➡ 100% Chocolate Cafe (p63)

For reviews, see p63.➡

Best Places to Shop

➡ Coredo Muromachi (p64)
➡ Mitsukoshi (p64)
➡ KITTE (p64)
➡ Muji (p64)

For reviews, see p64.➡

TOP SIGHT
IMPERIAL PALACE

The verdant grounds of Japan's Imperial Palace occupy the site of the original Edo-jō, the Tokugawa shogunate's castle when they ruled the land. In its heyday this was the largest fortress in the world, though little remains of it today apart from the moat and stone walls.

The present palace (Kyūden), completed in 1968, replaced the one built in 1888 and destroyed during WWII. Most of the complex is off-limits, but you can join a free tour organised by the Imperial Household Agency to see a small part of the inner compound. Tours (lasting around 1¼ hours) run at 10am and 1.30pm Tuesday through to Saturday, but not on public holidays or afternoons from late July through August (see the website for a detailed schedule). Reservations are taken – via the website, phone or by post – up to a month in advance. Alternatively, show up at least 30 minutes before the tour at the tour office at **Kikyō-mon** (桔梗門; Map p266; 1 Chiyoda, Chiyoda-ku; [S] Chiyoda line to Ōtemachi, exits C13b & C10) – if there is space you can take part. Bring photo ID.

If you're not on the tour, two palace bridges – the iron **Nijū-bashi** and the stone **Megane-bashi** – can be viewed from the southwest corner of **Imperial Palace Plaza**. Behind the bridges rises the Edo-era **Fushimi-yagura** watchtower. Part of the verdant palace grounds, the **Imperial Palace East Garden** (東御苑; Kōkyo Higashi-gyoen; Map p266; 🕒9am-4pm Nov-Feb, to 4.30pm Mar–mid-Apr, Sep & Oct, to 5pm mid-Apr–Aug, closed Mon & Fri year-round) [FREE] is open to the public; take a token upon arrival and return it when you leave. Free two-hour guided **walking tours** of the garden are offered on Wednesday, Saturday and Sunday; meet at the JNTO Tourist Information Center (p243) before 1pm.

DID YOU KNOW?

The palace grounds are open on 2 January and 23 December (the emperor's birthday). All well-wishers can come and greet the imperial family who stand and wave at specified times from a balcony in front of the palace.

PRACTICALITIES

- 皇居; Kōkyo
- Map p266, A4
- ☎03-5223-8071
- http://sankan.kunaicho.go.jp/english/guide/koukyo.html
- 1 Chiyoda, Chiyoda-ku
- tours usually 10am & 1.30pm Tue-Sat
- [S] Chiyoda line to Ōtemachi, exits C13b & C10

SIGHTS

Imperial Palace & Kitanomaru-kōen

IMPERIAL PALACE PALACE

See p56.

★NATIONAL MUSEUM OF MODERN ART (MOMAT) MUSEUM

Map p266 (国立近代美術館; Kokuritsu Kindai Bijutsukan; ☎03-5777-8600; www.momat.go.jp/english; 3-1 Kitanomaru-kōen, Chiyoda-ku; adult/student ¥430/130, extra for special exhibitions; ⏲10am-5pm Tue-Thu, Sat & Sun, to 8pm Fri; [S]Tōzai line to Takebashi, exit 1b) Regularly changing displays from the museum's superb collection of more than 12,000 works, by both local and international artists, are shown over floors two to four; special exhibitions are mounted on the ground floor. All pieces date from the Meiji period onward and impart a sense of how modern Japan has developed through portraits, photography, contemporary sculptures and video works. Don't miss the 'Room with a View' for a panorama of the Imperial Palace East Garden (p56).

CRAFTS GALLERY MUSEUM

Map p266 (東京国立近代美術館 工芸館; www.momat.go.jp/english; 1 Kitanomaru-kōen, Chiyoda-ku; adult/child ¥210/70, 1st Sun of month free; ⏲10am-5pm Tue-Sun; [S]Tōzai line to Takebashi, exit 1b) Housed in a vintage red-brick building, this annexe of MOMAT (p57) stages excellent changing exhibitions of *mingei* (folk crafts): ceramics, lacquerware, bamboo, textiles, dolls and much more. Artists range from living national treasures to contemporary artisans. The building was once the headquarters of the imperial guards, and was rebuilt after its destruction in WWII.

SCIENCE MUSEUM, TOKYO MUSEUM

Map p266 (科学技術館; ☎03-3212-8544; www.jsf.or.jp; 2-1 Kitanomaru-kōen, Chiyoda-ku; adult/child/student ¥720/260/410; ⏲9.30am-4pm Thu-Tue; 👪; [S]Tōzai line to Takebashi, exit 1b) Featuring a wide selection of exhibits aimed primarily at children and teenagers, the Science Museum has little in the way of English explanations, but you can ask for a free English pamphlet guide. Even without this or an understanding of Japanese, you can still have fun standing inside a soap bubble or watching a whole variety of scientific experiments.

Marunouchi

★INTERMEDIATHEQUE MUSEUM

Map p266 (☎03-5777-8600; www.intermediatheque.jp; 2nd & 3rd fl, JP Tower, 2-7-2 Marunouchi, Chiyoda-ku; ⏲11am-6pm Sun & Tue-Thu, to 8pm Fri & Sat; 🚆JR Yamanote line to Tokyo, Marunouchi exit) [FREE] Dedicated to interdisciplinary experimentation, Intermediatheque cherry picks from the vast collection of the University of Tokyo (Tōdai) to craft a fascinating, contemporary museum experience. Go from viewing the best ornithological taxidermy collection in Japan to a giant pop-art print or the beautifully encased skeleton of a dinosaur. A handsome Tōdai lecture hall is reconstituted as a forum for events, including the playing of 1920s jazz recordings on a gramophone or old movie screenings.

THE GREENING OF MARUNOUCHI

The ongoing rejuvenation of the Marunouchi, Ōtemachi and Yūrakuchō districts by Mitsubishi Estates incorporates a fair amount of greenery in the form of rooftop lawns at **KITTE** (p64), vertical gardens (at Marunouchi Brick Square) and trees (along Naka-dōri).

The greenest of the green, though, is local recruitment firm **Pasona** (パソナ; Map p266; ☎03-6734-1260; 2-6-4 Ōtemachi, Chiyoda-ku; ⏲9am-5.30pm Mon-Fri; [S]Tōzai line to Ōtemachi, exit B6) [FREE]. The exterior of its nine-storey office is clad in plants, while inside around 200 species of fruits, vegetables, rice and herbs make up its urban farm. Staff take meetings beneath trellises from which tomato plants and grape vines dangle, sitting on benches under which bean sprouts germinate. The company canteen, surrounded by water grasses and flowers, hosts classical-music miniconcerts each day at noon that are open to the public.

CHERRY BLOSSOM SPOT

The **Chidori-ga-fuchi moat** surrounding Kitanomaru-kōen explodes with cherry blossoms in spring, making it a prime *hanami* (cherry-blossom viewing) spot. You can also rent pedal boats here to view the blossoms from the water.

TOKYO STATION

LANDMARK

Map p266 (東京駅; www.tokyostationcity.com/en; 1-9 Marunouchi, Chiyoda-ku; ⏚JR lines to Tokyo Station) Tokyo Station celebrated its centenary in 2014 with a major renovation and expansion. Kingo Tatsuno's original elegant brick building on the Marunouchi side has been expertly restored to include domes faithful to the original design, decorated inside with relief sculptures. It's best viewed straight on from the plaza on Miyuki-dōri, the rooftop garden of the KITTE (p64) shopping mall, or the terrace on the 7th floor of the Shin-Maru Building.

TOKYO INTERNATIONAL FORUM

ARCHITECTURE

Map p266 (東京国際フォーラム; ☎03-5221-9000; www.t-i-forum.co.jp; 3-5-1 Marunouchi, Chiyoda-ku; ⏚JR Yamanote line to Yūrakuchō, central exit) FREE This architectural marvel designed by Rafael Viñoly houses a convention and arts centre, with eight auditoriums and a spacious courtyard in which concerts and events are held. The eastern wing looks like a glass ship plying the urban waters; take the lift to the 7th floor and look down on the tiny people below. Also look out for the statue of Ōta Dōkan, the samurai who first built the Edo Castle in 1457.

⊙ Nihombashi

NIHOMBASHI (NIHONBASHI)

BRIDGE

Map p266 (日本橋; www.nihonbashi-tokyo.jp; 1 Nihombashi, Chūō-ku; ⏚Ginza line to Mitsukoshimae, exits B5 & B6) Guarded by bronze lions and dragons, this handsome 1911-vintage granite bridge over Nihombashi-gawa is partly obscured by the overhead expressway. It's notable as the point from which all distances were measured during the Edo period and as the beginning of the great trunk roads (the Tōkaidō, the Nikkō

Kaidō etc) that took *daimyō* (feudal lords) between Edo and their home provinces.

MITSUI MEMORIAL MUSEUM

MUSEUM

Map p266 (三井記念美術館; www.mitsui-museum.jp; 7th fl, Mitsui Main Bldg, 2-1-1 Nihombashi-Muromachi, Chūō-ku; adult/student ¥1000/500; ⏰10am-5pm Tue-Sun; ⏚Ginza line to Mitsukoshimae, exit A7) Stately wood panelling surrounds a small collection of traditional Japanese art and artefacts, including ceramics, paintings and *nō* (stylised Japanese dance-drama) masks, amassed over three centuries by the families behind today's Mitsui conglomerate.

On permanent display is a reconstruction of the interior of the Jo-an tea-ceremony room; the original National Treasure is in Inuyama.

KITE MUSEUM

MUSEUM

Map p266 (凧の博物館; ☎03-3275-2704; www.tako.gr.jp/eng/museums_e/tokyo_e.html; 5th fl, 1-12-10 Nihombashi, Chūō-ku; adult/child ¥200/100; ⏰11am-5pm Mon-Sat; ⏚Ginza line to Nihombashi, exit C5) There are 300 or so kites in this small but fascinating museum, located above the restaurant Taimeiken (p58), including brilliantly painted ones based on folk characters, woodblock prints or samurai armour. None are particularly old (they're made of paper, after all), but they're amazing to admire nonetheless. Ask for an English booklet at reception.

✖ EATING

★ DHABA INDIA

SOUTH INDIAN ¥

Map p266 (ダバ インディア; ☎03-3272-7160; http://dhabaindia.com/dhaba/index.html; 2-7-9 Yaesu, Chūō-ku; lunch from ¥850, mains from ¥1370; ⏰11.15am-3pm & 5-11pm Mon-Fri, noon-3pm & 5-10pm Sat & Sun; ⏚Ginza line to Kyōbashi, exit 5) Indian meals in Tokyo don't come much better than those served at this long-established restaurant with deep-indigo plaster walls. The food is very authentic, particularly the curries served with basmati rice, naan or crispy *dosa* (giant lentil-flour pancakes). Set lunches are spectacularly good value.

★ TAIMEIKEN

JAPANESE ¥

Map p266 (たいめいけん; ☎03-3271-2464; www.taimeiken.co.jp; 1-12-10 Nihombashi, Chūō-ku; lunch from ¥800, omelette ¥1950; ⏰11am-

8.30pm Mon Sat, to 8pm Sun; S Ginza line to Nihombashi, exit C5) *Yoshoku*, Western cuisine adapted to Japanese tastes, has been the draw here since 1931, in particular its borscht and coleslaw (a bargain ¥50 each). For the food movie *Tampopo* (1985), directed by Itami Jūzō, it created *Tampopo omuraisu* (an omelette wrapped around tomato-flavoured rice) and it's been a signature dish ever since.

★ HŌNEN MANPUKU   JAPANESE ¥

Map p266 (豊年萬福; ☎03-3277-3330; www.hounenmanpuku.jp; 1-8-16 Nihombashi-Muromachi, Chūō-ku; mains ¥1280-1850; ⊗11.30am-2.30pm & 5-11pm Mon-Sat, 5-10pm Sun; S Ginza line to Mitsukoshimae, exit A1) Hōnen Manpuku's interior is dominated by giant *washi* (Japanese handmade paper) lanterns, beneath which patrons tuck into bargain-priced beef or pork sukiyaki and other traditional dishes. Ingredients are sourced from gourmet retailers in Nihombashi. Lunchtime set menus are great value, and there's a riverside terrace in the warmer months.

NIHONBASHI DASHI BAR   JAPANESE ¥

Map p266 (日本橋だし場 はなれ; ☎03-5205-8704; www.ninben.co.jp; 1st fl, Coredo Muromachi 2-3-1 Nihombashi-Muromachi, Chūō-ku; mains from ¥840, lunch/dinner set course from ¥950/1500; ⊗11am-10pm; S Ginza line to Mitsukoshimae, exit A4) A key ingredient of the stock *dashi* is flakes of *katsuobushi* (dried bonito), which the Nihombashi-based Ninben has been making and selling since the Edo period. In this restaurant the company showcases its product in myriad delicious ways, including soups, salads and rice dishes.

TOKYO RĀMEN STREET   RAMEN ¥

Map p266 (東京ラーメンストリート; www.tokyoeki-1bangai.co.jp/ramenstreet; B1 First Avenue Tokyo Station, 1-9-1 Marunouchi, Chiyoda-ku; ramen from ¥800; ⊗7.30am-10.30pm; ⩇JR lines to Tokyo Station, Yaesu south exit) Eight hand-picked *rāmen-ya* operate branches in this basement arcade on the Yaesu side of Tokyo Station (p58). All the major styles are covered – from *shōyu* (soy-sauce base) to *tsukemen* (cold noodles served on the side). Long lines form outside the most popular shops, but they tend to move quickly.

WORTH A DETOUR

NINGYŌCHŌ & BAKUROCHŌ

East of Nihombashi, towards the Sumida-gawa, are Ningyōchō and Bakurochō, two Shitamachi (low city) areas that are worth exploring, if you have more time in Tokyo.

Ningyō means doll – these and puppets were once made here when Ningyōchō was a base for performing arts, including kabuki and bunraku. Kabuki is still performed at the neighbourhood's **Meiji-za theatre** (p63). Zone in on the charming shopping street Amazake Yokochō lined with age-old businesses and named after the sweet, milky sake drink *amazake*; you can sample it at **Futaba** (双葉; Map p266; www.futaba-tofu.jp; 2-4-9 Nihombashi-ningyōchō, Chūō-ku; ⊗7am-7pm; S Hibiya line to Ningyōchō, exit A1), along with various sweet and savoury eats made from tofu.

There are also plenty of craft shops and food stalls, selling freshly made rice crackers and *taiyaki* (fish-shaped hot cakes stuffed with sweet *azuki* bean paste), another tasty local speciality. West across Ningyōchō-dōri from **Amazake Yokochō** (甘酒横丁; Map p266; S Hibiya line to Ningyōchō, exit A1), you'll easily spot **Tamahide** (Map p266; ☎03-3668-7651; www.tamahide.co.jp; 1-17-1 Nihombashi-Ningyōchō, Chūō-ku; oyakodon from ¥1500, dinner set-course menu from ¥6800; ⊗11.30am-1pm daily, 5-10pm Mon-Fri, 4-10pm Sat & Sun; S Hibiya line to Ningyōchō, exit A1) by the line of customers waiting for a space inside the restaurant; it has been serving up its signature *oyakodon* (chicken cooked in a sweet soy sauce with egg and served over a bowl of rice) since 1760.

Further north, the wholesale district of Bakurochō has morphed into a mini-hub for small galleries and craft shops. Standouts include the various businesses in the **Agata Takezawa Building** such as the gallery-cafe **Art + Eat** (Map p266; ☎03-6413-8049; www.art-eat.com; 2nd fl, Agata Takezawa Bldg, 1-2-11 Higashi-kanda, Chiyoda-ku; ⊗11am-7pm Tue-Thu, to 9pm Fri & Sat; ⩇JR Sobu line to Bakurochō, exit 2), and the elegant craft shop **Starnet** (Map p266; ☎03-5809-3336; www.starnet-bkds.com; 1-3-9 Higashi-Kanda, Chiyoda-ku; ⊗11am-7pm Tue-Sun; ⩇JR Sobu line to Bakurochō, exit 2).

1. Tokyo International Forum (p58)
Architectural marvel designed by Rafael Viñoly.

2. Kite Museum (p58)
Small but fascinating museum featuring around 300 paper kites.

3. Nihombashi lion (p58)
Detail on the granite bridge over Nihombashi-gawa.

4. KITTE (p64)
Shopping mall incorporating the restored facade of the Tokyo Central Post Office.

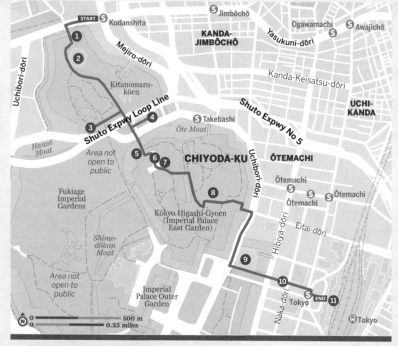

Neighbourhood Walk
Imperial Palace Grounds

START KUDANSHITA SUBWAY STATION, EXIT 2
END TOKYO STATION
LENGTH 1.5KM; TWO TO THREE HOURS

From the subway exit, walk uphill and across the Ushiga-fuchi moat to ❶**Tayasu-mon**. Dating from 1635, the northern gate to Kitanomaru-kōen was once part of the castle Edo-jō. Just inside the park is the ❷**Nippon Budōkan** (p63), a concert and martial-arts hall originally built for the 1964 Olympics.

Follow the road south branching off to the right to find the ❸**Crafts Gallery** (p57), a handsome recreation of a red-brick building that was once the headquarters of the imperial guards. Next, view some exceptional artworks at the ❹**National Museum of Modern Art (MOMAT)** (p57); on the 4th floor, the 'Room with a View' provides a beautiful multi-layered panorama of your next destination: the Imperial Palace East Garden.

Cross the Ōte Moat and enter the palace gardens via ❺**Kitahanebashi-mon**, a drawbridge gate that was the principal entrance to Edo Castle's north side. Beyond the gate is ❻**Tenshudai**, all that remains of the castle's *donjon* (main keep). Climb the stone base for views across the lawn towards the octagonal ❼**Tōkagakudō Concert Hall**, built in 1966 for the 60th birthday of Empress Kojun.

Meander down the Bairin-zaka, a slope lined with more than 50 plum trees to the ❽**Ninomaru Grove**, one of the prettiest parts of the garden with a pond and the elegant Suwano-chaya teahouse.

Exit the gardens via the Ōte-mon, the old main gate to the castle. Across the road, next to the Palace Hotel is ❾**Wadakura Fountain Park** and next door, the pedestrianised central reservation of ginko-tree-lined ❿**Gyoko-dōri**. It provides the perfect frame from which to admire the elegant brick facade and twin domes of ⓫**Tokyo Station** (p58).

DRINKING & NIGHTLIFE

★NIHOMBASHI TOYAMA BAR

Map p266 (日本橋とやま館; ☎03-6262-2723; http://toyamakan.jp; 1-2-6 Nihombashi-muromachi, Chūō-ku; 🕐11am-9pm; [S]Ginza line to Mitsukoshimae, exit B5) Scattered around central Tokyo you'll find many places like this that promote the products of a region of Japan. At this slickly designed outlet, there's a a great bar offering a selection of Toyama's best sakes from 17 different breweries. A set of three 30mL cups costs a bargain ¥700 (90mL cups from ¥600 each). English tasting notes are available.

MANPUKU SHOKUDŌ PUB

Map p266 (まんぷく食堂; ☎03-3211-6001; www.manpukushokudo.com; 2-4-1 Yūrakuchō, Chiyoda-ku; cover charge ¥300; 🕐24hr; 🚆JR Yamanote line to Yūrakuchō, central exit) Down your beer or sake as trains rattle overhead on the tracks that span Harumi-dōri at Yūrakuchō. This convivial *izakaya* (Japanese pub-eatery), plastered with old movie posters, is open round the clock and has bags of atmosphere.

Happy hour, when beers are ¥280, runs from 11am to 8pm Monday to Friday and 3pm to 8pm Saturday.

PETER: THE BAR COCKTAIL BAR

Map p266 (☎03-6270-2763; http://tokyo.peninsula.com/en/fine-dining/peter-lounge-bar; 24th fl, 1-8-1 Yūrakuchō, Chiyoda-ku; 🕐noon-midnight, to 1am Fri & Sat; [S]Hibiya line to Hibiya, exits A6 & A7) The Peninsula hotel's Peter: the Bar distinguishes itself with dress-circle views across the Imperial Palace (p56), Hibiya Park and Ginza as well as a generous happy hour (5pm to 8pm Sunday to Thursday), when drinks and snacks are all ¥800. You can also sample the Peninsula's famous afternoon tea up here.

100% CHOCOLATE CAFE CAFE

Map p266 (☎03-3273-3184; www.meiji.co.jp/sweets/choco-cafe; 2-4-16 Kyōbashi, Chūō-ku; 🕐8am-8pm Mon-Fri, 11am-7pm Sat & Sun; [S]Ginza line to Kyōbashi, exit 5) Meiji is one of Japan's top confectionery companies and this cafe, at its Tokyo headquarters, showcases the brand's range of chocolate. Fittingly, the interior sports a ceiling that mimics a slab of chocolate. Sample three types of drinking chocolate for ¥500, then peruse the scores of different flavoured bars that you can take away.

CRAFT BEER MARKET MITSUKOSHIMAE BEER HALL

Map p266 (Craft Beer Market三越前店; ☎03-6262-3145; www.craftbeermarket.jp; Coredo Muromachi 3, 1-5-5 Nihombashi-Muromachi, Chūō-ku; cover ¥300, beer small/large ¥480/780; 🕐11am-2pm & 5-11.30pm Mon-Fri, 11am-11.30pm Sat & Sun; [S]Ginza line to Mitsukoshimae, exit A4) If trawling Nihombashi's shops has given you a thirst, this craft-beer pub has some 30 kinds of ales and Japanese snacks such as fried chicken. It has some outdoor seating.

☆ ENTERTAINMENT

COTTON CLUB JAZZ

Map p266 (コットンクラブ; ☎03-3215-1555; www.cottonclubjapan.co.jp; 2F Tokia, Tokyo Building, 2-7-3 Marunouchi, Chiyoda-ku; 🕐shows 7pm & 9.30pm Mon-Sat, 5pm & 8pm Sun; 🚆JR lines to Tokyo Station, Marunouchi south exit) You're more likely to hear contemporary international jazz stars here than musicians harking back to the 1920s New York club it honours. Also on the roster is a medley of interesting Japanese artists such as saxophonist Itō Takeshi. Check the website for schedules.

NIPPON BUDŌKAN LIVE MUSIC

Map p266 (日本武道館; ☎03-3216-5100; www.nipponbudokan.or.jp; 2-3 Kitanomaru-kōen, Chiyoda-ku; [S]Hanzōmon line to Kudanshita, exit 2) The 14,000-plus-seat Budōkan, a legendary concert hall for big acts from the Beatles to Beck, was originally built for the martial-arts championships (judo, karate, kendō, aikidō) of the 1964 Olympics (*budō* means 'martial arts') and will be pressed into service again for the 2020 event.

MEIJI-ZA THEATRE

Map p266 (明治座; ☎03-3666-6666; www.meijiza.co.jp; 2-31-1 Nihonbashi-Hamachō, Chūō-ku; [S]Shinjuku line to Hamachō, exit A2) There's been a kabuki theatre here since the late 19th century. Concerts are also held here, along with the dance, music and animation show *Sakura – Japan in the Box* (http://sakura-meijiza.com/en).

SHOPPING

★COREDO MUROMACHI

MALL

Map p266 (コレド室町; http://31urban.jp/lng/eng/muromachi.html; 2-2-1 Nihonbashi-Muromachi, Chūō-ku; 🕒most shops 11am-7pm; [S]Ginza line to Mitsukoshimae, exit A4) Spread over three buildings, this stylish development hits its stride at Coredo Muromachi 3. This section houses several well-curated floors of top-class, Japanese-crafted goods including cosmetics, fashion, homewares, eyeglasses and speciality food.

★MITSUKOSHI

DEPARTMENT STORE

Map p266 (三越; ☎03-3241-3311; www.mitsukoshi.co.jp; 1-4-1 Nihombashi-Muromachi, Chūō-ku; 🕒10am-7pm; [S]Ginza line to Mitsukoshimae, exit A2) Mitsukoshi's venerable Nihombashi branch was Japan's first department store. It's a grand affair with an entrance guarded by bronze lions and a magnificent statue of Magokoro, the Goddess of Sincerity, rising up from the centre of the ground floor. For the full effect, arrive at 10am for the bells and bows that accompany each day's opening.

★KITTE

MALL

Map p266 (https://jptower-kitte.jp/en; 2-7-2 Marunouchi, Chiyoda-ku; 🕒11am-9pm Mon-Sat, to 8pm Sun; [R]JR lines to Tokyo, Marunouchi south exit) This well-designed shopping mall at the foot of JP Tower incorporates the restored facade of the former Tokyo Central Post Office. It is notable for its atrium, around which is arrayed a quality selection of craft-oriented Japanese-brand shops selling homewares, fashion, accessories and lifestyle goods.

★MUJI

HOMEWARES

Map p266 (無印良品; ☎03-5208-8241; www.muji.com; 3-8-3 Marunouchi, Chiyoda-ku; 🕒10am-9pm; [R]JR Yamanote line to Yūrakuchō, Kyōbashi exit) The flagship store of the famously understated brand sells elegant, simple clothing, accessories and homewares. There are scores of other outlets across Tokyo, including a good one in Tokyo Midtown, but the Yūrakuchō store is the largest with the biggest range. It also offers tax-free shopping, bicycle rental (¥1080 a day from 10am to 8pm) and a great cafeteria.

ŌEDO ANTIQUE MARKET

ANTIQUES

Map p266 (大江戸骨董市; ☎03-6407-6011; www.antique-market.jp; 3-5-1 Marunouchi, Chiyoda-ku; 🕒9am-4pm 1st & 3rd Sun of month; [R]JR Yamanote line to Yūrakuchō, Kokusai Forum exit) Held in the courtyard of Tokyo International Forum (p58), usually on the first and third Sunday of every month (check the website before you head out), this is a colourful event with hundreds of dealers and a good chance to bargain for retro and antique Japanese goods, from old ceramics to kitsch plastic figurines.

TOKYO CHARACTER STREET

TOYS

Map p266 (東京キャラクターストリート; www.tokyoeki-1bangai.co.jp; B1 First Avenue Tokyo Station, 1-9-1 Marunouchi, Chiyoda-ku; 🕒10am-8.30pm; [R]JR lines to Tokyo Station, Yaesu exit) From Doraemon to Hello Kitty and Ultraman, Japan knows *kawaii* (cute) and how to merchandise it. In the basement on the Yaesu side of Tokyo Station (p58), some 15 Japanese TV networks and toy manufacturers operate stalls selling official plush toys, sweets, accessories and the all-important miniature character to dangle from your mobile phone.

TAKASHIMAYA

DEPARTMENT STORE

Map p266 (高島屋; www.takashimaya.co.jp/tokyo/store_information; 2-4-1 Nihombashi, Chūō-ku; 🕒10am-8pm; [S]Ginza line to Nihombashi, Takashimaya exit) The design of Takashimaya's flagship store (1933) tips its pillbox hat to New York's Gilded Age with marble columns, chandeliers and uniformed female elevator operators announcing each floor in high-pitched sing-song voices.

SPORTS & ACTIVITIES

IMPERIAL PALACE CYCLING COURSE

CYCLING

Map p266 (パレスサイクリングコース; www.jbpi.or.jp/english/pc1.html; Babasakimon Police Box; 🕒10am-3pm Sun; [S]Chiyoda line to Nijūbashimae, exit 2) Every Sunday (bar rainy days), 150 free bicycles are provided for use along this 3.3km cycling course between **Iwaida Bridge** and **Hirakawa Gate**. Bikes are given on a first-come, first-served basis and can be picked up next to the Babasakimon police box in Imperial Palace Plaza (p56).

Ginza & Tsukiji

Neighbourhood Top Five

❶ Tsukiji Outer Market (p67) Rising early to catch the best of the city's seafood and other delicious eats at this bustling market area next to the old wholesale market.

❷ Dover Street Market Ginza (p74) Browsing some of Japan's top designers at this boutique that's like a

contemporary art gallery, then continuing shopping at Ginza's poshest shops and department stores.

❸ Kabukiza Theatre (p69) Lining up for a one-act ticket and being entertained by the Technicolor spectacle of kabuki drama.

❹ Hama-rikyū Onshi-teien (p68) Strolling past

immaculately manicured trees, some hundreds of years old, and sipping green tea in this beautiful bayside garden.

❺ Yūrakuchō Sanchoku Inshokugai (p70) Snacking on *yakitori* (chicken skewers) with salarymen and women under the railway tracks.

For more detail of this area see Map p268 ➡

Lonely Planet's Top Tip

Besides visiting Hama-rikyū Onshi-teien (p68) as a side trip from Ginza or Tsukiji, consider travelling by boat (p236) to or from Asakusa via the Sumida-gawa (Sumida River).

Best Places to Eat

➤ Kyūbey (p70)

➤ Trattoria Tsukiji Paradiso! (p70)

➤ Apollo (p69)

➤ Kagari (p69)

For reviews, see p69. ➡

Best Places to Drink

➤ Cha Ginza (p71)

➤ Cafe de l'Ambre (p71)

➤ Turret Coffee (p71)

➤ Bistro Marx (p71)

➤ Kagaya (p71)

For reviews, see p71. ➡

Best Places to Shop

➤ Takumi (p74)

➤ Itōya (p74)

➤ Akomeya (p74)

➤ Dover Street Market Ginza (p74)

For reviews, see p74. ➡

Explore Ginza & Tsukiji

Proudly ranking alongside Fifth Avenue and the Champs-Élysées, Ginza is among the world's most famous shopping districts, though it's not as exclusive as it used to be: now alongside Mikimoto Pearls and Louis Vuitton you'll also find the likes of Uniqlo. Amid the expense-account establishments, there's also plenty of affordable dining and drinking options, including classy ramen bars and stand-up joints serving everything from fancy French dishes to sushi.

Speaking of sushi, next to Ginza is Tsukiji. The wholesale fish, fruit and vegetable market, where the famous bluefin tuna auctions are held, may still move across Tokyo Bay to a new home in Toyosu in 2017 (or possibly later). Meanwhile, business is booming for the mouth-watering array of food-related businesses of the outer market (p67), which are here to stay. The good news is that you don't need to be up before the crack of dawn to sample the best of Tsukiji or the surrounding area, which includes the bayside garden Hama-rikyū Onshi-teien (p68).

Providing a 21st-century backdrop to the manicured greenery of Hama-rikyū are the skyscrapers of Shiodome and the monorail running through it from Shimbashi (also spelled Shinbashi), the birthplace of Japan's railways. The vaulted spaces beneath the train lines here remain one of Tokyo's most atmospheric spots for a night of drinking and dining.

Local Life

➤**Eating** Explore Mitsukoshi's (p75) and other department stores' *depachika* – basement food floors with plenty of free samples on offer.

➤**Promenading** Go for a stroll along Chūō-dōri each weekend, when a long section of the road is traffic-free from noon to 5pm (until 6pm, April to September).

➤**People-watching** Spot high-class hostesses, clad in kimonos, greeting salarymen at *ryōtei* (exclusive traditional restaurants); you may even see one of Tokyo's rare geisha in Shimbashi.

Getting There & Away

➤**Train** The JR Yamanote line stops at Shimbashi Station and Yūrakuchō Station.

➤**Subway** The Ginza, Hibiya and Marunouchi lines connect at Ginza Station, in the heart of Ginza. For Tsukiji, take either the Hibiya line to Tsukiji or the Ōedo line to Tsukijishijō.

➤**Water Bus** Ferries stop at Hama-rikyū Onshi-teien (p68) and go to Asakusa and Odaiba.

FI) PHOTO / SHUTTERSTOCK ©

TOP SIGHT
TSUKIJI OUTER MARKET

Tsukiji Outer Market (*jōgai-shijō*) is a one-stop shop for anything you need to prepare and serve a great Japanese meal. When (or even if) the neighbouring wholesale market moves on, this atmospheric and justifiably popular area will remain a top attraction for food lovers.

Come hungry, as rows of vendors hawk goods, from dried fish and seaweed to green tea and pickles, with many free samples on offer. There are plenty of snack foods on the go, too, including freshly shucked oysters, fat slices of *tamago-yaki* (sweet and savoury rolled omelettes) on a stick from **Yamachō** (山長; Map p268; ☑03-3248-6002; 4-16-1 Tsukiji; omlette slices ¥100; ◷6am-3.30pm), delicious fish-paste treats from **Tsukugon** (つくごん; Map p268; www.tsukugon.co.jp; 4-12-5 Tsukiji, Chūō-ku; snacks from ¥210; ◷6.30am-2pm Tue-Sun), and *maguro-yaki* (tuna-shaped pancakes, filled with sweet beans) from **Sanokiya** (さのきや; Map p268; 4-11-9 Tsukiji, Chūō-ku; pancakes ¥200-220; ◷8.30am-2pm Thu-Tue). If you'd prefer a sit-down meal, there are tons of restaurants and cafes.

A few vendors from the **intermediate wholesalers' market** (p68) have stalls in **Tsukiji Uogashi** (築地魚河岸; Map p268; www.tsukiji-market.or.jp; 6-chōme Tsukiji, Chūō-ku); this new complex in the outer market lacks the atmosphere of the older structures but the rooftop, open to the public, is a nice place to escape the crowds.

The market is also well stocked with non-edible goods, including crockery and fine-quality kitchen knives: try **Tsukiji Hitachiya** (つきじ常陸屋; Map p268; 4-14-18 Tsukiji, Chūō-ku; ◷8am-3pm Mon-Sat, 10am-2pm Sun) for a great selection of useful kitchen implements.

Before leaving, drop by **Namiyoke-jinja** (波除神社; Map p268; ☑03-3541-8451; www.nami yoke.or.jp; 6-20-37 Tsukiji, Chūō-ku), the Shintō shrine where Tsukiji's workers and residents come to pray. Giant lion masks used in the area's annual festival flank the entrance and there are dragon-shaped taps over the purification basins.

DON'T MISS

➡ Sushi for breakfast or lunch
➡ Delicious street food
➡ Shopping for kitchen gear and gadgets
➡ Namiyoke-jinja

PRACTICALITIES

➡ 場外市場; Jōgai Shijō
➡ Map p268, E3
➡ 6-chōme Tsukiji, Chūō-ku
➡ ◷5am-2pm
➡ Ⓢ Hibiya line to Tsukiji, exit 1

◉ SIGHTS

TSUKIJI OUTER MARKET   MARKET
See p67.

★ TSUKIJI MARKET   MARKET
Map p268 (東京都中央卸売市場, Tokyo Metropolitan Central Wholesale Produce; ☑03-3261-8326; www.tsukiji-market.or.jp; 5-2-1 Tsukiji, Chūō-ku; ⊙5am-1pm, closed Sun, most Wed & all public holidays; Ⓢ Hibiya line to Tsukiji, exit 1) FREE Fruit, vegetables, flowers and meat are sold here, but it's seafood – around 2000 tonnes of it traded daily – that Tsukiji is most famous for. The frenetic **inner market** *(jōnai-shijō)* is slated to move to Toyosu in 2017 or possibly later; the equally fascinating outer market (p67), comprising hundreds of food stalls and restaurants, will stay put.

Before coming here, check the market's online calendar to make sure it's open, and for instructions on attending the **tuna auctions**, which start around 5am.

Tsukiji's star attraction is *maguro* (bluefin tuna) as big as submarine torpedoes and weighing up to 300kg: the sight (and sound) of these flash-frozen whoppers being auctioned is a classic Tokyo experience, worth getting up early (or staying up late) for.

Visitors begin pitching up for one of the 120 allotted places for viewing the auctions from around 3.30am at the **Fish Information Center** (おさかな普及センター; Osakana Fukyū Senta; Map p268; Kachidoki Gate, 6-20-5 Tsukiji, Chūō-ku; ⊙1am-1pm; Ⓢ Hibiya line to Tsukiji, exit 1) in the northwest corner of the market. It's on a first-come, first-served basis. The first batch of 60 visitors go in to see the auctions between 5.25am and 5.50am; the second batch is from 5.50am to 6.15am. As public transport does not start running until around 5am, you will either need to walk or take a taxi to the market this early in the morning.

If you show up later, there's still plenty to see. Attending the **fruit and vegetable auction** (Map p268; ☑03-3261-8326; www.tsukiji-market.or.jp; 5-2-1 Tsukiji, Chūō-ku; ⊙8am market days; Ⓢ Ōedo line to Tsukijishijomae, exit A1) is far less fuss than the tuna auction; just turn up from around 7am. The incredibly perfect and pricey melons you see in department stores go on sale around 8am.

The Seafood Intermediate Wholesalers' Area (p67) opens to the public from 10am. This is where you can see all manner of sea creatures lain out in boxes and styrofoam crates. It's a photographer's paradise, but

you need to exercise caution to avoid getting in the way. Handcarts, forklifts and motorised vehicles perform a perfect high-speed choreography – not accounting for tourists. Don't come here in large groups, with small children or in nice shoes. By 11am the crowds have dwindled and the sprinkler trucks plough through to prep the empty market for tomorrow's sale.

Within the inner market is **Uogashi-yokochō** (魚がし横町; Map p268; sushi set ¥3150; ⊙5am-2pm), a block of tiny restaurants and food and souvenir stalls, set up originally to service market workers but now heavily patronised by visitors.

TSUKIJI HONGWAN-JI   BUDDHIST TEMPLE
Map p268 (築地本願寺; ☑03-3541-1131; www.tsukijihongwanji.jp; 3-15-1 Tsukiji, Chūō-ku; ⊙6am-5pm; Ⓢ Hibiya line to Tsukiji, exit 1) FREE When this impressive branch of the mother temple in Kyoto fell victim to the Great Kantō Earthquake of 1923, it was rebuilt in a classical Indian style, making it one of the most distinctive Buddhist places of worship in Tokyo. Talks in English about dharma are usually held on the last Saturday of the month from 5.30pm. See the temple website for more information.

NAKAGIN CAPSULE TOWER   ARCHITECTURE
Map p268 (中銀カプセルタワー; 8-16-10 Ginza, Chūō-ku; Ⓢ Ōedo line to Tsukijishijō, exit A3) A Facebook campaign has been started by some residents and fans to save Kurokawa Kishō's early-1970s building, which is a seminal work of Metabolist architecture. The tower's self-contained pods, which can be removed whole from a central core and replaced elsewhere, are in various states of decay and the building is swathed in netting, but it's still a very impressive design.

★ HAMA-RIKYŪ ONSHI-TEIEN   GARDENS
Map p268 (浜離宮恩賜庭園; Detached Palace Garden; www.tokyo-park.or.jp/park/format/index028.html; 1-1 Hama-rikyū-teien, Chūō-ku; adult/child ¥300/free; ⊙9am-5pm; Ⓢ Ōedo line to Shiodome, exit A1) This beautiful garden, one of Tokyo's finest, is all that remains of a shogunate palace that once extended into the area now occupied by Tsukiji Market (p68). The main features are a large duck pond with an island that's home to a charming tea pavilion, **Nakajima no Ochaya** (中島の御茶屋; Map p268; www.tokyo-park.or.jp/park/format/restaurant028.html; 1-1 Hama-rikyū Onshi-teien, Chūō-ku; tea

TOP SIGHT
KABUKIZA THEATRE

The flamboyant facade of this venerable theatre, which was completely reconstructed in 2013 to incorporate a tower block, makes a strong impression. It is a good indication of the extravagant dramatic flourishes that are integral to the traditional performing art of kabuki. Check the website for performance details and to book tickets; you'll also find an explanation about cheaper one-act, day seats.

A full kabuki performance comprises three or four acts (usually from different plays) over an afternoon or an evening (typically 11am to 3.30pm or 4.30pm to 9pm), with long intervals between the acts. Be sure to rent a headset (single act ¥500) for blow-by-blow explanations in English, and pick up a *bentō* (boxed meal) to snack on during the intervals.

If four-plus hours sounds too long, 90 sitting and 60 standing tickets are sold on the day for each single act. You'll be at the back of the auditorium but the views are still good. Some acts tend to be more popular than others, so ask ahead as to which to catch, and arrive at least 1½ hours before the start of the performance.

While you're here, stop for tea at Jugetsudo (p71).

➡ 歌舞伎座
➡ Map p268, D2
➡ ☑03-3545-6800
➡ www.kabuki-bito.jp/eng
➡ 4-12-15 Ginza, Chūō-ku
➡ tickets ¥4000-21,000, single-act tickets ¥800-2000
➡ ⓢHibiya line to Higashi-Ginza, exit 3

GINZA & TSUKIJI EATING

set ¥500; ⊘9am-4.30pm), as well as some wonderfully manicured trees (black pine, Japanese apricot, hydrangeas etc), some of which are hundreds of years old.

EATING

★ KAGARI
RAMEN ¥

Map p268 (籠; 4-4-1 Ginza; small/large ramen ¥950/1050; ⊘11am-3.30pm & 5.30-10.30pm; ⓢGinza line to Ginza, exit A10 or B1) Don't get confused – even though the English sign outside Kagari says 'Soba', this stands for *chūka soba*, meaning Chinese noodles, ie ramen. Kagari's luscious, flavoursome chicken broth makes all the difference here and has earned the shop a cult following; there's sure to be a long queue trailing from its tucked-away location on a Ginza alley.

A word to the wise: outside of the busy lunch period you can avoid lining up too long by heading to Kagari's branch in the underground arcade between the C1 and C2 exits of the Marunouchi line at Ginza. Look for it behind the Gano Delicatessen Bar.

ROSE BAKERY
BAKERY ¥

Map p268 (☑03-5537-5038; 7th fl, Ginza Komatsu West, 6-9-5 Ginza, Chūō-ku; baked goods from ¥400, meals from ¥1000; ⊘11am-9pm Mon-Fri, 9am-9pm Sat & Sun; ☑; ⓢGinza line to Ginza, exit A2) This chic branch of the top-class organic bakery chain is on the 7th floor of the same building as Dover Street Market Ginza (p74). Come here for great cakes, healthy salads and sandwiches as well as a full breakfast fry-up on weekends.

★ APOLLO
GREEK ¥¥

Map p268 (☑03-6264-5220; www.theapollo.jp; 11th fl, Tōkyū Plaza Ginza, 5-2-1 Ginza, Chūō-ku; mains ¥1800-5800; ⊘11.30am-10pm; ⓢGinza line to Ginza, exits C2 & C3) Ginza's glittering lights are the dazzling backdrop to this ace import from Sydney with its delicious take on modern Greek cuisine. The Mediterranean flavours come through strongly in dishes such as grilled octopus and fennel salad, taramasalata, and Kefalograviera cheese fried in a saganaki pan with honey, oregano and lemon juice. Portions are large and meant for sharing.

★ TRATTORIA TSUKIJI PARADISO! ITALIAN ¥¥

Map p268 (📞03-3545-5550; www.tsukiji-paradiso.com; 6-27-3 Tsukiji, Chūō-ku; mains ¥1500-3600; ⏰11am-2pm & 6-10pm; 🚇Hibiya line to Tsukiji, exit 2) Paradise for food lovers, indeed. This charming, aqua-painted trattoria serves seafood pasta dishes that will make you want to lick the plate clean. Its signature linguine is packed with shellfish in a scrumptious tomato, chilli and garlic sauce. Lunch (from ¥980) is a bargain, but you may well need to wait in line; book for dinner.

SUSHIKUNI JAPANESE ¥¥

Map p268 (鮨國; 📞03-3545-8234; 4-14-15 Tsukiji, Chūō-ku; seafood rice bowls from ¥3000; ⏰10am-3pm & 5-9pm Thu-Tue; 🚇Hibiya line to Tsukiji, exit 1) Specialising in bowls of sushi rice topped with seafood, this low-key spot is the place to indulge in the freshest of melt-in-the-mouth *uni* (sea urchin) and the salty pop of *ikura* (salmon roe) straight from the market. It's also open in the evenings.

YŪRAKUCHŌ SANCHOKU INSHOKUGAI JAPANESE ¥¥

Map p268 (有楽町産直飲食街; www.sanchoku-inshokugai.com/yurakucho; International Arcade, 2-1-1 Yūrakuchō, Chiyoda-ku; cover charge per person ¥400, dishes from ¥500; ⏰24hr; 🚉JR Yamanote line to Yūrakuchō, Yūrakuchō exit) Stalls dishing up *yakitori* (charcoal-grilled meat or vegetable skewers) have long huddled under the tracks here. This red-lantern-lit alleyway is a modern collective, which sticks to the cheap, cheerful and smoky formula, but uses quality ingredients sourced direct from producers around the country. Sample steak from Hokkaidō and seafood from Shizuoka.

MARU JAPANESE ¥¥

Map p268 (銀座圓; 📞03-5537-7420; www.maru-mayfont.jp/ginza; 2nd fl, Ichigo Ginza 612 Bldg, 6-12-15 Ginza, Chūō-ku; lunch/dinner from ¥1100/4800; ⏰11.30am-2pm & 5.30-9pm Mon-Sat; 🚇Ginza line to Ginza, exit A3) Maru offers a contemporary take on *kaiseki* (Japanese haute cuisine) fine dining. The chefs are young and inventive and the appealing space is dominated by a long, wooden, open kitchen counter across which you can watch them work. Its good-value lunches offer a choice of mainly fish dishes.

Maru's Harajuku branch (p112) is only open for dinner.

★ KYŪBEY SUSHI ¥¥¥

Map p268 (久兵衛; 📞03-3571-6523; www.kyubey.jp; 8-7-6 Ginza, Chūō-ku; lunch/dinner from ¥4000/10,000; ⏰11.30am-2pm & 5-10pm Mon-Sat; 🚇Ginza line to Shimbashi, exit 3) Since 1936, Kyūbey's quality and presentation has won it a moneyed and celebrity clientele. Even so, this is a supremely foreigner-friendly and relaxed restaurant. The friendly owner Imada-san speaks excellent English as do some of his team of talented chefs, who will make and serve your sushi, piece by piece.

GINZA GALLERIES

There are plenty of free shows to view at Ginza's galleries:

Gallery Koyanagi (ギャラリー小柳; Map p268; 📞03-3561-1896; www.gallerykoyanagi.com; 8th fl, 1-7-5 Ginza, Chūō-ku; ⏰11am-7pm Tue-Sat; 🚇Ginza line to Ginza, exit A9) FREE Exhibits notable local and international artists.

Ginza Graphic Gallery (ギンザ・グラフィック・ギャラリー; Map p268; 📞03-3571-5206; www.dnp.co.jp/gallery/ggg; 7-7-2 Ginza, Chūō-ku; ⏰11am-7pm Tue-Fri, to 6pm Sat; 🚇Ginza line to Ginza, exit A2) FREE Focuses on advertising and poster art.

METoA Ginza (Map p268; 📞03-5537-7411; www.metoa.jp/en; Tōkyū Plaza Ginza, 5-2-1 Ginza, Chūō-ku; ⏰11am-9pm; 🚇Ginza line to Ginza, exit C2) FREE Showcases some of Mitsubishi Electric's latest technologies in inventive collaborations with artists.

Shiseido Gallery (資生堂ギャラリー; Map p268; 📞03-3572-3901; www.shiseido.co.jp/e/gallery/html; basement fl, 8-8-3 Ginza, Chūō-ku; ⏰11am-7pm Tue-Sat, to 6pm Sun; 🚇Ginza line to Shimbashi, exit 1 or 3) FREE Specialises in experimental art.

Tokyo Gallery + BTAP (東京画廊; Map p268; 📞03-3571-1808; www.tokyo-gallery.com; 7th fl, 8-10-5 Ginza, Chūō-ku; ⏰11am-7pm Tue-Fri, to 5pm Sat; 🚇Ginza line to Shimbashi, exit 1 or 3) FREE Shows challenging, often political works by Japanese and Chinese artists.

DRINKING & NIGHTLIFE

★TURRET COFFEE CAFE

Map p268 (http://ja-jp.facebook.com/turretcoffee; 2-12-6 Tsukiji, Chūō-ku; ⏲7am-6pm Mon-Sat, noon-6pm Sun; [S]Hibiya line to Tsukiji, exit 2) Kawasaki Kiyoshi set up his plucky indie coffee shop next to Starbucks. It takes its name from the three-wheeled delivery trucks that beetle around Tsukiji Market (p68) – there's one on the premises. Ideal for an early-morning espresso en route to or from the outer market area.

★CAFE DE L'AMBRE CAFE

Map p268 (カフェ・ド・ランブル; ☎03-3571-1551; www.h6.dion.ne.jp/~lambre; 8-10-15 Ginza, Chūō-ku; coffee from ¥650; ⏲noon-10pm Mon-Sat, to 7pm Sun; [R]Ginza line to Ginza, exit A4) The sign over the door here reads 'Coffee Only' but, oh, what a selection. Sekiguchi Ichiro started the business in 1948 and – remarkably at the age of 100 – still runs it himself, sourcing and roasting aged beans from all over the world. It's dark, retro and classic Ginza.

★CHA GINZA TEAHOUSE

Map p268 (茶・銀座; ☎03-3571-1211; www.uogashi-meicha.co.jp/shop/ginza; 5-5-6 Ginza, Chūō-ku; ⏲11am-5pm, shop to 6pm Tue-Sun; [S]Ginza line to Ginza, exit B3) At this slick contemporary tea room, it costs ¥800 for either a cup of perfectly prepared *matcha* (green tea) and a small cake or two, or for a choice of *sencha* (premium green tea). Buy your token for tea at the shop on the ground floor, which sells top-quality teas from various growing regions in Japan.

BISTRO MARX CAFE

Map p268 (☎03-6280-6234; www.thierrymarx.jp; 7th fl, Ginza Place, 5-8-1 Ginza, Chūō-ku; ⏲11am-11pm, bar to 2am; 📶; [S]Ginza line to Ginza, exit A2) As well as French chef Thierry Marx' restaurant here, there's his casual bistro-bar where the outdoor terrace has a dress-circle view across to Ginza's iconic Wako department store. It's a fancy spot for an afternoon coffee and dessert above the throng, or a romantic setting for a drink later at night when it morphs into a bar.

JUGETSUDO TEAHOUSE

Map p268 (寿月堂; ☎03-6278-7626; www.jugestudo.fr; 5th fl, Kabuki-za Tower, 4-12-15 Ginza, Chūō-ku; ⏲10am-5.30pm; [S]Hibiya line to Higashi-Ginza, exit 3) This venerable tea seller's main branch is closer to Tsukiji, but this classy outlet in the Kabuki-za Tower has a Kengo Kuma–designed cafe where you can sample the various Japanese green teas, including *matcha*, along with food. Book for its tea-tasting experience (¥4000), which covers four different types of tea and runs from 10am to noon.

KAGAYA PUB

Map p268 (加賀屋; ☎03-3591-2347; http://kagayayy.sakura.ne.jp; B1 fl, Hanasada Bldg, 2-15-12 Shimbashi, Minato-ku; ⏲7pm-midnight Mon-Sat; [R]JR Yamanote line to Shimbashi, Shimbashi exit) It is safe to say that there is no other bar owner in Tokyo who can match Mark Kagaya for brilliant lunacy. His side-splitting antics are this humble *izakaya*'s star attraction although his mum's nourishing home cooking also hits the spot. Bookings are essential.

TOWN HOUSE TOKYO GAY

Map p268 (タウンハウス東京; ☎03-3289-8558; http://townhousetokyo.web.fc2.com; 6th fl, Koruteire Ginza Bldg, 1-11-5 Shimbashi, Minato-ku; cover incl 1 drink from ¥1000; ⏲6pm-midnight, to 4am Fri; [S]Ginza line to Shimbashi, exit 3) This long-running joint is friendly to *gaijin* (foreigners; literally 'outside people') and has been serving a wide-ranging crowd for years. It provides plenty of space and even a long balcony for a breather. It has karaoke on Fridays and the occasional underwear-only party on Saturday.

ENTERTAINMENT

KABUKIZA THEATRE

See p69.

TOKYO TAKARAZUKA THEATRE THEATRE

Map p268 (宝塚劇場; ☎03-5251-2001; http://kageki.hankyu.co.jp/english/index.html; 1-1-3 Yūrakuchō, Chiyoda-ku; tickets ¥3500-12,000; [S]Hibiya line to Hibiya, exits A5 & A13) If you love camp, this is for you. The all-female Takarazuka revue, going back to 1914, stages highly stylised musicals in Japanese (English synopses are available) where a mostly female audience swoons over actresses, some of whom are in drag.

1

1. Yūrakuchō Sanchoku Inshokugai (p70)
Yakatori alley near Shinjuku station.

2. Hama-rikyū Onshi-teien (p68)
One of Tokyo's finest gardens, all that remains of a shogunal palace.

3. Kabukiza Theatre (p69)
The last of Tokyo's dedicated kabuki theatres.

It's massively popular so shows often sell out. Fear not: there are 49 standing tickets (¥1500) sold daily for each show.

SHOPPING

★DOVER STREET MARKET GINZA — FASHION & ACCESSORIES

Map p268 (DSM; ☎03-6228-5080; http://ginza.doverstreetmarket.com; 6-9-5 Ginza, Chūō-ku; 🕐11am-8pm; [S]Ginza line to Ginza, exit A2) A department store as envisioned by Kawakubo Rei (of Comme des Garçons), DSM has seven floors of avant-garde brands, including several Japanese labels and everything in the Comme des Garçons line-up. The quirky art installations alone make it worth the visit.

★AKOMEYA — FOOD

Map p268 (☎03-6758-0271; www.akomeya.jp; 2-2-6 Ginza, Chūō-ku; 🕐shop 11am-9pm, restaurant 11.30am-10pm; [S]Yūrakuchō line to Ginza-itchōme, exit 4) Rice is at the core of Japanese cuisine and drink. This stylish store sells not only many types of the grain but also products made from it (such as sake), a vast range of quality cooking ingredients and a choice collection of kitchen, home and bath items.

★TAKUMI — ARTS & CRAFTS

Map p268 (たくみ; ☎03-3571-2017; www.ginza-takumi.co.jp; 8-4-2 Ginza, Chūō-ku; 🕐11am-7pm Mon-Sat; [S]Ginza line to Shimbashi, exit 5) You're unlikely to find a more elegant selection of traditional folk crafts, including toys, textiles and ceramics from around Japan. Ever thoughtful, this shop also encloses information detailing the origin and background of the pieces if you make a purchase.

★ITŌYA — ARTS & CRAFTS

Map p268 (伊東屋; www.ito-ya.co.jp; 2-7-15 Ginza, Chūō-ku; 🕐10.30am-8pm Mon-Sat, to 7pm Sun; [S]Ginza line to Ginza, exit A13) Nine floors (plus several more in the nearby annexe) of stationery-shop love await visual-art professionals and seekers of office accessories, with both everyday items and luxury such as fountain pens and Italian leather agendas. You'll also find *washi* (fine Japanese handmade paper), *tenugui* (beautifully hand-dyed thin cotton towels) and *furoshiki* (wrapping cloths).

GINZA SIX — MALL

Map p268 (http://ginza6.tokyo; 6-10 Ginza, Chūō-ku; 🕐10am-10pm; [S]Ginza line to Ginza, exit A2) Opened in April 2017 is Ginza's largest mixed-use development dedicated to maintaining and improving the area's luxury cachet. It includes international and local top-brand shops, restaurants, a superior food hall, a 4000-sq-metre rooftop garden and the **Kanze Nōgakudō**, a theatre specialising in *nō* dramas. Digital and contemporary art will feature in the public areas.

WORTH A DETOUR

TSUKUDA-JIMA & TSUKISHIMA

Where Harumi-dōri meets Kachidoki-bashi, there's a pleasant riverside walkway that runs past **St Luke's International Hospital** to **Tsukuda Ohashi**. Across this bridge, on the left side, is Tsukuda-jima (Island of Cultivated Rice Fields), a charming neighbourhood with traditional shops such as **Tenyasu Honten** (天安本店; Map p268; ☎03-3531-3457; http://tenyasu.jp; 1-3-14 Tsukuda, Chūō-ku; 🕐9am-6pm; [S]Tsukishima, exit 6) selling *tsukudani* (seafood, seaweed and meat preserved in a mixture of soy sauce, salt and sugar). There's also a small, old Shintō shrine, **Sumiyoshi-jinja** (住吉神社; Map p268; ☎03-3531-3500; 1-1-14 Tsukuda, Chūō-ku; 🕐dawn-dusk; [S]Ōedo line to Tsukishima, exit 6), and the attractive red-railed **Tsukudako-bashi** over a tidal inlet that is a popular filming location for TV shows and movies.

South of the Tsukuda Ohashi is Tsukishima, where the main shopping street – Monja-dōri – and the surrounding side streets are famous for their many restaurants serving the savoury dish *monjayaki*. Similar to the pancake *okonomiyaki*, *monjayaki* is a Tokyo original with a looser, scrambled-egg-like texture. **Monja Kondō** (もんじゃ近どう; Map p268; ☎03-3533-4555; 3-12-10 Tsukishima, Chūō-ku; monjayaki from ¥1000; 🕐5-10pm Mon-Fri, 11.30am-10pm Sat & Sun; [S]Ōedo line to Tsukishima, exit 8), in business since 1950, is said to be the area's oldest dedicated *monja* restaurant. It offers some 90 different toppings you can add to the basic mix, and the staff will help you get the hang of making *monjayaki* at your own table grill.

MATSUYA DEPARTMENT STORE

Map p268 (松屋; ☎03-3567-1211; www.matsuya.com; 3-6-1 Ginza; 🕐10am-8pm; [S]Ginza line to Ginza, exit 12A) One of Ginza's top department stores is packed with designer brands. Look out for the section on the 7th floor showcasing household products chosen by the Japan Design Committee, a group of leading designers, architects and critics.

SANRIOWORLD GINZA FASHION & ACCESSORIES

Map p268 (サンリオワールド ギンザ; ☎03-3566-4060; www.sanrio.co.jp/english/store/sh1703100; Nishi Ginza Department Store 4-1 Saki, Ginza, Chūō-ku; 🕐11am-8.30pm Mon, Tue & Sat, to 9pm Wed-Fri, to 8pm Sun; [S]Ginza line to Ginza, exit C5) Sanrio's flagship store is piled high with all the Hello Kitty merchandise your heart could desire, including some pretty blinged-up items of the famous feline fashion icon.

UNIQLO FASHION & ACCESSORIES

Map p268 (ユニクロ; www.uniqlo.com; 5-7-7 Ginza, Chūō-ku; 🕐11am-9pm; [S]Ginza line to Ginza, exit A2) This now-global brand has made its name by sticking to the basics and tweaking them with style. Offering inexpensive, quality clothing, this is the Tokyo flagship store with 11 floors and items you won't find elsewhere.

MITSUKOSHI DEPARTMENT STORE

Map p268 (三越; www.mitsukoshi.co.jp; 4-6-16 Ginza, Chūō-ku; 🕐10am-8pm; [S]Ginza line to Ginza, exits A7 & A11) One of Ginza's grande dames, Mitsukoshi embodies the essence of the Tokyo department store. Don't miss the basement food hall.

SPORTS & ACTIVITIES

TOKYO COOKING STUDIO COOKING

Map p268 (東京クッキングスタジオ; http://tokyo.cookingstudio.org; Hins Minato #004, 3-18-14 Minato, Chūō-ku; classes for up to 3 people from ¥30,000; [S]Yūrakuchō line to Shintomichō, exit 7) Genial English-speaking chef Inoue Akira is a master of soba – noodles made from nutty buckwheat flour. He's taught how to make and eat this classic Tokyo dish to chefs who have gone on to win Michelin stars for their cooking. Classes are held in a compact kitchen overlooking the Sumida River.

LOCAL KNOWLEDGE

GINZA BATHHOUSE

Join salarymen and women freshening up at **Komparu-yu** (金春湯; Map p268; ☎03-3571-5469; www002.upp.so-net.ne.jp/konparu; 8-7-5 Ginza, Chūō-ku; ¥460; 🕐2-10pm Mon-Sat; 🚆Ginza line to Shimbashi, exit 1 or 3), a simple bathhouse that's been located on a Ginza side street since 1863. Tile art includes old-school koi (carp) and the traditional Mt Fuji motifs.

TOKYO SUSHI ACADEMY COOKING

Map p268 (☎03-3362-2789; http://sushimaking.tokyo; 2nd fl, Tsukiji KY Bldg, 4-7-5 Tsukiji, Chūō-ku; per person ¥5400; 🕐9am-3pm Sat; [S]Hibiya line to Tsukiji, exit 1) English-speaking sushi chefs will give you a 30-minute crash course in making the vinegared rice speciality, after which you'll have an hour in which to make (and eat) as much of your favourite type of sushi as you like. Classes are held on Saturday (and sometimes Sunday) in a modern kitchen a stone's throw from the Tsukiji Outer Market (p67).

TSUKIJI MARKET INFORMATION CENTRE WALKING

Map p268 (☎03-3541-6521; www.tsukijitour.jp; 4-7-5 Tsukiji, Chūō-ku; tour per person from ¥8800; 🕐9am-3pm market days; [S]Hibiya line to Tsukiji, exit 2) This popular 2½-hour tour of Tsukiji Market (p68) for a minimum of two people starts with a video and finishes up with a sushi lunch in the area. When the market moves, it will continue tours in the Outer Market (p67) area and likely include a sushi-making class at a local restaurant.

Roppongi, Akasaka & Around

ROPPONGI | AKASAKA | SHIBA-KŌEN

Neighbourhood Top Five

❶ **Mori Art Museum** (p78) Enjoying contemporary art and Tokyo's urban panorama from this gallery that occupies the top of Mori Tower along with the observatory Tokyo City View.

❷ **21_21 Design Sight** (p79) Pondering cutting-edge art, architecture and design ideas at the Andō

Tadao–designed building in the park behind Tokyo Midtown.

❸ **Zōjō-ji** (p81) Walking through the massive entrance gate to this venerable temple and seeing Tokyo Tower in the background.

❹ **National Art Center Tokyo** (p79) Digging the very curvy architecture and

top-notch exhibitions at this Kurokawa Kishō–designed building.

❺ **Hotel New Ōtani Gardens** (p80) Strolling around this serene 400-year-old Japanese garden, which hides within the grounds of this 1960s hotel.

For more detail of this area see Map p270 ➡

Explore Roppongi, Akasaka & Around

Long one of Tokyo's prime nightlife districts, Roppongi has diversified over the last decade, with the successful mixed-use real-estate developments Roppongi Hills (p78) and Tokyo Midtown (p79) bringing arts, culture and high-end shopping to the neighbourhood.

You can easily spend a day exploring the Roppongi Art Triangle, its points anchored by the Mori Art Museum (p78), the Suntory Museum of Art (p79) and the National Art Center Tokyo (p79). As night falls, Roppongi Crossing becomes a magnet for an international crowd of hedonistic party-goers and club touts. Head downhill towards Nishi-Azabu or Azabu-Jūban for more sophisticated dining and drinking options.

Akasaka's proximity to the National Diet, Japan's parliament, defines it as establishment Tokyo. Attractions include Hie-jinja (p81), an important Shintō shrine; the Hotel New Ōtani's beautiful 400-year-old garden (p80); and the National Theatre (p86), the state-sponsored home of traditional performing arts. Further south, in and around Shiba-kōen (Shiba Park), you can ascend or just admire the retro-glam Tokyo Tower (p81) and pace the grounds of the grand Buddhist temple Zōjō-ji (p81).

Local Life

→**Markets** There's a small antiques flea market on the fourth Sunday of the month at Nogi-jinja (p79).

→**Networking** Attend PechaKucha (www.pechakucha.org/cities/tokyo) events at SuperDeluxe (p85) to discover what the local creatives are up to.

→**Events** The covered arena next to Roppongi Hills' Mohri Garden (p78) regularly hosts events and performances, such as those for Roppongi Art Night (www.roppongiartnight.com) and outdoor film screenings during the Tokyo International Film Festival (p27) in October.

Getting There & Away

→**Subway** The Hibiya and Ōedo subway lines run through Roppongi. The Ōedo line runs through Azabu-Jūban and near Shiba-kōen. The Yūrakuchō, Hanzōmon, Namboku, Chiyoda, Marunouchi and Ginza subway lines all converge in and around Akasaka.

→**Bus** The quickest way to get between Roppongi and Shibuya is on buses running along Roppongi-dōri.

Lonely Planet's Top Tip

Keep your ticket stub for Mori Art Museum (p78), Suntory Museum of Art (p79) or the National Art Center Tokyo (p79), and when you visit one of the other two galleries you'll be entitled to a discount on admission. At any of these venues, pick up the *Art Triangle Roppongi* walking map, which lists dozens of smaller galleries in the area.

✕ Best Places to Eat

→ Tofuya-Ukai (p85)
→ Honmura-An (p84)
→ Sougo (p84)
→ Kikunoi (p84)
→ Gogyo (p81)

For reviews, see p81.➡

⚊ Best Places to Drink

→ Brewdog (p85)
→ SuperDeluxe (p85)
→ These (p85)
→ The Garden (p85)

For reviews, see p85.➡

🔒 Best Places to Shop

→ Japan Traditional Crafts Aoyama Square (p86)
→ Souvenir From Tokyo (p86)
→ Axis Design (p86)
→ Tolman Collection (p86)

For reviews, see p86.➡

ROPPONGI, AKASAKA & AROUND

TOP SIGHT
ROPPONGI HILLS

DON'T MISS

- Mori Art Museum
- Tokyo City View
- Maman spider sculpture
- Mohri Garden

PRACTICALITIES

- 六本木ヒルズ
- Map p270, C6
- www.roppongihills.com/en
- 6-chōme Roppongi, Minato-ku
- 🕐11am-11pm
- [S]Hibiya line to Roppongi, exit 1

Roppongi Hills sprawls more than 11 hectares and is home to the city's leading contemporary art museum, a sky-high observatory, shops galore, dozens of restaurants and even a formal garden. It's imposing, upmarket and polarising – an architectural marvel, a grand vision realised or a crass shrine to conspicuous consumption? Explore this urban maze and decide for yourself.

The **Mori Art Museum** (www.mori.art.museum; 52nd fl, Mori Tower, Roppongi Hills, 6-10-1 Roppongi, Minato-ku; ☎10am-10pm Wed-Mon, to 5pm Tue, inside Sky Deck 10am-10pm; adult/child/student ¥1600/600/1100) occupies the 52nd and 53rd floors of Mori Tower. There's no permanent exhibition; instead, large-scale, original shows introduce major local and global artists and movements. Past exhibitions have focused on the works of Chinese artist and dissident Ai Weiwei and native son Murakami Takashi.

Admission to the Mori Art Museum is shared with **Tokyo City View** (東京シティビュー; Map p270; ☎03-6406-6652; www.roppongihills.com/tcv/en; 52nd fl, Mori Tower, 6-10-1 Roppongi, Minato-ku; adult/child/student ¥1800/600/1200; 🕐10am-11pm Mon-Thu & Sun, to 1am Fri & Sat), the observatory that wraps itself around the 52nd floor, 250m high. The view is particularly spectacular at night. Weather permitting, you can also pop out to the rooftop Sky Deck for alfresco views.

The open-air plaza near the street entrance is the lucky home of one of Louise Bourgeois' giant **Maman spider sculptures**. It has an amusing way of messing with the scale of the buildings, especially in photos. There are other sculptural wonders scattered around the complex, too.

Finally, don't miss **Mohri Garden**, modelled after the gardens popular during the Edo period. When juxtaposed with the gleaming towers, it creates a fascinating study of luxury then and now. Look for the cherry trees in spring.

SIGHTS

Roppongi

ROPPONGI HILLS LANDMARK
See p78.

COMPLEX 665 GALLERY
Map p270 (6-5-24 Roppongi, Minato-ku; 🕓11am-7pm Tue-Sat; [S]Hibiya line to Roppongi, exit 1) Opened in October 2016, this three-storey building tucked on a backstreet is the location of three major commercial art galleries: **Taka Ishii** (www.takaishiigallery.com), **ShugoArts** (https://shugoarts.com) and **Tomio Koyama Gallery** (www.tomiokoyamagallery.com). The free shows gather up an eclectic selection of Japanese contemporary works and are generally worth a look.

TOKYO MIDTOWN LANDMARK
Map p270 (東京ミッドタウン; www.tokyo-midtown.com/en; 9-7 Akasaka, Minato-ku; 🕓11am-11pm; [S]Ōedo line to Roppongi, exit 8) This sleek complex, the yin to nearby Roppongi Hills' (p78) yang, brims with sophisticated bars, restaurants, shops, art galleries, a hotel and leafy public spaces. Escalators ascend alongside constructed waterfalls of rock and glass, bridges in the air are lined with backlit *washi* (Japanese handmade paper), and planters full of soaring bamboo draw your eyes through skylights to the lofty heights of the towers above.

SUNTORY MUSEUM OF ART MUSEUM
Map p270 (サントリー美術館; ☎03-3479-8600; www.suntory.com/sma; 4th fl, Tokyo Midtown, 9-7-4 Akasaka, Minato-ku; admission varies, child free; 🕓10am-6pm Sun-Wed, to 8pm Fri & Sat; [S]Ōedo line to Roppongi, exit 8) Since its original 1961 opening, the Suntory Museum of Art has subscribed to an underlying philosophy of lifestyle art. Rotating exhibitions focus on the beauty of useful things: Japanese ceramics, lacquerware, glass, dyeing, weaving and such. Its current Tokyo Midtown (p79) digs, designed by architect Kuma Kengō, are both understated and breathtaking.

21_21 DESIGN SIGHT MUSEUM
Map p270 (21_21デザインサイト; ☎03-3475-2121; www.2121designsight.jp; Tokyo Midtown, 9-7-6 Akasaka, Minato-ku; admission varies; 🕓11am-8pm Wed-Mon; [S]Ōedo line to Roppongi, exit 8) An exhibition and discussion space dedicated to all forms of design, the 21_21 Design Sight acts as a beacon for local art enthusiasts, whether they be designers themselves or simply onlookers. The striking concrete and glass building, bursting out of the ground at sharp angles, was designed by Pritzker Prize–winning architect Andō Tadao.

FUJIFILM SQUARE MUSEUM
Map p270 (フジフイルム　スクエア; http://fujifilmsquare.jp/en; 9-7-3 Akasaka, Tokyo Midtown, Minato-ku; 🕓10am-7pm; 🚆Hibiya line to Roppongi, exit 4A) [FREE] This small gallery on the ground floor of the Tokyo Midtown (p79) West Tower is a fascinating look at the history of cameras, from 18th-century camera obscuras to zoetropes to the latest Fujifilm DSLRs. There are two galleries of photography, as well as a computer with a database of vintage Fujifilm TV ads starring Japanese celebs such as electronica group YMO.

NOGI-JINJA SHINTO SHRINE
Map p270 (乃木神社; ☎03-3478-3001; www.nogijinja.or.jp; 8-11-27 Akasaka, Minato-ku; 🕓9am-5pm; [S]Chiyoda line to Nogizaka, exit 1) This shrine honours General Nogi Maresuke, a famed commander in the Russo-Japanese War. Hours after Emperor Meiji's funerary procession in 1912, Nogi and his faithful wife committed ritual suicide, following their master into death. An **antiques flea market** is held on the shrine grounds on the fourth Sunday of each month (9am to 4pm).

General Nogi's Residence (旧乃木邸; Map p270; 8-11-32 Akasaka, Minato-ku; 🕓9am-4pm; 🚆Chiyoda line to Nogizaka, exit A1) [FREE] is up the hill from the shrine. This is where Nogi disembowelled himself and his wife slit her throat; it's open to the public only on 12 and 13 September, although you can peek through the windows the rest of the year.

NATIONAL ART CENTER TOKYO MUSEUM
Map p270 (国立新美術館; ☎03-5777-8600; www.nact.jp; 7-22-1 Roppongi, Minato-ku; admission varies by exhibition; 🕓10am-6pm Wed, Thu & Sat-Mon, to 8pm Fri; [S]Chiyoda line to Nogizaka, exit 6) Designed by Kurokawa Kishō, this architectural beauty has no permanent collection, but boasts the country's largest exhibition space for visiting shows, which have included titans such as Renoir and Modigliani. Apart from exhibitions, a visit here is recommended to admire the building's awesome undulating glass facade, its cafes atop

HIDDEN GARDENS OF AKASAKA

Akasaka's largest garden – attached to the **State Guest House, Akasaka Palace** – is mostly off-limits to commoners; even on a tour of the palace you will be allowed to see only a tiny portion of the vast area of greenery. Never mind; there are other lovely traditional gardens in the area, but you need to know where to look.

Nonguests are welcome to visit the beautiful 400-year-old garden at **Hotel New Ōtani** (ホテルニューオータニ; Map p270; www.newotani.co.jp; 4-1 Kioi-chō, Chiyoda-ku; 🕐6am-10pm; [S] Ginza line to Akasaka-mitsuke, exit D) [FREE], one of Tokyo's most enchanting outdoor spaces. Once part of the estate of a Tokugawa regent, this Japanese garden includes vermilion arched bridges, koi (carp) ponds and a mini Niagara waterfall. Ask at the hotel reception whether it's possible to access the rooftop **Rose Garden**, which is planted with tens of thousands of the flowers.

Across the road from the New Ōtani are the landscaped grounds wrapping around part of **Tokyo Garden Terrace** (Map p270; www.tgt-kioicho.jp.e.yu.hp.transer.com; 1-2 Kioi-chō, Chiyoda-ku; [S] Namboku line to Nagatachō, exit 9A). Dotted around the complex are large-scale sculptures, including *White Deer* by Nawa Kōhei and the giant metallic flowers of Ōmaki Shinji.

Sōgetsu Kaikan (草月会館; Map p270; ☎03-3408-1151; www.sogetsu.or.jp/e; 7-2-21 Akasaka, Minato-ku; 🕐9.30am-5.30pm Mon-Fri; [S] Ginza line to Aoyama-itchōme, exit 4) is one of Japan's leading schools of avant-garde ikebana (traditional flower arranging). Inside the building's lobby is a giant, climbable piece of installation art – a stone garden by the revered Japanese-American sculptor Isamu Noguchi. There's a cafe here too, on the 2nd floor, with a panoramic view of the trees in the Akasaka Palace garden.

Nearby is the most intriguing garden of all. Bring photo ID, sign in and take the escalator up to the entrance to the Canadian Embassy, which is fronted by the stark and brilliant **stone sculpture garden** (Map p270; 7-3-38 Akasaka, Minato-ko; 🕐garden 10am-5.30pm Mon-Fri; [S] Ginza line to Aoyama-itchōme, exit 4) [FREE]. Designed by the Zen priest Shunmyō Masuno, natural and cut stones from the Hiroshima region are used to represent Canada's geology. Over the balcony, Akasaka Palace's garden and the distant skyscrapers provide *shakkei*, the 'borrowed scenery' that's a key principle of Japanese garden design.

giant inverted cones and the great gift shop Souvenir from Tokyo (p86).

⊙ Akasaka

STATE GUEST HOUSE, AKASAKA PALACE PALACE

(迎賓館, 赤坂離宮; ☎03-3478-1111; www8.cao.go.jp/geihinkan/index-e.html; 2-1-1, Moto-Akasaka, Minato-ku; front garden free, palace & main garden adult/student ¥1000/500; 🕐10am-5pm according to opening schedule; [R] JR lines to Yotsuya) Check online for the opening schedule and somewhat complex admission details for this imperial palace and garden. Outside it's a dead ringer for London's Buckingham Palace. Inside, the tour route passes through four grandly decorated rooms – the most impressive being the **Kacho-no-Ma** (Room of Flowers and Birds), with Japanese ash panels inset with cloisonné panels – plus the entrance hall and main staircase.

Japan's only neo-baroque European-style palace was designed by Katayama Tōkuma, a pupil of British architect Josiah Conder, and completed in 1909. During its lifetime it's hardly been used by the imperial family and today serves duty as the State Guest House, providing accommodation and a diplomatic meeting space for visiting heads of state and other VIPs.

If you've not reserved an entry ticket online (which you will need to do around two months in advance), head to the front gate to bag one of the timed entry tickets, which are made available from 8am. It's very popular with locals so you may have to wait anything up to an hour to get in when your time slot comes up.

Online reservation is essential for the 120 places available on the six daily guided tours (lasting 40 minutes) around **Yushin-Tei**, the Japanese-style annexe building in a separate part of the grounds. The cost of this tour plus entry to the main palace is ¥1500.

HIE-JINJA SHINTO SHRINE

Map p270 (日枝神社; ☎03-3581-2471; www.hiejinja.net; 2-10-5 Nagatachō, Chiyoda-ku; 🕒5am-6pm Apr-Sep, 6am-5pm Oct-Mar; [S]Ginza line to Tameike-sannō, exits 5 & 7) [FREE] Enshrining the deity of sacred Mt Hiei, northeast of Kyoto, this hilltop shrine has been the protector shrine of Edo Castle, now the Imperial Palace (p56), since it was first built in 1478. Host of one of Tokyo's three liveliest *matsuri* (festivals), Sannō-sai (p25), it's an attractive place best approached by the tunnel of red *torii* (gates) on the hill's western side. There are also escalators up the hill from Tameike-sannō.

ATAGO-JINJA SHINTO SHRINE

Map p270 (愛宕神社; ☎03-3431-0327; www.atago-jinja.com; 1-5-3 Shiba, Minato-ku; 🕒dawn-dusk; [S]Hibiya line to Kamiyachō, exit 3) Climbing the 85 stone steps up to this rustically attractive shrine will give you a workout. They are known as *shussei-no-ishiden* (stone staircase of success) after a legend that a samurai managed to climb them on horseback to deliver plum blossoms to Tokugawa Ieyasu. The 1603-vintage shrine occupied the highest point in Edo, 26m above sea level.

MUSÉE TOMO MUSEUM

Map p270 (智美術館; ☎03-5733-5131; www.musee-tomo.or.jp; 4-1-35 Toranomon, Minato-ku; adult/student ¥1000/500; 🕒11am-6pm Tue-Sun; [S]Hibiya line to Kamiyachō, exit 4B) One of Tokyo's most elegant and tasteful museums is named after Kikuchi Tomo, whose collection of contemporary Japanese ceramics wowed them in Washington and London before finally being exhibited at home. Exhibitions change every few months but can be relied on to be atmospheric and beautiful.

⊙ Shiba-kōen

ZŌJŌ-JI BUDDHIST TEMPLE

Map p270 (増上寺; ☎03-3432-1431; www.zojoji.or.jp/en/index.html; 4-7-35 Shiba-kōen, Minato-ku; 🕒dawn-dusk; [S]Ōedo line to Daimon, exit A3) [FREE] One of the most important temples of the Jōdō (Pure Land) sect of Buddhism, Zōjō-ji dates from 1393 and was the funerary temple of the Tokugawa regime. It's an impressive sight, particularly the main gate, **Sangedatsumon** (三解脱門; Map p270), constructed in 1605, with its three sections designed to symbolise the three stages one must pass through to achieve nirvana. The **Daibonsho** (Big Bell; 1673) is a 15-tonne whopper considered one of the great three bells of the Edo period.

TOKYO TOWER TOWER

Map p270 (東京タワー; www.tokyotower.co.jp/english; 4-2-8 Shiba-kōen, Minato-ku; adult/child/student main deck ¥900/400/500, incl special deck ¥1600/800/1000; 🕒observation deck 9am-10pm; [S]Ōedo line to Akabanebashi, Akabanebashi exit) Something of a shameless tourist trap, this 1958-vintage tower remains a beloved symbol of the city's post-WWII rebirth. At 333m it's 13m taller than the Eiffel Tower, which was the inspiration for its design. It's also painted bright orange and white in order to comply with international aviation safety regulations.

The main observation deck is at 145m (there's another 'special' deck at 250m). There are loftier views at the more expensive Tokyo Sky Tree (p163).

🍴 EATING

🍴 Roppongi & Akasaka

★**GOGYŌ** RAMEN ¥

Map p270 (五行; ☎03-5775-5566; www.ramendining-gogyo.com; 1-4-36 Nish-Azabu, Minato-ku; ramen from ¥1290; 🕒11.30am-4pm & 5pm-3am, to midnight Sun; [S]Hibiya line to Roppongi, exit 2) Keep an eye on the open kitchen: no, that's not your dinner going up in flames but the cooking of *kogashi* (burnt) ramen, which this dark and stylish *izakaya* (Japanese pub-eatery) specialises in. It's the burnt lard that gives the broth its dark and intense flavour. There are plenty of other dishes on the menu, and a good range of drinks too.

GONPACHI IZAKAYA ¥

Map p270 (権八; ☎03-5771-0170; www.gonpachi.jp/nishiazabu; 1-13-11 Nishi-Azabu, Minato-ku; skewers ¥190-1500, set lunch weekday/weekend from ¥900/2200; 🕒11.30am-3.30am; [S]Hibiya line to Roppongi, exit 2) This cavernous old Edo-style space (said to have inspired a memorable set in Quentin Tarantino's *Kill Bill*) is a Tokyo dining institution, with other less-memorable branches scattered around the city. *Kushiyaki* (charcoal-grilled skewers) are served here alongside noodles, tempura and sushi.

1. 21_21 Design Sight (p79)
Design museum created by architect Tadao Ando and fashion designer Issey Miyake.

2. Hie-Jinja (p81)
Hilltop protector shrine of Edo Castle and host of Sannō-sai festival.

3. National Art Center Tokyo (p79)
Top-notch exhibitions at this Kurokawa Kishō-designed building.

LAUDERDALE
INTERNATIONAL ¥

Map p270 (☎03-3405-5533; www.lauderdale.
co.jp; 6-15-1 Roppongi, Minato-ku; mains from
¥1400; ◉7am-midnight Mon-Fri, from 8am Sat &
Sun; ☎; Ⓢ Hibiya line to Roppongi, exit 1) Just off
chic Keyaki-zaka and sporting a spacious
outdoor terrace, this is an on-trend, all-day
dining space that works as well for breakfast
as it does for dinner. Weekend brunch is very
popular here, particularly the egg dishes.

CHINESE CAFE 8
CHINESE ¥

Map p270 (中国茶房8; ☎03-5414-5708; http://
en.cceight.com/restaurant; 2nd fl, 3-2-13 Nishi-
Azabu, Minato-ku; dishes from ¥150; ◉24hr; ☎;
Ⓢ Hibiya line to Roppongi, exit 1) This cheap-
and-cheerful Chinese restaurant is known
for its cheeky decor, Peking duck (¥1280)
served at any hour and abrupt service (in
that order). Expect to wait in line for dinner
at weekends.

★SOUGO
VEGETARIAN ¥

Map p270 (宗胡; ☎03-5414-1133; www.sougo.to-
kyo; 3rd fl, Roppongi Green Bldg, 6-1-8 Roppongi,
Minato-ku; mains ¥600-2000, set lunch/dinner
from ¥1500/5000; ☑; Ⓢ Hibiya line to Roppongi,
exit 3) Sit at the long counter beside the open
kitchen or in booths and watch the expert
chefs prepare delicious and beautifully
presented *shōjin-ryōri* (vegetarian cuisine
as served at Buddhist temples). Reserve at
least one day in advance if you want them
to prepare a vegan meal. Look for it in the
building opposite the APA Hotel.

> ### ℹ️ ROPPONGI WARNING
>
> Roppongi is quite innocent, even
> upmarket, during the day. However,
> at night the footpaths along Gaien-
> Higashi-dōri, south of Tokyo Midtown
> (p79), become populated with hawkers
> trying to entice patrons into clubs,
> promising age-old entertainment such
> as massage and liquor. Some of these
> touts can be aggressive, others just
> chatty. Use caution if you follow them,
> as instances of spiked drinks followed
> by theft, beatings and blackouts have
> been reported, to the point that West-
> ern embassies have issued warnings.
> Exercise common sense and healthy
> scepticism. If someone offers you il-
> legal drugs, leave.

★HONMURA-AN
SOBA ¥

Map p270 (本むら庵; ☎03-5772-6657; www.hon-
muraantokyo.com; 7-14-18 Roppongi, Minato-ku;
soba from ¥900, set lunch/dinner ¥1600/7400;
◉noon-2.30pm & 5.30-10pm Tue-Sun, closed 1st
& 3rd Tue of month; ☎; Ⓢ Hibiya line to Roppongi,
exit 4) This fabled soba shop, once located in
Manhattan, now serves its handmade buckwheat noodles at this rustically contemporary noodle shop on a Roppongi side street.
The delicate flavour of these noodles is best
appreciated when served on a bamboo mat,
with tempura or with dainty slices of *kamo*
(duck).

JŌMON
IZAKAYA ¥¥

Map p270 (ジョウモン; ☎03-3405-2585; http://
teyandei.com/?page_id=18; 5-9-17 Roppongi,
Minato-ku; skewers ¥300-1000; ◉6pm-5am; ☑;
Ⓢ Hibiya line to Roppongi, exit 3) This wonderfully cosy kitchen has bar seating, rows of
ornate *shochu* (liquor) jugs lining the wall
and hundreds of freshly prepared skewers
splayed in front of the patrons – don't miss
the heavenly *zabuton* beef stick. It's almost
directly across from the Family Mart – look
for the name in Japanese on the door.

★KIKUNOI
KAISEKI ¥¥¥

Map p270 (菊乃井; ☎03-3568-6055; http://
kikunoi.jp; 6-13-8 Akasaka, Minato-ku; lunch/din-
ner set menu from ¥5940/17,820; ◉noon-1pm
Tue-Sat, 5-8pm Mon-Sat; Ⓢ Chiyoda line to Akasaka, exit 7) Exquisitely prepared seasonal
dishes are as beautiful as they are delicious
at this Michelin-starred Tokyo outpost of a
three-generation-old Kyoto-based *kaiseki*
(Japanese haute cuisine) restaurant. Kikunoi's chef Murata has written a book translated into English on *kaiseki* that the staff
helpfully use to explain the dishes you are
served, if you don't speak Japanese. Reservations are necessary.

🍴 Shiba-kōen

URAMAKIYA
SUSHI ¥

Map p270 (うらまきや; ☎03-5114-5590; www.
uramakiya.com; 2-4-7 Higashi-Azabu, Minato-
ku; rolls from ¥480, set lunch/dinner from
¥800/2000; ◉11.30am-3pm & 5.30-11pm Mon-
Sat; Ⓢ Ōedo line to Akabanebashi) Specialising
in California rolls (there are 50 different
types on the menu or you can invent your
own), this cosy diner is very foreigner-
friendly and does great lunch and dinner

deals. Check out the wonderful cartoon mural of Tokyo in the back dining room.

MORNINGTON CRESCENT
BAKERY ¥

Map p270 (http://mornington-crescent.co.jp; 1-14-3 Higashi-Azabu, Minato-ku; cakes from ¥380; ◷11am until sold out occasional Sat; Ⓢ Ōedo line to Akabanebashi) British baker Stacey Ward has caused a sensation with her authentic marzipan Battenburg cake and Victoria sponges – so much so that fans line up for anything up to an hour to purchase these and other sweet treats at her Saturday bake sales. Check the website for exact dates and for details of baking classes also held here.

★ TOFUYA-UKAI
KAISEKI ¥¥¥

Map p270 (とうふ屋うかい; ☏03-3436-1028; www.ukai.co.jp/english/shiba; 4-4-13 Shiba-kōen, Minato-ku; lunch/dinner set menu from ¥5500/8400; ◷11am-10pm, last order 8pm; ⃕; Ⓢ Ōedo line to Akabanebashi, exit 8) One of Tokyo's most gracious restaurants is located in a former sake brewery (moved from northern Japan), with an exquisite traditional garden, in the shadow of Tokyo Tower (p81). Seasonal preparations of tofu and accompanying dishes are served in the refined *kaiseki* style. Make reservations well in advance.

🍷 DRINKING & NIGHTLIFE

★ BREWDOG
CRAFT BEER

Map p270 (☏03-6447-4160; www.brewdog.com/bars/worldwide/roppongi; 5-3-2 Roppongi, Minato-ku; ◷5pm-midnight Mon-Fri, 3pm-midnight Sat & Sun; 🛜; Ⓢ Hibiya line to Roppongi, exit 3) This Scottish craft brewery's Tokyo outpost is nestled off the main drag. Apart from its own brews, there's a great selection of other beers, including Japanese ones on tap, mostly all served in small, regular or large (a full pint) portions. Tasty food and computer and board games to while away the evening round out a class operation.

★ THE GARDEN
CAFE

Map p270 (☏03-3470-4611; www.i-house.or.jp/eng/facilities/tealounge; International House of Japan, 5-11-16 Roppongi, Minato-ku; ◷7am-10pm; 🛜; Ⓢ Ōedo line to Azabu-Jūban, exit 7) Stare out from this serene tea lounge across the beautiful late-16th-century garden, hidden behind International House of Japan.

There are plenty of tempting pastries and cakes, as well as more substantial meals should you wish to linger – and who could blame you!

★ THESE
LOUNGE

Map p270 (テーゼ; ☏03-5466-7331; www.these-jp.com; 2-15-12 Nishi-Azabu, Minato-ku; cover charge ¥500; ◷7pm-4am, to 2am Sun; Ⓢ Hibiya line to Roppongi, exit 3) Pronounced *teh*-zeh, this delightfully quirky, nook-ridden 'library lounge' overflows with armchairs, sofas, and books on the shelves and on the bar. Imbibe champagne by the glass, whiskies or seasonal-fruit cocktails. Bites include escargot garlic toast, which goes down very nicely with a drink in the secret room on the 2nd floor. Look for the flaming torches outside.

★ SAKE PLAZA
SAKE

Map p268 (日本酒造会館; www.japansake.or.jp; 1-6-15 Nishi-Shimbashi, Minato-ku; ◷10am-6pm Mon-Fri; Ⓢ Ginza line to Toranomon, exit 9) Sake Plaza isn't a bar, but who cares when you can get 30mL thimbles of regionally brewed sake (some 36 types) or *shōchū* (16 types) for as little as ¥100 a shot. There are four tasting sets of three glasses from ¥200 to ¥500. This showroom and tasting space is an ideal place to learn about the national drink.

It's on the ground floor at the back of the Japan Sake Brewers Association Building (日本酒造会館).

★ SUPERDELUXE
CLUB

Map p270 (スーパー・デラックス; ☏03-5412-0515; www.super-deluxe.com; B1 fl, 3-1-25 Nishi-Azabu, Minato-ku; admission varies; Ⓢ Hibiya line to Roppongi, exit 1B) This groovy basement performance space, also a cocktail lounge and club of sorts, stages everything from electronic music to literary evenings and creative presentations in the 20 x 20 PechaKucha (20 slides x 20 seconds) format. Check the website for event details. It's in a brown-brick building by a shoe-repair shop.

AGAVE
BAR

Map p270 (アガヴェ; ☏03-3497-0229; www.agave.jp; B1 fl, 7-15-10 Roppongi, Minato-ku; ◷6.30pm-2am Mon-Thu, to 4am Fri & Sat; Ⓢ Hibiya or Ōedo line to Roppongi, exit 2) Rawhide chairs, *cruzas de rosas* (crosses decorated with roses) and tequila shots for the willing make Agave a good place for a long night in search of the sacred worm. Luckily, this gem in the jungle that is Roppongi is more about savouring the subtleties of its 400-plus varieties of tequila than tossing back shots of Cuervo.

ENTERTAINMENT

NATIONAL THEATRE THEATRE

(国立劇場, Kokuritsu Gekijō; ☎03-3265-7411; www.ntj.jac.go.jp/english; 4-1 Hayabusa-chō, Chiyoda-ku; tickets from ¥1500; [S]Hanzōmon line to Hanzōmon, exit 1) This is the capital's premier venue for traditional performing arts with a 1600-seat and a 590-seat auditorium. Performances include kabuki, *gagaku* (music of the imperial court) and *bunraku* (classic puppet theatre). Earphones with English translation are available for hire (¥650 plus ¥1000 deposit). Check the website for performance schedules.

SUNTORY HALL CLASSICAL MUSIC

Map p270 (☎03-3505-1001; www.suntory.com/culture-sports/suntoryhall; Ark Hills, 1-13-1 Akasaka, Minato-ku; [S]Ginza line to Tameike-sannō, exit 13) This is one of Tokyo's best venues for classical concerts with a busy schedule of accomplished musicians. Its 2000-seat main hall has one of the largest organs in the world.

SHOPPING

★JAPAN TRADITIONAL CRAFTS AOYAMA SQUARE ARTS & CRAFTS

Map p270 (伝統工芸 青山スクエア; ☎03-5785-1301; http://kougeihin.jp/home.shtml; 8-1-22 Akasaka, Minato-ku; ⏰11am-7pm; [S]Ginza line to Aoyama-itchōme, exit 4) Supported by the Japanese Ministry of Economy, Trade and Industry, this is as much a showroom as a shop exhibiting a broad range of traditional crafts, including lacquerwork boxes, woodwork, cut glass, paper, textiles and earthy pottery. The emphasis is on high-end pieces, but you can find beautiful things in all price ranges here.

SOUVENIR FROM TOKYO GIFTS & SOUVENIRS

Map p270 (スーベニアフロムトーキョー; ☎03-6812 9933; www.souvenirfromtokyo.jp; basement fl, National Art Center Tokyo, 7-22-2 Roppongi, Minato-ku; ⏰10am-6pm Sat-Mon, Wed & Thu, to 8pm Fri; [S]Chiyoda line to Nogizaka, exit 6) This shop, in the basement of the National Art Center Tokyo (p79), sells an expert selection of home-grown design bits and bobs that make for perfect, unique souvenirs: a mobile by Tempo, a bag made from fabric dyed using the *shibori* technique or a fun face pack with a kabuki design.

TOLMAN COLLECTION ARTS & CRAFTS

Map p270 (トールマンコレクション; ☎03-3434-1300; www.tolmantokyo.com; 2-2-18 Shiba-Daimon, Minato-ku; ⏰11am-7pm Wed-Mon; [S]Ōedo line to Daimon, exit A3) Based in a traditional wooden building, this reputable gallery represents nearly 50 leading Japanese artists of printing, lithography, etching, woodblock and more. Quality prints start at around ¥10,000 and rise steeply from there. From Daimon Station, walk west towards Zōjō-ji (p81). Turn left at the shop Create. You'll soon see the gallery on your left.

BLUE & WHITE ARTS & CRAFTS

Map p270 (ブルー アンド ホワイト; http://blueandwhitetokyo.com; 2-9-2 Azabu-Jūban, Minato-ku; ⏰11am-6pm; [S]Namboku or Ōedo line to Azabu-Jūban, exit 4) Expat American Amy Katoh sells traditional and contemporary items such as *tenugui* (hand-dyed towels), indigo-dyed *yukata* (light cotton kimonos), bolts of nubby cloth and painted chopsticks. Pick through dishes of ceramic beads or collect bundled-up swatches of fabric for your own creations.

AXIS DESIGN DESIGN

Map p270 (アクシスビル; www.axisinc.co.jp; 5-17-1 Roppongi, Minato-ku; ⏰11am-7pm; [S]Hibiya line to Roppongi, exit 3) Salivate over some of Japan's most innovative interior design at this high-end design complex of galleries and shops selling art books, cutting-edge furniture and other objets d'art.

SPORTS & ACTIVITIES

TOKYO COOK COOKING

Map p270 (☎03-5414-2727; www.tokyo-cook.com; 3rd fl, Roppongi Green Bldg, 6-1-8 Roppongi, Minato-ku; classes from ¥8640; [S]Hibiya line to Roppongi, exit 3) Among the several types of cooking classes on offer here in English are ones focusing on making vegetarian dishes, the temple food *shojin-ryori* and soba noodles. It's held inside the restaurant Sougo (p84).

Ebisu, Meguro & Around

EBISU | MEGURO | SHIROKANE & TAKANAWA | DAIKANYAMA & NAKA-MEGURO

Neighbourhood Top Five

❶ Daikanyama & Naka-Meguro (p92) Exploring the boutiques, cafes and leafy lanes of these fashionable neighbourhoods, far removed (spiritually, at least) from central Tokyo.

❷ Beer Museum Yebisu (p89) Learning about the history of beer in Japan at

the site of one of the country's first breweries.

❸ TOP Museum (p89) Catching an exhibition at Tokyo's leading photography museum, where the collection includes both the icons of Japanese photography and the up-and-comers.

❹ Bar Scene (p94) Squeezing into a space at

one of Ebisu's popular after-work watering holes, such as Buri.

❺ Happō-en (p89) Finding peace at the bottom of a bowl of *matcha* or alongside the koi (carp) pond inside this centuries-old strolling garden, now an urban oasis.

For more detail of this area see Map p274 ➡

Lonely Planet's Top Tip

Daikanyama and Naka-Meguro get a late start; don't expect cafes or boutiques to open before 11am (and sometimes not until noon). The exception is Daikanyama T-Site (p92), which opens from 7am.

✕ Best Places to Eat

➡ Tonki (p93)

➡ Afuri (p90)

➡ Ouca (p90)

For reviews, see p90.

🍷 Best Places to Drink

➡ Nakame Takkyū Lounge (p93)

➡ Buri (p94)

➡ Bar Trench (p93)

For reviews, see p93. ➡

🔒 Best Places to Shop

➡ Okura (p94)

➡ Kapital (p94)

➡ Daikanyama T-Site (p92)

For reviews, see p94. ➡

Explore Ebisu, Meguro & Around

Bookmark this area for a day when you're looking to take it easy. Ebisu and Meguro, both nodes on the Yamanote loop line, are gateways to largely residential (and often upscale) neighbourhoods, where Tokyo takes on a more human scale. Ebisu, named for the prominent beer manufacturer that once provided a lifeline for most of the neighbourhood's residents, is now a hip district anchored by Yebisu Garden Place (p89). Attractions here include the TOP Museum (p89), the city's principal photography museum, and the Beer Museum Yebisu (p89), in the old factory, which traces the history of beer in Japan.

From here it's a short walk to Daikanyama and Naka-Meguro. These adjacent neighbourhoods, with their uncrowded streets, are favourite haunts of fashion, art and media types, whose tastes are reflected in the shops and restaurants here. Alternatively, take the train one stop south to Meguro, where you can sip tea in a garden (p89), light incense at a historic temple (p90) or examine the centuries-old pottery used in tea ceremonies – and see nary another traveller.

Ebisu makes for a fun night out. The bars here, mostly tiny and clustered on a few strips, are a beacon for young professionals, which gives the neighbourhood a definite buzz.

Local Life

➡**Eating** Locals pile into retro arcade Ebisu-yokochō (p91) for grilled fish, fried noodles and copious amounts of beer.

➡**Events** Yebisu Garden Place (p89), with its wide open plaza, hosts weekend events year-round, including a twice-monthly farmers market (first and third Sundays) and open-air movie screenings during the summer.

➡**Shopping** Meguro-dōri (p94) is Tokyo's design district and is lined with furniture and homeware shops.

Getting There & Away

➡**Train** The JR Yamanote line stops at Ebisu, Meguro, Gotanda and Shinagawa Stations. The Tōkyū Tōyoko line runs from Shibuya to Daikanyama and Naka-Meguro; some Fukutoshin subway trains continue on the Tōyoko line.

➡**Subway** The Hibiya line runs through Ebisu to Naka-Meguro. The Namboku and Mita lines stop at Meguro and Shirokanedai. The Asakusa line runs from Gotanda Station to Takanawadai and Sengaku-ji.

SIGHTS

Ebisu

YEBISU GARDEN PLACE PLAZA

Map p274 (恵比寿ガーデンプレイス; www.gardenplace.jp; 4-20 Ebisu, Shibuya-ku; [R]JR Yamanote line to Ebisu, east exit) This shopping and cultural centre was built on the site of the original Yebisu Beer Brewery (1889) that gave the neighbourhood its name. Unlike most modern Tokyo malls, this one is short on shops and big on public space: the large central plaza regularly hosts events, including a farmers market on Sundays.

TOP MUSEUM MUSEUM

Map p274 (東京都写真美術館; Tokyo Photographic Arts Museum; ☎03-3280-0099; http://topmuseum.jp; 1-13-3 Mita, Meguro-ku; ¥500-1000; ⏲10am-6pm Tue, Wed, Sat & Sun, to 8pm Thu & Fri; [R]JR Yamanote line to Ebisu, east exit) Tokyo's principal photography museum reopened in 2016 after a two-year overhaul. In addition to drawing on its extensive collection, the museum also hosts travelling exhibitions. In autumn, it curates a show of up-and-coming Japanese photographers. Usually several exhibitions happen simultaneously; ticket prices depend on how many you see.

The museum is at the far end of Yebisu Garden Place, on the right side of the complex if you're coming from Ebisu Station.

BEER MUSEUM YEBISU MUSEUM

Map p274 (エビスビール記念館; ☎03-5423-7255; www.sapporoholdings.jp/english/guide/yebisu; 4-20-1 Ebisu, Shibuya-ku; ⏲11am-7pm Tue-Sun; [R]JR Yamanote line to Ebisu, east exit) [FREE] Photos, vintage bottles and posters document the rise of Yebisu, and beer in general, in Japan at this small museum located where the actual Yebisu brewery stood until 1988. At the 'tasting salon' you can sample four kinds of Yebisu beer (¥400 each). It's behind the Mitsukoshi department store at Yebisu Garden Place.

YAMATANE MUSEUM OF ART MUSEUM

Map p274 (山種美術館; ☎03-5777-8600; www.yamatane-museum.or.jp; 3-12-36 Hiroo, Shibuya-ku; adult/student/child ¥1000/800/free, special exhibits extra; ⏲10am-5pm Tue-Sun; [R]JR Yamanote line to Ebisu, west exit) When Western ideas entered Japan following the Meiji Restoration (1868), many artists set out to master oil and canvas. Others poured new energy into *nihonga* – Japanese-style painting, usually done with mineral pigments on silk or paper – and the masters of this latter movement are represented here. From the collection of 1800 works, a small number are displayed in thematic exhibitions.

Meguro

TOKYO METROPOLITAN TEIEN ART MUSEUM MUSEUM

Map p274 (東京都庭園美術館; www.teien-art-museum.ne.jp; 5-21-9 Shirokanedai, Minato-ku; adult/child ¥1100/800; ⏲10am-6pm, closed 2nd & 4th Wed each month; [R]JR Yamanote line to Meguro, east exit) Although the Teien museum hosts regular art exhibitions – usually of decorative arts – its appeal lies principally in the building itself: it's an art-deco structure, a former princely estate built in 1933, designed by French architect Henri Rapin. A lengthy renovation (in 2014) saw the addition of a modern annexe designed by artist Sugimoto Hiroshi.

Tip: budget time to lounge around on the perfectly manicured lawn.

INSTITUTE FOR NATURE STUDY PARK

Map p274 (自然教育園; Shizen Kyōiku-en; ☎03-3441-7176; www.ins.kahaku.go.jp; 5-21-5 Shirokanedai, Meguro-ku; adult/child ¥310/free; ⏲9am-4.30pm Tue-Sun Sep-Apr, to 5pm Tue-Sun May-Aug, last entry 4pm; [R]JR Yamanote line to Meguro, east exit) What would Tokyo look like left to its own natural devices? Since 1949 this park, affiliated with the Tokyo National Museum, has let the local flora go wild. There are wonderful walks through its forests, marshes and ponds. No more than 300 people are allowed in at a time, which makes for an even more peaceful setting.

Shirokane & Takanawa

HAPPŌ-EN GARDENS

(八芳園; ☎03-3443-3111; www.happo-en.com/english; 1-1-1 Shirokanedai, Minato-ku; ⏲10am-8.30pm; [S]Namboku line to Shirokanedai, exit 2) [FREE] Three centuries ago this gorgeous urban oasis was the backyard of a vassal to the shogun. Today its the grounds of a banquet hall, but usually anyone can enter to walk through the landscaped gardens (some areas are occasionally roped off for weddings). Highlights include the teahouse **Mujyōan** (無常庵; ☎03-3443-3775; 1-1-11

HARA MUSEUM OF CONTEMPORARY ART

The **Hara Museum of Contemporary Art** (原美術館; www.haramuseum.or.jp; 4-7-25 Kita-Shinagawa, Shinagawa-ku; adult/student/child ¥1100/700/free; ⊗11am-5pm Tue & Thu-Sun, to 8pm Wed; JR Yamanote line to Shinagawa, Takanawa exit) fills the rooms of a rare Bauhaus-style mansion from the 1930s, the residence of the founder's grandparents. It was taken over by the Allied occupation after WWII and used as an officer's residence. Left in a shambles, it was coaxed into its present form – as a museum on the vanguard of Tokyo's art scene – in 1979.

The permanent collection includes works from Japanese artists Morimura Yasumasa and Nara Yoshitomo, both of whom have created installations designed especially for the house's nooks and crannies. Exhibitions feature both domestic and international artists.

The patio cafe (which overlooks the sculpture garden) and excellent gift shop will make you extra glad you made the trip.

The museum is 1.5km from Shinagawa Station. You can walk or take bus 96 from platform six (¥210, every 20 minutes) one stop to Gotenyama, from where it's a three-minute walk.

Shirokanedai, Minato-ku; ⊗11am-4pm; Namboku line to Shirokanedai, exit 2), where you can sample *matcha* (powdered green tea), the row of bonsai (there's a 520-year-old pine!), and the air of serenity.

SENGAKU-JI
BUDDHIST TEMPLE

(泉岳寺; www.sengakuji.or.jp; 2-11-1 Takanawa, Minato-ku; ⊗7am-6pm Apr-Sep, to 5pm Oct-Mar; Asakusa line to Sengaku-ji, exit A2) The story of the 47 *rōnin* (masterless samurai) who avenged their master, Lord Asano – put to death after being tricked into pulling a sword on a rival – is legend in Japan. They were condemned to commit *seppuku* (ritual disembowelment) and their remains were buried at this temple. It's a sombre place, with fresh incense rising from the tombs, placed there by visitors moved by the loyalty of the samurai.

HATAKEYAMA COLLECTION
MUSEUM

(畠山記念館; www.ebara.co.jp/csr/hatakeyama; 2-20-12 Shirokanedai, Minato-ku; adult/student/child ¥700/500/free; ⊗10am-5pm Tue-Sun Apr-Sep, to 4.30pm Oct-Mar; Asakusa line to Takanawadai, exit A2) Get a feel for *wabi-sabi* – the aesthetic of perfect imperfections that guides the tea ceremony – at this museum specialising in the earthy pottery and art associated with the traditional ceremony. While the museum itself is rather small, it sits in a woodsy garden with several teahouses. A cup of *matcha* and a traditional sweet can be had for an extra ¥500. Note that the museum closes for weeks at a time in between exhibitions.

From exit A2 of Takanawadai station, hang a left at the police box (on your left) and keep going until you see the green-and-white sign (in Japanese) on the utility pole telling you to turn left.

EATING

Ebisu

★AFURI
RAMEN ¥

Map p274 (あふり; 1-1-7 Ebisu, Shibuya-ku; noodles from ¥880; ⊗11am-5am; JR Yamanote line to Ebisu, east exit) Hardly your typical, surly *rāmen-ya*, Afuri has upbeat young cooks and a hip industrial interior. The unorthodox menu might draw eye-rolls from purists, but house specialities such as *yuzu-shio* (a light, salty broth flavoured with yuzu, a type of citrus) draw lines at lunchtime. Order from the vending machine.

OUCA
ICE CREAM ¥

Map p274 (櫻花; www.ice-ouca.com; 1-6-6 Ebisu, Shibuya-ku; ice cream from ¥400; ⊗11am-11.30pm Mar-Oct, noon-11pm Nov-Feb; JR Yamanote line to Ebisu, east exit) Green tea isn't the only flavour Japan has contributed to the ice-cream playbook; other delicious innovations available (seasonally) at Ouca include *kuro-goma* (black sesame), *kinako kurosato* (roasted soy-bean flour and black sugar) and *beni imo* (purple sweet potato).

MEGUTAMA SHOKUDO ¥

Map p274 (めぐたま; http://megutama.com/; 3-2-7 Higashi, Shibuya-ku; lunch/dinner from ¥1000/1500; 🕐11.30am-2pm & 5-11pm Mon-Fri, noon-10pm Sat & Sun; 🚆JR Yamanote line to Ebisu, east exit) Megutama calls itself a 'photo books diner' – because thousands of photo tomes are shelved on its walls. Diners are free to flip through them (use the coloured card as a placeholder). The food here is good, too: classic home-cooking from a trio of very able women in aprons and kerchiefs. It's a modern wooden building with a red awning.

EBISU-YOKOCHŌ STREET FOOD ¥¥

Map p274 (恵比寿横町; www.ebisu-yokocho.com; 1-7-4 Ebisu, Shibuya-ku; dishes ¥500-1500; 🕐5pm-late; 🚆JR Yamanote line to Ebisu, east exit) Locals love this retro arcade chock-a-block with food stalls dishing up everything from humble *yaki soba* (fried buckwheat noodles) to decadent *hotate-yaki* (grilled scallops). Seating is on stools, while tables are fashioned from various items such as repurposed beer crates. It's a loud, lively (and smoky) place, especially on a Friday night; go early to get a table.

You won't find English menus, but the adventurous can get away with pointing at their fellow diners' dishes (you'll be sitting cheek-to-jowl with them). Even if you don't stop to eat, it's worth strolling through. The entrance is marked with a rainbow-coloured sign.

IPPO IZAKAYA ¥

Map p274 (一歩; ☎03-3445-8418; 2nd fl, 1-22-10 Ebisu, Shibuya-ku; dishes ¥500-1500; 🕐6pm-3am; 🚆JR Yamanote line to Ebisu, east exit) This mellow little *izakaya* (Japanese pub-eatery) specialises in simple pleasures: fish and sake (there's an English sign out front that says just that). The friendly chefs speak some English and can help you decide what to have grilled, steamed, simmered or fried (or if you can't decide, the ¥2500 set menu is great value). The entrance is up the wooden stairs.

YAKINIKU CHAMPION BARBECUE ¥¥

Map p274 (焼肉チャンピオン; ☎03-5768-6922; www.yakiniku-champion.com; 1-2-8 Ebisu, Shibuya-ku; dishes ¥780-3300, course from ¥5250; 🕐5pm-12.30am Mon-Fri, to 1am Sat, 4.30pm-midnight Sun; 🚆JR Yamanote line to Ebisu, west exit) Ready for an introduction into the Japanese cult of *yakiniku* (Korean barbecue)? Champion's sprawling menu includes everything from sweetbreads to the choicest cuts of grade A5 *wagyū* (Japanese beef); the menu even has a diagram of the cuts. You can't go wrong with popular dishes such as *kalbi* (short ribs, ¥980). It's very popular; best to reserve ahead.

TA-IM ISRAELI ¥¥

Map p274 (タイーム; ☎03-5424-2990; www.ta-imebisu.com; 1-29-16 Ebisu, Shibuya-ku; lunch set ¥1380-1780, dishes from ¥680-1980; 🕐11.30am-2.30pm & 6-11pm Thu-Tue; ✎; 🚆JR Yamanote line to Ebisu, east exit) This tiny Israeli bistro, run by expat Dan Zuckerman, regularly draws a crowd for its authentic felafel, schnitzel, hummus and more – washed down with Goldstar beer. Call ahead in the evening (in English is fine) as it's often full.

🍴 Daikanyama & Naka-Meguro

BOMBAY BAZAR INTERNATIONAL ¥

Map p274 (ボンベイバザー; www.bombaybazar.jp; 20-11 Sarugaku-chō; mains ¥1000-1300; 🕐11.30am-7.30pm; ✎; 🚆Tōkyū Tōyoko line to Daikanyama) Mismatched furniture and 'found' objects conspire to make this cafe look like something the Lost Boys of *Peter Pan* may have thrown together. The menu is similarly eclectic, with a spin-the-globe selection of pizza, pastas and curries (made with organic vegies). For just a snack, the *okura-yaki*, a chubby hotcake stuffed with red bean or blueberry jam, is delicious.

HIGASHI-YAMA JAPANESE ¥¥¥

(ヒガシヤマ; ☎03-5720-1300; www.higashiyama-tokyo.jp; 1-21-25 Higashiyama, Meguro-ku; lunch/dinner from ¥1650/4950; 🕐11.30am-2pm Tue-Sat, 6pm-1am Mon-Sat; [S]Hibiya line to Naka-Meguro) Higashi-Yama serves scrumptious modern Japanese cuisine paired with

LOCAL KNOWLEDGE

MEGURO-GAWA HANAMI

If you're in town during *hanami* (blossom-viewing) season, don't miss one of the city's best parties, along the **Meguro-gawa** (目黒川; Map p274; [S]Hibiya line to Naka-Meguro) in Naka-Meguro. Here vendors line the canal selling more upmarket treats than you'll find anywhere else. Rather than stake out a space to sit, visitors stroll under the blossoms, hot wine in hand.

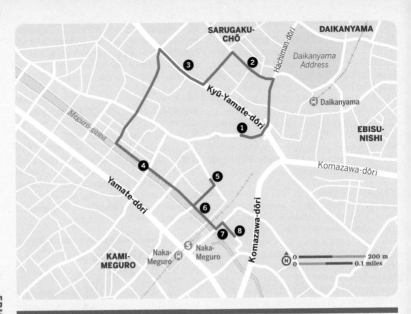

Local Life
Exploring Daikanyama & Naka-Meguro

Just one stop from Shibuya, but a world away, Daikanyama is an upscale residential enclave with sidewalk cafes, fashionable boutiques and an unhurried pace. Neighbouring Naka-Meguro is Daikanyama's bohemian little sister, home to secondhand shops and secret lounge bars. At the heart of the neighbourhood is the Meguro-gawa, a canal with a leafy promenade.

❶ Secret Garden

The **Kyū Asakura House** (旧朝倉家住宅; Kyū Asakura-ke Jūtaku; Map p274; 03-3476-1021; 29-20 Sarugaku-chō, Shibuya-ku; adult/child ¥100/50; ⊙10am-6pm Mar-Oct, to 4pm Nov-Feb; ⓡTōkyū Tōyoko line to Daikanyama) is a rare example of early-20th-century villa architecture (so hidden that many locals don't even know it exists) with tatami (reed mat) rooms and a garden with stone lanterns you can explore. It's a peek at what the neighbourhood looked like, before it was subsumed by the city.

❷ Bohemian Threads

Okura (p94), which sells boho-chic indigo-dyed goods, looks out of place in trendy Daikanyama (the shop looks like a farmhouse), but it's actually a neighbourhood landmark. If you're hungry, quirky cafe Bombay Bazar (p91), run by the same folks, is next door.

❸ Booklovers' Haunt

Locals love **Daikanyama T-Site** (代官山T-SITE; Map p274; http://tsite.jp/daikanyama; 17-5 Sarugaku-chō, Shibuya-ku; ⊙7am-2am; ⓡTōkyū Tōyoko line to Daikanyama). This stylish shrine to the printed word has fantastic books on travel, art, design and food (some in English). You can even sit at the in-house Starbucks and read all afternoon – if you can get a seat.

❹ Canalside Stroll

Lined with cherry trees and a walking path, the Meguro-gawa (p91), not so much a river as a canal, is what gives the neighbourhood Naka-Meguro its unlikely village vibe. On either side you'll find boutiques and a handful of eating and drinking spots.

❺ Hidden Art

Possibly the city's tiniest art gallery, the **Container** (Map p274; http://the-container.com; 1-8-30 Kami-Meguro, Meguro-ku; ⊙11am-9pm Wed-Mon, to 8pm Sat & Sun; ⓢHibiya line to Naka-Meguro) is literally a shipping con-

TOM BONAVENTURE / GETTY IMAGES ©

Cherry blossoms in Naka-Meguro

tainer within a hair salon. It doesn't get much more Tokyo than that.

6 Treasure Hunting

A perfect example of Naka-Meguro's tiny, impeccably curated boutiques, **Vase** (Map p274; vasenakameguro.com; 1-7-7 Kami-Meguro, Meguro-ku; 🕒noon-8pm; [S]Hibiya line to Naka-Meguro) stocks avant-garde designers and vintage pieces (for men and women). It's in a little white house set back from the Meguro-gawa.

7 Vintage Izakaya

Ōtaru (おおたる; Map p274; ☎03-3710-7439; 1-5-15 Naka-Meguro, Meguro-ku; dishes ¥330-600; 🕒11.30am-2am) isn't winning any Michelin stars, but we're giving it three stars of our own for atmosphere. This *izakaya*, in an old wooden building festooned with lanterns, stands out. Locals and visitors alike love it for its reasonable prices, canalside location and the fact that it opens before noon.

8 Hipster Lounge

Call it a day with a round of *takkyū* (ping pong) at Nakame Takkyū Lounge (p93) – the neighbourhood's best-known 'secret' bar.

gorgeous crockery. The interior, a rustic take on minimalism, is stunning too. The restaurant is all but hidden, on a side street with little signage; see the website for a map. Tasting courses make ordering easy; the 'chef's recommendation' course (¥9020) is a worthwhile splurge. Best to book ahead.

🍴 Meguro

★TONKI TONKATSU ¥

Map p274 (とんき; 1-2-1 Shimo-Meguro, Meguro-ku; meals ¥1900; 🕒4-10.45pm Wed-Mon, closed 3rd Mon of month; 🚉JR Yamanote line to Meguro, west exit) Tonki is a Tokyo *tonkatsu* (crumbed pork cutlet) legend, deep-frying pork cutlets, recipe unchanged, for nearly 80 years. The seats at the counter – where you can watch the perfectly choreographed chefs – are the most coveted, though there is usually a queue. There are tables upstairs.

From the station, walk down Meguro-dōri, take a left at the first alley and look for a white sign and *noren* (doorway curtains) across the sliding doors.

🍷 DRINKING & NIGHTLIFE

★NAKAME TAKKYŪ LOUNGE LOUNGE

Map p274 (中目卓球ラウンジ; 2nd fl, Lion House Naka-Meguro, 1-3-13 Kami-Meguro, Meguro-ku; cover before/after 10pm ¥500/800; 🕒6pm-2am Mon-Sat; [S]Hibiya line to Naka-Meguro) *Takkyū* means table tennis and it's a serious sport in Japan. This hilarious bar looks like a university table-tennis clubhouse – right down to the tatty furniture and posters of star players on the wall. It's in an apartment building next to a parking garage (go all the way down the corridor past the bikes); ring the doorbell for entry.

BAR TRENCH COCKTAIL BAR

Map p274 (バートレンチ; ☎03-3780-5291; http://small-axe.net/bar-trench/; 1-5-8 Ebisu-Nishi, Shibuya-ku; cover ¥500; 🕒7pm-2am Mon-Sat, 6pm-1am Sun; 🚉JR Yamanote line to Ebisu, west exit) One of the pioneers in Tokyo's new cocktail scene, Trench (named for the trench-like alley in which it is nestled) is a tiny place with the air of old-world bohemianism. It has a short but sweet menu of original tipples. Highlights include the 'Shady Samurai' (green-tea-infused gin with elderflower liquor, egg white and lime; ¥1620).

BURI
BAR

Map p274 (ぶり; ☎03-3496-7744; 1-14-1 Ebisu-nishi, Shibuya-ku; ⏰5pm-3am; ℝJR Yamanote line to Ebisu, west exit) Buri – the name means 'super' in Hiroshima dialect – is one of Ebisu's most popular *tachinomi-ya* (standing bars). On almost any night you can find a lively crowd packed in around the horseshoe-shaped counter here. Generous quantities of sake (more than 40 varieties; ¥770) are served semifrozen, like slushies in colourful jars.

BAR MARTHA
BAR

Map p274 (バー ・マーサ; www.martha-records. com; 1-22-23 Ebisu, Shibuya-ku; cover incl bar snacks ¥800; ⏰7pm-5am; ℝJR Yamanote line to Ebisu, east exit) It's hard to say which is more impressive at this dim, moody bar: the whiskey list or the collection of records. The latter are played on spot-lit turntables, amplified by a 1m-tall vintage Tannoy speaker. The cocktails, especially the *nama shōga mosuko myūru* (生生姜モスコミュール); fresh ginger moscow mule) are excellent, too. Drinks from ¥800.

SARUTAHIKO COFFEE
CAFE

Map p274 (猿田彦珈琲; http://sarutahiko.co; 1–6–6 Ebisu, Shibuya-ku; ⏰8am-12.30am Mon-Fri, 10am-12.30am Sat & Sun; ℝJR Yamanote line to Ebisu, east exit) Even though it has only a few seats inside, Sarutahiko Coffee is Ebisu's most popular caffeine pit stop, thanks to its aromatic, well-chosen beans. Both hand-drip and espresso drinks (from ¥400) are served.

⭐ ENTERTAINMENT

⭐ UNIT
LIVE MUSIC

Map p274 (ユニット; ☎03-5459-8630; www. unit-tokyo.com; 1-34-17 Ebisu-nishi, Shibuya-ku; ¥2500-5000; ℝTōkyū Tōyoko line to Daikanyama) On weekends, this subterranean club has two shows: live music in the evening and a DJ-hosted event that gets started around midnight. The solid line-up includes Japanese indie bands, veterans playing to a smaller crowd and overseas artists making their Japan debut. Unit is less grungy than other Tokyo live houses and, with high ceilings, doesn't get as smoky.

LIQUID ROOM
LIVE MUSIC

Map p274 (リキッドルーム; ☎03-5464-0800; www.liquidroom.net; 3-16-6 Higashi, Shibuya-ku; ℝJR Yamanote line to Ebisu, west exit) When

MEGURO INTERIOR SHOPS

Meguro-dōri, the broad boulevard that runs southwest from Meguro Station, is known as Tokyo's interior-design district. Some 30 shops punctuate a 3km stretch of the road, starting after the intersection with Yamate-dōri. Even if you're not planning to shop, it's interesting to poke around and imagine what Tokyo's concrete-box apartments might look like on the inside.

When you've had enough, simply hop on any bus heading back up Meguro-dōri; they all stop at Meguro Station. Note that many stores close on Wednesdays.

this storied concert hall moved to Ebisu from seedy Kabukichō, it cleaned up its act. Liquid Room is still a great place to catch big-name acts in an intimate setting. Both Japanese and international bands play here, and every once in a while there's an all-night gig. Tickets sell out fast.

SHOPPING

⭐ OKURA
FASHION & ACCESSORIES

Map p274 (オクラ; www.hrm.co.jp/okura; 20-11 Sarugaku-chō, Shibuya-ku; ⏰11.30am-8pm Mon-Fri, 11am-8.30pm Sat & Sun; ℝTōkyū Tōyoko line to Daikanyama) Almost everything in this enchanting shop is dyed a deep indigo blue – from contemporary tees and sweatshirts to classic work shirts. There are some beautiful, original items (though unfortunately most aren't cheap). The shop itself looks like a rural house, with worn, wooden floorboards and whitewashed walls. Note: there's no sign out the front, but the building stands out.

KAPITAL
FASHION & ACCESSORIES

Map p274 (キャピタル; ☎03-5725-3923; http:// kapital.jp; 2-20-2 Ebisu, Shibuya-ku; ⏰11am-8pm; ℝJR Yamanote line to Ebisu, west exit) Cult brand Kapital is hard to pin down, but perhaps a deconstructed mash-up of the American West and the centuries-old Japanese aesthetic of *boro* (tatty) chic comes close. Almost no two items are alike; most are unisex. The shop itself is like an art installation. The staff, not snobby at all, can point you towards the other two shops nearby.

Shibuya & Shimo-Kitazawa

Neighbourhood Top Five

1 Shibuya Crossing (p97) Losing yourself in the crowds at Japan's busiest intersection – and getting swept along in the beating heart of desire, aspiration and materialism that is Shibuya.

2 Shibuya Center-gai (p97) Eating, drinking and shopping your way down

the neighbourhood's always lively, neon-lit main drag.

3 Shimo-Kitazawa (p100) Getting lost in the tiny alleyways of this well-loved, bohemian neighbourhood, which offers a picture of how Tokyo might look if hippies – not bureaucrats – ran the city.

4 Dōgenzaka (p98) Scoping out the all-night club scene on the sloping stretch also known as Love Hotel Hill.

5 Tomigaya (p104) Checking out the hip hang-outs, such as Fuglen, in this 'un-Shibuya' neighbourhood, favoured by young creatives.

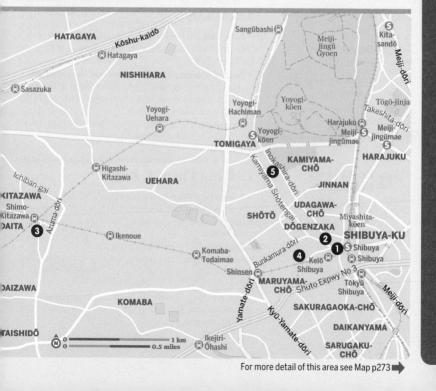

For more detail of this area see Map p273 ➡

Lonely Planet's Top Tip

Missed the last train? You're not alone – or stuck for options. Shibuya has plenty for night crawlers who were lured out late by the neighbourhood's charms but who'd rather not fork over the yen for a taxi ride home. In addition to love hotels and *manga kissa* (cafes where you pay by the hour to read manga, Japanese comic books), consider waiting for the first train at a karaoke parlour; most offer discounted all-night packages from midnight to 5am.

Best Places to Eat

➡ d47 Shokudō (p98)
➡ Shirube (p100)
➡ Matsukiya (p99)

For reviews, see p98. ➡

Best Places to Drink

➡ Good Beer Faucets (p99)
➡ Ghetto (p99)
➡ Fuglen Tokyo (p104)
➡ Womb (p100)

For reviews, see p99. ➡

Best Places to Shop

➡ Tokyu Hands (p105)
➡ Fake Tokyo (p105)
➡ Shibuya 109 (p105)

For reviews, see p105. ➡

SHIBUYA & SHIMO-KITAZAWA

Explore Shibuya & Shimo-Kitazawa

Shibuya is a neighbourhood that gets a late start – after all it was partying until the first trains started running in the morning. Come for lunch. Ease your way in by starting with the Shibuya of the future: Shibuya Hikarie (p105), a light and airy complex connected to the train station with views over the neighbourhood.

Then head down into the fray: exit the train station for Shibuya Crossing (p97), the epic neon-lit intersection that has become synonymous with Tokyo. From here, the pedestrian traffic flows onto Shibuya Center-gai (p97), the neighbourhood's lively main artery, lined with shops, cheap eateries and bars.

Shibuya is, above all, an entertainment district and it really comes alive at night. There are dance clubs, live-music venues, theatres and cinemas galore. While weekends are the busiest, you'll find people from all over Tokyo here any night of the week (and you may find yourself drawn back night after night). Bars and karaoke parlours stay open until dawn.

It's also worth spending some time in down-to-earth Shimo-Kitazawa, home to cafes and vintage shops, dive bars and underground live-music venues.

Local Life

➡**Teen Culture** Local teens love fashion hive Shibuya 109 (p105) and the 'print club' photo booths at Purikura no Mecca (p105).

➡**Record Stores** Shimo-Kitazawa and the Udagawa-chō neighbourhood of Shibuya are studded with tiny specialist record shops that are popular with local DJs. Pick up event fliers here.

➡**Hang-outs** The neighbourhood Tomigaya (p104) is the centre of a hip cafe and bistro scene.

Getting There & Away

➡**Train** The JR Yamanote line stops at Shibuya Station. The Keiō Inokashira line departs from Keiō Shibuya Station for Shinsen, Komaba-Todaimae and Shimo-Kitazawa.

➡**Subway** The Ginza, Hanzōmon and Fukutoshin lines stop in Shibuya. The Chiyoda line stops at Yoyogi-kōen Station (for Tomigaya); some trains continue on the Odakyū line for Shimo-Kitazawa.

➡**Bus** Bus No 1 departs for Roppongi from the east side of Shibuya Station, on the corner of Meiji-dōri and Miyamasu-zaka.

SEAN PAVONE / SHUTTERSTOCK ©

TOP SIGHT
SHIBUYA CROSSING

Rumoured to be the busiest intersection in the world (and definitely in Japan), Shibuya Crossing, also known as Shibuya Scramble, is like a giant beating heart, sending people in all directions with every pulsing light change. Perhaps nowhere else says 'Welcome to Tokyo' better than this.

Hundreds of people – and at peak times said to be more than 1000 people – cross at a time, coming from all directions at once yet still managing to dodge each other with a practised, nonchalant agility. Then, in the time that it takes for the light to go from red to green again, all corners have replenished their stock of people – like a video on loop. The intersection is most impressive after dark on a Friday or Saturday night, when the crowds pouring out of the station are dressed in their finest and neon-lit by the signs above. (Rainy days have their own visual appeal, with all the colourful umbrellas.)

The plaza in front of the station is a spectacle too: it's Shibuya's main rendezvous point and there are usually dozens (hundreds?) of people milling about. So much so that you might miss the famous **Hachikō statue** (ハチ公像), commemorating a loyal Akita dog. Hachikō came to Shibuya Station everyday to meet his owner, a professor, returning from work. The professor died in 1925, but Hachikō kept coming to the station until his own death 10 years later – a story that won the hearts of many Japanese.

Shibuya Crossing feeds into **Shibuya Center-gai** (渋谷センター街; Shibuya Sentā-gai; Map p273), the neighbourhood's main drag, closed to cars and chock-a-block with fast-food joints and high-street fashion shops. At night, lit bright as day, with a dozen competing soundtracks (coming from who knows where), wares spilling onto the streets, shady touts in sunglasses, and strutting teens, it feels like a block party – or Tokyo's version of a classic Asian night market.

DID YOU KNOW?

Shibuya Crossing sits over the confluence of two rivers, Shibuya-gawa and Uda-gawa, which were routed underground in the 1960s.

PRACTICALITIES

➤ 渋谷スクランブル交差点; Shibuya Scramble

➤ Map p273, C2

➤ ®JR Yamanote line to Shibuya, Hachikō exit

◉ SIGHTS

SHIBUYA CROSSING   STREET
See p97.

MYTH OF TOMORROW   PUBLIC ART
Map p273 (明日の神話; Asu no Shinwa; 🚇JR Yamanote line to Shibuya, Hachikō exit) Okamoto Tarō's mural, *Myth of Tomorrow* (1967), was commissioned by a Mexican luxury hotel but went missing two years later. It finally turned up in 2003 and, in 2008, the haunting 30m-long work, which depicts the atomic bomb exploding over Hiroshima, was installed inside Shibuya Station. It's on the 2nd floor, on the way to the Inokashira line.

SPAIN-ZAKA   AREA
Map p273 (スペイン坂; 🚇JR Yamanote line to Shibuya, Hachikō exit) Shibuya's most atmospheric little alley is typical Tokyo bricolage, with a Mediterranean flavour, a mismatch of architectural styles, cutesy clothing stores and a melting pot of restaurants all along a narrow, winding brick lane.

DŌGENZAKA   AREA
Map p273 (道玄坂; Love Hotel Hill; 🚇JR Yamanote line to Shibuya, Hachikō exit) Dōgenzaka, named for a 13th-century highway robber, is a maze of narrow streets. Home to one of Tokyo's largest clusters of hotels for amorous encounters, it's also known as Love Hotel Hill. It's more than a little seedy, but some of the older hotels have fantastical (if not a bit chipped and crumbling) facades.

TOGURI MUSEUM OF ART   MUSEUM
Map p273 (戸栗美術館; www.toguri-museum. or.jp; 1-11-3 Shōto, Shibuya-ku; adult/student/child ¥1000/700/400; ⊙10am-5pm Tue-Sun; 🚇JR Yamanote line to Shibuya, Hachikō exit) The Toguri Museum of Art has an excellent collection of Edo-era ceramics, displayed in informative, thematic exhibitions with English explanations – great for getting to know the symbolism of the different motifs and the techniques of the different styles. The museum is in the exclusive Shōto neighbourhood, 1km from Shibuya Station.

Head down the Kamiyama-chō *shōtengai* until the Kamiyama-chō Higashi (神山町東) intersection and then turn left; the museum will be on your right, after the bend.

D47 MUSEUM   MUSEUM
Map p273 (www.hikarie8.com/d47museum; 8th fl, Hikarie bldg, 2-21-1 Shibuya, Shibuya-ku; ⊙11am-8pm; 🚇JR Yamanote line to Shibuya, east exit) FREE Lifestyle brand D&Department combs the country for the platonic ideals of the utterly ordinary: the perfect broom, bottle opener or salt shaker (to name a few examples). See rotating exhibitions of its latest finds from all 47 prefectures at this one-room museum. The excellent d47 Design Travel shop is next door.

✗ EATING

★D47 SHOKUDŌ   JAPANESE ¥
Map p273 (d47食堂; www.hikarie8.com/d47shokudo/about.shtml; 8th fl, Shibuya Hikarie, 2-21-1 Shibuya, Shibuya-ku; meals ¥1200-1780; ⊙11am-2.30pm & 6-10.30pm; 🚇JR Yamanote line to Shibuya, east exit) There are 47 prefectures in Japan and d47 serves a changing line-up of *teishoku* (set meals) that evoke the specialities of each, from the fermented tofu of Okinawa to the stuffed squid of Hokkaido. A larger menu of small plates is available in the evening. Picture windows offer bird's-eye views over the trains coming and going at Shibuya Station.

GYŪKATSU MOTOMURA   TONKATSU ¥
Map p273 (牛かつ もと村; 03-3797-3735; basement fl, 3-18-10 Shibuya, Shibuya-ku; set meal ¥1200; ⊙10.30am-10.30pm Mon-Sat, 10.30am-8.30pm Sun; 🚇JR Yamanote line to Shibuya, east exit) You know *tonkatsu*, the deep-fried breaded pork cutlet that is a Japanese staple; meet *gyūkatsu*, the deep-fried breaded beef cutlet that is Tokyo's latest food craze. At Motomura, the beef is super-crisp on the outside and still very rare on the inside; diners get a small individual grill to finish the job to their liking. Set meals include cabbage, rice and soup.

Motomura is exceeding popular, with long queues common. It has since opened other shops in Shibuya and around Tokyo to handle the overflow; check inside for other locations.

SAGATANI   SOBA ¥
Map p273 (嵯峨谷; 2-25-7 Dōgenzaka, Shibuya-ku; noodles from ¥290; ⊙24hr; 🚇JR Yamanote line to Shibuya, Hachikō exit) Proving that Tokyo is only expensive to those who don't know better, this all-night joint serves up bamboo steamers of delicious noodles for just ¥290. You won't regret 'splurging' on the ごまだれそば (*goma-dare soba;* buckwheat noodles with sesame dipping sauce)

for ¥390. Look for the stone mill in the window and order from the vending machine.

FOOD SHOW
SUPERMARKET ¥

Map p273 (フードショー; basement fl, 2-24-1 Shibuya, Shibuya-ku; ⏰10am-9pm; 🅿; 🚇JR Yamanote line to Shibuya, Hachikō exit) This takeaway paradise in the basement of Shibuya Station has steamers of dumplings, crisp *karaage* (Japanese-style fried chicken), artfully arranged *bentō* (boxed meals), sushi sets, heaps of salads and cakes almost too pretty to eat. It's also home of the ¥10,000 melons. A green sign pointing downstairs marks the entrance at Hachikō Plaza.

NAGI SHOKUDŌ
VEGAN ¥

Map p273 (なぎ食堂; http://nagishokudo.com; 15-10 Uguisudani-chō, Shibuya-ku; lunch/dinner set menu ¥1050/1550; ⏰noon-4pm daily, 6-11pm Mon-Sat; 🅿; 🚇JR Yamanote line to Shibuya, west exit) A vegan haven in fast-food-laced Shibuya, Nagi serves up dishes such as falafel and coconut curry. The most popular thing on the menu is a set meal with three small dishes, miso soup and rice. It's a low-key, homey place with mismatched furniture, cater-corner from a post office (and hidden behind a concrete wall; look for the red sign).

KAIKAYA
SEAFOOD ¥¥

Map p273 (開花屋; ☎03-3770-0878; www.kaikaya.com; 23-7 Maruyama-chō, Shibuya-ku; lunch from ¥850, dishes ¥850-2300; ⏰11.30am-2pm & 5.30-10.30pm Mon-Fri, 5.30-10.30pm Sat & Sun; 🚇JR Yamanote line to Shibuya, Hachikō exit) 🌱 Traveller favourite Kaikaiya is one chef's attempt to bring the beach to Shibuya. Surfboards hang on the walls and much of what's on the menu is caught in nearby Sagami Bay. Seafood is served both Japanese- and Western-style. One must-try is the *maguro no kama* (tuna collar; ¥1200). Reservations recommended; there's a table charge of ¥400 per person.

From Dōgenzaka, turn right after the police box, and the restaurant, with a red awning, will be on your right.

MATSUKIYA
HOTPOT ¥¥¥

Map p273 (松木家; ☎03-3461-2651; 6-8 Maruyama-chō, Shibuya-ku; sukiyaki from ¥5400; ⏰5-11pm Mon-Sat; 🚇JR Yamanote line to Shibuya, Hachikō exit) Matsukiya has been making *sukiyaki* (thinly sliced beef, simmered and then dipped in raw egg) since 1890, and the chefs really, really know what they're doing. It's worth upgrading to the

NIHON MINGEI-KAN

The *mingei* (folk crafts) movement was launched in the early 20th century to promote the works of artisans over cheaper, mass-produced goods. Central to the *mingei* philosophy is *yo no bi* (beauty through use). The excellent **Japan Folk Crafts Museum** (日本民藝館; Mingeikan; http://mingeikan.x0.com; 4-3-33 Komaba, Meguro-ku; adult/student/child ¥1100/600/200; ⏰10am-4.30pm Tue-Sun; 🚇Keiō Inokashira line to Komaba-Todaimae, west exit), west of Shibuya, houses a collection of some 17,000 pieces in a farmhouse-like building designed by one of the movement's founders. From Komaba-Tōdaimae Station, walk with the train tracks on your left; when the road turns right (after about five minutes), the museum will be on your right. Note that it closes between exhibitions (check the schedule online).

premium course (¥7500) for even meltier meat. Prices are per person and for a full course that includes vegies and finishes with noodles cooked in the broth.

There's a white sign out front and the entrance is up some stairs. Reservations are recommended.

🍷 DRINKING & NIGHTLIFE

★GHETTO
BAR

(月灯; 1-45-16 Daizawa, Setagaya-ku; ⏰8.30pm-late; 🚇Keiō Inokashira line to Shimo-Kitazawa, south exit) What are the odds that the characters for 'moon' and 'light' could be pronounced together as 'ghetto'? It's not unlike the uncommon synergy that comes together nightly as musicians, travellers, and well-intentioned salarymen (and others) descend on this little bar in the rambling Suzunari theatre complex. By open until late we mean very, very late. No cover charge; drinks from ¥600.

★GOOD BEER FAUCETS
CRAFT BEER

Map p273 (グッドビアフォウセッツ; http://shibuya.goodbeerfaucets.jp; 2nd fl, 1-29-1 Shōtō, Shibuya-ku; pints from ¥800; ⏰5pm-midnight Mon-Thu & Sat, to 3am Fri, 4-11pm Sun; 🅿; 🚇JR Yamanote line to Shibuya, Hachikō exit) With 40 shiny taps, Good Beer Faucets has one of the city's best selections of Japanese craft brews and regularly draws a full house of locals and expats. The interior is chrome and concrete (and not at all grungy). Come for happy hour (5pm to 8pm Monday to Thursday, 1pm to 7pm Sunday) and get ¥200 off any pint.

CONTACT
CLUB

Map p273 (コンタクト; ☑03-6427-8107; www.contacttokyo.com; basement, 2-10-12 Dōgenzaka, Shibuya-ku; ¥2000-3500; ☒JR Yamanote line to Shibuya, Hachikō exit) This is Tokyo's newest hot spot, a stylish underground club that's keen on keeping up with the times (even if that means it's a little heavy on rules): the dance floor is no smoking and no photos (so you can dance with abandon). Weekends see big international names and a young, fashionable crowd. Under-23s get in for ¥2000. ID required.

Currently the club is 'members only', so to get in you have to sign up on the website. Look for the entrance in the back of a parking lot.

RHYTHM CAFE
BAR

Map p273 (リズムカフェ; ☑03-3770-0244; http://rhythmcafe.jp; 11-1 Udagawa-chō, Shibuya-ku; ◷6pm-2am; ☒JR Yamanote line to Shibuya, Hachikō exit) Run by a record label, fun and funky Rhythm Cafe often draws more customers than it can fit, meaning the party spills into the street. It's known for having off-beat event nights (such as the retro Japanese pop night on the fourth Thursday of the month). Drinks start at ¥700; when DJs spin, the cover is around ¥1000.

NONBEI-YOKOCHŌ
BAR

Map p273 (のんべえ横丁; www.nonbei.tokyo; Shibuya 1-chōme, Shibuya-ku; ☒JR Yamanote line to Shibuya, Hachikō exit) Nonbei-yokochō is one of Tokyo's anomalous – and endangered – strips of old wooden shanty bars, here in the shadow of the elevated JR tracks. There's a wonderfully eclectic assortment of teeny-tiny bars, though note that some have cover charges (usually ¥500 to ¥1000). **Tight** (タイト; Map p273; 2nd fl, 1-25-10 Shibuya, Shibuya-ku; ◷6pm-2am Mon-Sat, to midnight Sun) is one that doesn't.

WOMB
CLUB

Map p273 (ウーム; ☑03-5459-0039; www.womb.co.jp; 2-16 Maruyama-chō, Shibuya-ku; cover ¥1500-4000; ◷11pm-late Fri & Sat, 4-10pm Sun; ☒JR Yamanote line to Shibuya, Hachikō exit) A long-time (in club years, at least) club-scene

---

🏃 Local Life
A Night Out in Shimo-Kitazawa

For 50 years, Shimokita (as it's called here) has been a prism through which to see the city's alternative side. While other neighbourhoods go big, Shimokita fiercely defends its small stature, its narrow, crooked roads (the bane of taxi drivers) and its analogue vibe. Spend an evening here and raise your glass to (and with) the characters committed to keeping Shimokita weird.

❶ Step Out on the Southside
The **Minami-guchi shōtengai** (南口商店街), marked by an arch, is the main drag heading south from the station. It's here where the crowds get so thick that cars can't pass (though even without people it's still barely wide enough for cars to pass). As you walk, look out for the colourful murals on the shutters of shops that have closed for the day.

❷ Books and Beer
First stop: happy hour with the bookish crowd. **B&B** (http://bookandbeer.com; 2nd fl, 2-12-4 Kitazawa, Setagaya-ku; ◷noon-midnight; ☒Keiō Inokashira line to Shimo-Kitazawa, south exit) – which stands for books and beer – represents the new wave of Shimokita: a painfully hip bookstore that serves craft beer (from ¥500; or coffee, if that's how you roll). There is a small but good selection of English books on Tokyo here. Readings and acoustic performances take place some evenings.

❸ A Favourite Izakaya
Duck down a side street and look for the white door curtains that mark the entrance to **Shirube** (汁べゑ; ☑03-3413-3785; 2-18-2 Kitazawa, Setagaya-ku; dishes ¥730-1060; ◷5.30pm-midnight; ☑; ☒Keiō Inokashira line to Shimo-Kitazawa, south exit), a lively *izakaya* (Japanese-style pub) that is pretty much always packed. You'll want to book ahead if you've got a group or are out on a Friday or Saturday night.

❹ Rock Goddess
Step into **Mother** (マザー; ☑03-3421-9519; www.rock-mother.com; 5-36-14 Daizawa, Setagaya-ku; ◷5pm-2am Sun-Thu, 5pm-

5am Fri & Sat; ⒭Keiō Inokashira line to Shimo-Kitazawa, south exit), classic Shimo-Kitazawa and a work of art itself. The space, with undulating, mosaic walls, is definitely womblike (the better to incubate future rock'n'rollers); the soundtrack is '60s and '70s. Don't miss the made-in-house 'mori' liquor, served from a glass skull (drinks from ¥600).

❺ Shimokita Streetscape

Azuma-dōri (東通り), with its low-slung buildings, faux stained-glass street lamps and arching street signs, contains many of the elements that make up Shimokita's charmingly retro visual identity. As you turn on to the road, look to your left for the tiny shrine, **Kōshindō** (庚申堂), which is lovingly kept up by residents.

❻ A Classic Dive

Pretty much everything at **Trouble Peach** (トラブル・ピーチ; ☎03-3460-1468; 2nd fl, 2-9-18 Kitazawa, Setagaya-ku; cover ¥400; ⊗7pm-7am; ⒭Keiō Inokashira line to Shimo-Kitazawa, south exit) is chipped, frayed or torn – and none of it is artifice. This is a well-worn and well-loved bar, open for some 40-odd years, and still playing vinyl. It looks primed for demolition but has somehow managed to survive. Look for the neon sign by the tracks. Cover ¥400; drinks from ¥500.

❼ Late Night Gathering

Twinkling lights mark the entrance of late-night haunt **Never Never Land** (ネヴァーネヴァーランド; 2nd fl, 3-19-3 Kitazawa, Setagaya-ku; cover ¥200 per person; ⊗6pm-2am; ⒭Keiō Inokashira line to Shimo-Kitazawa, north exit), a long-running Shimokita bar that's consistently smoky, loud and filled with bohemian characters. The bar serves tasty Okinawan dishes along with beer and cocktails (food and drink from ¥500; cover charge ¥200 per person).

❽ A Local Legend

The Suzunari (ザ・スズナリ) is one of the neighbourhood's landmark fringe theatres. The sprawling (and rather dilapidated) building also includes a dozen or so tiny bars, including Ghetto (p99).

Alley in Shimo-Kitazawa

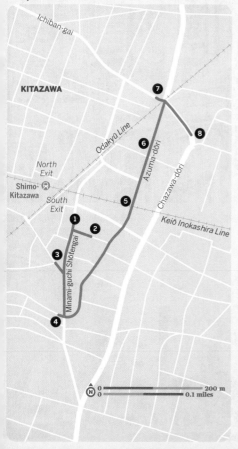

SHIBUYA & SHIMO-KITAZAWA

1. Shibuya Center-gai (p97)
Shibuya's lively main drag. .

2. Apparel shop, Shimo-kitazawa (p95)
Shimo-kitazawa is famous for its vintage shops, cafes and underground live-music venues.

3. Shibuya 109 (p105)
Cylindrical tower housing dozens of small boutiques; come here to understand Shibuya.

4. Hachikō statue (p97)
Famous statue of a loyal Akita dog that came every day to meet his owner at Shibuya station.

fixture, Womb gets a lot of big-name international DJs playing mostly house and techno on Friday and Saturday nights. Frenetic lasers and strobes splash across the heaving crowds, which usually jam all four floors. Weekdays are quieter, with local DJs playing EDM mix and ladies getting free entry (with flyer).

BEAT CAFE
BAR

Map p273 (www.facebook.com/beatcafe; basement fl, 2-13-5 Dōgenzaka, Shibuya-ku; ⏰7pm-5am; 🚃JR Yamanote line to Shibuya, Hachikō exit) Join an eclectic mix of local and international regulars at this comfortably shabby bar among the nightclubs and love hotels of Dōgenzaka. It's a known hang-out for musicians and music fans; check the website for info on parties (and after-parties). Look for Gateway Studio on the corner; the bar is in the basement. Drinks from ¥600.

SHIDAX VILLAGE
KARAOKE

Map p273 (シダックスビレッジ; 📞03-3461-9356; 1-12-13 Jinnan, Shibuya-ku; per person per 30min from ¥400; ⏰11am-5am Sun-Thu, to 6am Fri & Sat; 🚃JR Yamanote line to Shibuya, Hachikō exit) Shidax is a step up from the other karaoke chains, with roomier booths and hundreds of English songs. Note that prices go up by ¥50 to ¥100 on weekends and during holidays; if you stay longer than two hours (which often happens) the 'free time' plan (フリータイム; ¥1950, until 5am) is a good deal; with *nomihōdai* (all-you-can-drink; 飲み放題) it's ¥4950. Nonsmoking rooms available.

⭐ ENTERTAINMENT

★WWW
LIVE MUSIC

Map p273 (www.shibuya.jp/index.html; 13-17 Udagawa-chō, Shibuya-ku; tickets ¥2000-5000; 🚃JR Yamanote line to Shibuya, Hachikō exit) In a former arthouse cinema (with the tell-tale tiered floor still intact), this is one of those rare venues where you could turn up just about any night and hear something good. The line-up varies from indie pop to punk to electronica. Upstairs is the new WWW X, with more space.

UPLINK
CINEMA

Map p273 (アップリンク; www.uplink.co.jp; 37-18 Udagawa-chō, Shibuya-ku; adult/student ¥1800/1500; 🚃JR Yamanote line to Shibuya, Hachikō exit) Watching indies at Uplink feels a bit like hanging out in a friend's basement; with just 40 (comfy, mismatched) seats, it's officially Tokyo's smallest theatre. Artsy domestic and foreign films (subtitled in Japanese), including documentaries, are screened here. Uplink is also one of the few Tokyo cinemas that screens films with a political bent. On weekdays students pay just ¥1100.

SETAGAYA
PUBLIC THEATRE
PERFORMING ARTS

(世田谷パブリックシアター; 📞03-5432-1526; www.setagaya-pt.jp; 4-1-1 Taishidō, Setagaya-ku; tickets ¥3500-7500; 🚃Tōkyū Den-en-toshi line to Sangenjaya, Carrot Tower exit) The best of Tokyo's public theatres, Setagaya Pub-

---

HOT SPOT TOMIGAYA

Just a 15-minute walk away from the brash teen culture of Shibuya Center-gai, is Tomigaya, a fashionable enclave known for its bistros and cafes. Follow the Kamiyama *shōtengai* towards Yoyogi-kōen subway station.

Some of our favourite stops:

Camelback (キャメルバック; www.camelback.tokyo; 42-2 Kamiyama-chō, Shibuya-ku; sandwiches ¥410-900; ⏰10am-7pm Tue-Sun; 🖊; 🚇Chiyoda line to Yoyogi-kōen, exit) The speciality at this sandwich counter run by a former sushi chef is *tamago-yaki* (the kind of rolled omelette that you get at sushi shops) served on a fluffy roll with mayonnaise and a hint of hot mustard.

Fuglen Tokyo (www.fuglen.com; 1-16-11 Tomigaya, Shibuya-ku; coffee from ¥360; ⏰8am-10pm Mon & Tue, to 1am Wed-Sun; 📶; 🚇Chiyoda line to Yoyogi-kōen, exit 2) This Tokyo outpost of a long-running Oslo coffee shop serves Aeropress coffee by day and some of the city's most creative cocktails (from ¥1000) by night.

Shibuya Publishing Booksellers (SPBS; Map p273; www.shibuyabooks.co.jp; 17-3 Kamiyamachō, Shibuya-ku; ⏰noon-midnight Mon-Sat, noon-10pm Sun; 🚃JR Yamanote line to Shibuya, Hachikō exit) Open-late hangout with a decent offering of English-language books and a fine collection of artsy, photo-heavy Japanese magazines.

lic Theatre puts on contemporary dramas as well as modern *nō* (a stylised Japanese dance-drama, performed on a bare stage) and sometimes *butoh* (an avant-garde form of dance). The smaller **Theatre Tram** shows more experimental works. Both are located inside the Carrot Tower building connected to Sangenjaya Station, a five-minute train ride from Shibuya.

CLUB QUATTRO   LIVE MUSIC
Map p273 (クラブクアトロ; ☎03-3477-8750; www.club-quattro.com; 32-13-4 Udagawa-chō, Shibuya-ku; tickets ¥3000-4000; ⓡJR Yamanote line to Shibuya, Hachikō exit) This small, intimate venue has the feel of a slick nightclub and attracts a more grown-up, artsy crowd than the club's location – near Center-gai – might lead you to expect. Though there's no explicit musical focus, emphasis is on rock and world music, with many an indie darling passing through.

 SHOPPING

⭐**TOKYU HANDS**   DEPARTMENT STORE
Map p273 (東急ハンズ; http://shibuya.tokyu-hands.co.jp; 12-18 Udagawa-chō, Shibuya-ku; ⓣ10am-8.30pm; ⓡJR Yamanote line to Shibuya, Hachikō exit) This DIY and *zakka* (miscellaneous goods) store has eight fascinating floors of everything you didn't know you needed, including reflexology slippers, bee-venom face masks and cartoon-character-shaped rice-ball moulds. Most stuff is inexpensive, making it perfect for souvenir- and gift-hunting. Warning: you could lose hours in here.

FAKE TOKYO   FASHION & ACCESSORIES
Map p273 (☎03-5456-9892; www.faketokyo.com; 18-4 Udagawa-chō, Shibuya-ku; ⓣnoon-10pm; ⓡJR Yamanote line to Shibuya, Hachikō exit) This is one of the best places in the city to discover hot underground Japanese designers. It's actually two shops in one: downstairs is Candy, full of brash, unisex streetwear; upstairs is Sister, which specialises in more ladylike items, both new and vintage. Look for the 'Fake Tokyo' banners out front.

SHIBUYA 109   FASHION & ACCESSORIES
Map p273 (渋谷109; Ichimarukyū; www.shibuya109.jp/en/top; 2-29-1 Dōgenzaka, Shibuya-ku; ⓣ10am-9pm; ⓡJR Yamanote line to Shibuya, Hachikō exit) See all those dolled-up teens walking around Shibuya? This is where they

REIMAGINING SHIBUYA

Shibuya is right now undergoing a massive redevelopment. **Shibuya Hikarie** (渋谷ヒカリエ; Map p273; www.hikarie.jp; 2-21-1 Shibuya, Shibuya-ku; ⓣ10am-9pm; ⓡJR Yamanote line to Shibuya, east exit), completed in 2012, was just the first of several planned towers. By the time you read this, Shibuya Station South District (projected completion: 2018) and East Tower (projected completion: 2019) might already be open. Also in the works are a revitalisation of the Shibuya-gawa (currently mostly cloaked in concrete). The 11th-floor 'Sky Lobby' of Shibuya Hikarie has a scale model of what Shibuya will look like when everything is completed in 2027; there are good views from here, too.

shop. Nicknamed *marukyū*, this cylindrical tower houses dozens of small boutiques, each with its own carefully styled look (and competing soundtrack). Even if you don't intend to buy anything, you can't understand Shibuya without making a stop here.

LOFT   DEPARTMENT STORE
Map p273 (ロフト; ☎03-3462-3807; www.loft.co.jp; 18-2 Udagawa-chō, Shibuya-ku; ⓣ10am-9pm; ⓡJR Yamanote line to Shibuya, Hachikō exit) This emporium of homewares, stationery and accessories specialises in all that is cute and covetable. The 1st floor, which stocks seasonal stuff and gifts, is particularly ripe for souvenir-hunting.

 SPORTS & ACTIVITIES

PURIKURA NO MECCA   ARCADE
Map p273 (プリクラのメッカ; 3rd fl, 29-1 Udagawa-chō, Shibuya-ku; purikura ¥400; ⓣ24hr; ⓡJR Yamanote line to Shibuya, Hachikō exit) It's easy to see why teens get sucked into the cult of *purikura* ('print club', aka photo booths): the digitally enhanced photos automatically airbrush away blemishes and add doe eyes and long lashes for good measure (so you come out looking like an anime version of yourself). After primping and posing, decorate the images on screen with touch pens. Note that all-guy groups aren't allowed in.

SHIBUYA & SHIMO-KITAZAWA SHOPPING

Harajuku & Aoyama

HARAJUKU | AOYAMA & GAIENMAE

Neighbourhood Top Five

❶ Meiji-jingū (p108) Leaving the city behind as you pass through the towering cedar *torii* (gate), which marks the entrance to the abode of the gods, and following the wooded, gravel path to Tokyo's most impressive Shintō shrine.

❷ Omote-sandō (p110) Gawking at the contemporary architecture, the work of Japan's leading architects, and the eyebrow-raising consumerism along this wide, tree-lined boulevard.

❸ Yoyogi-kōen (p109) Stretching out on the grassy lawn or catching a food festival at the city's most popular park, which buzzes with life on weekends.

❹ Takeshita-dōri (p109) Scouting new looks while strolling through Harajuku's famous teen fashion bazaar.

❺ Nezu Museum (p111) Retreating into the calm galleries and gardens of this excellent antiquities museum.

For more detail of this area see Map p276 ➡

Explore Harajuku & Aoyama

Harajuku is a neighbourhood that rewards an early start: grab a coffee at Little Nap Coffee Stand (p113) and walk through Yoyogi-kōen (p109) to the shrine, Meiji-jingū (p108) – you'll beat the crowds this way. Then make your way up Omote-sandō (p110), before the shopping starts in earnest (the better to see the striking contemporary buildings that line this boulevard). For a retreat, step into the hushed environs of one of the excellent art museums here, like the Ukiyo-e Ōta Memorial Museum of Art (p109), for woodblock prints, or the Nezu Museum (p111), for antiquities.

Harajuku is Tokyo's real-life catwalk, a world-renowned shopping destination where the ultra-chic (and chic-in-training) come to browse and be seen – a sight in and of itself (and a must if shopping is on your itinerary). Work your way back through the snaking side alleys of Ura-Hara (the nickname for the side streets on either side of Omote-sandō, where the fashion is edgier than on the main drag), to Takeshita-dōri (p109). This trendy shopping strip, beloved by teens all over, should be heaving by now.

Once the shops close, Harajuku becomes eerily quiet. Aoyama too, though there are some swanky establishments here that fuel the well-heeled after hours. There are some excellent (and not unreasonable) dinner options here, if you've planned for a splurge night.

Local Life

→**Hang-outs** On sunny weekends, Yoyogi-kōen (p109) draws crowds of picnicking families, frisbee-tossing students and amateur musicians and dancers using the grassy lawn as free practice space.

→**Street Fashion** Photographers for street-fashion magazines line Omote-sandō looking for the next big thing. Teens and 20-somethings know it and dress for a shot at their 15 minutes of fame.

→**Markets** On weekends the most popular lunch spot is the cluster of food trucks at Aoyama's farmers market (p109).

Getting There & Away

→**Train** The JR Yamanote line stops at Harajuku Station.

→**Subway** The Chiyoda line runs beneath Omote-sandō, stopping at Meiji-jingūmae (for Harajuku) and Omote-sandō (for Aoyama). The Fukutoshin line stops at Meiji-jingūmae and Kita-Sandō. The Ginza and Hanzōmon lines both stop at Omote-sandō Station.

Lonely Planet's Top Tip

Harajuku, and especially the boulevard Omote-sandō, can get extremely crowded – with foot traffic moving at a slow, platform-shoe shuffle. If you want to seriously shop or zip around to see the museums and architecture, then head over on a weekday. If you want to get caught up in it all, check out the markets and people-watch, then come on a Saturday or Sunday afternoon.

✖ Best Places to Eat

→ Maisen (p111)

→ Harajuku Gyōza Rō (p111)

→ Yanmo (p112)

For reviews, see p111. →

⊟ Best Places to Drink

→ Two Rooms (p113)

→ Oath (p113)

→ Montoak (p113)

For reviews, see p113. →

🔒 Best Places to Shop

→ Dog (p116)

→ Sou-Sou (p116)

→ Laforet (p116)

→ Musubi (p116)

→ Bedrock (p117)

For reviews, see p116. →

MEIJI-JINGŪ (MEIJI SHRINE)

If you visit only one Shintō shrine in Tokyo, make it this one. Meiji-jingū is dedicated to the Emperor Meiji and Empress Shōken, whose reign (1868–1912) coincided with Japan's transformation from isolationist, feudal state to modern nation. The shrine is undergoing renovation in preparation for its centennial in 2020; some structures may be under wraps, but as a whole it will remain open.

Constructed in 1920 and destroyed in WWII air raids, the shrine was rebuilt in 1958; however, unlike so many of Japan's postwar reconstructions, Meiji-jingū has an authentic old-world feel. The main shrine is made of cypress from the Kiso region of Nagano. To make an offering, toss a ¥5 coin in the box, bow twice, clap your hands twice and then bow again. To the right, you'll see kiosks selling *ema* (wooden plaques on which prayers are written) and *omamori* (charms).

Several wooden *torii* (gates) mark the entrance to Meiji-jingū. The largest, created from a 1500-year-old Taiwanese cypress, stands 12m high. It's the custom to bow upon passing through a *torii*, which marks the boundary between the mundane world and the sacred one.

Before approaching the main shrine, visitors purify themselves by pouring water over their hands at the *temizuya* (font). Dip the ladle in the water and first rinse your left hand then your right. Pour some water into your left hand and rinse your mouth, then rinse your left hand again. Make sure none of this water gets back into the font!

The shrine itself occupies only a small fraction of the sprawling forested grounds, which contain some 120,000 trees collected from all over Japan. Along the path towards the main shrine, is the entrance to **Meiji-jingū Gyoen** (明治神宮御苑; Inner Garden; Map p276; ¥500; ◷9am-4.30pm, to 4pm Nov-Feb), a landscaped garden. It once belonged to a feudal estate; however, when the grounds passed into imperial hands, the emperor himself designed the iris garden to please the empress.

DON'T MISS

➡ The gates
➡ The font
➡ Main shrine
➡ Meiji-jingū Gyoen

PRACTICALITIES

➡ 明治神宮
➡ Map p276, C1
➡ www.meijijingu.or.jp
➡ 1-1 Yoyogi Kamizono-chō, Shibuya-ku
➡ admission free
➡ ◷dawn-dusk
➡ 🚃JR Yamanote line to Harajuku, Omote-sandō exit

SIGHTS

Harajuku

MEIJI-JINGŪ SHINTO SHRINE

See p108.

★YOYOGI-KŌEN PARK

Map p276 (代々木公園; www.yoyogipark.info; [R]JR Yamanote line to Harajuku, Omote-sandō exit) If it's a sunny and warm weekend afternoon, you can count on there being a crowd lazing around the large grassy expanse that is Yoyogi-kōen. You can also usually find revellers and noisemakers of all stripes, from hula-hoopers to African drum circles to a group of retro greasers dancing around a boom box. It's an excellent place for a picnic and probably the only place in the city where you can reasonably toss a frisbee without fear of hitting someone.

During the warmer months, festivals take place on the plaza across from the park (see website, in Japanese, for a schedule). Cherry blossoms draw huge crowds and parties that go late into the night.

YOYOGI NATIONAL STADIUM ARCHITECTURE

Map p276 (国立代々木競技場; Kokuritsu Yoyogi Kyōgi-jō; 2-1-1 Jinnan, Shibuya-ku; [R]JR Yamanote line to Harajuku, Omote-sandō exit) This early masterpiece by architect Tange Kenzō was built for the 1964 Olympics (and will be used again in the 2020 games). The stadium, which looks vaguely like a samurai helmet, uses suspension-bridge technology – rather than beams – to support the roof.

★TAKESHITA-DŌRI AREA

Map p276 (竹下通り; [R]JR Yamanote line to Harajuku, Takeshita exit) This is Tokyo's famously outré fashion bazaar, where trendy duds sit alongside the trappings of decades of fashion subcultures (plaid and safety pins for the punks; colourful tutus for the *decora;* Victorian dresses for the Gothic Lolitas). Be warned: this pedestrian alley is a pilgrimage site for teens from all over Japan, which means it can get packed.

UKIYO-E ŌTA MEMORIAL MUSEUM OF ART MUSEUM

Map p276 (浮世絵太田記念美術館; ☎03-5777-8600; www.ukiyoe-ota-muse.jp; 1-10-10 Jingūmae, Shibuya-ku; adult ¥700-1000, child free; ⏲10.30am-5.30pm Tue-Sun; [R]JR Yamanote line to Harajuku, Omote-sandō exit) Change into slippers to enter the peaceful, hushed museum that houses the excellent *ukiyo-e* (woodblock prints) collection of Ōta Seizo, the former head of the Toho Life Insurance Company. Seasonal, thematic exhibitions are easily digested in an hour and usually include a few works by masters such as Hokusai and Hiroshige. It's often closed the last few days of the month.

The shop in the basement sells beautifully printed *tenugui* (traditional hand-dyed thin cotton towels).

KAWAII MONSTER CAFE NOTABLE BUILDING

Map p276 (☎03-5413-6142; http://kawaiimonster.jp/pc/; 4th fl, YM Bldg, 4-31-10 Jingūmae, Shibuya-ku; cover charge ¥500, drinks from ¥800; ⏲11.30am-4.30pm & 6-10.30pm Mon-Sat, 11am-8pm Sun; [R]JR Yamanote line to Harajuku, Omote-sandō exit) Lurid colours, surrealist installations and out-of-this world costumes – this is the vision of Sebastian Masuda, stylist to pop star Kyary Pamyu Pamyu, who designed this new cafe. It's an embodiment of the now-reigning aesthetic of *guro-kawaii* (somewhat grotesque cuteness). Food and drink (not what you're here for, but you have to order something) are coloured to match the decor.

CAT STREET AREA

Map p276 (キャットストリート; [R]JR Yamanote line to Harajuku, Omote-sandō exit) Had enough

LOCAL KNOWLEDGE

AOYAMA'S MARKETS

On weekends a **farmers' market** (Map p276; www.farmersmarkets.jp; 5-53-7 Jingūmae, Shibuya-ku; ⏲10am-4pm Sat & Sun; [S]Ginza line to Omote-sandō, exit B2), with colourful produce and a dozen food trucks, sets up on the plaza in front of the United Nations University on Aoyama-dōri. It's as much a social event as a shopping stop. Events pop up, too, including the hipster flea market **Raw Tokyo** (Map p276; www.rawtokyo.jp; 5-53-7 Jingūmae, Shibuya-ku; ⏲11am-6pm, 1st Sat & Sun of the month; [S]Ginza line to Omote-sandō, exit B2) – with DJs and live painting. For a festival atmosphere any day of the week, check out the collection of food vendors at **Commune 246** (Map p276; http://commune246.com/; 3-13 Minami-Aoyama, Minato-ku; ⏲11am-10pm; 🖉; [S]Ginza line to Omote-sandō, exit A4).

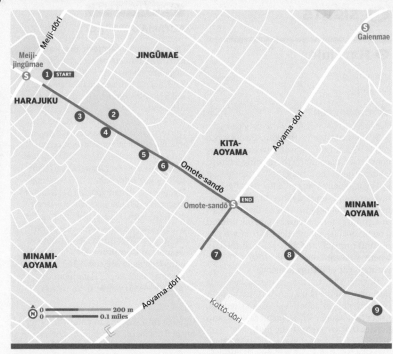

Neighbourhood Walk
Omote-sandō Architecture

START TOKYŪ PLAZA
END NEZU MUSEUM
LENGTH 1.5KM; 1½ HOURS

Omote-sandō is like a walk-through show-room of the who's who of contemporary architecture. Here you'll see buildings from four of Japan's six Pritzker Prize winners: Maki Fumihiko, Andō Tadao, SANAA (Sejima Kazuyo and Nishizawa Ryūe) and Itō Toyō.

Start at the intersection of Omote-sandō and Meiji-dōri, with ❶ **Tokyū Plaza**, a cas-tle-like structure built in 2012 and designed by up-and-coming architect Nakamura Hiro-shi. The entrance is a dizzying hall of mirrors and there's a roof garden on top.

Next up is something a little more understated: Andō's deceptively deep ❷ **Omotesandō Hills** (p226; 2003). This high-end shopping mall spirals around a sunken central atrium.

Across the street, ❸ **Dior Building** (2003), designed by SANAA, has a filmy exterior that seems to hang like a dress. Nearby, a glass cone marks the unlikely loca-

tion of the ❹ **Japan Nursing Association** (2004), designed by Kurokawa Kishō.

Aoki Jun's ❺ **Louis Vuitton Building** (2002) has offset panels of tinted glass behind sheets of metal mesh that are meant to evoke a stack of trunks. There's an art gallery on the 7th floor.

Climb onto the elevated crosswalk to bet-ter admire Itō's construction for ❻ **Tod's** boutique (2004). The criss-crossing strips of concrete take their inspiration from the zelkova trees below; they're also structural.

Fumihiko's 1985 ❼ **Spiral Building** (p226) is worth a detour down Aoyama-dōri. The patchwork, uncentred design is a nod to Tokyo's own incongruous landscape. Inside, a spiralling passage doubles as an art gallery.

You can't miss the convex glass fishbowl that is the ❽ **Prada Aoyama Building** (2003). Created by Herzog and de Meuron, it kicked off the design race down Omote-sandō.

A thicket of bamboo marks the entrance to the traditional-meets-modern Kuma Kengō building that houses the excellent ❾ **Nezu Museum** (p111).

of crowded Harajuku? Exit, stage right, for Cat Street, a windy road lined with a mishmash of boutiques and more room to move. The retail architecture is also quite a spectacle, as this is where smaller brands strike their monuments to consumerism if they can't afford to do so on the main drag.

DESIGN FESTA GALLERY

Map p276 (デザインフェスタ; ☏03-3479-1442; www.designfestagallery.com; 3-20-2 Jingūmae, Shibuya-ku; ◷11am-8pm; ⊠; ⊠JR Yamanote line to Harajuku, Takeshita exit) **FREE** Design Festa has been a leader in Tokyo's DIY art scene for nearly two decades. The madhouse building itself is worth a visit; it's always evolving. Inside there are dozens of small galleries rented by the day. More often than not, the artists themselves are hanging around, too.

Design Festa also sponsors a twice-yearly exhibition, actually Asia's largest art fair, at Tokyo Big Sight.

⊙ Aoyama & Gaienmae

★NEZU MUSEUM MUSEUM

Map p276 (根津美術館; ☏03-3400-2536; www.nezu-muse.or.jp; 6-5-1 Minami-Aoyama, Minato-ku; adult/student/child ¥1100/800/free, special exhibitions extra ¥200; ◷10am-5pm Tue-Sun; ⊠Ginza line to Omote-sandō, exit A5) Nezu Museum offers a striking blend of old and new: a renowned collection of Japanese, Chinese and Korean antiquities in a gallery space designed by contemporary architect Kuma Kengo. Select items from the extensive collection are displayed in seasonal exhibitions. The English explanations are usually pretty good. Behind the galleries is a woodsy strolling garden laced with stone paths and studded with teahouses and sculptures.

TARO OKAMOTO MEMORIAL MUSEUM MUSEUM

Map p276 (岡本太郎記念館; http://taro-oka-moto.or.jp; 6-1-19 Minami-Aoyama, Minato-ku; adult/child ¥620/310; ◷10am-6pm Wed-Mon; ⊠Ginza line to Omote-sandō, exit A5) A painter and sculpture, Okamoto Tarō was Japan's most recognised artist from the post-WWII period, a rare avant-garde figure with mass appeal. His works are both playful and sinister, life-affirming and chaotic. This small museum, which includes a sculpture garden, is inside the artist's home.

WATARI MUSEUM OF CONTEMPORARY ART MUSEUM

Map p276 (ワタリウム美術館; Watari Um; ☏03-3402-3001; www.watarium.co.jp; 3-7-6 Jingūmae, Shibuya-ku; adult/student ¥1000/800; ◷11am-7pm Tue & Thu-Sun, to 9pm Wed; ⊠Ginza line to Gaienmae, exit 3) This progressive and often provocative museum was built in 1990 to a design by Swiss architect Mario Botta. Exhibits range from retrospectives of established art-world figures (such as Yayoi Kusama and Nam June Paik) to graffiti and landscape artists – with some exhibitions spilling onto the surrounding streets. 'Pair' tickets cost ¥1600 for two.

There's an excellent art bookshop, **On Sundays** (www.watarium.co.jp; ◷11am-8pm), in the basement.

✕ EATING

✕ Harajuku

★HARAJUKU GYŌZA-RŌ DUMPLINGS ¥

Map p276 (原宿餃子楼; 6-4-2 Jingūmae, Shibuya-ku; 6 gyōza ¥290; ◷11.30am-4.30am; ⊠JR Yamanote line to Harajuku, Omote-sandō exit) *Gyōza* (dumplings) are the only thing on the menu here, but you won't hear any complaints from the regulars who queue up to get their fix. Have them *sui* (boiled) or *yaki* (pan-fried), with or without *niniku* (garlic) or *nira* (chives) – they're all delicious. Expect to wait on weekends, but the line moves quickly.

★MAISEN TONKATSU ¥

Map p276 (まい泉; http://mai-sen.com; 4-8-5 Jingūmae, Shibuya-ku; lunch/dinner from ¥995/1680; ◷11am-10pm; ⊠Ginza line to Omote-sandō, exit A2) You could order something else (maybe fried shrimp), but everyone else will be ordering the famous *tonkatsu* (breaded, deep-fried pork cutlets). There are different grades of pork on the menu, including prized *kurobuta* (black pig), but even the cheapest is melt-in-your-mouth divine. The restaurant is housed in an old public bathhouse. A takeaway window serves delicious *tonkatsu sando* (sandwich).

SAKURA-TEI OKONOMIYAKI ¥

Map p276 (さくら亭; ☏03-3479-0039; www.sakuratei.co.jp; 3-20-1 Jingūmae, Shibuya-ku; okonomiyaki ¥950-1500; ◷11am-midnight; ⊠✎;

LOCAL KNOWLEDGE

GOLDEN GINGKOS

While Japan as a whole is world famous for its *sakura* (cherry trees), Tokyo's official tree is the *ichō* (gingko). In late fall, the trees along Ichō Namiki (Gingko Avenue) in Gaienmae turn a glorious shade of gold. Locals know to grab a seat at **Royal Garden Café** (ローヤルガーデンカフェ; Map p270; ☎03-5414-6170; www.royal-gardencafe.com; 2-1-19 Kita-Aoyama, Minato-ku; ⏰11am-11pm; 📶; [S]Ginza line to Gaienmae, exit 4A) for the best views.

[R]JR Yamanote line to Harajuku, Takeshita exit) Grill your own *okonomiyaki* (savoury pancakes) at this funky place inside the gallery Design Festa (p111). In addition to classic options (with pork, squid and cabbage), there are some wacky innovations (try taco or carbonara *okonomiyaki*). There's also a great value 90-minute all-you-can-eat plan (lunch/dinner ¥1250/2100).

KYŪSYŪ JANGARA RAMEN ¥

Map p276 (九州じゃんがら; 1-13-21 Jingūmae, Shibuya-ku; ramen ¥630-1130; ⏰10.45am-midnight Mon-Fri, from 10am Sat & Sun; 📝; [R]JR Yamanote line to Harajuku, Omote-sandō exit) Come sample the elegantly thin noodles, silky *chāshū* (roast pork) and righteous *karashi takana* (hot pickled greens) for which Kyūshū-style ramen is famous. You can't go wrong with ordering *zembu-iri* (everything in). Vegetarians and vegans take note: Kyūsyū Jangara recently debuted a bowl just for you, which, against all odds, is actually pretty good.

MOMINOKI HOUSE JAPANESE ¥¥

Map p276 (もみの木ハウス; www.mominoki-house.net; 2-18-5 Jingūmae, Shibuya-ku; lunch/dinner set menu from ¥980/2500; ⏰11am-3pm & 5-11pm; 📝; [R]JR Yamanote line to Harajuku, Takeshita exit) 🌿 Boho Tokyoites have been coming here for tasty macrobiotic fare since 1976. The casual dining room, which looks like a grown-up (indoor) tree fort and features several cosy, semi-private booths, has seen some famous visitors too, such as Paul McCartney. Chef Yamada's menu is heavily vegan, but also includes free-range chicken and *Ezo shika* (Hokkaidō venison, ¥4800).

🍴 Aoyama & Gaienmae

HIGASHIYA MAN SWEETS ¥

Map p276 (ひがしや　まん; ☎03-5414-3881; www.higashiya.com/shop/man/; 3-17-14 Minami-Aoyama, Minato-ku; sweets ¥300; ⏰11am-7pm; 📝; [S]Ginza line to Omote-sandō, exit A4) *Manjū* (まんじゅう) – that's where the shop's name comes from; it's not just for men! – are hot buns stuffed with sweetened red-bean paste. They're steamed fresh at this takeaway counter, a popular pit-stop for Aoyama shoppers. Inside the tiny shop, there's a greater selection of traditional Japanese sweets, many packaged beautifully for gifts.

KINOKUNIYA INTERNATIONAL SUPERMARKET SUPERMARKET ¥

Map p276 (紀ノ国屋 インターナショナル; www.super-kinokuniya.jp/store/international; basement fl, AO bldg, 3-11-7 Kita-Aoyama, Minato-ku; ⏰9.30am-9pm; 📝; [S]Ginza line to Omote-sandō, exit B2) Kinokuniya carries expat lifesavers such as Marmite and peanut butter; crusty, wholegrain bread; and cheeses galore (at a price of course).

YANMO SEAFOOD ¥¥¥

Map p276 (やんも; ☎03-5466-0636; www.yanmo.co.jp/aoyama/index.html; basement fl, T Place bldg, 5-5-25 Minami-Aoyama, Minato-ku; lunch/dinner set menu from ¥1100/7560; ⏰11.30am-2pm & 6-10.30pm Mon-Sat; [S]Ginza line to Omote-sandō, exit A5) Freshly caught seafood from the nearby Izu Peninsula is the speciality at this upscale, yet unpretentious restaurant. If you're looking to splash out on a seafood dinner, this is a great place to do so. The reasonably priced set menus include sashimi and steamed and grilled fish. Reservations are essential for dinner. Lunch is a bargain, but you might have to queue.

MARU JAPANESE ¥¥¥

Map p276 (圓; ☎03-6418-5572; www.maru-mayfont.jp; basement fl, 5-50-8 Jingūmae, Shibuya-ku; dinner course from ¥6600; ⏰6pm-1am Mon-Fri, 5pm-1am Sat, 5pm-midnight Sun; [S]Ginza line to Omote-sandō, exit B2) Maru's chef trained at one of Kyoto's top *kaiseki* (Japanese haute cuisine) restaurants and then decided he'd rather run a down-to-earth, accessible restaurant. The 10-course meal (which changes monthly) is a great deal and Maru is deservedly popular; reservations are recommended.

LOCAL KNOWLEDGE

MEIJI-JINGŪ GAIEN BEER GARDENS

Summer beer gardens are a Tokyo tradition (typically running late May to early September). Two of the city's best are within Meiji-jingū Gaien (the 'Outer Garden' of Meiji-jingū). **Mori-no Beer Garden** (森のビアガーデン; Map p270; www.rkfs.co.jp/brand/beer_garden_detail.html; 1-7-5 Kita-Aoyama, Minato-ku; ⊙5-10pm Mon-Fri, 3-10pm Sat & Sun; 📍JR Sōbu line to Shinanomachi) hosts up to 1000 revellers for all-you-can-eat-and-drink spreads of beer and barbecue under a century-old tree.

At the more patrician **Sekirei** (鶺鴒; Map p270; ☎03-3746-7723; www.meijikinenkan.gr.jp/restaurant/company/sekirei; Meiji Kinenkan, 2-2-23 Moto-Akasaka, Minato-ku; cover charge ¥500; ⊙5-10.30pm; 📍JR Sōbu line to Shinanomachi), you can quaff beer on the neatly clipped lawn of the stately Meiji Kinenkan (a hall used for weddings); traditional Japanese dance is performed nightly around 8pm.

DRINKING & NIGHTLIFE

LITTLE NAP COFFEE STAND `CAFE`
Map p276 (リトルナップコーヒースタンド; www.littlenap.jp; 5-65-4 Yoyogi, Shibuya-ku; ⊙9am-7pm Tue-Sun; 📍Chiyoda line to Yoyogi-kōen, exit 3) Few people enter Yoyogi-kōen from the entrance near the subway stop of the same name, except those who live nearby. Odds are, on their way, they've stopped by Little Nap for a well-crafted latte (¥400). On Sundays, there's always a crowd loitering out front.

OATH `BAR`
(http://bar-oath.com; 4-5-9 Shibuya, Shibuya-ku; ⊙9pm-5am Mon-Thu, to 8am Fri & Sat, 5-11pm Sun; 📍Ginza line to Omote-sandō, exit B1) A tiny space along a somewhat forlorn strip of highway, Oath is a favourite after-hours destination for clubbers – helped no doubt by the ¥500 drinks and lack of cover charge. Underground DJs spin here sometimes, too.

TWO ROOMS `BAR`
Map p276 (トゥールームス; ☎03-3498-0002; www.tworooms.jp; 5th fl, AO bldg, 3-11-7 Kita-Aoyama, Minato-ku; ⊙11.30am-2am Mon-Sat, to 10pm Sun; 📍Ginza line to Omote-sandō, exit B2) Expect a crowd dressed like they don't care that wine by the glass starts at ¥1600. You can eat here too, but the real scene is at night by the bar. Call ahead (staff speak English) on Friday or Saturday night to reserve a table on the terrace, which has sweeping views towards the Shinjuku skyline.

MONTOAK `CAFE`
Map p276 (モントーク; 6-1-9 Jingūmae, Shibuya-ku; ⊙11am-3am; 📍JR Yamanote line to Harajuku, Omote-sandō exit) This stylish, tinted-glass cube is a calm, dimly lit retreat from the busy streets. It's perfect for holing up with a pot of tea or carafe of wine and watching the crowds go by. Or, if the weather is nice, score a seat on the terrace. Drinks from ¥700.

HARAJUKU TAPROOM `PUB`
Map p276 (原宿タップルーム; http://bairdbeer.com/en/taproom; 2nd fl, 1-20-13 Jingūmae, Shibuya-ku; ⊙5pm-midnight Mon-Fri, noon-midnight Sat & Sun; 📍JR Yamanote line to Harajuku, Takeshita exit) Baird's Brewery is one of Japan's most successful and consistently good craft breweries. This is one of its two Tokyo outposts, where you can sample more than a dozen of its beers on tap; try the top-selling Rising Sun Pale Ale (pints ¥1000). Japanese pub-style food is served as well.

A TO Z CAFE `CAFE`
Map p276 (エートゥーゼットカフェ; 5th fl, 5-8-3 Minami-Aoyama, Minato-ku; ⊙11.30am-11.30pm; 📍Ginza line to Omote-sandō, exit B3) Artist Yoshitomo Nara (known for his portraits of punkish tots) teamed up with design firm Graf to create this spacious and only slightly off-kilter cafe. Along with wooden schoolhouse chairs, whitewashed walls and a small cottage, you can find a few scattered examples of Nara's work. Drinks from ¥600.

ENTERTAINMENT

JINGŪ BASEBALL STADIUM `BASEBALL`
Map p276 (神宮球場; Jingū Kyūjo; ☎0180-993-589; www.jingu-stadium.com; 3-1 Kasumigaoka-machi, Shinjuku-ku; tickets ¥1600-4600; 📍Ginza line to Gaienmae, exit 3) Jingū Baseball Stadium, built in 1926, is home to the Yakult Swallows, Tokyo's number-two team (but

1. Prada Aoyama Building (p110)
Main entrance to the Prada building designed by architects Herzog and de Meuron in 2003.

2. Nezu Museum gardens (p111)
The gardens, studded with teahouses and sculptures, of Nezu Museum, which houses Asian antiques.

3. Yoyogi-kōen (p109)
Tokyoites enjoy the blossoming cherry trees in Yoyogi-kōen park.

4. Takeshita-dōri (p109)
Famous teen fashion bazaar.

number-one when it comes to fan loyalty). Night games start at 6pm; weekend games start around 2pm. Pick up tickets from the booth next to Gate 9, which is open 11am to 5pm (or until 20 minutes after the game starts).

Same-day outfield tickets cost just ¥1600 to ¥1900 (¥500 for children) and are usually available – unless the Swallows are playing crosstown rivals, the Yomiuri Giants.

NATIONAL NŌ THEATRE THEATRE

(国立能楽堂; Kokuritsu Nō-gakudō; ☎03-3230-3000; www.ntj.jac.go.jp/english; 4-18-1 Sendagaya, Shibuya-ku; adult ¥2600-4900, student ¥1900-2200; [R]JR Sōbu line to Sendagaya) The traditional music, poetry and dances that *nō* is famous for unfold here on an elegant cypress stage. Each seat has a small screen displaying an English translation of the dialogue. Shows take place only a few times a month and can sell out fast; purchase tickets one month in advance through the Japan Arts Council website.

The theatre is 400m from Sendagaya Station; from the exit, walk right along the main road and turn left at the traffic light.

CROCODILE LIVE MUSIC, COMEDY

Map p276 (クロコダイル; www.crocodile-live.jp; basement fl, 6-18-8 Jingūmae, Shibuya-ku; ⏲6pm-1am; [S]Chiyoda line to Meiji-jingūmae, exit 1) Decked out in neon, mirrors and chrome, Crocodile is a classic dive. Live music of all sorts plays here nightly, but the most popular event is the English comedy night put on by Tokyo Comedy Store on the last Friday of the month (admission ¥1500, plus drink order). Advanced bookings are recommended; see www.tokyocomedy.com/improvazilla_main_stage_show.

LOCAL KNOWLEDGE

URA-HARA

The recent arrival of fast-fashion megachains (such as H&M) hasn't pushed Harajuku fashion off the map; it's just pushed it further into the backstreets. Ura-Hara (literally 'behind Harajuku') is the nickname for the maze of backstreets behind Omote-sandō. Here you'll find the tiny, eccentric shops and secondhand stores from which Harajuku hipsters cobble together their head-turning looks. Whether your aim is acquisitive or more of the anthropological sort, it's worth spending some time exploring these streets. Some places to start include club-kid favourite **Dog** (p116) and cutesy pioneer **6% Doki Doki** (p117).

SHOPPING

★DOG FASHION, VINTAGE

Map p276 (ドッグ; www.dog-hjk.com/index.html; basement fl, 3-23-3 Jingūmae, Shibuya-ku; ⏲noon-8pm; [R]JR Yamanote line to Harajuku, Takeshita exit) Club kids and stylists love the showpiece items at legendary Ura-Hara boutique Dog. The store itself, which is decorated to look like a derelict carnival funhouse, is much of the appeal: it looks like an art installation.

It's a tiny place, though, and it has taken to charging admission for tour groups, but ordinary browsers are welcome. Look for graffiti over the entrance and head down the stairs.

★SOU-SOU FASHION & ACCESSORIES

Map p276 (そうそう; ☎03-3407-7877; http://sousounetshop.jp; 5-3-10 Minami-Aoyama, Minato-ku; ⏲11am-8pm; [S]Ginza line to Omote-sandō, exit A5) Kyoto brand Sou-Sou gives traditional Japanese clothing items – such as split-toed *tabi* socks and *haori* (coats with kimono-like sleeves) – a contemporary spin. It is best known for producing the steel-toed, rubber-soled *tabi* shoes worn by Japanese construction workers in fun, playful designs, but it also carries bags, tees and super-adorable children's clothing.

★MUSUBI ARTS & CRAFTS

Map p276 (むす美; http://kyoto-musubi.com; 2-31-8 Jingūmae, Shibuya-ku; ⏲11am-7pm Thu-Tue; [R]JR Yamanote line to Harajuku, Takeshita exit) *Furoshiki* are versatile squares of cloth that can be folded and knotted to make shopping bags and gift wrap. This shop sells pretty ones in both traditional and contemporary patterns. There is usually an English-speaking clerk who can show you how to tie them, or pick up one of the English-language books sold here.

★LAFORET FASHION & ACCESSORIES

Map p276 (ラフォーレ; www.laforet.ne.jp; 1-11-6 Jingūmae, Shibuya-ku; ⏲11am-8pm; [R]JR Yamanote line to Harajuku, Omote-sandō exit) Laforet has been a beacon of cutting-edge

Harajuku style for decades and lots of quirky, cult favourite brands still cut their teeth here (you'll find some examples at the ground-floor boutique, Wall). A range of looks are represented here from *ame-kaji* (American casual) to gothic (in the basement).

ARTS & SCIENCE FASHION & ACCESSORIES

Map p276 (http://arts-science.com/; 101, 103, 105 & 109 Palace Aoyama, 6-1-6 Minami-Aoyama, Minato-ku; 🕒noon-8pm; [S]Ginza line to Omote-sandō, exit A5) Strung along the 1st floor of a mid-century apartment (across from the Nezu Museum) is a collection of small boutiques from celebrity stylist Sonya Park. Park's signature style is a vintage-inspired minimalism in luxurious, natural fabrics. Homewares, too.

COMME DES GARÇONS FASHION & ACCESSORIES

Map p276 (コム・デ・ギャルソン; www.comme-des-garcons.com; 5-2-1 Minami-Aoyama, Minato-ku; 🕒11am-8pm; [S]Ginza line to Omote-sandō, exit A5) Designer Kawakubo Rei threw a wrench in the fashion machine in the early '80s with her dark, asymmetrical designs. That her work doesn't appear as shocking today as it once did speaks volumes for her far-reaching success. This eccentric, vaguely disorienting architectural creation is her brand's flagship store.

GALLERY KAWANO CLOTHING

Map p276 (ギャラリー川野; www.gallery-kawano.com; 4-4-9 Jingūmae, Shibuya-ku; 🕒11am-6pm; 🚆Ginza line to Omote-sandō, exit A2) Gallery Kawano has a good selection of vintage kimonos in decent shape, priced reasonably (about ¥5000 to ¥15,000). The knowledgeable staff will help you try them on and pick out a matching *obi* (sash); they're less excited about helping customers who try things on but don't intend to buy.

BEDROCK FASHION & ACCESSORIES

Map p276 (ベッドロック; 4-12-10 Jingūmae, Shibuya-ku; 🕒11am-9pm, to 8pm Sun; [S]Ginza line to Omote-sandō, exit A2) Walking into Bedrock is like stepping into Keith Richards' boudoir, or the costume closet for *Pirates of the Caribbean* – all leather, feathers and lace. Enter through a secret staircase in the back of the Forbidden Fruit juice bar.

6% DOKI DOKI FASHION & ACCESSORIES

Map p276 (ロクパーセントドキドキ; www.dokidoki6.com; 2nd fl, 4-28-16 Jingūmae, Shibuya-ku; 🕒noon-8pm; 🚆JR Yamanote line to Harajuku, Omote-sandō exit) Tucked away on an Ura-Hara backstreet, this bubblegum-pink store sells acid-bright accessories that are part raver, part schoolgirl and, according to the shop's name, 'six percent exciting'. We wonder what more excitement would look like! Anyway, it's 100% Harajuku.

KIDDYLAND TOYS

Map p276 (キデイランド; www.kiddyland.co.jp/en/index.html; 6-1-9 Jingūmae, Shibuya-ku; 🕒10am-9pm; 🚆JR Yamanote line to Harajuku, Omote-sandō exit) This multistorey toy emporium is packed to the rafters with character goods, including all your Studio Ghibli, Sanrio and Disney faves. It's not just for kids either; you'll spot plenty of adults on a nostalgia trip down the Hello Kitty aisle.

CHICAGO THRIFT STORE VINTAGE

Map p276 (シカゴ; 6-31-21 Jingūmae, Shibuya-ku; 🕒10am-8pm; 🚆JR Yamanote line to Harajuku, Omote-sandō exit) Chicago is crammed with all sorts of vintage clothing, but best of all is the extensive collection of used kimonos and *yukata*, priced very low, in the back.

SPORTS & ACTIVITIES

OHARA SCHOOL OF IKEBANA IKEBANA

Map p276 (小原流いけばな; ☎03-5774-5097; www.ohararyu.or.jp; 5-7-17 Minami-Aoyama, Minato-ku; per class ¥4000; [S]Ginza line to Omote-sandō, exit B1) Every Thursday, from 10.30am to 12.30pm, this well-regarded, modern ikebana school teaches introductory flower-arrangement classes in English. Sign up via email by 3pm the Tuesday before.

SHIMIZU-YU SENTO

Map p276 (清水湯; ☎03-3401-4404; http://shimizuyu.jp/; 3-12-3 Minami-Aoyama, Minato-ku; with/without sauna ¥1000/460; 🕒noon-midnight Mon-Thu, to 11pm Sat & Sun; 🚆Ginza line to Omote-sandō, exit A4) Not all *sentō* (public bathhouses) are historical relics: Shimizu-yu has ultramodern tubs of glistening white tile, jet baths and a sauna. It's just as likely to be filled with young shoppers – perhaps transitioning to a night out – as local grandmas. You can rent a towel (¥300) and purchase soap and shampoo (¥310) at the counter.

West Tokyo

NAKANO & KŌENJI | KICHIJŌJI & MITAKA | OGIKUBO | KICHIJŌJI

Neighbourhood Top Five

1. **Ghibli Museum** (p120) Delighting in the creativity of Japan's legendary animator, Miyazaki Hayao, and savouring the magic and wonder of his films in a museum he designed.

2. **Inokashira-kōen** (p121) Ambling through the woodsy grounds of a beloved park, past buskers and performance artists, and paying your respects to the sea goddess enshrined here.

3. **Nakano Broadway** (p121) Wandering the halls of this vintage 1960s shopping mall, a collectors' paradise and favourite of *otaku* (fans of anime and manga).

4. **Kita-Kore Building** (p124) Getting a glimpse of Tokyo's raw, unpolished side at Kōenji's colourful (counter) cultural centre.

5. **Reversible Destiny Lofts** (p121) Experiencing the topsy-turvy tactile world of one of Tokyo's more eccentric contemporary buildings.

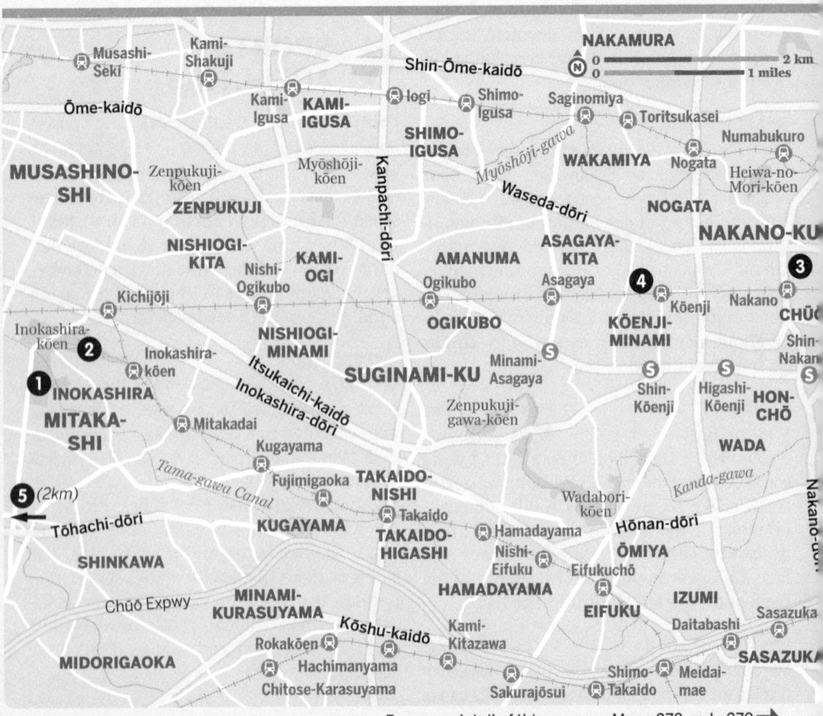

For more detail of this area see Map p278 and p279

Explore West Tokyo

West Tokyo here is defined by the largely residential neighbourhoods along the Chūō line, Tokyo's central rail line, west of Shinjuku. Over the decades, each node on the line has developed its own local culture and atmosphere: Nakano is a draw for *otaku* (fans of anime and manga); Kōenji attracts punks and social activists; many who work in the anime industry live in Asagaya; students love Kichijōji. These are generalisations, of course, but spending an hour or two (or more!) in each gives you a picture of the many possible lives of Tokyoites.

The area's top sight is the enchanting Ghibli Museum (p120), in far-west Mitaka. We recommend booking your visit at 10am or 2pm so that your visit can coincide with a leisurely detour through Inokashira-kōen (p121) and lunch in Kichijōji. Spend the rest of the afternoon wandering around Nakano, with its stubbornly mid-20th-century shopping arcades and collectors' shops, or Kōenji, with its colourful (and sometimes a little crumbly) counter-culture spaces. Most of the neighbourhoods here have nomiyagai (p123), strips crammed with tiny bars and restaurants that come alive in the evenings – proof that these suburbs are anything but sleepy.

Local Life

→**Hang-outs** On weekends Inokashira-kōen (p121) fills with performance artists and craft vendors, drawing families and students.

→**Music** Kōenji is the locus of Tokyo's punk scene and has several underground music venues.

→**Living** Kichijōji, with its park, department stores and commuting convenience, is routinely voted one of the best places to live in Tokyo.

Getting There & Away

→**Train** The JR Sōbu (local) and Chūō (rapid) lines run on the same lines west from Shinjuku to Nakano, Kōenji (local trains only on weekdays), Ogikubo, Kichijōji and Mitaka. Beware of the 'special' rapid and 'Ome liner' trains, which go nonstop from Shinjuku to Mitaka. The Keiō Inokashira line runs from Shibuya to Kichijōji, stopping at Inokashira-kōen-mae (for the park).

→**Subway** The Tōzai line continues west from Takadanobaba to Nakano. The Marunouchi line runs from Shinjuku to Ogikubo, south of (but parallel to) the Sōbu-Chūō line.

Lonely Planet's Top Tip

Two of the highlights here, the Ghibli Museum (p120) and the Reversible Destiny Lofts (p121), require advanced reservations. We recommend booking Ghibli tickets as early as possible (up to three months in advance) with a travel agent in your home country – otherwise you may find yourself out of luck. If there are no tours of the Reversible Destiny Lofts taking place during your visit, you can always stay (p197) there.

WEST TOKYO

✕ Best Places to Eat

→ Tensuke (p122)

→ Okajōki (p122)

→ Harukiya (p122)

For reviews, see p122.➡

⊖ Best Places to Drink

→ Cocktail Shobō (p123)

→ Nantoka Bar (p123)

→ Uni Stand (p123)

For reviews, see p123.➡

⌂ Best Places to Shop

→ Mandarake (p124)

→ PukuPuku (p124)

→ Sokkyō (p124)

For reviews, see p124.➡

TOP SIGHT
STUDIO GHIBLI

Master animator Miyazaki Hayao and his Studio Ghibli (pronounced 'jiburi') have been responsible for some of the best-loved films in Japan – and the world. Miyazaki designed this museum himself, and it's redolent of the dreamy, vaguely steampunk atmosphere that makes his animations so enchanting.

The building itself looks like an illustration from a European fairy tale. Inside there is an imagined workshop filled with the kinds of books and artworks that inspired the creator, as well as vintage machines from animation's history. It rewards curiosity and exploration; peer through a small window, for example, and you'll see little soot sprites (as seen in *Spirited Away*; 2001). A spiral staircase leads to a purposefully overgrown rooftop terrace with a 5m tall statue of the Robot Soldier from Laputa (*Castle in the Sky*; 1986).

A highlight for children (sorry grown-ups!) is a giant, plush replica of the cat bus from the classic *My Neighbor Totoro* (1988) that kids can climb on. There's also a small theatre where original animated shorts – which can only be seen here! – are screened (you'll get a ticket for this when you enter). The film changes monthly to keep fans coming back.

Getting to Ghibli is all part of the adventure. A minibus (round trip/one way ¥320/210) leaves for the museum every 20 minutes from Mitaka Station (bus stop 9). The museum is on the western edge of Inokashira-kōen, so you can also walk there or back through the park from Kichijōji Station in about 30 minutes. Check the website for details on how to secure tickets.

DID YOU KNOW?

Spirited Away (2001) won the Academy Award for Best Animated Feature – the only Japanese animated film and only hand-drawn film ever to win.

PRACTICALITIES

➤ ジブリ美術館
➤ Map p279, A4
➤ www.ghibli-museum.jp
➤ 1-1-83 Shimo-Renjaku, Mitaka-shi
➤ adult ¥1000, child ¥100-700
➤ ⊙10am-6pm, closed Tue
➤ ⓡJR Sōbu-Chūō line to Mitaka, south exit

👁 SIGHTS

👁 Nakano & Kōenji

⭐**NAKANO BROADWAY**   NOTABLE BUILDING
Map p278 (中野ブロードウェイ; www.nbw.jp;
5-25-15 Nakano, Nakano-ku; ⊘varies by shop; 📷;
🚉JR Sōbu-Chūō line to Nakano, north exit) This
vintage 1960s shopping mall – at the end of
the equally vintage Nakano Sun Mall (p124)
covered arcade – helped cement Nakano's
reputation as an underground Akihabara.
It's filled with small shops aimed at collectors of all sorts; many sell manga (Japanese
comics) and vintage toys, but there are
also those specialising in antique watches,
darts...you name it.

GARTER   GALLERY
Map p278 (http://chimpom.jp/; Kita-Kore Bldg,
3-4-13 Kōenji-kita, Suginami-ku; ⊘3.30-9pm Thu-
Tue; 🚉JR Sōbu line to Kōenji, north exit) FREE
Inside the Kita-Kore Building (p124), this
space is run by Tokyo-based art collective
ChimPom. The group is known to be overt-
ly political (and sometimes un-PC), which
makes this an interesting space to watch.
Closed between exhibits.

👁 Kichijōji & Mitaka

GHIBLI MUSEUM   MUSEUM
See p120.

⭐**INOKASHIRA-KŌEN**   PARK
Map p279 (井の頭公園; www.kensetsu.metro.
tokyo.jp/seibuk/inokashira/index.html; 1-18-31
Gotenyama, Musashino-shi; 🚉JR Sōbu-Chūō
line to Kichijōji, Kōen exit) One of Tokyo's best
parks, Inokashira-kōen has a big pond in
the middle flanked by woodsy strolling
paths. You can rent row boats and swan-
shaped pedal boats to take out onto the
water (¥700 per hour). On weekends performance artists and craft vendors gather here
(along with lots of Tokyoites of all ages).
Don't miss the ancient shrine to the sea
goddess Benzaiten.

To reach the park, walk straight from
the Kōen exit of Kichijōji Station, cross at
the light and veer right at Marui ('0101')
department store; the park is at the end of
the lane. Along the way, you'll pass shops
selling takeaway items such as *yakitori*
(grilled chicken skewers) and hot dogs.

WORTH A DETOUR

EDO-TOKYO OPEN AIR MUSEUM

The fantastic, yet little-known **Edo-
Tokyo Open Air Architecture
Museum** (江戸東京たてもの園; www.
tatemonoen.jp/english; 3-7-1 Sakura-
chō, Koganei-shi; adult/child ¥400/free;
⊘9.30am-5.30pm Tue-Sun Apr-Sep, to
4.30pm Oct-Mar; 👶; 🚉JR Chūō line to
Musashi-Koganei) has a collection of historic buildings rescued from Tokyo's
modernising zeal. Among them are an
Edo-era farmhouse, a modernist villa
and a whole strip of early-20th-century
shops, all of which you can enter. Take
the Chūō line west to Musashi-Koganei
(four stops past Kichijōji); from the
station's north exit, take bus 2 or 3 for
Koganei-kōen Nishi-guchi. It's a short
walk through Koganei-kōen (Tokyo's
second-largest park) to the museum.

INOKASHIRA BENZAITEN   SHINTO SHRINE
Map p279 (井の頭弁財天; Inokashira-kōen,
Musashino-shi; ⊘7am-4.30pm; 🚉JR Sōbu-Chūō
line to Kichijōji, Kōen exit) FREE Benzaiten, one
of Japan's eight lucky gods, is actually the
octet's sole goddess (she's also the Japanese
incarnation of the Hindi goddess Sarasvati
and a patron of the arts). Her realm is the
waters, which is why you'll find this shrine
– said to have been founded in 1197 – on an
island in Inokashira-kōen's central pond.

A warning to couples thinking of taking a
row boat out on the waters: though Benzait-
en has many positive qualities, she is known
to be a jealous goddess and urban legend has
it that couples break up after rowing here.

HARMONICA-YOKOCHŌ   MARKET
Map p279 (ハーモニカ横丁; http://hamoyoko.
com; 1-2 Kichijōji-Honchō, Musashino-shi; 🚉JR
Sōbu-Chūō line to Kichijōji, north exit) This covered market, with low ceilings and red paper
chōchin (lanterns), originated as a black market after WWII. Some of the vendors – the
fishmongers, for example – have been around
for decades, but there are some trendy new
boutiques and bars here too. There's a morning market every third Sunday (7am to 10am).

REVERSIBLE DESTINY LOFTS   ARCHITECTURE
(天命反転住宅; Tenmei Hanten Jūtaku; 📞0422-
26-4966; www.rdloftsmitaka.com/english; 2-2-8
Ōsawa, Mitaka-shi; adult/child ¥2700/1000;

WEST TOKYO EATING

🔊; 🚉JR Sōbu-Chūō line to Mitaka, south exit)
Designed by husband and wife Arakawa Shūsaku (1936–2010) and Madeleine Gins (1941–2014) and completed in 2005, this housing complex certainly strikes against the mould: Created 'in memory of Helen Keller' the nine units have undulating, ridged floors, spherical dens and ceiling hooks for hammocks and swings. All this is meant to create a sensory experience beyond the visual (though the building is plenty colourful). Inside access is by tour only (check the website); the guides can speak some English.

Some units are occupied by residents, but others are available for short-term stays (p197).

From JR Mitaka Station, take bus 51 or 52 (¥220, 15 minutes, every 10 to 15 minutes) from bus stop 2 on the station's south side and get off at Ōsawa Jūjiro (大沢十字路); you can see the building from the bus stop. Not all buses go this far, so show the driver where you want to go. Bus 1 (¥220, 25 minutes, every 10 to 15 minutes) goes here from Kichijōji Station (south exit, bus stop 3), alongside Inokashira-kōen.

🍴 EATING

🍴 Nakano & Kōenji

⭐TENSUKE   TEMPURA ¥
Map p278 (天すけ; ☎03-3223-8505; 3-22-7 Kōenji-kita, Suginami-ku; lunch/dinner from ¥1100/1600; ◷noon-2.15pm & 6-10pm Tue-Fri, 11.30am-3pm & 6-10pm Sat & Sun; 🚉JR Sōbu line to Kōenji, north exit) An entirely legitimate candidate for eighth wonder of the modern world is Tensuke's *tamago* (egg) tempura. We don't know how the chef (who is quite a showman) does it, but the egg comes out batter-crisp on the outside and runny in the middle. It's served on rice with seafood and vegetable tempura as part of the *tamago tempura teishoku* (玉子天ぷら定食).

There's a blue and orange sign out front; expect to queue.

DAILY CHIKO   ICE CREAM ¥
Map p278 (デイリーチコ; basement fl, Nakano Broadway, Nakano-ku; cone from ¥280; ◷10am-8pm; 🚉JR Sōbu-Chūō line to Nakano, north exit) A Nakano legend and one of Nakano Broadway's few original shops, this ice-cream counter features eight flavours of soft-serve –

and you can get them all in one towering cone (¥490). Or just two or three, if you believe in moderation. The only-in-Japan *yuzu* (柚子; a kind of citrus) and *ramune* (ラムネ; cider) flavours are delicious.

⭐OKAJŌKI   IZAKAYA ¥¥
Map p278 (陸蒸気; ☎03-3228-1230; www.nakano-okajoki.com; 5-59-3 Nakano, Nakano-ku; lunch/dinner set menu ¥900/3980; ◷11.30am-3pm & 4-10pm Mon-Fri, 4-10pm Sat & Sun; 🚉JR Sōbu-Chūō line to Nakano, north exit) The *yaki-zakana* (焼き魚; grilled fish) lunch here is legendary. The fish are roasted around a large central hearth, and are served as a set with rice, miso soup and pickles. There's no English menu, but some common fish are *shake* (しゃけ; salmon), *nishin* (にしん; Pacific herring) and *saba* (さば; mackerel). Order at the kiosk at the entrance and expect a line.

For dinner, a set menu, which includes sashimi and grilled fish, makes ordering easy. Reservations recommended for dinner.

🍴 Ogikubo

HARUKIYA   RAMEN ¥
(春木屋; www.haruki-ya.co.jp; 1-4-6 Kami-Ogi, Suginami-ku; ramen from ¥850; ◷11am-9pm; 🚉JR Sōbu-Chūō line to Ogikubo, north exit) Harukiya, open since 1949, is one of Tokyo's oldest ramen shops – so old that the menu here says 'chuka-soba' ('Chinese' soba, which the egg noodle dish was called when it was still an exotic import). The shop serves what has since come to be known as classic Tokyo-style ramen: a light chicken and fish stock seasoned with soy sauce.

🍴 Kichijōji

TETCHAN   YAKITORI ¥
Map p279 (てっちゃん; 1-1-2 Kichijōji-Honchō, Musashino-shi; skewers from ¥110; ◷4-11pm; 🚉JR Sōbu-Chūō line to Kichijōji, north exit) Located inside the labyrinthine covered market Harmonica-yokochō, Tetchan has been drawing locals for years. But it's now become something of a tourist destination too, thanks to its new interior of acrylic 'ice' by architect Kuma Kengo (known for his more establishment works). There's no English menu, but safe bets include *tsukune* (chicken meatballs), *buta bara* (pork belly) and *motsu-ni* (stewed offal).

MANBOSHI IZAKAYA ¥

Map p279 (万星; ☎0422-44-2305; 3-31-16 Inokashira, Mitaka-shi; dishes ¥380-980, charge after 7pm ¥300; ⊙5.30pm-3am; ⏻Keiō Inokashira line to Inokashira-kōen) Right at the tip of Inokashira-kōen (and steps from Inokashira-kōen Station) is this little tavern whose name means '10,000 stars'. Work your way through the park and then stop here for its sundown special: an assortment of three small dishes and a beer or cocktail (for ¥1000, 5pm to 7pm). There's no sign, but look for the red lantern out front.

STEAK HOUSE SATOU STEAK ¥¥

Map p279 (ステーキハウス　さとう; ☎0422-21-6464; www.shop-satou.com; 1-1-8 Kichijōji Honchō, Mitaka-shi; lunch set ¥1200-4000; dinner set ¥2600-10,000; ⊙11am-2.30pm & 5-8.30pm Mon-Fri, 11am-8.30pm Sat & Sun; ⏻JR Sōbu-Chūō line to Kichijōji, north exit) This is a classic Japanese-style steak house, where the meat is cooked at the counter on a *teppanyaki* (iron hot plate), diced before serving and paired with rice, miso soup and pickles. It's also excellent value, considering the quality of the beef; even a 'splurge' on the chef's choice (lunch/dinner ¥4000/7000) is reasonable.

On the ground floor, there's a counter selling *menchi-katsu* (メンチカツ; ¥220), deep-fried, minced-beef croquettes. You can spot the shop by the regular queue for these.

🍷 DRINKING & NIGHTLIFE

★**COCKTAIL SHOBŌ** BAR

Map p278 (コクテイル書房; 3-8-13 Kōenji-kita, Suginami-ku; ⊙11.30am-3pm Wed-Sun, 5pm-midnight Mon-Sun; ⏻JR Sōbu line to Kōenji, north exit) At this bar-bookstore mash-up, the wooden counter doubles as a bookshelf and the local crowd comes as much to sip cocktails (from ¥450) as it does to flip through the selection of worn paperbacks. It's a cosy place, and like most bars in Kōenji, a labour of love. During lunch hours, curry and coffee are served.

NANTOKA BAR BAR

Map p278 (なんとかバー; http://trio4.nobody.jp/keita/shop/16_nantoka.html; 3-4-12 Kōenji-kita, Suginami-ku; drinks from ¥400; ⊙7pm-late; ⏻JR Sōbu line to Kōenji, north exit) Part of the

EATING & DRINKING STREETS

Neighbourhoods on the Chūō line are known for their cheerfully shabby *nomiyagai* (literally 'bar streets', but you can get food here, too). These are strips of tiny bars and eateries, often with no more than a few seats – sometimes with a makeshift table outside. The buildings date to the postwar reconstruction days, and though some have been spruced up, others look (much to the delight of customers) like they're held together with duct tape. For maximum Chūō-line atmosphere, check out **Yanagi-dōri** (柳通り; Nishi-Ogikubo, Suginami-ku; ⊙5pm-late; ⏻JR Sōbu-Chūō line to Nishi-Ogikubo, south exit), in Nishi-Ogikubo, and **Kōenji Gādo-shita** (高円寺ガード下; Map p278; Kōenji, Suginami-ku; ⊙5pm-late; ⏻JR Sōbu line to Kōenji, north exit), under the train tracks in Kōenji.

collective of spaces run by the Kōenji-based activist group Shirōto no Ran (Amateur Revolt), Nantoka Bar is about as uncommercial as a place selling drinks can get: there's no cover charge, drinks are generous and cheap and it's run on any given day by whoever feels like running it (which is sometimes no one at all).

BLUE SKY COFFEE CAFE

Map p279 (ブルースカイコーヒー; 4-12 Inokashira, Mitaka-shi; coffee from ¥250; ⊙1-5pm; ⏻Keiō Inokashira line to Inokashira-kōen) This tiny cafe looks like it could be the work of Studio Ghibli: a wooden cottage secreted in the woodsy perimeter of Inokashira-kōen concealing a shiny, state-of-the-art coffee roaster. The coffee is made with care, and is the cheapest around.

UNI STAND TEAHOUSE

Map p279 (ユニスタンド; http://unistand.jp/; 1-16-1 Shimorenjaku, Mitaka-shi; drinks ¥480-560; ⊙10am-7pm Wed-Mon; ⏻JR Sōbu-Chūō line to Mitaka, south exit) Taking a cue from the third-wave coffee movement, Uni Stand sells single-origin teas and carefully crafted *matcha* lattes (with high-grade powdered green tea from Uji). A little pretentious, sure, but also a welcome addition – a good cup of tea is surprisingly hard to find on the go in Tokyo.

⭐ ENTERTAINMENT

STAR PINE'S CAFE LIVE MUSIC

Map p279 (スターパインズカフェ; ☎0422-23-2251; www.mandala.gr.jp/spc.html; basement fl, 1-20-16 Kichijōji Honchō, Musashino-shi; tickets ¥2500-4000; 🚆JR Sōbu-Chūō line to Kichijōji, north exit) This is an attractive, intimate venue, sunk deep so the ceiling feels refreshingly high. The line-up is jazz, but that's a wide net, encompassing everything from standards to the quirky, avant-garde and experimental. The audience will likely be multi-generational and attentive. One drink minimum order (but the drinks are actually decent).

NI MAN DEN ATSU LIVE MUSIC

Map p278 (二万電圧; www.den-atsu.com; basement fl, 1-7-23 Kōenji-Minami, Suginami-ku; tickets ¥1800-4000; 🚇Marunouchi line to Higashi-Kōenji, exit 3) Kōenji's notorious punk venue has something loud going on most nights. This is a good place to start digging into the city's underground scene. Oddly enough, it's in the basement of a large, nondescript apartment complex. One drink (¥500) minimum order.

🛍 SHOPPING

MANDARAKE COMPLEX ANIME, MANGA

Map p278 (まんだらけ; www.mandarake.co.jp; 5-52-15 Nakano, Nakano-ku; ⏰noon-8pm; 🚆JR Sōbu-Chūō line to Nakano, north exit) This is the original Mandarake – the go-to store for all things manga and anime – and the origin of Nakano Broadway's transformation into a geek's paradise. Once a small, secondhand comic-book store, Mandarake now has some 25 shops just inside Nakano Broadway. Each specialises in something different, be it books, cell art or figurines.

KITA-KORE BUILDING FASHION & ACCESSORIES

Map p278 (キタコレビル; 3-4-11 Kōenji-kita, Suginami-ku; ⏰1-8pm; 🚆JR Sōbu line to Kōenji, north exit) A must-see in Kōenji, the Kita-Kore Building is a dilapidated shack of a structure housing a handful of seriously outré shops. Really, it's more art installation than shopping destination, though we do know of at least one person who's actually bought stuff here – Lady Gaga.

SHOPPING STREETS

Shōtengai (商店街), shopping streets, have traditionally been the lifeblood of Japanese neighbourhoods. These often pedestrian-only strips, usually connect to a train station, are lined with sundries shops and takeaway counters. Their supremacy has been challenged (often successfully) in the past few decades by supermarkets and big-box stores but *shōtengai* loyalists remain.

While *shōtengai* can be nothing more than a short alley, in some neighbourhoods along the Chūō line they are grand covered arcades with high ceilings and (what now appear very retro) decorative flourishes. **Nakano Sun Mall** (中野サンモール; Map p278; 5-64 Nakano, Nakano-ku; 🚆JR Sōbu-Chūō line to Nakano, north exit) and **Asagaya Pearl Centre** (阿佐ヶ谷パールセンター; www.asagaya.or.jp; Asagaya-Minami, Suginami-ku; 🚆JR Sōbu-Chūō line to Asagaya, south exit) are the two most famous ones.

PUKUPUKU ANTIQUES

Map p279 (ぷくぷく; http://pukupukukichi.blogspot.jp/; 2-26-2 Kichijōji Honchō, Musashino-shi; ⏰11.30am-7.30pm; 🚆JR Sōbu-Chūō line to Kichijōji, north exit) This cluttered little antiques shop stocks ceramics from the early Shōwa (昭和; 1926–89) period, through Taishō (大正; 1912–26) and Meiji (明治; 1868–1912) and all the way back to old Edo (江戸; 1603–1868). Flip the dishes over for a sticker that indicates the period. Hundred-year-old saucers can be had for as little as ¥1000.

SOKKYŌ VINTAGE

Map p278 (即興; www.sokkyou.net; 102 Nakanishi Apt Bldg, 3-59-14 Kōenji-minami, Suginami-ku; ⏰1-9pm, holidays irregular; 🚆JR Sōbu line to Kōenji, south exit) As far as vintage shops go, Sokkyō is more like a gallery of cool. The stock is impeccably edited down to a look that is both dreamy and modern. That said, we may have sent you on an impossible mission: the shop is unmarked in an ordinary house down a tiny alley. When it's open, however, an article of clothing will be hanging outside.

Shinjuku & Northwest Tokyo

NISHI-SHINJUKU | SHINJUKU | MEJIRO & IKEBUKURO | NISHI-SHINJUKU & SHINJUKU

Neighbourhood Top Five

1 Shinjuku at Night (p131) Exploring the crackling neon canyons of Tokyo's biggest and most colourful nightlife district, where the vivacity and sheer volume of dining, drinking and entertainment options are something to behold.

2 Tokyo Metropolitan Government Building (p127) Taking in the immensity of the metropolis, which extends to the horizon, from the (free!) observatories atop Tokyo's city hall.

3 Shinjuku-gyoen (p127) Lazing on the lawn with a *bentō* (boxed meal) while gazing up at the surrounding skyscrapers.

4 Golden Gai (p134) Getting cosy in the tiny, ramshackle bars of Shinjuku's literary and artistic hang-out spot.

5 Classic Izakaya (p132) Joining the after-work crowd at a Japanese-style pub, such as Donjaca, in Shinjuku-sanchōme.

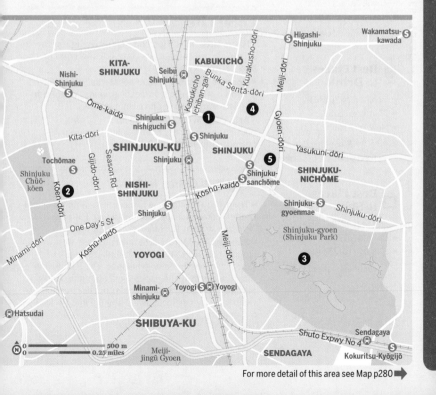

For more detail of this area see Map p280 ➡

Lonely Planet's Top Tip

Even Tokyoites get confused in Shinjuku Station. While it might seem natural to go with the flow, when it comes to reaching your intended destination, your battle begins on the platform: make sure you pick the right exit; otherwise you could wind up completely on the other side of the neighbourhood, having to circumnavigate the huge train station. Coin lockers abound inside the station, but use them at your peril: you might never find your stuff again.

Best Places to Eat

➡ Nagi (p130)

➡ Donjaca (p132)

➡ Kozue (p132)

➡ Nakajima (p130)

For reviews, see p130.➡

Best Places to Drink

➡ BenFiddich (p132)

➡ Zoetrope (p133)

➡ New York Bar (p133)

➡ Aiiro Cafe (p133)

For reviews, see p132.➡

Best Places to Shop

➡ Isetan (p135)

➡ Beams (p135)

➡ Bingoya (p135)

For reviews, see p135.➡

Explore Shinjuku & Northwest Tokyo

Shinjuku works neatly as a day-to-night destination. Start with the skyscrapers of Nishi-Shinjuku (west of the train station). Morning is usually the best time of day to see Mt Fuji from the observatories atop the Tokyo Metropolitan Government Building (p127). For lunch, join the office workers at Shinjuku I-Land (p127), where cheap eateries surround an open courtyard, or hop on the subway for Shinjuku-gyoen (p127) – picking up a *bentō* (boxed meal) on the way – and have a picnic in the park.

Shinjuku has many department stores with fun and fashionable wares, which are a big draw for shoppers. You can also take this opportunity to visit a couple of the city's under-appreciated sights north of Shinjuku, such as the architectural masterpieces St Mary's Cathedral Tokyo (p130) and Myōnichikan (p130).

Shinjuku's east side really shines at night – quite literally, with myriad bars, *izakaya* (Japanese-style pubs), karaoke parlours, and jazz haunts that await. While Friday nights are the most crowded, Shinjuku buzzes every night of the week. Beware the crush of the last train – between midnight and 1am – when packed in like sardines is an understatement.

Local Life

➡ **Hang-outs** Tokyo's gay community comes together at Aiiro Cafe (p133) for happy hour; creative types hit the bars of Golden Gai (p134).

➡ **Noodles** Shinjuku, Takadanobaba and Ikebukuro are three oft-cited ramen 'battlegrounds', where cult favourites are born of fierce competition.

➡ **Arts** Place M (p127) is a hub for the city's photographers; gritty Shinjuku has long been a favourite subject of theirs.

Getting There & Away

➡ **Train** The JR Yamanote line connects Shinjuku, Shin-Ōkubo, Takadanobaba and Ikebukuro. The private Keiō New line stops at Hatsudai, west of Shinjuku.

➡ **Subway** The Marunouchi line runs east–west, stopping at Nishi-Shinjuku, Shinjuku, Shinjuku-sanchōme and Shinjuku-gyoenmae. The Fukutoshin line runs north–south, stopping at Shinjuku, Higashi-Shinjuku, Zōshigaya and Ikebukuro. The circuitous Ōedo line stops at Tochōmae, Shinjuku and Higashi-Shinjuku.

◉ SIGHTS

◉ Nishi-Shinjuku

★ TOKYO METROPOLITAN GOVERNMENT BUILDING   NOTABLE BUILDING

Map p280 (東京都庁; Tokyo Tochō; http://www.metro.tokyo.jp/english/offices/observat.htm; 2-8-1 Nishi-Shinjuku, Shinjuku-ku; ⊘observatories 9.30am-11pm; Ⓢ Ōedo line to Tochōmae, exit A4) FREE Tokyo's seat of power, designed by Tange Kenzō and completed in 1991, looms large and looks somewhat like a pixelated cathedral (or the lair of an animated villain). Take an elevator from the ground floor of Building 1 to one of the twin 202m-high observatories for panoramic views over the never-ending cityscape (the views are virtually the same from either tower). On a clear day (morning is best), you may catch a glimpse of Mt Fuji to the west.

SHINJUKU I-LAND   PUBLIC ART

Map p280 (新宿アイランド; 6-5-1 Nishi-Shinjuku, Shinjuku-ku; Ⓢ Marunouchi line to Nishi-Shinjuku) An otherwise ordinary office complex, Shinjuku I-Land (completed in 1995 but conceived before the bursting of the economic bubble) is home to more than a dozen public artworks, including one of Robert Indiana's *Love* sculptures and two *Tokyo Brushstroke* sculptures by Roy Liechtenstein. The open-air courtyard, with stonework by Giulio Paolini and several reasonably priced restaurants, makes for an attractive lunch or coffee stop.

JAPANESE SWORD MUSEUM   MUSEUM

(刀剣博物館; www.touken.or.jp; 4-25-10 Yoyogi, Shibuya-ku; adult/student/child ¥600/300/free; ⊘9am-4.30pm Tue-Sun; Ⓡ Keiō New line to Hatsudai, east exit) In 1948, after American forces returned the *katana* (Japanese swords) they'd confiscated during the postwar occupation, the national Ministry of Education established a society, and this museum, to preserve the feudal art of Japanese sword-making. There are dozens of swords on display here, accompanied by excellent English explanations.

The museum's location, in a residential neighbourhood, is not obvious. Head down Kōshū-kaidō to the Park Hyatt and make a left, then the second right under the highway, followed by another quick right and left in succession. There's a map on the website.

NTT INTERCOMMUNICATION CENTRE   MUSEUM

(ICC; www.ntticc.or.jp; 4th fl, Tokyo Opera City 3-20-2 Nishi-Shinjuku, Shinjuku-ku; admission charged for special exhibitions; ⊘11am-6pm Tue-Sun; Ⓡ Keiō New line to Hatsudai) FREE The ICC shows challenging, conceptual works that explore the intersection between art and technology. Make sure to check out the changing installations that make use of the museum's eerie, echo-free chamber (experienced one at a time; pick up a reservation ticket from museum staff). Every summer the museum does a program for kids with lots of hands-on, sensory stuff.

◉ Shinjuku

★ SHINJUKU-GYOEN   PARK

Map p280 (新宿御苑; ☎03-3350-0151; www.env.go.jp/garden/shinjukugyoen; 11 Naito-chō, Shinjuku-ku; adult/child ¥200/50; ⊘9am-4.30pm Tue-Sun; Ⓢ Marunouchi line to Shinjuku-gyoenmae, exit 1) Though Shinjuku-gyoen was designed as an imperial retreat (completed 1906), it's now definitively a park for everyone. The wide lawns make it a favourite for urbanites in need of a quick escape from the hurly-burly of city life. Don't miss the greenhouse, with its giant lily pads and perfectly formed orchids, and the cherry blossoms in spring.

HANAZONO-JINJA   SHINTO SHRINE

Map p280 (花園神社; www.hanazono-jinja.or.jp; 5-17-3 Shinjuku, Shinjuku-ku; ⊘24hr; Ⓢ Marunouchi line to Shinjuku-sanchōme, exits B10 & E2) During the day, merchants from nearby Kabukichō come to this Shintō shrine to pray for the solvency of their business ventures. (Founded in the 17th century, the shrine is dedicated to the god Inari, whose specialities include fertility and worldly success). At night, despite signs asking revellers to refrain, drinking and merrymaking carry over from the nearby bars onto the stairs here. Most Sundays, the shrine hosts a **flea market** (青空骨董市; Aozora Kottō-ichi; Map p280; http://kottou-ichi.jp; Hanazono-jinja, 5-17 Shinjuku, Shinjuku-ku; ⊘dawn-dusk Sun).

PLACE M   GALLERY

Map p280 (www.placem.com; 3rd fl, 1-2-11 Shinjuku, Shinjuku-ku; ⊘noon-7pm; Ⓢ Marunouchi line to Shinjuku-gyoenmae, exit 2) FREE Run by four

1. Shinjuku-gyoen (p127)

Designed as an Imperial retreat, it's now popular with urbanites keen to escape the hurly-burly of city life.

2. Restaurant on Omoide-Yokochō (p130)

Omoide-Yokochō (Memory Lane) is lined with *yakatori* stalls and restaurants.

3. Shinjuku (p125)

Crowds of shoppers on a busy Shinjuku street.

4. Tokyo Metropolitan Government Building (p127)

Government buildings in Nishi-Shinjuku.

veteran photographers (including pioneering street photographer Moriyama Daido), this gallery is a key player in the local scene, hosting exhibitions as well as workshops to nurture new photographers; it also runs a press. There are a few other small photography galleries in the neighbourhood – you'll find tons of flyers by the door.

Mejiro & Ikebukuro

MYŌNICHIKAN ARCHITECTURE

Map p280 (明日館; House of Tomorrow; www.jiyu.jp; 2-31-3 Nishi-Ikebukuro, Toshima-ku; with/without coffee ¥600/400; ⏰10am-4pm Tue-Sun; 🚆JR Yamanote line to Ikebukuro, Metropolitan exit) Lucky are the girls who attended the Frank Lloyd Wright–designed 'School of the Free Spirit' (Jiyū Gakuen; 自由学園). Built in 1921, Myōnichikan functioned as the school's main structure until the 1970s. After restoration, it was reopened as a public space in 2001. Visitors can tour the facilities and have coffee in the the light-filled hall, sitting at low tables on (mostly) original chairs.

It can be tricky to find, though there are beige and green directional signs (in Japanese) on nearby utility poles.

ST MARY'S CATHEDRAL TOKYO CHURCH

(東京カテドラル聖マリア大聖堂; Sekiguchi Cathedral; www.tokyo.catholic.jp; 3-16-15 Sekiguchi, Bunkyō-ku; ⏰9am-5pm; [S]Yurakuchō line to Edogawabashi, exit 1A) [FREE] Rising nearly 40m high and glistening in the sun, this stainless-steel contemporary cathedral was completed in 1955. It's the work of Japan's foremost modern architect, Tange Kenzō, and structural and acoustic engineers from the University of Tokyo. If you're lucky, you'll catch someone practising on the pipe organ, the largest in Japan and specially designed for the cathedral; concerts take place here occasionally, too.

IKEBUKURO EARTHQUAKE HALL MUSEUM

Map p280 (池袋防災館; Ikebukuro Bōsai-kan; www.tfd.metro.tokyo.jp/hp-ikbskan; 2-37-8 Nishi-Ikebukuro, Tōshima-ku; ⏰9am-5pm Wed-Mon, closed 3rd Wed of month; 🚆JR Yamanote line to Ikebukuro, Metropolitan exit) [FREE] This public safety centre has a room that simulates a real earthquake, which is no joke – on our last visit we experienced a re-enactment of the 1923 Kantō quake that was thoroughly rattling. It's obviously intended for school children (who get to experience gentler shakes), but travellers are welcome here, too. Sessions start at 11.10am (50 minutes, including a short subtitled video) and noon (30 minutes, without the video). Reservations not necessary.

🍴 EATING

🍴 Nishi-Shinjuku & Shinjuku

★NAGI RAMEN ¥

Map p280 (凪; www.n-nagi.com; 2nd fl, Golden Gai G2, 1-1-10 Kabukichō, Shinjuku-ku; ramen from ¥850; ⏰24hr; 🚆JR Yamanote line to Shinjuku, east exit) Nagi, once an upstart, has done well and now has branches around the city – and around Asia. This tiny shop, one of the originals, up a treacherous stairway in Golden Gai, is still our favourite. (It's many people's favourite and often has a line.) The house speciality is *niboshi* ramen (egg noodles in a broth flavoured with dried sardines).

Look for the sign with a red circle.

NAKAJIMA KAISEKI ¥

Map p280 (中嶋; ☎03-3356-4534; www.shinjyuku-nakajima.com; basement fl, 3-32-5 Shinjuku, Shinjuku-ku; lunch/dinner from ¥800/8640; ⏰11.30am-2pm & 5.30-10pm Mon-Sat; [S]Marunouchi line to Shinjuku-sanchōme, exit A1) In the evening, this Michelin-starred restaurant serves exquisite *kaiseki* (Japanese haute cuisine) dinners. On weekdays, it also serves a set lunch of humble *iwashi* (sardines) for one-tenth the price; in the hands of Nakajima's chefs they're divine. The line for lunch starts to form shortly before the restaurant opens at 11.30am. Look for the white sign at the top of the stairs.

OMOIDE-YOKOCHŌ YAKITORI ¥

Map p280 (思い出横丁; Nishi-Shinjuku 1-chōme, Shinjuku-ku; skewers from ¥150; ⏰noon-midnight, vary by shop; 🚆JR Yamanote line to Shinjuku, west exit) Since the postwar days, smoke has been billowing night and day from the rickety, wooden *yakitori* stalls that line this alley by the train tracks, literally translated as 'Memory Lane' (and less politely known as Shonben-yokochō, or 'Piss Alley'). Several stalls have English menus. See if you can't spot the one that has appeared on an earlier edition of Lonely Planet's *Tokyo* guide.

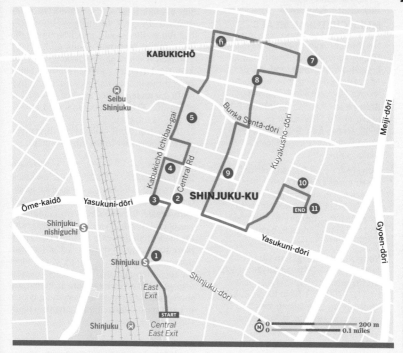

🏃 Neighbourhood Walk
Shinjuku at Night

START SHINJUKU STATION (EAST EXIT)
END HANAZONO-JINJA
LENGTH 2KM; TWO HOURS

Shinjuku's east side is lively any night of the week (and busiest on Fridays). Take the east exit and follow the signs out of the station for Kabukichō. Above ground, you'll spot the big screen of **1 Studio Alta** (スタジオアルタ), a popular Shinjuku meeting spot.

Take the pedestrian street on your left to Yasukuni-dōri, Shinjuku's main drag, where *izakaya* (Japanese pub-eateries) are stacked several storeys high. At all-night emporium **2 Don Quijote** (1-16-5 Kabukichō; www.donki.com; ⏲24hr) you can pick up everything from a bottle of wine to a nurse's costume.

One block west, is the flashing red **3 torii** (gate) that marks the entrance to Kabukichō, Tokyo's biggest red-light district. **4 Kabukichō Ichiban-gai**, the lane that leads into the heart of the neighbourhood, is a strange mix of 'hostess bars' (staffed by sexily clad, flirtatious young women), 'information centres' (which match customers with establishments that suit their particular, uh, needs) and otherwise ordinary restaurants.

Peak around the corner for a spot-on view of **5 Shinjuku TOHO building**, a new landmark, with its enormous Godzilla statue.

There are innocent ways to blow off steam in Kabukichō, too. Look for **6 Oslo Batting Centre** on the corner. It's ¥400 for 20 pitches if you feel like taking a swing.

To the right is a row of **7 love hotels** (hotels for amorous encounters). Kabukichō is also known for **8 host bars**, where bleach-blond pretty boys wait on the gals. You'll see plenty of signs for these.

On your left you'll pass the eye-searing entrance to the **9 Robot Restaurant** (p134), home to one of Kabukichō's most bizarre spectacles (which is saying something). Back on Yasukuni-dōri, turn left. Look for the stone-paved, tree-lined path on your left that leads to atmospheric **10 Golden Gai** (p134) and get yourself a drink. Before calling it a night, pay your respects at **11 Hanazono-jinja** (p127).

LOCAL KNOWLEDGE

MULTICULTURAL MEALS

Northwest Tokyo is home to several foreign communities. If you need a break from Japanese food, you'll find some tempting options in these 'hoods. Here are a few local favourites:

Shin-chan (辛ちゃん; Map p280; 1-2-9 Hyakunin-chō, Shinjuku-ku; dishes from ¥980; 🕒noon-5am; 🚉JR Yamanote line to Shin-Ōkubo) Spicy fried chicken in Shin-Ōkubo's Koreatown.

Ruby (ルビー; 3-8-5 Takadanobaba, Toshima-ku; mains ¥750-1000; 🕒11.30am-2.30pm & 5pm-midnight Mon-Fri, 5pm-5am Sat & Sun; 🚉JR Yamanote line to Takadanobaba, Waseda exit) Noodles and more in Takadanobaba's Little Myanmar.

Yong Xiang Sheng Jian Guan (永祥生煎館; Map p280; 1st fl, Sun City Hotel, 1-29-2 Nishi-Ikebukuro, Toshima-ku; 4 dumplings for ¥400; 🕒11.30am-10pm; 🚉JR Yamanote line to Ikebukuro, west exit) Shanghai street food in Ikebukuro's Chinatown.

NUMAZUKŌ SUSHI ¥

Map p280 (沼津港; 3-34-16 Shinjuku, Shinjuku-ku; plates ¥100-550; 🕒11am-10.30pm; 📶; 🚉JR Yamanote line to Shinjuku, east exit) Shinjuku's best *kaiten-sushi* (conveyor-belt sushi) restaurant is pricier than many, but the quality is worth it. It's popularity means that few plates make it around the long, snaking belt without getting snatched up (you can also order off the menu, if you don't see what you want). This is a good choice if you don't want a full meal.

SHINJUKU ASIA-YOKOCHŌ ASIAN ¥

Map p280 (新宿アジア横丁; ☎03-3207-7218; rooftop, 2nd Toa Hall bldg, 1-21-1 Kabukichō, Shinjuku-ku; dishes ¥450-1250; 🕒5pm-midnight Tue-Thu & Sun, 5pm-5am Fri & Sat; 🚉JR Yamanote line to Shinjuku, east exit) A rooftop night market that spans the Asian continent, Asia-yokochō has vendors dishing out everything from Korean *bibimbap* to Vietnamese *pho*. It's noisy, a bit chaotic and particularly fun in a group.

★**DONJACA** IZAKAYA ¥

Map p280 (呑者家; ☎03-3341-2497; 3-9-10 Shinjuku, Shinjuku-ku; dishes ¥350-850; 🕒5pm-7am; [S]Marunouchi line to Shinjuku-sanchōme, exit C6) The platonic ideal of a Shōwa-era (1926–89) *izakaya*, Donjaca, in business since 1979, has red leather stools, paper-lantern lighting and hand-written menus on the wall. The food is equal parts classic (grilled fish and fried chicken) and inventive: house specialities include *natto gyoza* (dumplings stuffed with fermented soy beans) and *mochi* gratin. Excellent sake is served in convenient tasting sets.

If it's full, staff will likely direct you around the corner to the larger annexe.

TSUNAHACHI TEMPURA ¥¥

Map p280 (つな八; ☎03-3352-1012; www.tunahachi.co.jp; 3-31-8 Shinjuku, Shinjuku-ku; lunch/dinner from ¥1512/2484; 🕒11am-10.30pm; 🚉JR Yamanote line to Shinjuku, east exit) Tsunahachi has been expertly frying prawns and vegies for more than 90 years and is an excellent place to get initiated in the art of tempura (foreign tourists get a handy cheat sheet on the different condiments). Set menus (except for the cheaper ones at lunch) are served piece by piece, so everything comes hot and crisp. Indigo *noren* (curtains) mark the entrance.

KOZUE JAPANESE ¥¥¥

Map p280 (梢; ☎03-5323-3460; http://tokyo.park.hyatt.jp/en/hotel/dining/Kozue.html; 40th fl, Park Hyatt, 3-7-1-2 Nishi-Shinjuku, Shinjuku-ku; lunch set menu ¥2850-12,400, dinner set menu ¥12,400-27,300; 🕒11.30am-2.30pm & 5.30-9.30pm; [S]Ōedo line to Tochōmae, exit A4) It's hard to beat Kozue's combination of well-executed, seasonal Japanese cuisine, artisan crockery and soaring views over Shinjuku from the floor-to-ceiling windows. As the (kimono-clad) staff speak English and the restaurant caters well to allergies and personal preferences, this is a good splurge spot for diners who don't want to give up complete control. Reservations are essential.

DRINKING & NIGHTLIFE

★**BENFIDDICH** COCKTAIL BAR

Map p280 (ベンフィディック; ☎03-6279-4223; 9th fl, 1-13-7 Nishi-Shinjuku, Shinjuku-ku; 🕒6pm-3am Mon-Sat; 🚉JR Yamanote line to Shinjuku, west exit) Step into the magical space that is BenFiddich. It's dark, it's tiny, and vials of infusions line the shelves, while herbs hang drying from the ceiling. Classical music simmers and soars. The barman, Kayama Hiroyasu, in a white suit, moves like a magician. There's no menu, but cocktails run about ¥1500; service charge is 10%.

★ ZOETROPE   BAR
Map p280 (ゾートロープ; http://homepage2. nifty.com/zoetrope; 3rd fl, 7-10-14 Nishi-Shinjuku, Shinjuku-ku; ☺7pm-4am Mon-Sat; ℝJR Yamanote line to Shinjuku, west exit) A must-visit for whisky fans, Zoetrope has some 300 varieties of Japanese whisky behind its small counter – including hard-to-find bottles from cult favourite Chichibu Distillery. The owner speaks English and can help you pick from the daunting menu. Cover charge ¥1000; whisky by the glass from ¥400 to ¥19,000, though most are reasonable.

SAMURAI   BAR
Map p280 (サムライ; http://jazz-samurai.seesaa. net; 5th fl, 3-35-5 Shinjuku, Shinjuku-ku; ☺6pm-1am; ℝJR Yamanote line to Shinjuku, southeast exit) Never mind the impressive record collection, this eccentric jazz *kissa* (cafe where jazz records are played) is worth a visit just for the owner's overwhelming collection of 2500 *maneki-neko* (beckoning cats). Look for the sign next door to Disc Union and take the elevator. There's a ¥300 cover charge (¥500 after 9pm); drinks from ¥650.

BAR GOLDFINGER   LESBIAN
Map p280 (✆03-6383-4649; www.goldfingerparty.com; 2-12-11 Shinjuku, Shinjuku-ku; ☺6pm-late; ⓈMarunouchi line to Shinjuku-sanchōme, exit C8) Goldfinger has long been a ladies' haven in Shinjuku-nichōme, though these days just Saturdays are still women-only. It's got a lowbrow-chic decor – designed to look like a '70s motel – and a friendly vibe. Drinks from ¥700; no cover unless there's a special event.

AIIRO CAFE   GAY & LESBIAN
Map p280 (アイイロ カフェ; http://aliving.net/airocafe/; 2-18-1 Shinjuku, Shinjuku-ku; ☺6pm-2am Mon-Thu, 6pm-5am Fri & Sat, 6pm-midnight Sun; ⓈMarunouchi line to Shinjuku-sanchōme, exit C8) Occupying the former spot of Ni-chome institution Advocates (and many old-time regulars still call it that), Aiiro is the best place to start any night out in the neighbourhood (thanks to the all-you-can-drink beer for ¥1000 happy-hour special). The bar itself is teeny-tiny; the action happens on the street corner outside, which swells to block-party proportions in the summer.

NEW YORK BAR   BAR
Map p280 (ニューヨークバー; ✆03-5323-3458; http://tokyo.park.hyatt.com; 52nd fl, Park Hyatt, 3-7-1-2 Nishi-Shinjuku, Shinjuku-ku; ☺5pm-midnight Sun-Wed, to 1am Thu-Sat; ℝŌedo line to Tochōmae, exit A4) Head to the Park Hyatt's 52nd floor to swoon over the sweeping nightscape from the floor-to-ceiling windows at this bar (of *Lost in Translation* fame). There's a cover charge of ¥2400 if you visit or stay past 8pm (7pm Sunday); go earlier and watch the sky fade to black. Cocktails start at ¥2000. Note: dress code enforced and 20% service charge levied.

DEPARTMENT STORE FOOD COURTS & ROOFTOPS

Should you want to grab a quick bite to eat – without having to brave the crowded streets – head to one of the food courts on the top floors of the shopping centres in and around Shinjuku Station. **Takashimaya Times Square** (高島屋タイムズスクエア; Map p280; 5-24-2 Sendagaya, Shibuya-ku; ☺11am-11pm; ℝJR Yamanote line to Shinjuku, New South exit) has the nicest one, though it is also the priciest, with meals starting around ¥2000 per person. **Lumine** (ルミネ; Map p280; www.lumine.ne.jp/shinjuku; ☺11am-11pm) and **Mylord** (ミロード; Map p280; www.shinjuku-mylord.com; ☺11am-11pm), near the south exit, are cheaper, catering to young shoppers.

Within Shinjuku Station, before you reach the New South exit ticket gates, there are a number of good takeaway vendors – perfect when you're catching the Narita Express or a long-distance bus; you can also sit and eat on the terrace outside the ticket gates, adjacent to the **NEWoMan** (Map p280; www.newoman.jp; 4-1-6 Shinjuku, Shinjuku-ku; ☺11am-10pm, food hall 8am-10pm) mall.

From Shinjuku-sanchōme subway station you can directly access **Isetan** (p135), which has a fantastic basement food hall, with *bentō*, fresh bread and more. The department store also has a little known, free rooftop garden where you can sit and eat.

ARTY FARTY GAY & LESBIAN

Map p280 (アーティファーティ; www.arty-farty.net; 2nd fl, 2-11-7 Shinjuku, Shinjuku-ku; 🕒6pm-1am; [S]Marunouchi line to Shinjuku-sanchōme, exit C8) A fixture on Tokyo's gay scene for many a moon, Arty Farty welcomes all in the community to come shake a tail feather on the dance floor here. It usually gets going later in the evening.

REN BAR

Map p280 (蓮; 1-10-10 Kabukichō, Shinjuku-ku; 🕒6pm-6am; 🚆JR Yamanote line to Shinjuku, east exit) An over-the-top lounge bar brought to you by the folks behind the equally over-the-top Robot Restaurant. After midnight, there's a ¥1000 table charge for groups with men and a 20% service charge added to the bill. Drinks start at ¥500.

☆ ENTERTAINMENT

TOKYO OPERA CITY CONCERT HALL CLASSICAL MUSIC

(東京オペラシティコンサートホール; ☎03-5353-9999; www.operacity.jp; 3rd fl, Tokyo Opera City, 3-20-2 Nishi-Shinjuku, Shinjuku-ku; ¥3000-5000; 🚆Keiō New line to Hatsudai) This beautiful, oak-panelled, A-frame concert hall, with legendary acoustics, hosts the Tokyo Philharmonic Orchestra among other well-regarded ensembles, including the occasional *bugaku* (classical Japanese music) group. Free lunchtime organ performances take place monthly, usually on Fridays. Information and tickets can be acquired at the box office next to the entrance to the Tokyo Opera City Art Gallery.

ROBOT RESTAURANT CABARET

Map p280 (ロボットレストラン; ☎03-3200-5500; www.shinjuku-robot.com; 1-7-1 Kabukichō, Shinjuku-ku; tickets ¥8000; 🕒shows at 4pm, 5.55pm, 7.50pm & 9.45pm; 🚆JR Yamanote line to Shinjuku, east exit) This Kabukichō spectacle is wacky Japan at its finest, with giant robots operated by bikini-clad women and enough neon to light all of Shinjuku – though it's become more family-friendly in recent years. Reservations aren't necessary but are recommended: the show's popularity is evinced by the ever-creeping ticket price. Look for discount tickets at hotels around town.

If the price makes you think twice, you can still swing by for a photo-op with two of the robots parked outside. You can also grab a drink (and a taste of Robot Restaurant's signature gilded plastic, game-show-set aesthetic) at new sister bar Ren around the corner.

SHINJUKU PIT INN JAZZ

Map p280 (新宿ピットイン; ☎03-3354-2024; www.pit-inn.com; basement, 2-12-4 Shinjuku, Shinjuku-ku; from ¥3000; 🕒matinee 2.30pm, evening show 7.30pm; [S]Marunouchi line to Shinjuku-sanchōme, exit C5) This is not the kind of place you come to talk over the music. It's the kind of place you come to sit in thrall of Japan's best jazz performers (as Tokyoites have been doing for half a century now). Weekday matinees feature up-and-coming artists and cost only ¥1300.

GOLDEN GAI

Golden Gai, a warren of tiny alleys and narrow, two-storey wooden buildings, began as a black market following WWII. It later functioned as a licensed quarter, until prostitution was outlawed in 1958. Now those same buildings are filled with more than a hundred closet-sized bars. Each is as unique and eccentric as the 'master' or 'mama' who runs it. That Golden Gai – prime real estate – has so far resisted the kind of development seen elsewhere in Shinjuku is a credit to these stubbornly bohemian characters.

The best way to experience Golden Gai is to stroll the lanes and pick a place that suits your mood. Bars here usually have a theme – from punk rock to photography – and draw customers with matching expertise and obsessions (many of whom work in the media and entertainment industries). Since regular customers are their bread and butter, some establishments are likely to give tourists a cool reception. Don't take it personally. Japanese visitors unaccompanied by a regular get the same treatment; this is Golden Gai's peculiar, invisible velvet rope. However, there are also an increasing number of bars that expressly welcome tourists (with English signs posted on their doors). Note that many bars have a cover charge (usually ¥500 to ¥1500).

🛍 SHOPPING

POKEMON CENTER
MEGA TOKYO
TOYS

Map p280 (ポケモンセンターメガトウキョー; ☎03-5927-9290; www.pokemon.co.jp/gp/pokecen/english/megatokyo_access.html; Sunshine City, 3-1-2 Higashi-Ikebukuro, Toshima-ku; ⊙10am-10pm; Ⓢ Yūrakuchō line to Higashi-Ikebukuro, exit 2) Japan's largest Pokémon centre sells every piece of the series' merchandise. You can also pose with several large statues around the store, including the one that is the store's mascot: Pikachu riding on the back of a Mega Charizard Y.

BEAMS
FASHION & ACCESSORIES

Map p280 (ビームス; www.beams.co.jp; 3-32-6 Shinjuku, Shinjuku-ku; ⊙11am-8pm; Ⓡ JR Yamanote line to Shinjuku, east exit) Beams, a national chain of boutiques, is a cultural force in Japan. This multistorey Shinjuku shop is particularly good for the latest Japanese streetwear labels and work from designers giving traditional looks a modern twist (including men, women and unisex fashions). Also sometimes available: crafts, housewares and original artwork (the line-up is always changing).

ISETAN
DEPARTMENT STORE

Map p280 (伊勢丹; www.isetan.co.jp; 3-14-1 Shinjuku, Shinjuku-ku; ⊙10am-8pm; Ⓢ Marunouchi line to Shinjuku-sanchōme, exits B3, B4 & B5) Most department stores play to conservative tastes, but this one doesn't. For an always changing line-up of up-and-coming Japanese womenswear designers, check out the Tokyo Closet (2nd floor) and Re-Style (3rd floor) boutiques. Men get a whole building of their own (connected by a passageway). Don't miss the basement food hall, featuring famous purveyors of sweet and savoury goodies.

BINGOYA
ARTS & CRAFTS

Map p280 (備後屋; www.quasar.nu/bingoya; 10-6 Wakamatsu-chō, Shinjuku-ku; ⊙10am-7pm Tue-Sun, closed 3rd Sat & Sun of the month; Ⓢ Toei Ōedo line to Wakamatsu-Kawada) Bingoya has five floors of quality, unpretentious crafts sourced from all over Japan. There's a particularly good selection of folksy pottery and textiles. Since it's a little out of the way, it's better for buyers than browsers; the store can help arrange shipping overseas. It's just in front of Wakamatsu-Kawa-

da Station; look across the main street, to the right.

KINOKUNIYA
BOOKS

Map p280 (紀伊國屋書店; www.kinokuniya.co.jp; Takashimaya Times Sq, 5-24-2 Sendagaya, Shibuya-ku; ⊙10am-8pm; Ⓡ JR Yamanote line to Shinjuku, south exit) The 6th floor here has a broad selection of foreign-language books and magazines, including many titles on Japan and English-teaching texts. Note that the rest of the store is currently closed for renovation.

LOCAL KNOWLEDGE
OTOME ROAD

Ikebukuro's Otome Rd, literally 'Maiden Road', has many of the same anime and manga stores that you see in Akihabara – but they're full of goods that girl geeks love. One of our favourites is **Acos** (Map p280; www.acos.me; 3-2-1 Higashi Ikebukuro, Toshima-ku; ⊙11am-8pm; Ⓡ JR Yamanote line to Ikebukuro, east exit), *otaku* superstore Animate's *cosplay* speciality shop, which stocks a mesmerising selection of reasonably good-quality wigs (in all the colours of the rainbow), coloured contact lenses and accessories (including stick-on tear drops). Otome Rd is across the street from the west edge of the enormous Sunshine City shopping complex, just beyond the highway overpass.

🏃 SPORTS & ACTIVITIES

THERMAE-YU
ONSEN

Map p280 (テルマー湯; ☎03-5285-1726; www.thermae-yu.jp; 1-1-2 Kabukichō, Shinjuku-ku; weekdays/weekends & holidays ¥2360/2690; ⊙11am-9am; 🔊; Ⓡ JR Yamanote line to Shinjuku, east exit) The best (and most literal) example to date that red-light district Kabukichō is cleaning up its act: the 2016 opening of this gleaming onsen complex. The tubs, which include several indoor and outdoor ones (sex-segregated), are filled with honest-to-goodness natural hot-spring water. There are several saunas, including a hot-stone sauna (*ganbanyoku*, ¥810 extra). Sorry, no tattoos allowed.

Kōrakuen & Akihabara

KŌRAKUEN & KUDANSHITA | KANDA & AKIHABARA | KAGURAZAKA

Neighbourhood Top Five

❶ **Koishikawa Kōrakuen** (p138) Slipping into the beautiful verdant world of this classic traditional garden with its central pond, charming bridges and seasonal flowerings.

❷ **Akiba Kart** (p146) Experiencing the blazing neon and wacky *otaku* (geek) vibe of 'Akiba' while taking a go-kart for a spin dressed in a Super Mario *cosplay* outfit.

❸ **3331 Arts Chiyoda** (p139) Encountering dinosaurs made from old plastic toys amid the contemporary art galleries in this former school turned arts-and-culture centre.

❹ **2k540 Aki-Oka Artisan** (p144) Browsing a choice selection of Japanese crafts at this beneath-the-train-tracks mall between Akihabara and Ueno.

❺ **Akagi-jinja** (p143) Threading your way through the stone-flagged streets of Kagurazaka, with its atmospheric shops and bars, to find this thoroughly modern shrine.

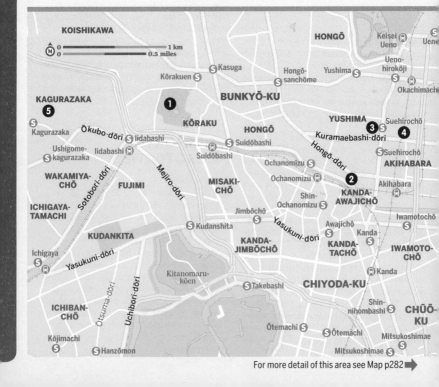

For more detail of this area see Map p282 ➡

Explore Kōrakuen & Akihabara

Kōrakuen has two big hitter sights: the traditional garden Koishikawa Kōrakuen (p138) and the entertainment complex Tokyo Dome City (p146). South of Kōrakuen, in Kudanshita, are two controversial attractions: the shrine Yasukuni-jinja (p138) and its adjacent museum Yūshūkan (p138), which covers Japan's warring past. Anyone with an interest in Japanese history (or Asian geopolitics) should make a stop here. On a lighter note, there are also some pleasant strolls nearby, along the Imperial Palace moats, Hanzo-bōri and Soto-bōri. Also worth a detour: the neighbourhood of Kagurazaka (p142), with its narrow cobblestone lanes, presents a charming alternative picture of Tokyo.

Heading east, the neighbourhood of Kanda, has an interesting trio of religious buildings: the Shintō shrine Kanda Myōjin (p138), the Confucian shrine Yushima Seidō (p139) and the Russian Orthodox Nikolai Cathedral (p139). Then throw yourself headfirst into 21st-century Tokyo in Akihabara, the electronics district that has become synonymous with *otaku* (geeks) and their love of anime (Japanese animation), manga (Japanese comics) and J-pop culture. Akiba, as it's popularly known, also has artisan-goods shopping malls and the contemporary arts centre 3331 Arts Chiyoda (p139).

Local Life

➡ **Cosplay** Catch anime fans dressed as their favourite characters along Akihabara's Chūō-dōri on Sundays (1pm to 6pm April to September, to 5pm October to March), when it becomes a pedestrian zone.

➡ **Festivals** The area bursts with extra creativity during Trans Arts Tokyo (www.kanda-tat.com), a contemporary arts fest held in autumn.

➡ **Video Games** Go old-school and join enthusiasts playing Pac-Man and Street Fighter at Super Potato Retro-kan (p146).

Getting There & Away

➡ **Train** The JR Sōbu line runs east–west, stopping at Iidabashi (for Kagurazaka), Suidōbashi (for Kōrakuen), Ochanomizu and Akihabara. Rapid-service JR Chūō line trains stop at Ochanomizu and Kanda. Kanda and Akihabara are stops on the JR Yamanote line.

➡ **Subway** Many lines converge in Iidabashi (Nanboku, Yūrakuchō, Tōzai and Ōedo lines). The Hibiya line stops in Akihabara, while the Ginza line stops at Suehirochō and Kanda.

Lonely Planet's Top Tip

Check electronics prices in your home country online before buying big-ticket items in Akihabara; they may or may not be a good deal. If you do buy, have your passport handy since travellers spending more than ¥10,000 in a single day at selected shops can get a refund of the consumption tax (8%). For a list of duty-free shops offering this service, see www.akiba.or.jp.

✕ Best Places to Eat

➡ Kanda Yabu Soba (p143)
➡ Botan (p143)
➡ Ethiopia (p139)
➡ Kado (p139)

For reviews, see p139. ➡

🍷 Best Places to Drink

➡ Imasa (p143)
➡ N3331 (p144)
➡ Craft Beer Server Land (p144)
➡ Mugimaru 2 (p142)

For reviews, see p143. ➡

🔒 Best Places to Shop

➡ 2k540 Aki-Oka Artisan (p144)
➡ mAAch ecute (p145)
➡ Mandarake Complex (p145)
➡ Kukuli (p142)

For reviews, see p144. ➡

KŌRAKUEN & AKIHABARA

◉ SIGHTS

◉ Kōrakuen & Kudanshita

★ KOISHIKAWA KŌRAKUEN
GARDENS

Map p282 (小石川後楽園; ☎03-3811-3015; http://teien.tokyo-park.or.jp/en/koishikawa; 1-6-6 Kōraku, Bunkyō-ku; adult/child ¥300/free; ⊙9am-5pm; ⓡŌedo line to Iidabashi, exit C3) Established in the mid-17th century as the property of the Tokugawa clan, this formal strolling garden incorporates elements of Chinese and Japanese landscaping. It's among Tokyo's most attractive gardens, although nowadays the *shakkei* (borrowed scenery) also includes the other-worldly Tokyo Dome (p144).

Don't miss the **Engetsu-kyō** (Full-Moon Bridge), which dates from the early Edo period (the name will make sense when you see it), and the beautiful vermilion wooden bridge **Tsuten-kyō**. The garden is particularly well known for its plum blossoms in February, irises in June and autumn leaves.

YASUKUNI-JINJA
SHINTO SHRINE

Map p282 (靖国神社; ☎03-3261-8326; www.yasukuni.or.jp; 3-1-1 Kudan-kita, Chiyoda-ku; ⊙6am-5pm; ⓢHanzōmon line to Kudanshita, exit 1) Literally 'For the Peace of the Country Shrine', Yasukuni is the memorial shrine to Japan's war dead, around 2.5 million souls. First built in 1869, it is also incredibly controversial: in 1979, 14 class-A war criminals, including WWII general Hideki Tōjō, were enshrined here. The main approach is fronted by a 25m-tall *torii* (entrance gate) made of steel and bronze; behind the main shrine, seek out the serene grove of mossy trees and the ornamental pond.

For politicians, a visit to Yasukuni, particularly on 15 August, the anniversary of Japan's defeat in WWII, is considered a political statement. It's a move that pleases hawkish constituents but also one that draws a strong rebuke from Japan's Asian neighbours, who suffered greatly in Japan's wars of expansion during the 20th century.

YŪSHŪ-KAN
MUSEUM

Map p282 (遊就館; ☎03-3261-8326; www.yasukuni.or.jp; 3-1-1 Kudankita, Chiyoda-ku; adult/student ¥800/500; ⊙9am-4pm; ⓢHanzōmon line to Kudanshita, exit 1) Most history museums in Japan skirt the issue of war or focus on the burden of the common people.

Not so here: Yūshū-kan begins with Japan's samurai tradition and ends with its defeat in WWII. It is also unapologetic and has been known to boil the blood of some visitors with its particular view of history.

There are also some emotionally harrowing exhibits, such as the messages (translated into English) of kamikaze pilots written to their families before their final missions.

NATIONAL SHŌWA MEMORIAL MUSEUM
MUSEUM

Map p282 (昭和館; Shōwa-kan; ☎03-3222-2577; www.showakan.go.jp; 1-6-1 Kudan-minami, Chiyoda-ku; adult/child/student ¥300/80/150; ⊙10am-5.30pm Tue-Sun; ⓡHanzōmon line to Kudanshita, exit 4) This museum of WWII-era Tokyo gives a sense of everyday life for the common people: how they ate, slept, dressed, studied, prepared for war and endured martial law, famine and loss of loved ones. An English audio guide (free) fills in a lot.

◉ Kanda & Akihabara

ORIGAMI KAIKAN
GALLERY

Map p283 (おりがみ会館; ☎03-3811-4025; www.origamikaikan.co.jp; 1-7-14 Yushima, Bunkyō-ku; ⊙shop 9am-6pm, gallery 10am-5.30pm Mon-Sat; ⓡ; ⓡJR Chūō or Sōbu lines to Ochanomizu, Hijiri-bashi exit) FREE This exhibition centre and workshop is dedicated to the quintessential Japanese art of origami, which you can learn to do yourself in classes here. There's a shop-gallery on the 1st floor, a gallery on the 2nd, and a workshop on the 4th where you can watch the process of making, dyeing and decorating origami paper.

Admission is free, but origami lessons (offered most days in Japanese) cost ¥1000 to ¥2500 for one to two hours, depending on the complexity of that day's design. First-timers would do well to try for a class with the centre's director, Kobayashi Kazuo.

KANDA MYŌJIN (KANDA SHRINE)
SHINTO SHRINE

Map p283 (神田明神; ☎03-3254-0753; www.kandamyoujin.or.jp; 2-16-2 Soto-kanda, Chiyoda-ku; ⓡJR Chūō or Sōbu lines to Ochanomizu, Hijiri-bashi exit) FREE Tracing its history back to AD 730, this splendid Shintō shrine boasts vermilion-lacquered halls surrounding a stately courtyard, where you'll also find the pet pony Akari. Its present location dates from 1616 and the *kami* (gods) enshrined here are said to bring luck in business and in finding a spouse. There are also plenty of anime characters, since this is Akiba's local shrine.

YUSHIMA SEIDŌ
(YUSHIMA SHRINE) CONFUCIAN SITE
Map p283 (湯島聖堂; ☎03-3251-4606; www.seido.or.jp; 1-4-25 Yushima, Bunkyō-ku; ⏰9.30am-5pm Apr-Sep, to 4pm Oct-Mar; 🚉JR Chūō or Sōbu lines to Ochanomizu, Hijiri-bashi exit) **FREE** Established in 1691 and later used as a school for the sons of the powerful during the Tokugawa regime, this is one of Tokyo's handful of Confucian shrines. There's a Ming-dynasty bronze statue of Confucius in its black-lacquered main hall (Taisei-den), rebuilt in 1935. The sculpture is visible only from 1 to 4 January and on the fourth Sunday in April, but on weekends and holidays the interior of Taisei-den is accessible; at other times you can only look around the shrine grounds.

NIKOLAI CATHEDRAL CHURCH
Map p283 (ニコライ堂; ☎03-3295-6879; www.orthodoxjapan.jp; 4-1-3 Kanda-Surugadai, Chiyoda-ku; ¥300; ⏰1-4pm Apr-Sep, 1-3.30pm Oct-Mar, 1-6pm every Mon; 🚇Chiyoda line to Shin-Ochanomizu, exit 2) This Russian Orthodox cathedral, complete with distinctive Byzantine-style architecture, was first built in 1891 under the supervision of English architect Josiah Conder. The original copper dome was damaged in the 1923 earthquake, forcing the church to downsize to the (still enormous) dome that's now in place.

3331 ARTS CHIYODA GALLERY
Map p283 (☎03-6803 2441; www.3331.jp/en; 6-11-14 Soto-Kanda, Chiyoda-ku; ⏰noon-7pm Wed-Mon; 📶🚻; 🚉Ginza line to Suehirochō, exit 4) **FREE** A major exhibition space, smaller art galleries and creative studios now occupy this former high school, which has morphed into a forward-thinking arts hub for Akiba. It's a fascinating place to explore. There's a good cafe and shop selling cute design items, as well as a play area for kids stocked with recycled toys and colourful giant dinosaurs made of old plastic toys.

EATING

🍴 Kagurazaka

KADO JAPANESE ¥¥
Map p282 (カド; ☎03-3268-2410; http://kagurazaka-kado.com; 1-32 Akagi-Motomachi, Shin-juku-ku; lunch/dinner set menus from ¥800/3150; ⏰11.30am-2.30pm & 5-11pm; 🚇Tōzai line to Kagurazaka exit 1) Set in an old wooden house with a white lantern out front, Kado specialises in *katei-ryōri* (home-cooking). Dinner is a set course of seasonal dishes (such as grilled quail or crab soup). At lunch there's no English menu, so your best bet is the カド定食 *(kado teishoku)*, the daily house special. Bookings are required for dinner. In the entrance is a standing bar, where you can order dishes à la carte, paired with sake.

CANAL CAFE ITALIAN ¥¥
Map p282 (カナルカフェ; ☎03-3260-8068; www.canalcafe.jp; 1-9 Kagurazaka, Shinjuku-ku; lunch from ¥1600, dinner mains ¥1500-2800; ⏰11.30am-11pm Tue-Sat, to 9.30pm Sun; 📶; 🚉JR Sōbu line to Iidabashi, west exit) Along the languid moat that forms the edge of Kitanomaru-kōen, this is one of Tokyo's best alfresco dining spots. The restaurant serves tasty wood-fired pizzas, seafood pastas and grilled meats, while over on the self-service 'deck side' you can settle in with a sandwich, muffin or just a cup of coffee.

🍴 Kanda & Akihabara

⭐ETHIOPIA JAPANESE ¥
Map p283 (エチオピア; ☎03-3295-4310; 3-10-6 Kanda-ogawamachi, Chiyoda-ku; curry from ¥900; ⏰11am-10pm Mon-Fri, to 8.30pm Sat & Sun; 🚇Hanzōmon line to Jimbōchō, exit A5) In studenty Jimbōchō, Japanese curry cafes are 10 a penny and fiercely competitive. Ethiopia is a seasoned champ, offering jumbo serves and curries packed with meat and vegetables. The spice level goes from zero to a nuclear-thermal 70! Pay at the machine as you enter the wonderfully retro shop.

KIKANBŌ RAMEN ¥
Map p283 (鬼金棒; http://karashibi.com; 2-10-8 Kaji-chō, Chiyoda-ku; ramen from ¥800; ⏰11am-9.30pm Mon-Sat, to 4pm Sun; 🚉JR Yamanote line to Kanda, north exit) The *karashibi* (カラシビ) spicy miso ramen here has a cult following. Choose your level of *kara* (spice) and *shibi* (a strange mouth-numbing sensation created by Japanese *sanshō* pepper). We recommend *futsu-futsu* (regular for both) for first-timers; *oni* (devil) level costs an extra ¥100. Look for the red door curtains and buy an order ticket from the vending machine.

1. Kanda Myōjin (p138)
Splended Shintō shrine housing gods said to bring luck in business and love.

2. Koishikawa Kōrakuen (p138)
Classic traditional garden with a central pond, charming bridges and seasonal flowering.

3. Nikolai Cathedral (p139)
Russian Orthodox cathedral, with Byzantine-style architecture, built in 1923.

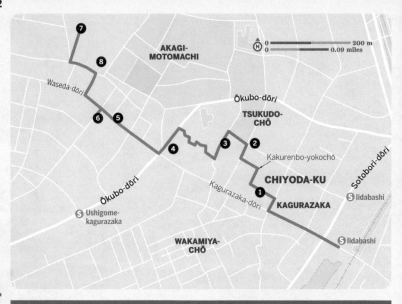

🏃 Local Life
A Stroll Through Kagurazaka

At the start of the 20th century, Kagurazaka was a fashionable *hanamachi* – a pleasure quarter where geisha entertained. Though there are far fewer geisha these days (they're seldom seen by tourists), the neighbourhood retains its glamour and charm. It's a popular destination for Tokyoites, who enjoy wandering the cobblestone lanes or whiling away time in one of the area's many cafes.

❶ In The Footsteps of Geisha

Walk up Kagurazaka-dōri, turn right at Royal Host restaurant and then take the first left onto **Geisha Shinmichi**. This narrow lane was once where geisha lived and worked. Though it's now home to residences and restaurants, the paving stones remain.

❷ Traditional Crafts

At the end of attractive side-street Honta-yokochō is **Kukuli** (くくり; Map p282; ☎03-6280-8462; www.kukuli.co.jp; 1-10 Tsukudo-chō, Shinjuku-ku; ◎11am-7pm; 🚃JR Yamanote line to Iidabashi, west exit), one of several shops specialising in traditional craftwork. It has hand-dyed textiles (such as scarves and tea towels) with a modern touch.

❸ Cobblestone Alleyways

Winding cobblestone alley **Hyogo-yokochō** is the neighbourhood's oldest and most atmospheric lane, often used in TV and movie shoots. You'll see *ryōtei* here: exclusive,

traditional Japanese restaurants (for which Kagurazaka is famous).

❹ Tea Break in an Old House

Follow the twisting stone-paved road. The old house almost covered in ivy is **Mugi-maru 2** (ムギマル2; Map p282; ☎03-5228-6393; www.mugimaru2.com; 5-20 Kagurazaka, Shinjuku-ku; coffee ¥550; ◎noon-8pm Thu-Tue; 🚇Tozai line to Kagurazaka, exit 1), a favourite local hang-out. Climb the narrow staircase and grab a spot on the floor beside a low table. The speciality is *manjū* (steamed buns).

❺ Confectioners at Work

Award-winning, 80-year-old confectioner **Baikatei** (梅花亭; Map p282; ☎03-5228-0727; www.baikatei.co.jp; 6-15 Kagurazaka, Shinjuku-ku; ◎10am-8pm, to 7.30pm Sun; 🚇Tōzai line to Kagurazaka, exit 1) turns out gorgeous *wagashi* (Japanese-style sweets). Watch the chefs at work, whipping humble beans and rice into pastel flowers, from the window in the back.

Wagashi (Japanese-style sweets)

❻ Handmade Accessories

The ever-changing selection at **Sada** (貞; Map p282; ☎03-3513-0851; www.sadakagura.com; 6-58 Kagurazaka, Shinjuku-ku; 🕓noon-7pm; [S]Tōzai line to Kagurazaka, exit 1) includes clothes and pretty accessories handmade in Japan. Some items are contemporary; others have a traditional Japanese feel, made with kimono material.

❼ A Contemporary Shrine

Akagi-jinja (赤城神社; Map p282; ☎03-3260-5071; www.akagi-jinja.jp; 1-10 Akagi-Motomachi, Shinjuku-ku; [S]Tōzai line to Kagurazaka, exit 1), Kagurazaka's signature shrine, only bears a passing resemblance to the traditional ones around the city. In 2010 the shrine, which can trace its history back centuries, was remodelled by Kengo Kuma, one of Japan's most prominent architects. The result is a sleek glass box.

❽ Dinner at Kado

Set in a gorgeous home, half-hidden by a wooden facade, Kado (p139) serves delicious seasonal courses (try the firefly squid in vinegar miso dressing); reservations recommended. For something light, the bar in the foyer serves dishes à la carte.

KANDA YABU SOBA SOBA ¥

Map p283 (神田やぶそば; ☎03-3251-0287; www.yabusoba.net; 2-10 Kanda Awajichō, Chiyoda-ku; noodles ¥670-1910; 🕓11.30am-8.30pm; [S]Marunouchi line to Awajichō, exit A3) Totally rebuilt following a fire in 2013, this is one of Tokyo's most venerable buckwheat noodle shops, in business since 1880. Come here for classic handmade noodles and accompaniments such as shrimp tempura *(ten-seiro soba)* or slices of duck *(kamo-nanban soba)*.

KOMAKI SHOKUDŌ VEGAN ¥

Map p283 (こまきしょくどう; ☎03-5577-5358; http://konnichiha.net/fushikian; Chabara, 8-2 Kanda Neribei-chō, Chiyoda-ku; set meals from ¥980; 🕓11am-7.30pm; 🚆JR Yamanote line to Akihabara, Electric Town exit) A Kamakura cooking school specialising in *shōjin-ryōri* (Buddhist-style vegan cuisine) runs this cafe within the Chabara (p145) food market. Its nonmeat dishes are very tasty and it sells some of the ingredients used. Round off your meal with excellent coffee from Yanaka Coffee opposite.

BOTAN HOTPOT ¥¥¥

Map p283 (ぼたん; ☎03-3251-0577; http://r.gnavi.co.jp/g198900; 1-15 Kanda-Sudachō, Chiyoda-ku; set meals from ¥7300; 🕓11.30am-9pm Mon-Sat; [S]Marunouchi line to Awajichō, exit A3) Botan has been making a single, perfect dish in the same traditional wooden house since the 1890s. Sit cross-legged on rattan mats as chicken *nabe* (meat cooked in broth with vegetables) simmers over a charcoal brazier next to you, allowing you to take in the scent of prewar Tokyo. Try to get a seat in the handsome upstairs dining room.

🍷 DRINKING & NIGHTLIFE

★IMASA CAFE

Map p283 (井政; ☎03-3255-3565; www.kanda-imasa.co.jp; 2-16 Soto-Kanda, Chiyoda-ku; drinks ¥600; 🕓11am-4pm Mon-Fri; 🚆JR Chūō or Sōbu lines to Ochanomizu, Hijiri-bashi exit) It's not every day that you get to sip your coffee or tea in a cultural property. Imasa is the real deal, an old timber merchant's shophouse dating from 1927 but with Edo-era design and detail, and a few pieces of contemporary furniture. Very few houses like this exist in Tokyo or are open to the public.

★ CRAFT BEER

SERVER LAND
CRAFT BEER

Map p282 (☎03-6228-1891; Okawa Bldg B1F, 2-9 Kagurazaka, Shinjuku-ku; service charge ¥380; ⏰5pm-midnight Mon-Fri, noon-midnight Sat & Sun; 🛜; 🚃JR Sōbu line to Iidabashi, west exit) With some 14 Japanese craft beers on tap, going for a reasonable ¥500/840 a glass/ pint, plus good food (the fish and chips is excellent), this brightly lit basement bar with wooden furniture and a slight Scandi feel is a winner.

Look for the English sign as you head up the slope.

CAFE ASAN
CAFE

Map p283 (☎03-6803-0502; www.cafeasan. jp; 2k540 Aki-Oka Artisan, 5-9-9 Ueno, Taitō-ku; ⏰11.30am-7pm Thu-Tue; 🛜; 🚇Ginza line to Suehirochō, exit 2) With hammock-style chairs, free wi-fi and plugs for computers and smartphones, this is a popular cafe with the digital generation. Manga and anime are a subtle design theme, fitting for Akiba, but the real draw is the made-to-order soufflé hotcakes, deliciously sweet treats that are well worth waiting the 20 minutes or so they take to make.

N3331
CAFE

Map p283 (☎03-5295-2788; http://n3331.com; 2nd fl, mAAch ecute, 1-25-4 Kanda-Sudachō, Chiyoda-ku; ⏰11am-10.30pm Mon-Sat, to 8.30pm Sun; 🚃JR Yamamote line to Akihabara, Electric Town exit) Climb the original white-tile-clad stairs to the former platform of Mansei-bashi Station to find this ultimate trains-potters' cafe. Through floor-to-ceiling windows, watch commuter trains stream by while you sip coffee, craft beer or sake and enjoy snacks.

@HOME CAFE
CAFE

Map p283 (@ほぉ〜むカフェ; www.cafe-athome.com; 4th-7th fl, 1-11-4 Soto-Kanda, Chiyo-da-ku; drinks from ¥500; ⏰11.30am-10pm Mon-Fri, 10.30am-10pm Sat & Sun; 🚃JR Yamanote line to Akihabara, Electric Town exit) 'Maid cafes' with *kawaii* (cute) waitresses, dressed as saucy French or prim Victorian maids, are a stock-in-trade of Akiba. @Home is one of the more 'wholesome' of them. You'll be welcomed as *go-shujinsama* (master) or *o-jōsama* (miss) the minute you enter. The maids serve drinks and dishes, such as cur-ried rice, topped with smiley faces.

⭐ ENTERTAINMENT

★ TOKYO DOME
BASEBALL

Map p282 (東京ドーム; www.tokyo-dome.co.jp/e; 1-3 Kōraku, Bunkyō-ku; tickets ¥2200-6100; 🚃JR Chūō line to Suidōbashi, west exit) Tokyo Dome (aka 'Big Egg') is home to the Yomiuri Gi-ants. Love 'em or hate 'em, they're the most consistently successful team in Japanese baseball. If you're looking to see the Giants in action, the baseball season runs from the end of March to the end of October. Tickets sell out in advance; get them early at www. giants.jp/en.

P.A.R.M.S
LIVE PERFORMANCE

(☎012-075-9835; www.pasela.co.jp; 7th fl, Pasela Resorts Akihabara-Denkigai, 1-13-2 Soto-kanda, Chiyoda-ku; admission incl 1 drink Mon-Fri ¥1500, Sat & Sun ¥3500; ⏰shows 5.30pm & 8.15pm Mon-Fri, 10.30am Sat & Sun; 🚃JR Yamanote line to Akihabara, Electric Town exit) Shows by the girl group Kamen Joshi – singing and danc-ing young women wearing cute outfits and hockey masks – are all the rage at this live-music show in the Pasela Resort's karaoke emporium. It's a chance to swing around a light sabre (handed out to audience mem-bers) in a thoroughly Akiba night out.

CLUB GOODMAN
LIVE MUSIC

(☎03-3862-9010; http://clubgoodman.com; B1 fl, AS Bldg, 55 Kanda-Sakumagashi, Chiyoda-ku; cover from ¥1500; 🚃JR Yamanote line to Aki-habara, Electric Town exit) In the basement of a building with a guitar shop and recording studios, it's no surprise that this live house is a favourite with Tokyo's indie-scene bands and their fans.

🛍 SHOPPING

★ 2K540 AKI-OKA ARTISAN
ARTS & CRAFTS

Map p283 (アキオカアルチザン; www.jrtk. jp/2k540; 5-9-23 Ueno, Taitō-ku; ⏰11am-7pm Thu-Tue; 🚇Ginza line to Suehirochō, exit 2) This ace arcade under the JR tracks (its name refers to the distance from Tokyo Station) offers an eclectic range of stores selling Japanese-made goods – everything from pottery and leatherwork to cute aliens, a nod to Akihabara from a mall that is more akin to Kyoto than Electric Town. The best for colourful crafts is **Nippon Hyakkuten** (日本百貨店; http://nippon-dept.jp).

THE EVOLUTION OF AKIBA

Post WWII, a black market for radio parts and other electronics developed around Akihabara Station; if you look carefully you'll still find the legacy of this former life in the **Akihabara Radio Center** (秋葉原ラジオセンター; Map p283; 1-14-2 Soto-Kanda, Chiyoda-ku; ⏰generally 10am-6pm; 🚉JR Yamanote line to Akihabara, Electric Town exit), a two-storey warren of several dozen stalls dealing in connectors, jacks, LEDs, switches, semiconductors and other components, under the elevated railway tracks. This is the original, still-beating heart of Akihabara, and it's worth a peek, mainly as a cultural study.

After the 1960s and '70s, when the district was the place to hunt for bargain new and used electronics, Akihabara saw its top shopping mantle increasingly usurped by discount stores elsewhere in the city. It has long since bounced back by reinventing itself as the centre of the *otaku* (geek) universe, catching J-pop culture fans in its gravitational pull.

These days you are as likely to find intricately designed plastic models of anime characters, self-penned pornographic comics and *cosplay* (costume play) outfits as you are electrical circuits, fuses and wires in the place locals call Akiba. Along neon-lined Chūō-dōri, west of the station, you're sure to encounter *cosplay* maids enticing customers into maid cafes. To make some sense of it all, pick up an English map at **Akiba Info** (Map p283; ☎080-3413-4800; www.animecenter.jp; 2nd fl, Akihabara UDX Bldg, 4-14-1 Soto-Kanda, Chiyoda-ku; ⏰11am-5.30pm Tue, Wed & Fri-Sun; 🈂; 🚉JR Yamanote line to Akihabara, Electric Town exit); the helpful staff here speak English.

★**MANDARAKE COMPLEX**   MANGA, ANIME

Map p283 (まんだらけコンプレックス; www.mandarake.co.jp; 3-11-2 Soto-Kanda, Chiyoda-ku; ⏰noon-8pm; 🚉JR Yamanote line to Akihabara, Electric Town exit) When *otaku* (geeks) dream of heaven, it probably looks a lot like this giant go-to store for manga and anime. Eight storeys are piled high with comic books and DVDs, action figures and cell art just for starters. The 5th floor, in all its pink splendour, is devoted to women's comics, while the 4th floor is for men.

CHABARA   FOOD

Map p283 (ちゃばら; www.jrtk.jp/chabara; 8-2 Kanda Neribei-chō, Chiyoda-ku; ⏰11am-8pm; 🚉JR Yamanote line to Akihabara, Electric Town exit) This under-the-train-tracks shopping mall focuses on artisan food and drinks from across Japan, including premium sake, soy sauce, sweets, teas and crackers – all great souvenirs and presents.

MAACH ECUTE   MALL

Map p283 (☎03-3257-8910; www.maach-ecute.jp; 1-25-4 Kanda-Sudachō, Chiyoda-ku; ⏰11am-9pm Mon-Sat, to 8pm Sun; 🚉Chūō or Sōbu lines to Akihabara, Electric Town exit) JR has another shopping and dining hit on its hands with this complex crafted from the old station and red-brick railway arches at Manseibashi. Crafts, homewares, fashions and food from across Japan are sold here; look

out for craft beers from **Hitachino Brewing Lab** and freshly roasted beans from **Obscura Coffee Roasters**.

YODOBASHI AKIBA   ELECTRONICS

Map p283 (ヨドバシカメラAkiba; www.yodobashi-akiba.com; 1-1 Kanda Hanaoka-chō, Chiyoda-ku; ⏰9.30am-10pm; 🚉JR Yamanote line to Akihabara, Shōwa-tōriguchi exit) This is the monster branch of Yodobashi Camera where many locals shop. It has eight floors of electronics, cameras, toys, appliances; CDs and DVDs on the 7th-floor branch of Tower Records; and even restaurants. Ask about export models and VAT-free purchases.

AKIHABARA RADIO KAIKAN   MANGA, ANIME

Map p283 (秋葉原ラジオ会館; http://akihabara-radiokaikan.co.jp; 1-15-6 Soto-kanda, Chiyoda-ku; ⏰11am-8pm; 🚉JR Yamanote line to Akihabara, Electronic Town exit) Despite its name, Radio Kaikan has nothing to do with radios and everything to do with Japanese pop culture. It was completely rebuilt in 2014 to include nine floors of shops selling manga, anime, collectables such as models and figurines, fanzines, costumes and gear. Shops include **Volks** for dolls, **K-Books** and **Kaiyōdō Hobby Lobby**.

JIMBŌCHŌ BOOKSTORES   BOOKS

Map p283 (Kanda-Jimbōchō, Chiyoda-ku; 🚇Hanzōmon line to Jimbōchō, exits A1, A6 or A7) This fascinating neighbourhood of more than 170 new and secondhand booksellers is proof that the printed word is alive and well in Tokyo. Amid tottering stacks of volumes, you'll find everything from antique guidebooks of the Yoshiwara pleasure district to obscure sheet music from your favourite symphony.

Recommended stores to target are **Ohya Shobō** (大屋書房; Map p283; ☎03-3291-0062; www.ohya-shobo.com; 1-1 Kanda-Jimbōchō, Chiyoda-ku; 🕑10am-6pm Mon-Sat), purveyor of antique books, maps and original *ukiyo-e* prints, and **Komiyama Shoten** (小宮山書店; Map p283; ☎03-3291-0495; www.book-komiyama.co.jp; 1-7 Kanda-Jimbōchō, Chiyoda-ku; 🕑11am-6.30pm Mon-Sat, to 5.30pm Sun) for art books, prints and posters.

SPORTS & ACTIVITIES

★BUDDHA BELLIES — COOKING

Map p282 (http://buddhabelliestokyo.jimdo.com; 2nd fl, Uekuri Bldg, 22-4-3 Kanda-Jimbōchō, Chiyoda-ku; courses from ¥7500; [S]Shinjuku line to Jimbōchō, exit A2) Professional sushi chef and sake sommelier Ayuko leads small hands-on classes in sushi, *bentō* (boxed lunch) and udon making. Prices start at ¥7500 per person for a 2½-hour course.

★AKIBA KART — SCENIC DRIVE

Map p283 (アキバカート; ☎03-6206-4752; http://akibanavi.net; 2-4-6 Soto-kanda, Chiyoda-ku; 1hr from ¥2700; 🕑10am-8pm; 🚆JR Yamanote line to Akihabara, Electric Town exit) Naturally, it was a no-brainer for this *cosplay* (costume play) plus go-karting operation to set up in Akiba. Reserve in advance and make sure you have an international driver's licence handy if you wish to motor around Tokyo in a go-kart dressed as a character from *Super Mario Brothers* – you know you want to!

★SPA LAQUA — ONSEN

Map p282 (スパ ラクーア; ☎03-5800-9999; www.laqua.jp; 5th-9th fl, Tokyo Dome City, 1-1-1 Kasuga, Bunkyō-ku; weekday/weekend ¥2635/2960; 🕑11am-9am; [S]Marunouchi line to Kōrakuen, exit 2) One of Tokyo's few true onsen, this chic spa complex relies on natural hot-spring water from 1700m below ground. There are indoor and outdoor baths, saunas and a bunch of add-on options, such as *akasuri* (Korean-style whole-body exfoliation). It's a fascinating introduction to Japanese health and beauty rituals.

An extra ¥865 gives you access to the Healing Baden area, with even more varieties of saunas and a lounge area styled like a Balinese resort; here men and women can hang out together (everyone gets a pair of rental pyjamas).

TOKYO DOME CITY ATTRACTIONS — AMUSEMENT PARK

Map p282 (東京ドームシティアトラクションズ; ☎03-3817-6001; www.tokyo-dome.co.jp/e/attractions; 1-3-61 Kōraku, Bunkyō-ku; day pass adult/child/teenager ¥3900/2100/3400; 🕑10am-9pm; 👪; 🚆JR Chūō line to Suidōbashi, west exit) The top attraction at this amusement park next to Tokyo Dome (p144) is the 'Thunder Dolphin' (¥1030), a roller coaster that cuts a heart-in-your-throat course in and around the tightly packed buildings of downtown. There are plenty of low-key, child-friendly rides as well. You can buy individual-ride tickets, day passes, night passes (valid from 5pm) and a five-ride pass (¥2600).

SUPER POTATO RETRO-KAN — ARCADE

Map p283 (スーパーポテトレトロ館; www.superpotato.com; 1-11-2 Soto-kanda, Chiyoda-ku; 🕑11am-8pm Mon-Fri, from 10am Sat & Sun; 🚆JR Yamanote line to Akihabara, Electric Town exit) Are you a gamer keen to sample retro computer games? On the 5th floor of this store specialising in used video games, there's a retro video arcade where you can get your hands on some old-fashioned consoles at a bargain ¥100 per game.

ICHIGAYA FISH CENTRE — FISHING

Map p282 (市ヶ谷フィッシュセンター; ☎03-3260-1325; www.ichigaya-fc.com; 1-1 Ichigaya Tamachi, Shinjuku-ku; per hr ¥750, rod and bait ¥100; 🕑9.30am-7.30pm Mon-Fri, 9am-8pm Sat & Sun; 👪; 🚆JR lines to Ichigaya) There's something charming and totally Tokyo about this fishing centre on the Sotobori moat beneath Ichigaya Station. You can watch trains whizz by as you dangle your rod in the fish pools waiting for the tiddlers to bite. Kids will love it, and there are more-exotic species to spot in the aquarium shop here.

Ueno & Yanesen

UENO | YANESEN

Neighbourhood Top Five

❶ Tokyo National Museum (p149) Getting schooled in Japanese art history at the finest collection of Japanese art and cultural artefacts in the world, home to samurai swords, *ukiyo-e* (woodblock prints) and gilded screens.

❷ Rikugi-en (p152) Admiring the inspired views across one of Tokyo's most beautiful formal gardens with its central pond, teahouses, stone bridges and manicured foliage.

❸ Ueno-kōen (p153) Strolling through this expansive park chock-a-block with museums, temples and a zoo.

❹ Nezu-jinja (p154) Paying your respects at this picturesque shrine with its corridor of mini red *torii* (gates) and azalea bushes, then explore the wider Yanesen area.

❺ Ameya-yokochō (p158) Absorbing the sights, sounds and smells of this old-fashioned partially outdoor market; also a great spot for street food.

For more detail of this area see Map p284 ➡

Lonely Planet's Top Tip

While it's possible to get around Ueno and Yanesen on foot, the 'tōzai' (東西; east–west) route of the **Megurin** (www.city.taito.lg.jp/index/kurashi/kotsu/megurin) community bus does a helpful loop around the area. Useful stops include No 2, across from the Ueno Park exit at Ueno Station, No 9 in front of Yanaka Cemetery (Yanaka Rei-en Iriguchi) and No 12 for Yanaka Ginza (Yanaka Ginza Yomise-dōri). Stops are announced on the bus, which runs approximately every 15 minutes from 7am to 7pm.

◉ Best Museums

➡ Tokyo National Museum (p149)

➡ Asakura Museum of Sculpture, Taitō (p154)

➡ Shitamachi Museum (p153)

For reviews, see p149. ➡

◉ Best Places to Stroll

➡ Ueno-kōen (p153)

➡ Yanaka Ginza (p154)

➡ Ameya-yokochō (p158)

➡ Yanaka-reien (p154)

For reviews, see p153. ➡

✕ Best Places to Eat

➡ Shinsuke (p155)

➡ Hantei (p157)

➡ Innsyoutei (p155)

➡ Kamachiku (p155)

For reviews, see p155. ➡

Explore Ueno & Yanesen

You could easily spend a whole day in Ueno-kōen (p153), one of Tokyo's top draws. Start at the Tokyo National Museum (p149) then wend your way southward, hitting a few other museums, the zoo and the centuries-old shrines and temples that dot the park. Temporary exhibitions can draw huge crowds, but you'll find the permanent collections of most museums blissfully quiet. Finish up at Ameya-yokochō (p158).

Within walking distance of Ueno is a trio of neighbourhoods that time seemingly forgot. Much of Yanaka, Nezu and Sendagi, collectively known as Yanesen, miraculously survived the Great Kantō Earthquake and the allied fire-bombing of WWII (not to mention the slash-and-burn modernising of the postwar years). Yanaka, in particular, has a high concentration of vintage wooden structures and more than a hundred temples and shrines. It's a fantastic place to wander and is popular with Tokyoites, too, so can get crowded on weekends.

Last but far from least, don't miss Rikugi-en (p152), in the northern neighbourhood Komagome, perhaps Tokyo's most spectacular traditional garden.

Local Life

➡**Park Life** On weekends, look for buskers, acrobats and food vendors in Ueno-kōen (p153). The park is also Tokyo's most famous cherry-blossom-viewing place.

➡**Night Market** Many casual restaurants in and around Ameya-yokochō (p158) open up onto the street. It's a fun place to dine in the evening.

➡**Cycling** Join the locals getting around Yanesen by bicycle with a rental from Tokyobike Rental Service (p155). If you're staying nearby, many accommodations also have bicycles to lend.

➡**Hang-outs** Join Yanesen's artsy crowd for coffee at Kayaba Coffee (p157) or cocktails at bookstore-bar Bousingot (p157).

Getting There & Away

➡**Train** The JR Yamanote line stops at Ueno, Nippori (for Yanaka) and Komagome (for Rikugi-en) (p152). Keisei line trains from Narita Airport stop at Keisei Ueno Station (just south of JR Ueno Station).

➡**Subway** The Ginza and Hibiya lines stop at Ueno. The Chiyoda line runs along the west side of Ueno-kōen (p153), stopping at Yushima, Nezu and Sendagi; the latter two stops are convenient for Yanaka. The Namboku line runs to Komagome for Rikugi-en.

UENO & YANESEN

TOKYO NATIONAL MUSEUM

If you visit only one museum in Tokyo, make it this one. Established in 1872, this unprecedented collection of Japanese art covers ancient pottery, Buddhist sculpture, samurai swords, colourful *ukiyo-e* (woodblock prints), gorgeous kimonos and much, much more.

The museum is divided into several buildings, the most important of which is the **Honkan** (Japanese Gallery), which houses the collection of Japanese art. Visitors with only an hour or two should hone in on the galleries here. The building itself is in the Imperial Style of the 1930s, with art-deco flourishes throughout inside.

Next on the priority list is the enchanting **Gallery of Hōryū-ji Treasures** (法隆寺宝物館), which displays masks, scrolls and gilt Buddhas from Hōryū-ji (in Nara Prefecture, dating from 607) in a spare, elegant, box-shaped contemporary building (1999) by Taniguchi Yoshio. Nearby, to the west of the main gate, is the **Kuro-mon** (Black Gate), transported from the Edo-era mansion of a feudal lord. On weekends it opens for visitors to pass through.

Visitors with more time can explore the three-storied **Tōyōkan** (Gallery of Asian Art), with its collection of Buddhist sculptures from around Asia and delicate Chinese ceramics. The **Heiseikan** (平成館), accessed via a passage on the 1st floor of the Honkan, houses the Japanese Archaeological Gallery, full of pottery, talismans and articles of daily life from Japan's paleolithic and neolithic periods.

The museum also regularly hosts temporary exhibitions (which cost extra), within the Heiseikan; these can be fantastic, but sometimes lack the English signage found throughout the rest of the museum.

DON'T MISS

➜ Honkan
➜ Gallery of Hōryū-ji Treasures
➜ Kuro-mon
➜ Tōyōkan

PRACTICALITIES

➜ 東京国立博物館; Tokyo Kokuritsu Hakubutsukan
➜ Map p284, D4
➜ ☑03-3822-1111
➜ www.tnm.jp
➜ 13-9 Ueno-kōen, Taitō-ku
➜ adult/child & senior/ student ¥620/free/410
➜ ⊘9.30am-5pm Tue-Sun year-round, to 8pm Fri Mar-Dec, to 6pm Sat & Sun Mar-Aug
➜ Ⓡ JR lines to Ueno, Ueno-kōen exit

Tokyo National Museum

HISTORIC HIGHLIGHTS

It would be a challenge to take in everything the sprawling Tokyo National Museum has to offer in a day. Fortunately, the Honkan (Japanese Gallery) is designed to give visitors a crash course in Japanese art history from the Jōmon era (13,000–300 BC) to the Edo era (AD 1603–1868). The works on display here are rotated regularly, to protect fragile ones and to create seasonal exhibitions – you're always guaranteed to see something new.

Buy your ticket from outside the main gate then head straight to the Honkan with its sloping tile roof. Stow your coat in a locker and take the central staircase up to the 2nd floor, where the exhibitions are arranged chronologically. Allow two hours for this tour of the highlights.

The first room on your right starts from the beginning with **ancient Japanese art ❶**. Be sure to pick up a copy of the brochure Highlights of Japanese Art at the entrance.

Continue to the **National Treasure Gallery ❷**. 'National Treasure' is the highest distinction awarded to a work of art in Japan. Keep an eye out for more National Treasures, labelled in red, on display in other rooms throughout the museum.

Moving on, stop to admire the **courtly art gallery ❸**, the **samurai armour and swords ❹** and the **ukiyo-e and kimono ❺**.

Next, take the stairs down to the 1st floor, where each room is dedicated to a different decorative art, such as lacquerware or ceramics. Don't miss the excellent examples of **religious sculpture ❻** and **folk art ❼**.

Finish your visit with a look inside the enchanting **Gallery of Hōryū-ji Treasures ❽**.

Ukiyo-e & Kimono (Room 10)
Chic silken kimono and lushly coloured *ukiyo-e* (woodblock prints) are two icons of the Edo era (AD 1603–1868) *ukiyo* – the 'floating world', or world of fleeting beauty and pleasure.

Japanese Sculpture (Room 11)
Many of Japan's most famous sculptures, religious in nature, are locked away in temple reliquaries. This is a rare chance to see them up close.

MUSEUM GARDEN
Don't miss the garden if you visit during the few weeks it's open to the public in spring and autumn.

Heiseikan & Japanese Archaeology Gallery

Research & Information Centre

Hyōkeikan

Kuro-mon

Main Gate

Gallery of Hōryū-ji Treasures
Surround yourself with miniature gilt Buddhas from Hōryū-ji, said to be one of Japan's oldest Buddhist temples, founded in 607. Don't miss the graceful Pitcher with Dragon Head, a National Treasure.

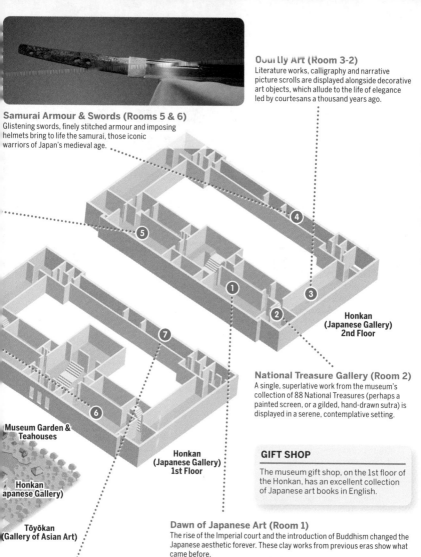

Courtly Art (Room 3-2)

Literature works, calligraphy and narrative picture scrolls are displayed alongside decorative art objects, which allude to the life of elegance led by courtesans a thousand years ago.

Samurai Armour & Swords (Rooms 5 & 6)

Glistening swords, finely stitched armour and imposing helmets bring to life the samurai, those iconic warriors of Japan's medieval age.

Honkan (Japanese Gallery) 2nd Floor

National Treasure Gallery (Room 2)

A single, superlative work from the museum's collection of 88 National Treasures (perhaps a painted screen, or a gilded, hand-drawn sutra) is displayed in a serene, contemplative setting.

Museum Garden & Teahouses

Honkan (Japanese Gallery)

Tōyōkan (Gallery of Asian Art)

Honkan (Japanese Gallery) 1st Floor

GIFT SHOP

The museum gift shop, on the 1st floor of the Honkan, has an excellent collection of Japanese art books in English.

Dawn of Japanese Art (Room 1)

The rise of the Imperial court and the introduction of Buddhism changed the Japanese aesthetic forever. These clay works from previous eras show what came before.

Folk Culture (Room 15)

See artefacts from Japan's historical minorities – the indigenous Ainu of Hokkaidō and the former Ryūkyū Empire, now Okinawa.

DADEROT ©

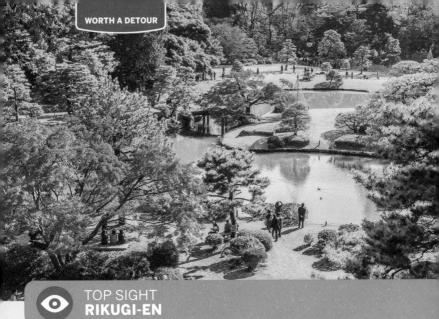

TOP SIGHT
RIKUGI-EN

Tokyo's most beautiful garden is hidden in the city's north. Built by a feudal lord in 1702, with a large central pond, it was designed to reflect the aesthetic of traditional Waka poetry. Walkways pass over hills, stone bridges, trickling streams and scenes inspired by famous poems.

The bridge, **Togetsukyō**, created from two huge stone slabs, references a poem about a crane flying over a moon-lit field. Stone markers around the garden make note of other scenic views, many of which reference famous works of Japanese or Chinese literature. Climb to the top of the **Fujishiro-tōge**, a hill named after a real one in Wakayama Prefecture, for panoramic views across the garden.

Rikugi-en has two vintage teahouses, where you can sit and rest, taking in the scenery. The **Tsutsuji-chaya** dates to the Meiji period and is perfectly primed for viewing the maples in autumn. The **Takimi-chaya** is perched on the edge of the stream where you can enjoy the view of a mini waterfall over rocks and giant *koi* (carp) swimming in the water.

Something is almost always in bloom at Rikugi-en, though the garden is most famous for its maple leaves, which turn bright red usually around late November or early December. During this time, the park stays open until 9pm and the trees are illuminated after sunset.

In early spring you can catch plum blossoms, followed by the flowering of the magnificent weeping cherry tree near the entrance.

DON'T MISS

➡ Teahouses
➡ Togetsukyō
➡ View from Fujishiro-tōge
➡ Maples in late autumn

PRACTICALITIES

➡ 六義園
➡ ☏03-3941-2222
➡ http://teien.tokyo-park.or.jp/en/rikugien
➡ 6-16-3 Hon-Komagome, Bunkyō-ku
➡ adult/child ¥300/free
➡ ⊙9am-5pm
➡ ⮔JR Yamanote line to Komagome, south exit

⊙ SIGHTS

TOKYO NATIONAL MUSEUM MUSEUM
See p110.

RIKUGI-EN GARDENS
See p152.

⊙ Ueno

UENO-KŌEN PARK
Map p284 (上野公園; http://ueno-bunka.
jp; Ueno-kōen, Taitō-ku; ⓡJR lines to Ueno,
Ueno-kōen & Shinobazu exits) Best known
for its profusion of cherry trees that burst
into blossom in spring (making this one of
Tokyo's top *hanami* – blossom-viewing –
spots), sprawling Ueno-kōen is also the
location of the city's highest concentration of museums. At the southern tip is the
large scenic pond, **Shinobazu-ike** (不忍池),
choked with lotus flowers.

UENO ZOO ZOO
Map p284 (上野動物園; Ueno Dōbutsu-en; ☑03-
3828-5171; www.tokyo-zoo.net; 9-83 Ueno-kōen,
Taitō-ku; adult/child ¥600/free; ⊙9.30am-5pm
Tue-Sun; ⓡJR lines to Ueno, Ueno-kōen exit)
Japan's oldest zoo, established in 1882, is
home to animals from around the globe,
but the biggest attractions are two giant
pandas that arrived from China in 2011 –
Rī Rī and Shin Shin. There's also a whole
area devoted to lemurs, which makes sense
given Tokyoites' love of all things cute.

UENO TŌSHŌ-GŪ SHINTO SHRINE
Map p284 (上野東照宮; ☑03-3822-3455; www.
uenotoshogu.com; 9-88 Ueno-kōen, Taitō-ku;
¥500; ⊙9am-5.30pm Mar-Sep, to 4.30pm Oct-
Feb; ⓡJR lines to Ueno, Shinobazu exit) This
shrine inside Ueno-kōen (p153) was built
in honour of Tokugawa Ieyasu, the warlord
who unified Japan. Resplendent in gold
leaf and ornate details, it dates from 1651
(though it has had recent touch-ups). You
can get a pretty good look from outside the
gate, if you want to skip the admission fee.

In January and February there is a spectacular peony garden; from mid-September
to 30 October the same garden blooms with
dahlias. Entry to either is an additional ¥500.

KIYŌMIZU KANNON-DŌ BUDDHIST TEMPLE
Map p284 (清水観音堂; ☑03-3821-4749; 1-29
Ueno-kōen, Taitō-ku; ⊙9am-4pm; ⓡJR lines to
Ueno, Shinobazu exit) Ueno-kōen's Kiyōmizu
Kannon-dō is one of Tokyo's oldest structures: established in 1631 and in its present
position since 1698, it has survived every
disaster that has come its way. A miniature
of the famous Kiyomizu-dera in Kyoto, it's
a pilgrimage site for women hoping to con-
ceive as it enshrines Kosodate Kannon, the
protector of childbearing and child-raising.

KURODA MEMORIAL HALL GALLERY
Map p284 (黒田記念室; ☑03-5777-8600; www.
tobunken.go.jp/kuroda/index_e.html; 13-9 Ueno-
kōen, Taitō-ku; ⊙9.30am-5pm Tue-Sun; ⓡJR
lines to Ueno, Ueno-kōen exit) FREE Kuroda
Seiki (1866–1924) is considered the father of
modern Western-style painting in Japan. In
this 1928-vintage hall, an annexe to Tokyo
National Museum (p149), some of his works
are displayed, including key pieces such as
Maiko Girl and *Wisdom, Impression and
Sentiment*, a striking triptych of three nude
women on canvases coated with ground gold.

**NATIONAL MUSEUM OF
NATURE & SCIENCE** MUSEUM
Map p284 (国立科学博物館; ☑03-5777-8600;
www.kahaku.go.jp/english; 7-20 Ueno-kōen, Taitō-
ku; adult/child ¥600/free; ⊙9am-5pm Tue-Thu,
Sat & Sun, to 8pm Fri; ⓡJR lines to Ueno, Ueno-kōen
exit) The **Japan Gallery** here showcases the
rich and varied wildlife of the Japanese archipelago, from the bears of Hokkaidō to the
giant beetles of Okinawa. Elsewhere in the
museum: a rocket launcher, a giant squid,
an Edo-era mummy, and a digital seismo-
graph that charts earthquakes in real time.
There's English signage throughout, plus an
English-language audio guide (¥300).

**NATIONAL MUSEUM OF
WESTERN ART** MUSEUM
Map p284 (国立西洋美術館; ☑03-5777-8600;
www.nmwa.go.jp; 7-7 Ueno-kōen, Taitō-ku; adult/
student ¥430/130, 2nd & 4th Sat free; ⊙9.30am-
5.30pm Tue-Thu, Sat & Sun, to 8pm Fri; ⓡJR lines
to Ueno, Ueno-kōen exit) The permanent collection here runs from medieval Madonna-
and-child images to 20th-century abstract
expressionism, but is strongest in French
impressionism, including a whole gallery
of Monet. The main building, completed
in 1959, was designed by Le Corbusier, and
is Unesco World Heritage listed. Ask at the
information desk for the *Discover Architecture* map (in English), which notes key
aspects of the building.

SHITAMACHI MUSEUM MUSEUM
Map p284 (下町風俗資料館; ☑03-3823-7451;
www.taitocity.net/taito/shitamachi; 2-1 Ueno-
kōen, Taitō-ku; adult/child ¥300/100; ⊙9.30am-
4.30pm Tue-Sun; ⓡJR lines to Ueno, Shinobazu

exit) This small museum recreates life in the plebeian quarters of Tokyo during the Meiji and Taishō periods (1868–1926), before the city was twice destroyed by the Great Kantō Earthquake and WWII. There are old tenement houses and shops that you can enter.

KYŪ IWASAKI-TEIEN HISTORIC BUILDING
Map p284 (旧岩崎邸庭園; ☎03-3823-8340; http://teien.tokyo-park.or.jp/en/kyu-iwasaki/index.html; 1-3-45 Ike-no-hata, Taitō-ku; adult/child ¥400/free; ⌚9am-5pm; [S]Chiyoda line to Yushima, exit 1) This grand residence combines a Western-style mansion designed by Josiah Conder in 1896, a Japanese house built by Ōkawa Kijuro at the same time, and gardens. It was once the villa of Hisaya Iwasaki, son of the founder of Mitsubishi, and is a fascinating example of how the cultural elite of the early Meiji period tried to straddle east and west.

YUSHIMA TENJIN SHINTO SHRINE
Map p284 (湯島天神; Yushima Tenmangu; ☎03-3836-0753; www.yushimatenjin.or.jp; 3-30-1 Yushima, Bunkyō-ku; ⌚6am-8pm; [S]Chiyoda line to Yushima, exit 1) In the 14th century, the spirit of a renowned scholar was enshrined here, leading to the shrine's current popularity: it receives countless students who come to pray for academic success, especially during school-entrance-exam season. It's an attractive shrine that's famous for its display of *ume* (plum) blossoms in February and March.

Yanesen

★NEZU-JINJA SHINTO SHRINE
Map p284 (根津神社; ☎03-3822-0753; www.nedujinja.or.jp; 1-28-9 Nezu, Bunkyō-ku; ⌚24hr; [S]Chiyoda line to Nezu, exit 1) Not only is this one of Japan's oldest shrines, it is also easily the most beautiful in a district packed with attractive religious buildings. The opulently decorated structure, which dates from the early 18th century, is one of the city's miraculous survivors and is offset by a long corridor of small red *torii* (gates) that makes for great photos.

YANAKA GINZA AREA
Map p284 (谷中銀座; 🚉JR Yamanote line to Nippori, north exit) Yanaka Ginza is pure, vintage mid-20th-century Tokyo, a pedestrian street lined with butcher shops, vegetable vendors and the like. Most Tokyo neighbourhoods once had stretches like these (until supermarkets took over). It's popular with Tokyoites from all over the city, who come to soak up the nostalgic atmosphere, plus the locals who shop here.

YANAKA-REIEN CEMETERY
Map p284 (谷中霊園; 7-5-24 Yanaka, Taitō-ku; 🚉JR Yamanote line to Nippori, west exit) One of Tokyo's largest graveyards, Yanaka-reien is the final resting place of more than 7000 souls, many of whom were quite well known in their day. It's also where you'll find the tomb of Yoshinobu Tokugawa (徳川慶喜の墓), the last shogun. Come spring it is also one of Tokyo's main cherry-blossom-viewing spots.

★ASAKURA MUSEUM OF SCULPTURE, TAITŌ MUSEUM
Map p284 (朝倉彫塑館; www.taitocity.net/taito/asakura; 7-16-10 Yanaka, Taitō-ku; adult/student ¥500/250; ⌚9.30am-4.30pm Tue, Wed & Fri-Sun; 🚉JR Yamanote line to Nippori, north exit) Sculptor Asakura Fumio (artist name Chōso; 1883–1964) designed this atmospheric house himself. It combined his original Japanese home and garden with a large studio that incorporated vaulted ceilings, a 'sunrise room' and a rooftop garden with wonderful neighbourhood views. It's now a reverential museum with many of the artist's signature realist works, mostly of people and cats, on display.

SCAI THE BATHHOUSE GALLERY
Map p284 (スカイザバスハウス; ☎03-3821-1144; www.scaithebathhouse.com; 6-1-23 Yanaka, Taitō-ku; ⌚noon-6pm Tue-Sat; [S]Chiyoda line to Nezu, exit 1) [FREE] This 200-year-old bathhouse has for several decades been an avant-garde gallery space, showcasing Japanese and international artists in its austere vaulted space.

SHITAMACHI MUSEUM ANNEX HISTORIC BUILDING
Map p284 (下町風俗資料館; 2-10-6 Uenosakuragi, Taitō-ku; ⌚9.30am-4.30pm Tue-Sun; [S]Chiyoda line to Nezu, exit 1) [FREE] This century-old liquor shop (which operated until 1986) has been returned to its original state, but as a museum of bygone Tokyo, with old sake barrels, weights, measures and posters.

🍴 EATING

🍴 Ueno

★SHINSUKE IZAKAYA ¥¥

Map p284 (シンスケ; ☎03-3832-0469; 3-31-5 Yushima, Bunkyō-ku; ⏰5-9.30pm Mon-Fri, to 9pm Sat; [S]Chiyoda line to Yushima, exit 3) In business since 1925, Shinsuke has honed the concept of an ideal *izakaya* to perfection: long cedar counter, 'master' in *happi* (traditional short coat) and *hachimaki* (traditional headband), and smooth-as-silk *dai-ginjo* (premium-grade sake). The food – contemporary updates of classics – is fantastic. Don't miss the *kitsune raclette* – deep-fried tofu stuffed with raclette cheese.

Also, unlike other storied *izakaya* that can be intimidating to foreigners, the staff here are friendly and go out of their way to explain the menu in English.

★INNSYOUTEI JAPANESE ¥

Map p284 (韻松亭; ☎03-3821-8126; www.innsyoutei.jp; 4-59 Ueno-kōen, Taitō-ku; lunch/dinner from ¥1680/5500; ⏰restaurant 11am-3pm & 5-9.30pm, tearoom 11am-5pm; 🚆JR lines to Ueno, Ueno-kōen exit) In a gorgeous wooden building dating back to 1875, Innsyoutei (pronounced 'inshotei' and meaning 'rhyme of the pine cottage') has long been a favourite spot for fancy *kaiseki*-style meals while visiting Ueno-kōen (p153). Without a booking (essential for dinner) you'll have a long wait but it's worth it. Lunchtime *bentō* (boxed meals) offer beautifully presented morsels and are great value.

There's an attached rustic teahouse serving *matcha* (powdered green tea) and traditional desserts from ¥600.

SASA-NO-YUKI TOFU ¥¥

Map p284 (笹乃雪; ☎03-3873-1145; 2-15-10 Negishi, Taitō-ku; dishes ¥400-700, lunch/dinner course from ¥2200/5000; ⏰11.30am-8.30pm Tue-Sun; 📝; 🚆JR Yamanote line to Uguisudani, north exit) 🌿 Sasa-no-Yuki opened its doors in the Edo period, and continues to serve its signature dishes with tofu made fresh every morning using water from the shop's own well. Some treats to expect: *ankake-dofu* (tofu in a thick, sweet sauce) and *goma-dofu* (sesame tofu). The best seats overlook a tiny garden with a koi (carp) pond.

> **ⓘ BICYCLE RENTAL**
>
> Ueno-kōen (p153) and Yanesen are great places to stroll; they're also great places to cycle. Hipster bicycle manufacturer **Tokyobike Rental Services** (Map p284; ☎03-3827-4819; www.tokyobike.com/rental; 6-3-12 Yanaka, Taitō-ku; per day ¥2500; ⏰10am-7pm Wed-Sun; 🚆JR Yamanote line to Nippori, west exit) in Yanaka rents seven-speed city bikes. Reserve one in advance by sending an email with your name, and desired day and height.

Vegetarians should not assume everything is purely vegie – ask before ordering. There is bamboo out front.

KINGYOZAKA JAPANESE ¥¥

(金魚坂; ☎03-3815-7088; www.kingyozaka.com; 5-3-15 Hongo, Bunkyō-ku; set lunch from ¥1400, dinner mains from ¥1800; ⏰11.30am-9.30pm Tue-Fri, to 8pm Sat & Sun; [S]Ōedo line to Hongō-sanchōme, exit 3) They've been selling ornamental fish from this spot for some 350 years, so it's only fitting that the attached restaurant and cafe take a goldfish theme (*kingyo* means goldfish). It's a charming place in a timber-framed building. The star dish is a Japanese-style beef curry with a thick sauce and sizeable chunks of meat. It also serves tea and cakes and *kaiseki*-style meals.

🍴 Yanesen

★KAMACHIKU UDON ¥

Map p284 (釜竹; ☎03-5815-4675; http://kamachiku.com/top_en; 2-14-18 Nezu, Bunkyō-ku; noodles from ¥850, small dishes ¥350-850; ⏰11.30am-2pm Tue-Sun, 5.30-9pm Tue-Sat; [S]Chiyoda line to Nezu, exit 1) Udon (thick wheat noodles) made fresh daily is the speciality at this popular restaurant, in a beautifully restored brick warehouse from 1910 with a view onto a garden. In addition to noodles, the menu includes lots of *izakaya*-style small dishes (such as grilled fish and vegies). Expect to queue on weekends.

HAGISO JAPANESE ¥

Map p284 (☎03-5832-9808; http://hanare.hagiso.jp; 3-10-25 Yanaka, Taitō-ku; mains ¥815-1300; ⏰8-10.30am & noon-9pm; [S]Chiyoda line to

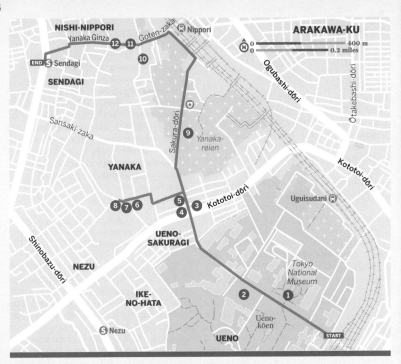

🏃 Neighbourhood Walk
An Afternoon in Yanaka

START TOKYO NATIONAL MUSEUM
END SENDAGI STATION
LENGTH 3KM; TWO HOURS

If you have time, visit the ❶ **Tokyo National Museum** (p149) before you start exploring Yanaka, with its temples, galleries and old wooden buildings. If not, simply follow the road northwest out of ❷ **Ueno-kōen** (p153) until you hit Kototoi-dōri. At the corner is the ❸ **Shitamachi Museum Annex** (p154), actually a preserved, century-old liquor store. Across the street is ❹ **Kayaba Coffee** (p157), if you need a pick-me-up.

From here, it's a short walk to ❺ **SCAI the Bathhouse** (p154), a classic old public bathhouse turned contemporary art gallery. It's a worthwhile detour to continue down to ❻ **Edokoro** (p158), the studio of painter Allan West, and to see the ancient, thick-trunked ❼ **Himalayan cedar tree** on the corner. In and around here, you'll pass many temples, including ❽ **Enju-ji**, where Nichika-sama, the 'god of strong legs' is

enshrined; it's popular with runners. Feel free to stop in any of the temples; just be respectful and keep your voice low.

Now double back towards the entrance of ❾ **Yanaka-reien** (p154), one of Tokyo's most atmospheric and prestigious cemeteries. When you exit the cemetery, continue with the train tracks on your right, climbing until you reach the bridge, which overlooks the tracks (a favourite destination for trainspotters).

Head left and look for the sign pointing towards the ❿ **Asakura Museum of Sculpture, Taitō** (p154), the home studio of an early-20th-century sculptor and now an attractive museum. Back on the main drag, continue down the ⓫ **Yūyake Dandan** – literally the 'Sunset Stairs' – to the classic mid-20th-century shopping street ⓬ **Yanaka Ginza** (p154). Pick up some snacks from the vendors here, then sit down on a milk crate on the side of the road with the locals and wash it all down with a beer. Walk west and you can pick up the subway at Sendagi Station.

Sendagi, exit 2) This attractive new cafe and gallery, run by students from Tokyo University of the Arts (Geidai), is a good all-rounder for meals, drinks and sweets in the heart of Yanaka. Its Japanese-style breakfast is a great deal at ¥325, while lunch set menus may include a hearty vegetable curry or Japanese-style hamburger steak. Expect to wait on weekends as it's popular.

NAGOMI YAKITORI ¥

Map p284 (和味; ☎03-3821-5972; 3-11-11 Yanaka, Taitō-ku; skewers from ¥180; 🕒5pm-midnight; 🚉JR Yamanote line to Nippori, north exit) On Yanaka Ginza (p154), Nagomi deals in juicy skewers of *ji-dori* (free-range chicken). There are plenty of grilled vegie options, too. Wash it all down with a bowl of chicken-soup ramen. Look for the sake bottles in the window.

NEZU NO TAIYAKI SWEETS ¥

Map p284 (根津のたいやき; 1-23-9-104 Nezu, Bunkyō-ku; taiyaki ¥170; 🕒10.30am until sold out, closed irregularly; 🚭; [S]Chiyoda line to Nezu, exit 1) This street stall, beloved of locals for half a century, sells just one thing: *taiyaki* – hot, sweet, bean-jam buns shaped like *tai* (sea bream), a fish considered to be lucky. Come early before they sell out (always by 2pm, and sometimes by noon).

★HANTEI JAPANESE ¥¥

Map p284 (はん亭; ☎03-3828-1440; http://hantei.co.jp; 2-12-15 Nezu, Bunkyō-ku; meals from ¥3000; 🕒noon-3pm & 5-10pm Tue-Sun; [S]Chiyoda line to Nezu, exit 2) Housed in a beautifully maintained, century-old traditional wooden building, Hantei is a local landmark. Delectable skewers of seasonal *kushiage* (fried meat, fish and vegetables) are served with small, refreshing side dishes. Lunch includes eight or 12 sticks and dinner starts with six, after which you'll continue to receive additional rounds (¥210 per skewer) until you say stop.

DRINKING & NIGHTLIFE

★YANAKA BEER HALL CRAFT BEER

Map p284 (☎03-5834-2381; www.facebook.com/yanakabeerhall; 2-15-6 Ueno-sakuragi, Taitō-ku; 🕒noon-8.30pm Tue-Fri, 11am-8.30pm Sat & Sun; 📶; [S]Chiyoda line to Nezu, exit 1) Exploring Yanesen can be thirsty work so thank heavens for this craft-beer bar, a cosy place with some outdoor seating. It's part of a charming complex of old wooden buildings that also house a bakery-cafe, bistro and events space. It has several brews on tap, including a Yanaka lager that's only available here.

TORINDŌ TEAHOUSE

Map p284 (桃林堂; 1-5-7 Ueno-Sakuragi, Taitō-ku; tea ¥450; 🕒9am-5pm Tue-Sun; [S]Chiyoda line to Nezu, exit 1) Sample a cup of paint-thick *matcha* (powdered green tea) at this tiny teahouse on the edge of Ueno-kōen (p153). Tradition dictates that the bitter tea be paired with something sweet, so choose from the artful desserts in the glass counter, then pull up a stool at the communal table. It's a white building on a corner.

BOUSINGOT BAR

Map p284 (ブーザンゴ; ☎03-3823-5501; www.bousingot.com; 2-33-2 Sendagi, Bunkyō-ku; drinks from ¥450; 🕒6-11pm Wed-Mon; [S]Chiyoda line to Sendagi, exit 1) It's fitting that Yanaka, which refuses to trash the past, would have a bar that doubles as a used bookstore. Sure, the books are in Japanese but you can still enjoy soaking up the atmosphere with some resident book lovers.

KAYABA COFFEE CAFE

Map p284 (カヤバ珈琲; ☎03-3823-3545; http://kayaba-coffee.com; 6-1-29 Yanaka, Taitō-ku; drinks from ¥450; 🕒8am-11pm Mon-Sat, to 6pm Sun; [S]Chiyoda line to Nezu, exit 1) This vintage 1930s coffee shop in Yanaka is a hang-out for local students and artists. Come early for the 'morning set' (coffee and a sandwich for ¥800). In the evenings, Kayaba morphs into a bar.

☆ ENTERTAINMENT

TOKYO BUNKA KAIKAN CLASSICAL MUSIC

Map p284 (東京文化会館; www.t-bunka.jp/en; 5-45 Ueno-kōen, Taitō-ku; 🕒library 1-8pm Tue-Sat, to 5pm Sun; 🚉JR lines to Ueno, Ueno-kōen exit) The Tokyo Metropolitan Symphony Orchestra and the Tokyo Ballet both make regular appearances at this concrete bunker of a building designed by Maekawa Kunio, an apprentice of Le Corbusier. Prices vary wildly; look out for monthly morning classical-music performances that cost only ¥500. The gorgeously decorated auditorium has superb acoustics.

Tokyo Bunka Kaikan is the main venue for **Tokyo Haru-sai** (東京春祭; www.tokyo-harusai.com/index_e.html), a classical-music festival that takes place every spring. There's also a **music library** where it's free to listen to vinyl platters (mainly classical but also Japanese and various other ethnic and folk music) on old LP players.

 # SHOPPING

★ AMEYA-YOKOCHŌ   MARKET
Map p284 (アメヤ横町; www.ameyoko.net; 4 Ueno, Taitō-ku; ⊙10am-7pm, some shops close Wed; ℝJR lines to Okachimachi, north exit) Step into this partially open-air market paralleling and beneath the JR line tracks, and ritzy, glitzy Tokyo feels like a distant memory. It got its start as a black market, post-WWII, when American goods were sold here. Today, it's packed with vendors selling everything from fresh seafood and exotic cooking spices to jeans, sneakers and elaborately embroidered bomber jackets.

★ YANAKA MATSUNOYA   HOMEWARES
Map p284 (谷中松野屋; www.yanakamatsunoya. jp; 3-14-14 Nishi-Nippori, Arakawa-ku; ⊙11am-7pm Mon & Wed-Fri, 10am-7pm Sat & Sun; ℝJR Yamanote line to Nippori, west exit) At the top of Yanaka Ginza (p154), Matsunoya sells household goods – baskets, brooms and canvas totes, for example – simple in beauty and form, and handmade by local artisans.

SHOKICHI   ARTS & CRAFTS
Map p284 (☑03-3821-1837; http://shokichi. main.jp; 3-2-6 Yanaka, Bunkyō-ku; ⊙10am-6pm Wed-Sun; ⓢChiyoda line to Sendagi, exit 1) Mitsuaki Tsuyuki makes and sells his incredible hand puppets here – look out for lifelike renditions of Japanese celebs and, natch, Elvis. He can hand-make a portrait puppet from a photograph (¥40,000). Far more affordable are the quick portraits he draws via one of his hand puppets (¥1000).

If you can get a group of three or more together, he'll put on a 30-minute puppet show for ¥1000 per person.

EDOKORO ALLAN WEST   ART
Map p284 (繪処アランウエスト; ☑03-3827-1907; www.allanwest.jp; 1-6-17 Yanaka, Taitō-ku; ⊙1-5pm, from 3pm Sun, closed irregularly; ⓢChiyoda line to Nezu, exit 1) FREE In this masterfully converted garage, long-time Yanaka resident Allan West paints gorgeous screens and scrolls in the traditional Japanese style, making his paints from scratch just as local artists have done for centuries. Smaller votive-shaped paintings start at ¥5000; the screens clock in at a cool ¥6 million.

ISETATSU   ARTS & CRAFTS
Map p284 (いせ辰; ☑03-3823-1453; 2-18-9 Yanaka, Taitō-ku; ⊙10am-6pm; ⓢChiyoda line to Sendagi, exit 1) Dating back to 1864, this venerable stationery shop specialises in *chiyogami* – gorgeous, colourful paper made using woodblocks – as well as papier-mâché figures and masks.

 # ACTIVITIES

★ ROKURYU KŌSEN   BATHHOUSE
Map p284 (六龍鉱泉; ☑03-3821-3826; 3-4-20 Ikenohata, Taitō-ku; ¥460; ⊙3.30-11pm Tue-Sun; ⓢChiyoda line to Nezu, exit 2) Dating from 1931, this gem of a neighbourhood *sentō* (public bath) has a beautiful mural of the wooden arched bridge Kintai-kyo in Iwasaki on the bathhouse wall. The amber-hued water is packed with minerals that are reputed to be excellent for your skin, if you can stand the water temperature – a scalding-hot 45°C in the cooler of the two pools!

The bathhouse is located down a small lane next to a shop with a green awning.

UENO FREE WALKING TOUR   WALKING
Map p284 (https://tokyosgg.jp/guide.html; 7-47 Ueno-kōen, Taitō-ku; ℝJR lines to Ueno, Ueno-kōen exit) FREE Free tours of Ueno, conducted in English by volunteer guides, leave from in front of the Green Salon (グリーンサロン) cafe every Sunday, Wednesday and Friday at 10.30am and 1pm. No sign-up is necessary.

YANESEN TOURIST INFORMATION & CULTURE CENTER   ART
Map p284 (☑03-3828-7878; www.ti-yanesen.jp/ en; 3-16-6 Yanaka, Taitō-ku; ⊙9am-5pm; ⓢChiyoda line to Sendagi, exit 2) Check the website for information on cultural experiences and guided tours of the Yanesen area. Some activities such as *shodō* (calligraphy), *sadō* (tea ceremony), noodle making and wearing a kimono or *yukata* can be arranged on the day.

Asakusa & Sumida River

ASAKUSA | OSHIAGE | RYŌGOKU | KIYOSUMI & FUKAGAWA | ASAKUSA & OSHIAGE | RYŌGOKU, KIYOSUMI & SHIRAKAWA

Neighbourhood Top Five

1 **Sensō-ji** (p161) Browsing the craft stalls of Nakamise-dōri and soaking up the atmosphere (and the incense) at Asakusa's centuries-old temple complex.

2 **Ryōgoku Kokugikan** (p168) Catching the salt-slinging, belly-slapping ritual of sumo at one of the city's four annual tournaments.

3 **Edo-Tokyo Museum** (p164) Learning about life in old Edo at this excellent history museum with full-scale reconstructions of famous buildings.

4 **Tokyo Sky Tree** (p163) Scaling the world's tallest communication tower, seeing the capital at your feet, then browsing the Solamachi mall at the base afterwards.

5 **Fukagawa Fudō-dō** (p164) Being blown away by the theatre of the fire ritual at this Shingon sect temple, which also has a trippy corridor lined with 9500 mini Buddhas.

For more detail of this area see Maps p286 and p287 ➡

Lonely Planet's Top Tip

Tokyo Mizube Cruising Line (www.tokyo-park.or.jp/waterbus) water buses depart from Niten-mon Pier in Asakusa for Odaiba, via Ryōgoku. It's actually the most convenient way to get between Asakusa and Ryōgoku (¥310, one way 10 minutes) and is the perfect way for travellers short on time to sample a river cruise.

Best Places to Eat

➡ Otafuku (p167)
➡ Kappō Yoshiba (p168)
➡ Asakusa Imahan (p167)
➡ Onigiri Yadoroku (p165)

For reviews, see p165. ➡

Best Places to Drink

➡ Popeye (p168)
➡ Café Otonova (p168)
➡ Camera (p169)
➡ 'Cuzn Homeground (p168)

For reviews, see p168. ➡

Best Places to Shop

➡ Marugoto Nippon (p169)
➡ Tokyo Hotarudo (p169)
➡ Bengara (p170)
➡ Kakimori (p169)

For reviews, see p169. ➡

Explore Asakusa & Sumida River

Welcome to the area long known as Shitamachi (the 'Low City'), where the city's merchants and artisans lived during the Edo period (1603–1868). Asakusa (ah-saku-sah), with its bustling temple complex, is one of Tokyo's principal tourist destinations. During the day, and especially at weekends, Sensō-ji (p161) is jam-packed. Step off the main drags though and you'll find far fewer tourists, and the craft shops and mum-and-dad restaurants that have long defined these quarters.

The neighbourhoods east of the Sumida-gawa – Oshiage, Ryōgoku, Fukagawa and Kiyosumi – look much like they have for decades, having experienced little of the development seen elsewhere in the city; Tokyo Sky Tree (p163), just across the river from Asakusa, is the exception. Make it your last stop of the day, to see the city all lit up at night.

Ryōgoku has two key sights, the sumo stadium (p168) and the Edo-Tokyo Museum (p164). Further south, Fukagawa and Kiyosumi have a handful of worthy sights (a temple, a shrine and a garden) yet remain fairly off the radar. Exploring these peaceful neighbourhoods can give you a feel for the old-Tokyo culture of the city's east side.

Local Life

➡**Street Food** Asakusa brims with street food vendors (p165), especially along Nakamise-dōri.

➡**Festivals** The 15th and 28th of each month are festival days at Fukagawa Fudō-dō (p164) and Tomioka Hachiman-gū (p165), with food stalls and a flea market.

➡**Parks** Sumida-kōen, on both sides of the river around Asakusa, is a cherry-blossom-viewing hot spot and also gets packed for the summer **fireworks festival** (隅田川花火大会, Sumida-gawa Hanabi Taikai).

Getting There & Away

➡**Train** The Tōbu Sky Tree line leaves from Tōbu Asakusa Station for Tokyo Sky Tree Station. The JR Sōbu line goes to Ryōgoku.

➡**Subway** The Ginza and Asakasa line stops at separate Asakusa stations. The Asakusa and Hanzōmon lines stop at Oshiage. The Ōedo line connects Ryōgoku, Kiyosumi (Kiyosumi-Shirakawa Station) and Fukagawa (Monzen-Nakachō Station).

➡**Water Bus** Tokyo Cruise (p236) and Tokyo Mizube Cruising Line (p236) ferries stop at separate piers in Asakusa; Tokyo Mizube Cruising Line also stops in Ryōgoku.

TOP SIGHT
SENSŌ-JI

Sensō-ji is the capital's oldest temple, far older than Tokyo itself. According to legend, in AD 628, two fishermen brothers pulled out a golden image of Kannon (the Bodhisattva of compassion) from the nearby Sumida-gawa. Sensō-ji was built to enshrine it. Today the temple stands out for its old-world atmosphere – a glimpse of a bygone Japan rarely visible in Tokyo today.

Kaminari-mon

The temple precinct begins at the majestic **Kaminari-mon** (雷門), which means Thunder Gate. An enormous *chōchin* (lantern), which weighs 670kg, hangs from the centre. On either side are a pair of ferocious protective deities: Fūjin, the god of wind, on the right; and Raijin, the god of thunder, on the left. Kaminari-mon has burnt down countless times over the centuries; the current gate dates to 1970.

Nakamise-dōri Shopping Street

Beyond Kaminari-mon is the bustling shopping street Nakamise-dōri. With its lines of souvenir stands it is very touristy, though that's nothing new: Sensō-ji has been Tokyo's top tourist sight for centuries, since travel was restricted to religious pilgrimages during the feudal era. In addition to the usual T-shirts, you can find Edo-style crafts and oddities (such as wigs done up in traditional hairstyles). There are also numerous snack vendors serving up crunchy *sembei* (rice crackers) and *age-manju* (deep-fried *anko* – bean-paste – buns).

At the end of Nakamise-dōri is **Hōzō-mon** (宝蔵門), another gate with fierce guardians. On the gate's back side are a pair of 2500kg, 4.5m-tall *waraji* (straw sandals) crafted for

DON'T MISS

- Kaminari-mon
- Nakamise-dōri stalls
- Incense cauldron at the Main Hall
- Temple lights at sunset
- *Omikuji* (fortune telling)

PRACTICALITIES

- 浅草寺
- Map p286, C2
- ☎03-3842-0181
- www.senso-ji.jp
- 2-3-1 Asakusa, Taitō-ku
- admission free
- 🕘24hr
- [S]Ginza line to Asakusa, exit 1

FORTUNE TELLING

Don't miss getting your fortune told by an *omikuji* (paper fortune). Drop ¥100 into the slots by the wooden drawers at either side of the approach to the Main Hall, grab a silver canister and shake it. Extract a stick and note its number (in kanji). Replace the stick, find the matching drawer and withdraw a paper fortune (there's English on the back). If you pull out 大凶 (*dai-kyō*, Great Curse), never fear. Just tie the paper on the nearby rack, ask the gods for better luck, and try again!

During the first three days of the New Year more than 2.5 million people visit Sensō-ji to pray for the year to come.

FESTIVALS

Asakusa-jinja hosts one of Tokyo's most important festivals, May's Sanja Matsuri, which draws 1.5 million visitors. On 8 February Awashima-dō holds a curious ceremony: *hari-kuyō* (the needle funeral) when monks perform last rites for broken or old sewing needles and kimono makers show gratitude to the needles by sticking them in blocks of tofu.

Sensō-ji by some 800 villagers in northern Yamagata Prefecture. These are meant to symbolise the Buddha's power, and it's believed that evil spirits will be scared off by the giant footwear.

Main Hall

In front of the grand **Hondō** (Main Hall), with its dramatic sloping roof, is a large cauldron with smoking incense. The smoke is said to bestow health and you'll see people wafting it over their bodies. The current Hondō was constructed in 1958, replacing the one destroyed in WWII air raids. The style is similar to the previous one, though the roof tiles are made of titanium.

The **Kannon image** (a tiny 6cm) is cloistered away from view deep inside the Main Hall (and admittedly may not exist at all). Nonetheless, a steady stream of worshippers visits the temple to cast coins, pray and bow in a gesture of respect. Do feel free to join in.

Off the courtyard stands a 53m-high **Five-Storey Pagoda** (五重塔), a 1973 reconstruction of a pagoda built by Tokugawa Iemitsu; it's due to be renovated in 2017. The current structure is the second-highest pagoda in Japan.

Asakusa-jinja

On the east side of the temple complex is **Asakusa-jinja** (浅草神社; ☎03-3844-1575; ◷9am-4.30pm), built in honour of the brothers who discovered the Kannon statue that inspired the construction of Sensō-ji. (Historically, Japan's two religions, Buddhism and Shintō were intertwined and it was not uncommon for temples to include shrines and vice versa.) This section of Sensō-ji survived WWII and Asakusa-jinja's current structure dates to 1649. Painted a deep shade of red, it is a rare example of early Edo architecture.

Next to the shrine is the temple complex's eastern gate, **Niten-mon** (二天門), standing since 1618. Though it appears minor today, this gate was the point of entry for visitors arriving in Asakusa via boat – the main form of transport during the Edo period.

Awashima-dō & Chingo-dō

Sensō-ji includes many other smaller temples. One to visit is **Awashima-dō** (あわしま堂), on the western edge of the temple grounds, which dates to the late 17th century. Another is **Chingo-dō** (鎮護堂), which has a separate entrance on Dembō-in-dōri. It pays tribute to the *tanuki* (racoon-like folkloric characters), who figure in Japanese myth as mystical shape-shifters and merry pranksters.

SIGHTS

Asakusa

SENSŌ-JI BUDDHIST TEMPLE

See p161.

SUPER DRY HALL ARCHITECTURE

Map p286 (フラムドール; Flamme d'Or; www.asahibeer.co.jp/aboutus/summary/#headQuarter; 1-23-1 Azuma-bashi, Sumida-ku; [S]Ginza line to Asakusa, exit 4) Also known as Asahi Beer Hall, the headquarters of the brewery was designed by Philippe Starck and completed in 1989 and remains one of the city's most distinctive buildings. The tower, with its golden glass facade and white top floors, is supposed to evoke a giant mug of beer, while the golden blob atop the lower jet-black building is the flame (locals, however, refer to it as the 'golden turd').

AMUSE MUSEUM MUSEUM

Map p286 (アミューズミュージアム; www.amuse-museum.com; 2-34-3 Asakusa, Taitō-ku; adult/student ¥1080/540; 🕓10am-6pm; [S]Ginza line to Asakusa, exit 1) Here you'll find a fascinating collection of Japanese folk articles, mainly patched clothing and pieces of fabric, known as *boro*, gathered by famed ethnologist Tanaka Chūzaburō. Many of the pieces are like fine works of contemporary art.

On another floor there's a video tutorial (with English subtitles) on how to find secret meaning in *ukiyo-e* (woodblock prints). Don't miss the roof terrace, which looks over the Sensō-ji (p161) temple complex.

EDO SHITAMACHI TRADITIONAL CRAFTS MUSEUM MUSEUM

Map p286 (江戸下町伝統工芸館; Edo Shitamachi Dentō Kōgeikan; ☎03-3842-1990; 2-22-13 Asakusa, Taitō-ku; 🕓10am-8pm; [S]Ginza line to Asakusa, exit 1) [FREE] Asakusa has a long artisan tradition, and changing exhibitions of local crafts – such as Edo-*kiriko* (cut glass) – are on display at this museum in a covered shopping arcade. Demonstrations are held on Saturdays and Sundays (between 11am and 5pm).

TAIKO DRUM MUSEUM MUSEUM

Map p286 (太鼓館; Taiko-kan; ☎03-3844-2141; www.miyamoto-unosuke.co.jp/taikokan; 4th fl, 2-1-1 Nishi-Asakusa, Taitō-ku; adult/child ¥500/150; 🕓museum 10am-5pm Wed-Sun, shop 9am-6pm; [S]Ginza line to Tawaramachi, exit 3) There are hundreds of drums from around the world here, including several traditional Japanese *taiko*. The best part is that you can actually play most of them (those marked with a music note). The shop downstairs sells drums and a lot of other associated traditional crafts.

Oshiage

TOKYO SKY TREE TOWER

Map p286 (東京スカイツリー; www.tokyo-skytree.jp; 1-1-2 Oshiage, Sumida-ku; 350m/450m observation decks ¥2060/3090; 🕓8am-10pm; [S]Hanzōmon line to Oshiage, Sky Tree exit) Tokyo Sky Tree opened in May 2012 as the world's tallest 'free-standing tower' at 634m. Its silvery exterior of steel mesh morphs from a triangle at the base to a circle at 300m. There are two observation decks, at 350m and 450m. You can see more of the city during daylight hours – at peak visibility you can see up to 100km away, all the way to Mt Fuji – but it is at night that Tokyo appears truly beautiful.

Sky Tree isn't the world's tallest built structure (that honour goes to Dubai's Burj Khalifa at 829.8m), but the panorama from the lower observatory, the Tembō Deck, is spectacular. Don't miss the small section of glass floor panels, where you can see – dizzyingly – all the way to the ground. The upper observatory, the Tembō Galleria, beneath the digital broadcasting antennas, features a circular glass corridor for more

[i] ASAKUSA INFO CENTRE

The roof terrace of the **Asakusa Culture Tourist Information Center** (浅草文化観光センター; Map p286; ☎03-3842-5566; http://taitonavi.jp; 2-18-9 Kaminarimon, Taitō-ku; 🕓9am-8pm; 📶; [S]Ginza line to Asakusa, exit 2) has fantastic views of **Tokyo Sky Tree** (p163) and the Nakamise-dōri approach to **Sensō-ji** (p161). Free guided tours of Asakusa depart from the centre on Saturdays and Sundays at 11am and 1.15pm. Also check to see if its program of **geisha entertainment** is running: it usually happens in April, June, July, October and November on Saturday at 1pm and 2.30pm with free tickets being issued at the centre from 10am.

ASAKUSA & SUMIDA RIVER SIGHTS

WORTH A DETOUR

WATCHING SUMO PRACTICE

Not in town for a sumo tournament? You can still catch an early-morning practice session at a 'stable' – where the wrestlers live and practise. Overseas visitors are welcome at **Arashio Stable** (荒汐部屋, Arashio-beya; Map p266; ☑03-3666-7646; www.arashio.net/tour_e.html; 2-47-2 Hama-chō, Nihombashi, Chūō-ku; ⓈToei Shinjuku line to Hamachō, exit A2) FREE, so long as they mind the rules (check the website). Visit between 7.30am and 10am – you can watch through the window or on a bench outside the door. There is no practice during tournament weeks.

vertiginous thrills. The elevator between the two has a glass front, so you can see yourself racing up the tower as the city grows smaller below.

The ticket counter is on the 4th floor. You'll see signs in English noting the wait and the current visibility. Try to avoid visiting on the weekend, when you might have to wait in line.

At the base is Tokyo Sky Tree Town, which includes the shopping centre **Solamachi** (ソラマチ; Map p286; www.tokyo-solamachi.jp; Ⓣ10am-9pm). Shops on the 4th floor here offer a better-than-usual selection of Japanese-y souvenirs, including pretty trinkets made from kimono fabric and quirky fashion items. On the 5th floor, **Sumida City Point** (Map p286; ☑03-6796-6341; http://machidokoro.com; 5F Tokyo Skytree Town Solamachiu; Ⓣ10am-9pm), which promotes the many artisans and craft businesses of Sumida ward. There's a cafe where you can sample food specialities, usually craftspeople providing demonstations, and experts on hand to guide you to specific shops outside of the gravitational pull of the Sky Tree.

◉ Ryōgoku

★EDO-TOKYO MUSEUM   MUSEUM

Map p287 (江戸東京博物館; ☑03-3626-9974; www.edo-tokyo-museum.or.jp; 1-4-1 Yokoami, Sumida-ku; adult/child ¥600/free; Ⓣ9.30am-5.30pm, to 7.30pm Sat, closed Mon; ⒿJR Sōbu line to Ryōgoku, west exit) This history museum, in a cavernous building, does an excellent job laying out Tokyo's miraculous

transformation from feudal city to modern capital, through city models, miniatures of real buildings, reproductions of old maps and *ukiyo-e* (woodblock prints). It starts with a bang as you cross the life-sized partial replica of the original Nihombashi bridge and gaze down on facades of a kabuki theatre and Meiji-era bank. There is English signage throughout and a free audio guide available (¥1000 deposit).

On Saturdays there may be free traditional culture programs for tourists offered here, including magic tricks, paper cutting and acrobatics; see www.tokyo-tradition.jp/eng for details.

SUMIDA HOKUSAI MUSEUM   MUSEUM

Map p287 (すみだ北斎美術館; ☑03-6658-8931; http://hokusai-museum.jp; 2-7-2 Kamezawa, Sumida-ku; adult/child/student ¥1200/400/900; Ⓣ9.30am-5.30pm Tue-Sun; ⓈOedo line to Ryōgoku, exit A4) The artist Katsushika Hokusai was born and died close to the location of this new museum, opened in 2016. The striking aluminium-clad building is designed by Pritzker Prize–winning architect Kazuyo Sejima. The museum's collection numbers more than 1500 pieces and includes some of the master's most famous images, such as *The Great Wave off Kanagawa* from his series *Thirty-six Views of Mount Fuji*.

◉ Kiyosumi & Fukagawa

KIYOSUMI-TEIEN   GARDENS

Map p287 (清澄庭園; http://teien.tokyo-park.or.jp/en/kiyosumi/index.html; 3-3-9 Kiyosumi, Kōtō-ku; adult/child ¥150/free; Ⓣ9am-5pm; ⓈOedo line to Kiyosumi-Shirakawa, exit A3) One of Tokyo's most picturesque retreats, Kiyosumi-teien started out in 1721 as the villa of a *daimyō* (domain lord; regional lord under the shoguns). After the villa was destroyed in the 1923 earthquake, Iwasaki Yatarō, founder of the Mitsubishi Corporation, purchased the property. He used company ships to transport prize stones here from all over Japan, which are set around a pond ringed with Japanese black pine, hydrangeas and Taiwanese cherry trees.

★FUKAGAWA FUDŌ-DŌ   BUDDHIST TEMPLE

Map p287 (深川不動尊; ☑03-3630-7020; www.fukagawafudou.gr.jp; 1-17-13 Tomioka, Kōtō-ku; Ⓣ8am-6pm, to 8pm on festival days; ⓈOedo line to Monzen-Nakachō, exit 1) Belonging to the esoteric Shingon sect, this is very much an active temple where you can attend one of the city's most spectacular religious rituals. *Goma* (fire rituals) take place daily in an auditorium in the Hondō (Main Hall) at 9am, 11am, 1pm, 3pm and 5pm, plus 7pm on festival days (1st, 15th and 28th of each month). Sutras are chanted, giant *taiko* drums are pounded and flames are raised on the main altar as an offering to the deity.

At the end of the 30-minute ceremony, people line up to have their bags and other possessions passed over the dying flames as a blessing.

While here, don't miss the trippy **prayer corridor** with 9500 miniature Fudōmyō (a fierce-looking representation of Buddha's determination) crystal statues. Upstairs is also a beautifully decorated gallery (open until 4pm) depicting all 88 temples of the 1400km pilgrimage route on the island of Shikoku; it is said that offering a prayer at each alcove has the same effect as visiting each temple.

TOMIOKA HACHIMAN-GŪ SHINTO SHRINE
Map p287 (富岡八幡宮; ☎03-3642-1315; 1-20-3 Tomioka, Kōtō-ku; [S]Ōedo line to Monzen-Nakachō, exit 1) Founded in 1627, this shrine is famous as the birthplace of the sumo tournament. Around the back of the main building is the *yokozuna* stone, carved with the names of each of these champion wrestlers. Near the entrance are the two gilded, jewel-studded *mikoshi* (portable shrines), used in the Fukagawa Hachiman (p26) festival in mid-August; the larger one weighs 4.5 tonnes.

🍴 EATING

🍴 Asakusa & Oshiage

★ONIGIRI YADOROKU JAPANESE ¥
Map p286 (おにぎり 浅草 宿六; ☎03-3874-1615; http://onigiriyadoroku.com; 3-9-10 Asakusa, Taitō-ku; set lunch ¥660 & ¥900, onigiri ¥200-600; 🕒11.30am-5pm Mon-Sat, 6pm-2am Thu-Tue; [R]Tsukuba Express to Asakusa, exit 1) *Onigiri* (rice-ball snacks), usually wrapped in crispy sheets of *nori* (seaweed) are a great Japanese culinary invention and this humbly decorated and friendly place specialises in them. The set lunches, including a choice of two or three *onigiri*, are a great deal. At night there's a large range of flavours to choose from along with alcohol.

ROKURINSHA RAMEN ¥
Map p286 (六厘舎; www.rokurinsha.com; 6th fl, Solamachi, 1-1-2 Oshiage, Sumida-ku; ramen from ¥850; 🕒10.30am-11pm; [S]Hanzōmon line to Oshiage, exit B3) Rokurinsha's speciality is *tsukemen* – ramen noodles served on the side with a bowl of concentrated soup for dipping. The noodles here are thick and perfectly al dente and the soup has a rich *tonkotsu* (pork bone) base. It's an addictive combination that draws lines to this outpost in Tokyo Sky Tree Town.

KOMAGATA DOZEU JAPANESE ¥
Map p286 (駒形どぜう; ☎03-3842-4001; www.dozeu.com/en; 1-7-12 Komagata, Taitō-ku; mains from ¥1550; 🕒11am-9pm; [S]Ginza line to

ASAKUSA STREET FOOD

Asakusa is great for street food. Here are some local favourites:

Iriyama Sembei (入山煎餅; Map p286; 1-13-4 Asakusa, Taitō-ku; sembei from ¥130; 🕒10am-6pm Fri-Wed; [R]Tsukuba Express to Asakusa, exit 4) At this century-old shop you can watch *sembei* (flavoured rice crackers) being hand-toasted on charcoal grills. Get them hot as takeaway or packaged as souvenirs.

Hoppy-dōri (ホッピー通り; Map p286; 2-5 Asakusa, Taitō-ku; skewers from ¥120; [R]Tsukuba Express to Asakusa, exit 4) Along either side of the street popularly known as Hoppy-dōri – 'hoppy' is a cheap malt beverage – food vendors set out stools and tables for customers to nosh on cheap *yakitori* (skewers of grilled meat or vegetables) from noon until late.

Chōchin Monaka (ちょうちんもなか; Map p286; 2-3-1 Asakusa, Taitō-ku; ice cream ¥330; 🕒10am-5pm; [S]Ginza line to Asakusa, exit 1) Traditionally, *monaka* are wafers filled with sweet bean jam. At this little stand on Nakamise-dōri, they're filled with ice cream instead – in flavours such as *matcha* (powdered green tea) and *kuro-goma* (black sesame).

Neighbourhood Walk
Shitamachi Tour

START ASAKUSA STATION, EXIT 4
END EF
LENGTH 2.5KM; 2½ HOURS, PLUS LUNCH

This walk takes in the major sights in Asakusa, while giving you a feel for the flavour of Shitamachi (the old Edo-era 'Low City'). First head over to ❶**Azuma-bashi** (2 Kaminarimon, Taitō-ku). Originally built in 1774, it was once the point of departure for boat trips to the Yoshiwara pleasure district, north of Asakusa. From here you can get a good look at the golden flame of Super Dry Hall and the even more incongruent Tokyo Sky Tree, both across the river.

Retrace your steps to ❷**Kaminari-mon** (p161), the entrance to the grand temple complex ❸**Sensō-ji** (p161). Spend some time exploring the temple's highlights. Afterwards, walk past the nostalgic amusement park ❹**Hanayashiki** (p170), an Asakusa fixture since 1853.

Next take a detour up the covered arcade to the ❺**Edo Shitamachi Traditional**

Crafts Museum (p163), where you can see the work of local artisans. Then head down the lane called ❻**Hoppy-dōri** (p165), lined with *yakitori* stalls. Go on, have a few skewers and a beer.

Pop over to look at lantern-lit ❼**Asakusa Engei Hall** (p169), reminiscent of the vaudeville halls that were once common here. The theatre is part of the Rokku district of Asakusa, a famous (and famously bawdy) entertainment district during the century before WWII. Pay a visit to vintage store ❽**Tokyo Hotarudo** (p169), where the goods pay homage to this era, when Asakusa was thought of as the Montmartre of Tokyo.

If you resisted the charms of Hoppy-dōri you can have a meal at ❾**Daikokuya** (p167), an old-school tempura restaurant, along Dembō-in-dōri, a strip with crafty stores. Don't miss the centuries-old comb store ❿**Yonoya Kushiho** (p170).

Take one of the roads parallel to Nakamise – a world away from the tourist hordes – and finish up at ⓫**Ef** (p168), a cafe in a 19th-century wooden warehouse.

Asakusa, exits A2 & A4) Since 1801, Komagata Dozeu has been simmering and stewing *dojō* (Japanese loach, which looks something like a miniature eel). *Dojō-nabe* (loach hotpot), served here on individual *hibachi* (charcoal stoves), was a common dish in the days of Edo, but few restaurants serve it today. The open seating around wide, wooden planks heightens the traditional flavour. There are lanterns out front.

DAIKOKUYA   TEMPURA ¥

Map p286 (大黒家; ☏03-3844-1111; www.tempura.co.jp/english/index.html; 1-38-10 Asakusa, Taitō-ku; meals ¥1550-2100; ☉11am-8.30pm Sun-Fri, to 9pm Sat; ⓈGinza line to Asakusa, exit 1) Near Nakamise-dōri, this is the place to get old-fashioned tempura fried in pure sesame oil, an Asakusa speciality. It's in a white building with a tile roof. If there's a queue (and there often is), you can try your luck at the annexe one block over, where they also serve set-course meals.

SOMETARŌ   OKONOMIYAKI ¥

Map p286 (染太郎; ☏03-3844-9502; 2-2-2 Nishi-Asakusa, Taitō-ku; mains from ¥650; ☉noon-10pm; ⓈGinza line to Tawaramachi, exit 3) Sometarō is a fun and funky place to try *okonomiyaki* (savoury Japanese-style pancakes filled with meat, seafood and vegetables that you cook yourself). This historic, vine-covered house is a friendly spot where the menu includes a how-to guide for novice cooks.

★OTAFUKU   JAPANESE ¥¥

Map p286 (大多福; ☏03-3871-2521; www.otafuku.ne.jp; 1-6-2 Senzoku, Taitō-ku; oden ¥110-550; ☉5-11pm Tue-Sat, to 10pm Sun; ⓇTsukuba Express to Asakusa, exit 1) Over a century old, Otafuku specialises in *oden* (a classic Japanese stew). It's simmered at the counter and diners pick what they want from the pot. You can dine cheaply on radishes and kelp, or splash out on scallops and tuna or a full-course menu for ¥5400 – whichever way you go, you get to soak up Otafuku's convivial, old-time atmosphere.

Look for a shack-like entrance and lantern on the northern side of Kototoi-dōri.

ASAKUSA UNAGI SANSHO   JAPANESE ¥¥

Map p286 (浅草 うなぎ さんしょ; ☏03-3843-0344; 2-25-7 Nishi-Asakusa, Taitō-ku; eel ¥2700-4300; ☉11.30am-2pm & 4-8pm Fri-Wed; ⓇTsukuba Express to Asakusa, exit 4) At this superfriendly and simple *unagi* (eel) restaurant the grilled eel is served in three different

KAPPABASHI KITCHENWARE TOWN

Kappabashi-dōri (合羽橋通り; Map p286; ⓈGinza line to Tawaramachi, exit 3) is the country's largest wholesale restaurant-supply and kitchenware district. Gourmet accessories include bamboo steamer baskets, lacquer trays, neon signs and *chōchin* (paper lanterns). It's also where restaurants get their freakishly realistic plastic food models. **Ganso Shokuhin Sample-ya** (元祖食品サンプル屋; Map p286; ☏0120-17-1839; www.ganso-sample.com; 3-7-6 Nishi-Asakusa, Taitō-ku; ☉10am-5.30pm; ⓈGinza line to Tawaramachi, exit 3) has a showroom of tongue-in-cheek ones, plus key chains and kits to make your own.

sizes: only go for large if you're *really* hungry. On the walls hang detailed traditional embroidery done by the mum, while the dad cooks the eels to perfection.

★ASAKUSA IMAHAN   JAPANESE ¥¥¥

Map p286 (浅草今半; ☏03-3841-1114; www.asakusaimahan.co.jp; 3-1-12 Nishi-Asakusa, Taitō-ku; lunch/dinner set menu from ¥3800/10,000; ☉11.30am-9.30pm; ⓇTsukuba Express to Asakusa, exit 4) For a meal to remember, swing by this famous beef restaurant, in business since 1895. Choose between courses of sukiyaki (sauteed beef dipped in raw egg) and *shabu-shabu* (beef blanched in broth); prices rise according to the grade of meat. For diners on a budget, Imahan sells a limited number of cheaper lunch sets (from ¥1500).

✕ Ryōgoku, Kiyosumi & Shirakawa

KINTAME   JAPANESE ¥

Map p287 (近為; ☏03-3641-2740; www.kintame.co.jp; 1-14-5 Tomioka, Kōtō-ku; meals from ¥1390; ☉11am-5pm Tue-Sun; ⓈŌedo line to Monzen-Nakachō, exit 1) This branch of the famous Kyoto-based pickle shop provides tastings of its traditional preserves done in a variety of ways, including with salt, vinegar miso and soy sauce. At a communal table you can also try its filling and good-value meals of fish marinated in sake lees (the deposits produced during the alcohol's fermentation).

At the end of the shopping street leading to Fukagawa Fudō-dō (p164), it's a good place for lunch when visiting the temple.

⭐**KAPPŌ YOSHIBA**   JAPANESE ¥¥
(割烹吉葉; ☏03-3623-4480; www.kapou-yoshiba.jp/english/index.html; 2-14-5 Yokoami, Sumida-ku; dishes ¥600-6600; ⊙11.30am-2pm & 5-10pm Mon-Sat; 🚇Ōedo line to Ryōgoku Station, exit 1) The former Miyagino sumo stable is the location for this one-of-a-kind restaurant that has preserved the *dōyo* (practice ring) as its centrepiece. Playing up to its sumo roots, you can order the protein-packed stew *chanko-nabe* (for two people from ¥4600), but Yoshiba's real strength is its sushi, which is freshly prepared in jumbo portions.

DRINKING & NIGHTLIFE

⭐**CAFÉ OTONOVA**   CAFE
Map p286 (カフェ・オトノヴァ; ☏03-5830-7663; www.cafeotonova.net/#3eme; 3-10-4 Nishi-Asakusa; ⊙noon-11pm, to 9pm Sun; 🚇) Tucked away on an alley running parallel to Kappabashi-dōri (p167), this charming cafe occupies an old house. Exposed beams are whitewashed and an atrium has been created, with cosy booths upstairs and a big communal table downstairs in front of the DJ booth. It's a stylish cafe by day and a romantic bolthole for drinks at night, with no table charge.

⭐**POPEYE**   PUB
Map p287 (ポパイ; ☏03-3633-2120; www.40beersontap.com; 2-18-7 Ryōgoku, Sumida-ku; ⊙11.30am-4pm & 5-11pm Mon-Sat; 🚃JR Sōbu line to Ryōgoku, west exit) Popeye boasts an astounding 70 beers on tap, including the world's largest selection of Japanese beers – from Echigo Weizen to Hitachino Nest Espresso Stout. The happy-hour deal (5pm to 8pm) offers select brews with free plates of pizza, sausages and other munchables. It's extremely popular and fills up fast; get here early to grab a seat. From the station's west exit, take a left on the main road and pass under the tracks; take the second left and look for Popeye on the right.

'CUZN HOMEGROUND   BAR
Map p286 (www.homeground.jpn.com; 2-17-9 Asakusa, Taitō-ku; beer ¥800; ⊙11am-6am; 🛜; 🚇Ginza line to Tawaramachi, exit 3) Run by a wild gang of local hippies, 'Cuzn is the kind of bar where anything can happen: a barbecue, a jam session or all-night karaoke, for example.

EF   CAFE
Map p286 (エフ; ☏03-3841-0442; www.gallery-ef.com; 2-19-18 Kaminari-mon, Taitō-ku; coffee ¥550; ⊙11am-midnight Mon, Wed, Thu & Sat, to 2am Fri, to 10pm Sun; 🚇Ginza line to Asakusa, exit 2) Set in a 19th-century wooden warehouse that beat the 1923 earthquake and WWII, this wonderfully cosy space serves coffee, tea and, after 6pm, cocktails and beer. Be sure to check out the gallery in the stone *kura* (storeroom) out back.

KAMIYA BAR   BAR
Map p286 (神谷バー; ☏03-3841-5400; www.kamiya-bar.com; 1-1-1 Asakusa, Taitō-ku; ⊙11.30am-10pm Wed-Mon; 🚇Ginza line to Asakusa, exit 3) One of Tokyo's oldest Western-style bars, Kamiya opened in 1880 and is still hugely popular – though probably more so today for its enormous, cheap draught beer (¥1050 for a litre). Its real speciality, however, is Denki Bran (¥270), a herbal liquor that's been produced in-house for more than a century. Order at the counter, then give your tickets to the server.

ASAHI SKY ROOM   BAR
Map p286 (アサヒスカイルーム; ☏03-5608-5277; http://r.gnavi.co.jp/a170900/menu10; 22F, Asahi Super Dry Bldg, 1-23-1 Azuma-bashi, Sumida-ku; beer ¥720; ⊙10am-9pm; 🚇Ginza line to Asakusa, exit 4) Spend the day at the religious sites and end at the Asahi altar, on the 22nd floor of the golden-tinged Asahi Super Dry Building. The venue itself isn't noteworthy, but the views over the Sumida River are spectacular, especially at sunset.

☆ ENTERTAINMENT

⭐**RYŌGOKU KOKUGIKAN**   SPECTATOR SPORT
Map p287 (両国国技館; Ryōgoku Sumo Stadium; ☏03-3623-5111; www.sumo.or.jp; 1-3-28 Yokoami, Sumida-ku; ¥2200-14,800; 🚃JR Sōbu line to Ryōgoku, west exit) If you're in town when a tournament is on – for 15 days each January, May and September – catch the big boys in action at Japan's largest sumo stadium. Doors open at 8am, but the action doesn't heat up until the senior wrestlers hit the ring around 2pm. Tickets can be bought online one month before the start of the tournament.

Around 200 general-admission tickets are sold on the day of the match from the box office in front of the stadium. You'll have to line up very early (say 6am) on the last couple of days of the tournament to snag one.

If you get there in the morning when the stadium is still pretty empty, you can usually sneak down to the box seats. You can rent a radio (¥100 fee, plus ¥2000 deposit) to listen to commentary in English. Stop by the basement banquet hall to sample *chanko-nabe* (the protein-rich stew eaten by the wrestlers) for just ¥300 a bowl.

OIWAKE   TRADITIONAL MUSIC
Map p286 (追分; ☑03-3844-6283; www.oiwake. info; 3-28-11 Nishi-Asakusa, Taitō-ku; admission ¥2000 plus 1 food item & 1 drink; ⏰5.30pm-midnight; ℝTsukuba Express to Asakusa, exit 1) Oiwake is one of Tokyo's few *minyō izakaya*, pubs where traditional folk music is performed. It's a homey place, where the waitstaff and the musicians – who play *tsugaru-jamisen* (a banjo-like instrument), hand drums and bamboo flute – are one and the same. Sets start at 7pm and 9pm; children are welcome for the early show. Seating is on tatami.

ASAKUSA ENGEI HALL   COMEDY
Map p286 (浅草演芸ホール; ☑03-3841-6545; www.asakusaengei.com; 1-43-12 Asakusa, Taitō-ku; adult/student ¥2800/2300; ⏰shows 11.40am-4.30pm & 4.40-9pm; ⓢGinza line to Tawaramachi, exit 3) Asakusa was once full of theatres like this one, where traditional *rakugo* (comedic monologues) and other forms of comedy are performed. There are also jugglers, magicians and the like. It's all in Japanese, but the linguistic confusion is mitigated by lively facial expressions and props, which help translate comic takes on universal human experiences.

🛍 SHOPPING

★MARUGOTO NIPPON   FOOD & DRINKS
Map p286 (まるごとにっぽん; ☑03-3845-0510; www.marugotonippon.com; 2-6-7 Asakusa, Taitō-ku; ⏰10am-8pm; ⓢGinza line to Tawaramachi, exit 3) Think of this as a modern mini department store, showcasing the best of Japan's best in terms of speciality food and drink (ground floor) and arts and crafts (2nd floor). There are also plenty of tasting samples, and cafes and restaurants on the 3rd and 4th floors should you want something more substantial.

★TOKYO HOTARUDO   VINTAGE
Map p286 (東京蛍堂; ☑03-3845-7563; http://tokyohotarudo.com; 1-41-8 Asakusa, Taitō-ku; ⏰11am-8pm Wed-Sun; ℝTsukuba Express to Asakusa, exit 5) This curio shop is run by an eccentric young man who prefers to dress as if the 20th century hasn't come and gone already. If you think that sounds marvellous, then you'll want to check out his collection of vintage dresses and bags, antique lamps, watches and decorative *objet*.

The entrance is tricky: look for a vertical black sign with a pointing finger.

KURAMAE'S CRAFTSHOPS

A short walk south of Asakusa and beside the Sumida-gawa is Tokyo's old rice granary district of Kuramae (蔵前). The low rents and ingrained culture of craftsmanship here have inspired a new generation of entrepreneurs to make traditional crafts but with a contemporary twist. As it eschews the flash of other Tokyo shopping districts, an amble around the small boutiques and ateliers here is a pleasure. Start with **Koncent** (☑03-3862-6018; www.koncent.net; 2-4-5 Kuramae, Taitō-ku; ⏰11am-7pm; ⓢAsakusa line to Kuramae, exit A3), a trendy homewares and gift boutique on Edo-dōri, stocking mainly Japanese design products. It serves coffee and produces a detailed, free map (in Japanese) that covers many of the area's interesting businesses. Move on to Kokusai-dōri to shop for customised notebooks and other stationery at **Kakimori** (カキモリ; ☑03-3864-3898; www.kakimori.com; 4-20-12 Kuramae, Taitō-ku; ⓢAsakusa line to Kuramae, exit 3); naturally dyed clothing and accessories at **Maito** (マイト; ☑03-3863-1128; www.maito.info; 4-14-2 Kuramae, Taitō-ku; ⓢAsakusa line to Kuramae, exit A3); and lovely leather goods at **Camera** (☑03-5825-4170; http://camera1010.tokyo; 4-21-8 Kuramae, Taitō-ku; ⏰11am-6pm Tue-Sun; ⓢAsakusa line to Kuramae, exit A3), where you can also have something to drink and eat.

KURODAYA
STATIONERY

Map p286 (黒田屋; ☎03-3844-7511; 1-2-5 Asakusa, Taitō-ku; ⏰10am-6pm; ⒮Ginza line to Asakusa, exit 3) Since 1856, Kurodaya has been specialising in *washi* (traditional Japanese paper) and products made from paper such as cards, kites and papier-mâché folk-art figures. It sells its own designs and many others from across Japan.

YONOYA KUSHIHO
FASHION & ACCESSORIES

Map p286 (よのや櫛舗; 1-37-10 Asakusa, Taitō-ku; ⏰10.30am-6pm Thu-Tue; ⒮Ginza line to Asakusa, exit 1) Even in a neighbourhood where old is not out of place, Yonoya Kushiho stands out: this little shop has been selling handmade boxwood combs since 1717. Yonoya also sells old-fashioned hair ornaments (worn with the elaborate up-dos of courtesans in the past) and modern trinkets.

FUJIYA
ARTS & CRAFTS

Map p286 (ふじ屋; ☎03-3841-2283; www.asakusa-noren.ne.jp/tenugui-fujiya/sp.html; 2-2-15 Asakusa, Taitō-ku; ⏰10am-6pm Wed-Mon; ⒮Ginza line to Asakusa, exit 1) Fujiya specialises in *tenugui:* dyed cloths of thin cotton that can be used as tea towels, handkerchiefs, gift wrapping (the list goes on – they're surprisingly versatile). Here they come in traditional designs and humorous modern ones.

BENGARA
ARTS & CRAFTS

Map p286 (べんがら; ☎03-3841-6613; www.bengara.com; 1-35-6 Asakusa, Taitō-ku; ⏰10am-6pm Mon-Fri, to 7pm Sat & Sun, closed 3rd Thu of month; ⒮Ginza line to Asakusa, exit 1) *Noren* are the curtains that hang in front of shop doors. This store sells beautiful ones, made of linen and coloured with natural dyes (such as indigo or persimmon) or decorated with ink-brush paintings. There are smaller items too, such as pouches and book covers, made of traditional textiles.

🏃 ACTIVITIES

★ WANARIYA
TRADITIONAL CRAFT

Map p286 (和なり屋; ☎03-5603-9169; www.wanariya.jp; 1-8-10 Senzoku, Taitō-ku; indigo dyeing/weaving from ¥1920/1980; ⏰10am-5pm Thu-Tue; ⒮Hibiya line to Iriya, exit 1) A team of young and friendly Japanese runs this indigo dyeing and traditional handloom-weaving workshop where you can learn the crafts and have a go yourself in under an hour or so. It's a fantastic way to make your own unique souvenir, with a whole range of items you can dye, from *tenugui* (thin cotton towels) to canvas sneakers.

★ MOKUHANKAN
TRADITIONAL CRAFT

Map p286 (木版館; ☎070-5011-1418; http://mokuhankan.com/parties; 2nd fl, 1-41-8 Asakusa, Taitō-ku; per person ¥2000; ⏰10am-5.30pm Wed-Mon; ⒭Tsukuba Express to Asakusa, exit 5) Try your hand at making *ukiyo-e* (woodblock prints) at this studio run by expat David Bull. Hour-long 'print parties' are great fun and take place daily; sign up online. There's a shop here too, where you can see Bull's and Jed Henry's humorous *Ukiyo-e Heroes* series – prints featuring video-game characters in traditional settings.

TOKYO KITCHEN
COOKING

Map p286 (☎090-9104-4329; www.asakusa-tokyokitchen.com; 502 Ayumi Bldg, 1-11-3 Hanakawa-do, Taitō-ku; course from ¥7560; ⒮Ginza line to Asakusa, exit 4A) English-speaking Yoshimi is an Asakusa-based cook who teaches small groups of visitors how to make a range of Japanese dishes. Her menu list is broad and includes mosaic sushi rolls, tempura, ramen and *gyōza*. Vegetarians and those with gluten intolerance are catered for too. Yoshimi will also meet you at the subway exit and guide you to her kitchen.

JAKOTSU-YU
BATHHOUSE

Map p286 (蛇骨湯; ☎03-3841-8645; www.jakotsuyu.co.jp; 1-11-11 Asakusa, Taitō-ku; adult/child ¥460/180; ⏰1pm-midnight Wed-Mon; ⒮Ginza line to Tawaramachi, exit 3) Unlike most *sentō* (public baths), the tubs here are filled with pure hot-spring water, naturally the colour of weak tea. Another treat is the lovely, lantern-lit, rock-framed *rotemburo* (outdoor bath). Jakotsu-yu is a welcoming place; it has English signage and doesn't have a policy against tattoos. It's an extra ¥200 for the sauna, ¥140 for a small towel.

HANAYASHIKI
AMUSEMENT PARK

Map p286 (花やしき; ☎03-3842-8780; www.hanayashiki.net/index.html; 2-28-1 Asakusa, Taitō-ku; adult/child ¥1000/500; ⏰10am-6pm; ⒮Ginza line to Asakusa, exit 1) Japan's oldest amusement park has creaky old carnival rides and heaps of vintage charm. Once you're inside, you can buy tickets for rides (which cost a few hundred yen each). A haunted-house attraction here allegedly housed a real ghost that is said to still appear on the grounds.

Ōdaiba & Tokyo Bay

ŌDAIBA | TENNŌZU ISLE

Neighbourhood Top Five

1 **Ōdaiba Kaihin-kōen** (p173) Seeing Tokyo's glittering waterfront and the lantern-festooned pleasure boats gliding languidly across the water from this seaside promenade.

2 **Ōedo Onsen Monogatari** (p173) Soaking in some honest-to-goodness natural hot springs (and experienc-

ing an onsen theme park) right here on the bay.

3 **National Museum of Emerging Science & Innovation** (p173) Meeting the robots of the future at this museum of cutting-edge technology.

4 **Archi-Depot** (p174) Getting an up-close look at more than 100 works by

leading Japanese architects – all in one room, at this museum for architectural models.

5 **Bay Cruises** (p175) Gliding atop Tokyo Bay on a traditional flat-bottomed boat *(yakatabune)* or on the manga-inspired party cruise ship, Jicoo the Floating Bar.

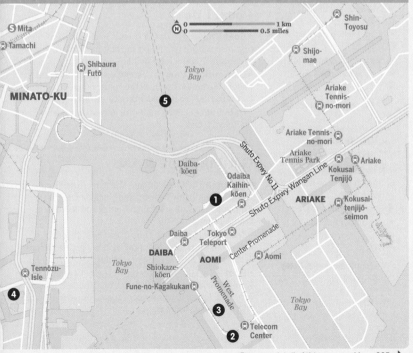

For more detail of this area see Map p265 ➡

Lonely Planet's Top Tip

One of the most exhilarating (if not mildly terrifying) ways to experience Odaiba is by driving a go-kart over Rainbow Bridge. If you want to sign up for a tour with Maricar (p175), you must have a valid international driver's license – which you'll need to acquire from your home country.

Best Places to Eat

➡ TY Harbor Brewery (p174)

➡ Bills (p174)

➡ Hibiki (p174)

For reviews, see p174.➡

Best Views

➡ Odaiba Kaihin-kōen (p173)

➡ Jicoo the Floating Bar (p175)

➡ Fuji TV Building (p174)

➡ Yurikamome line (p175)

➡ Dai-kanransha (p176)

For reviews, see p173.➡

Best for Kids

➡ National Museum of Emerging Science & Innovation (p173)

➡ Tokyo Joypolis (p176)

➡ Mega Web (p173)

➡ Tokyo Disney Resort (p176)

For reviews, see p173.➡

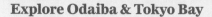

Explore Odaiba & Tokyo Bay

In central Tokyo, it's easy to forget that the city started as a seaside town. Not so on Odaiba, a collection of artificial islands on Tokyo Bay tethered to the mainland by the 798m Rainbow Bridge. Visit in the evening for romantic twinkling views of the city skyline. The bay can also be appreciated from the water on pleasure cruises.

Odaiba, largely developed in the 1990s, is an alternative vision of Tokyo; one with buildings on a grand scale, broad streets, spacious parks and waterfront views – even a beach! There are major attractions here, such as Ōedo Onsen Monogatari (p173) and the National Museum of Emerging Science & Innovation (p173); both can easily take up a half-day. Tokyo's youngsters and families can't get enough of Odaiba's several malls, with masses of chain stores, restaurants and amusements under one roof. They're less interesting for foreign tourists; however, if you're travelling with kids, these all-in-one complexes can be excellent on rainy days.

Tennōzu Isle, historically a warehouse district, offers a different vibe, with the new Archi-Depot museum, galleries, street art and canalside eateries. Several of the new sites for the 2020 Summer Olympics will be also be on Tokyo Bay; the new fish market will be in Toyosu, should the move from Tsukiji go ahead.

Local Life

➡**Boat Cruises** Groups of friends and colleagues organise private parties on the bay, particularly during the summer and winter holidays.

➡**Conventions** Crowds descend on Tokyo Big Sight for major conventions such as the comic market Comiket (www.comiket.co.jp) and Tokyo Game Show.

➡**Date Spot** Odaiba's malls are classic date destinations for Tokyo teens.

Getting There & Away

➡**Monorail** The Yurikamome line runs from Shimbashi through Odaiba to Toyosu; stops include Odaiba Kaihin-kōen, Daiba, Telecom Center and Kokusai-tenjijō-seimon.

➡**Train** The Rinkai line runs from Ōsaki through Odaiba to Shin-Kiba, stopping at Tennōzu Isle, Tokyo Teleport and Kokusai-tenjijō stations.

➡**Boat** Tokyo Cruise water buses run between Odaiba Kaihin-kōen (Odaiba Seaside Park), Hinode Pier and Asakusa. A shorter, infrequent route connects Palette Town and Tokyo Big Sight.

SIGHTS

✪ Odaiba

★ NATIONAL MUSEUM OF EMERGING SCIENCE & INNOVATION (MIRAIKAN)   MUSEUM

Map p265 (未来館; www.miraikan.jst.go.jp; 2-3-6 Aomi, Kōtō-ku; adult/child ¥620/210; ◷10am-5pm Wed-Mon; 🐾; ℝYurikamome line to Telecom Center) *Miraikan* means 'hall of the future', and exhibits here present the science and technology that will (possibly!) shape the years to come. Lots of hands-on displays make this a great place for kids, while a new multilingual smartphone app makes a game out of visiting. Don't miss the demonstrations of humanoid robot ASIMO and the lifelike android Otonaroid. The Gaia dome theatre/planetarium (adult/child ¥300/100) has an English audio option and is popular; book online one week in advance.

ODAIBA KAIHIN-KŌEN   PARK

Map p265 (お台場海浜公園; Odaiba Marine Park; http://www.tptc.co.jp/en/c_park/01_02; 1-4-1 Daiba, Minato-ku; ◷24hr; ℝYurikamome line to Odaiba Kaihin-kōen) One of the best views of Tokyo is from this park's promenades and elevated walkways – especially at night when old-fashioned *yakatabune* (low-slung wooden pleasure boats), decorated with lanterns, traverse the bay. Also here you'll find an 800m-long artificial **beach** and an 11m replica of the **Statue of Liberty**, plus plenty of teens and students kicking around.

CHIHIRAJUNCO   ROBOT

Map p265 (地平ジュンこ; 3rd fl, Aqua City, 1-7-1 Daiba, Minato-ku; ◷11am-9pm; ℝYurikamome line to Odaiba Kaihin-kōen) FREE The future is here. Maybe. ChihiraJunco is a demure lady android created by Toshiba who has her own information counter adjacent to the people-staffed information counter at the Aqua City shopping mall. At the time of research, she was not (yet?) able to answer spoken questions; however, she does answer questions entered into the touch panel – in Japanese, English or Chinese.

MEGA WEB   SHOWROOM

Map p265 (メガウェブ; ☎03-3599-0808; www.megaweb.gr.jp; Palette Town, 1-3-12 Aomi, Kōtō-ku; ◷11am-9pm; ℝYurikamome line to Aomi) FREE The highlight of visiting this Toyota

---

👁 TOP SIGHT
ŌEDO ONSEN MONOGATARI

Just to experience the truly Japanese phenomenon that is an amusement park centred on bathing is reason enough to visit. The baths here are filled with real hot-spring water, pumped from 1400m below Tokyo Bay. It's touristy, yes, but for visitors making their first foray into Japanese-style communal bathing, the light and kitschy atmosphere makes the actual bathing part much less intimidating.

Upon entering, visitors change into colourful *yukata* (light cotton kimonos) to wear while they stroll around the complex, which is a lantern-lit re-creation of an old Tokyo downtown area, with food stalls and carnival games. There's a huge variety of baths here, including jet baths, pools of natural rock and, on the ladies' side, personal bucket-shaped baths made of cedar. These are segregated by gender, but there's also a communal outdoor foot bath, set in a garden, where mixed groups and families can hang out together (the town area is also communal).

Come after 6pm for a ¥500 discount. Visitors with tattoos will be denied admission. You can also crash here overnight, sleeping on reclining chairs in the lounge, bathing at whim if you want to dig deep into the onsen experience; there's a surcharge of ¥2000 per person if you stay between 2am and 5am.

➔ 大江戸温泉物語
➔ Map p265, B4
➔ www.ooedoonsen.jp
➔ 2-6-3 Aomi, Kōtō-ku
➔ adult/child ¥2280/980, surcharge Sat & Sun ¥200
➔ ◷11am-9am, last entry 7am
➔ ℝYurikamome line to Telecom Center, Rinkai line to Tokyo Teleport with free shuttle bus

showroom is getting to try out prototypes of the car company's Segway-like personal mobility device, Winglet. English instruction takes place daily from 2pm to 3pm. Riders must be over 140cm. Littler ones can practise driving (very slowly in a very controlled environment) tiny Lexus convertibles at the **Ride Studio** (11am to 6.15pm; rides ¥200 to ¥300).

Map p265 (フジテレビ; ☑0180-993-188; 2-4-8 Daiba, Minato-ku; adult/child ¥550/300; ⊘Tue-Sun 10am-6pm; ㉠Yurikamome line to Daiba) Designed by the late, great Kenzō Tange, the Fuji TV headquarters building is easily recognisable by the 1200-tonne orb suspended from the scaffolding-like structure. It's free to take the escalators up to the 7th floor; admission is for the observatories inside the orb.

⊙ Tennōzu Isle

★ARCHI-DEPOT   GALLERY
Map p265 (建築倉庫; Kenchiku Sōko; ☑03-5769-2133; http://archi-depot.com; Warehouse Terrada, 2-6-10 Higashi-Shinagawa, Shinagawa-ku; adult/child ¥1000/500; ⊘11am-9pm Tue-Sun; ㉠Rinkai line to Tennōzu Isle, exit B) This is brilliant: a facility that lets architects store the miniature models they make to conceptualise buildings (thus preserving them) and the public to see them up close. Many of the big names of Japanese architecture are represented here (Ban Shigero, Kuma Kengo). It looks very much like a storage room too, with the models sitting on rows of metal shelves (and not behind glass). Information about the architects can be accessed through QR codes.

NEW TOYOSU MARKET

The Tokyo Metropolitan Government has been planning to move Tsukiji Market to a new facility in Toyosu, one of Tokyo Bay's artificial islands, for years. The new structure, called **Toyosu Market** (豊洲市場), was ready to go – when it was discovered that officials in charge had cut corners on work to decontaminate the land (where a gas refinery once stood). The move was halted, and plans were still suspended, awaiting review, at the time of research.

TERRADA ART COMPLEX   GALLERY
Map p265 (http://art.terrada.co.jp; 3rd fl, 1-33-10 Higashi-Shinagawa, Shinagawa-ku; ⊘11am-6pm Tue-Thu & Sat, to 8pm Fri; ㉠Rinkai line to Tennōzu Isle, exit B) Part of the fashioning of the Tennōzu Isle warehouse district, this new art space contains five contemporary galleries – Kodama Gallery, Urano, Yamamoto Gendai, and Yuka Tsuruno Gallery – relocated under one roof from other parts of the city. It's on the 3rd floor of a charcoal-grey warehouse; look for the English sign by the elevator.

✗ EATING

BILLS   INTERNATIONAL ¥
Map p265 (ビルズ; www.bills-jp.net; 3rd fl, Seaside Mall, DECKS Tokyo Beach, 1-6-1 Daiba, Minato-ku; mains from ¥1400; ⊘9am-10pm Mon-Fri, 8am-10pm Sat & Sun; 🛜📶; ㉠Yurikamome line to Odaiba Kaihin-kōen) Australian chef Bill Granger has had a big hit with his restaurant chain in Japan – unsurprising given how inviting and spacious a place this is. The menu includes his classics such as ricotta hotcakes, and lunch and dinner mains such as *wagyū* burgers. The terrace also has great bay views.

ODAIBA TAKOYAKI MUSEUM   JAPANESE ¥
Map p265 (お台場たこ焼きミュージアム; 4th fl, Seaside Mall, DECKS Tokyo Beach, 1-6-1 Daiba, Minato-ku; takoyaki from ¥420; ⊘11am-9pm; ㉠Yurikamome line to Odaiba Kaihin-kōen) Seven different stalls dish up variations on the classic fried batter and octopus balls usually served from street stalls at festivals and events.

TY HARBOR BREWERY   AMERICAN ¥¥
Map p265 (☑03-5479-4555; www.tyharborbrewing.co.jp; 2-1-3 Higashi-Shinagawa, Shinagawa-ku; lunch set meal ¥1200-1700, dinner mains from ¥1700; ⊘11.30am-2pm & 5.30-10pm; ⓈRinkai line to Tennōzu Isle, exit B) In a former warehouse on the waterfront, TY Harbor serves up excellent burgers, steaks and crab cakes and offers views of the canals around Tennōzu Isle. It also brews its own beer on the premises and is a favourite brunch spot for expats. Call ahead to book a seat on the terrace.

HIBIKI   JAPANESE ¥¥
Map p265 (響; ☑03-3599-5500; www.dynacjapan.com/hibiki; 6th fl, Aqua City, 1-7-1 Daiba, Minato-ku; lunch set menu ¥1000-2000, dishes ¥650-2700; ⊘11am-3pm & 5-11pm; ㉠Yurika-

mome line to Daiba, south exit) Hibiki has glittering views across the bay, and a menu featuring seasonal dishes, hearty grilled meats and fresh tofu along with *sake* and *shōchū* (strong distilled alcohol often made from potatoes). The lunch set is a good deal and includes a small salad bar; choose your main dish from the samples out the front. There's a ¥550 seating charge at dinner.

DRINKING & NIGHTLIFE

JICOO THE FLOATING BAR · COCKTAIL BAR
Map p265 (ジークザフローティングバー; ☎0120-049-490; www.jicoofloatingbar.com; cover from ¥2600; ⊙8-10.30pm Thu-Sat; ⒭Yurikamome line to Hinode or Odaiba Kaihin-kōen) For a few nights a week, the futuristic cruise-boat Himiko, designed by manga and anime artist Leiji Matsumoto, morphs into this floating bar. Board on the hour at Hinode pier and the half-hour at Odaiba Kaihin-kōen. The evening-long 'floating pass' usually includes live music; check the schedule online.

AGEHA · CLUB
(アゲハ; www.ageha.com; 2-2-10 Shin-Kiba, Kōtō-ku; cover ¥2500-4000; ⊙11pm-5am Fri & Sat; ⒮Yūrakuchō line to Shin-Kiba, main exit) This gigantic waterside club, the largest in Tokyo, rivals any you'd find in LA or Ibiza. Top international and Japanese DJs appear here. Free buses run between the club and a bus stop on the east side of Shibuya Station (on Roppongi-dōri) all night. Events vary widely; check the website for details and bring photo ID.

SHOPPING

★PIGMENT · ARTS & CRAFTS
Map p265 (☎03-5781-9550; https://pigment. tokyo; Terrada Harbor One Bldg., 2-5-5 Higashi-Shinagawa, Shinagawa-ku; ⊙11am-8pm, closed Mon & Thu; ⒭Rinkai line to Tennōzu Isle, exit B) This is an art supply store to make you go weak in the knees: the walls are lined with vials of pigments – including the crushed mineral pigments used in traditional Japanese painting – in shades from vermilion to *matcha* (green tea). There are drawers of brushes, rolls of *washi* (Japanese paper) and displays of weighty ink stones.

ⓘ **GETTING AROUND ODAIBA**

Odaiba has a vastness that fools you after a few days in central Tokyo. While it is walkable, there can be some long slogs. The automated (driverless) Yurikamome line monorail runs around Odaiba, connecting the artificial islands to 'mainland' Tokyo. While principally a means of getting around, the ride itself is a treat: from Shimbashi (the central Tokyo terminus) the elevated tracks wend in-between skyscrapers before doing a loop to reach Rainbow Bridge, which it then takes over the waters to Odaiba. Fares are from ¥190 to ¥360; a one-day pass costs ¥820/¥410 per adult/child. Alternatively, there's Kōtō-ku's **bike sharing scheme** (☎customer support 0120-116-819; http://docomo-cycle.jp/koto; per day ¥1500). It's a little tricky to work out (sign up for membership in advance), but your effort is rewarded with access to nifty electric-hybrid bicycles for zipping around Odaiba's wide, flat streets.

STRANGE LOVE · ANTIQUES
Map p265 (ストレンジラブ; www.strangelove. co.jp; 2nd fl, Venus Fort, 1-3-15 Aomi, Kōtō-ku; ⊙11am-9pm; ⒭Yurikamome line to Aomi) Ding the ship's bell to gain access to this warehouse-like antiques and curio store, stocking items for those with adult or macabre tastes.

🏃 SPORTS & ACTIVITIES

ŌEDO ONSEN MONOGATARI · ONSEN
See p173.

MARICAR · SCENIC DRIVE
Map p265 (マリカー; ☎080-9999-2525, 0120-81-9999; http://maricar.jp; 1-23-15 Kita-Shinagawa, Shinagawa-ku; per person from ¥3500; ⒭Keikyū line to Kita-Shinagawa) We're not sure how this is legal (and Nintendo has had words to say about copyright infringement), but at the time of writing it still is: go-karting on the streets of Tokyo dressed as your favourite Mario Kart character. It brings the idea of Tokyo as a real-life video game experience to a whole new level. You must, however, have a valid international (or Japanese) driver's license.

The operation feels a little slap-dash and there's no practising on the go-karts, which

YAKATABUNE BAY CRUISES

Those low-slung wooden boats out on the bay, bedecked with lanterns, are *yakatabune* and they've been a Tokyo tradition since the days of Edo. They're usually used for private parties, which typically include all-you-can-eat-and-drink banquets and karaoke.

Usually they are chartered affairs (requiring groups of 15 or more); however, **Tsukishima Monja Yakatabune** (月島もんじゃ屋形船; ☎03-3533-6699; www.4900yen.com; 2-6-3 Shin-Kiba, Kōtō-ku; per person from ¥5000; [S]Yūrakuchō line to Shin-Kiba, main exit) accepts bookings for as few as two people, to join shared cruises. The two-hour (day or night) cruise includes free-flowing beer and all-you-can-eat *monja-yaki* (a savoury, scrambled batter-style dish and Tokyo speciality). The departure point is far-flung Shin-Kiba pier, a short (and free) shuttle-bus ride from Shin-Kiba Station.

More upscale **Funasei** (船清; Map p265; ☎03-5479-2731; www.funasei.com; 1-16-8 Kita-Shinagawa, Shinagawa-ku; per person ¥10,800; 🚉Keikyū line to Kita-Shinagawa), a charter company, also runs shared cruises several times a month, which you can book if you have at least two people. Their 2½-hour cruises come with sashimi and tempura dinners and all-you-can-drink beer and sake. There's a schedule of departures on the website (in Japanese).

Reservations are essential for both, and you'll need a Japanese speaker to help you book. There's also the option to take the modern-day booze cruise that is Jicoo the Floating Bar (p175) – no reservation required.

can be tricky at first, before you're on the road with trucks and buses, so absolutely speak up if you're not comfortable; one of the English-speaking guides will hang back with you, or re-route the course. While daytime is best for snapping photos, the night course over the Rainbow Bridge across Tokyo Bay to Odaiba wins for sheer thrill.

TOKYO DISNEY RESORT AMUSEMENT PARK

(東京ディズニーリゾート; ☎domestic calls 0570-00-8632, from overseas +81-45-330-5211; www.tokyodisneyresort.co.jp; 1-1 Maihama, Urayasu-shi, Chiba-ken; 1-day ticket for 1 park adult/child ¥7400/4800, after 6pm ¥4200; 🕒varies by season; 🚉JR Keiyō line to Maihama) Here you'll find not only Tokyo Disneyland, modelled after the one in California, but also Tokyo DisneySea, an original theme park with seven 'ports' evoking locales real and imagined (the Mediterranean and 'Mermaid Lagoon', for example). DisneySea targets a more grown-up crowd, but still has many attractions for kids. Both resorts get extremely crowded, especially on weekends and during summer holidays; you'll have to be strategic with your fast passes. Book admission tickets online to save time.

TOKYO JOYPOLIS AMUSEMENT PARK

Map p265 (東京ジョイポリス; http://tokyo-joypolis.com; 3rd-5th fl, DECKS Tokyo Beach, 1-6-1 Daiba, Minato-ku; adult/child ¥800/300, all-rides passport ¥4300/3300, passport after 5pm ¥3300/2300; 🕒10am-10pm; 🚉Yurikamome line to Odaiba Kaihin-kōen) This indoor amusement park is stacked with virtual-reality attractions and adult thrill rides, such as the video-enhanced Half-pipe Canyon; there are rides for little ones, too. Separate admission and individual ride tickets (¥500 to ¥800) are available, but if you plan to go on more than half a dozen attractions, the unlimited 'passport' makes sense.

DAI-KANRANSHA FERRIS WHEEL

Map p265 (大観覧車; www.daikanransha.com; 1-3-10 Aomi, Kōtō-ku; ¥920; 🕒10am-10pm Sun-Thu, to 11pm Fri & Sat; 🚉Yurikamome line to Aomi) The world's tallest Ferris wheel when it opened in 1999 (it lost that title in 2000), this Odaiba landmark offers glorious views over the city and the bay. It's also great eye-candy when illuminated at night in a rainbow of colours.

★**T-ART ACADEMY** ART & CRAFTS

Map p265 (https://pigment.tokyo/academy; Terrada Harbor One Bldg, 2-5-5 Higashi-Shinagawa, Shinagawa-ku; per person from ¥4000; 🚉Rinkai line to Tennōzu Isle, exit B) Run in conjunction with art supply store Pigment (p175), these artist-led workshops include topics such as 'intro to calligraphy' and 'how to mix traditional paints' (with mineral pigments and animal fat). Some are held in English (you can join the Japanese classes, too); if you've got a group you can request a workshop with a translator (at extra cost). Reservations necessary.

Day Trips from Tokyo

Mt Fuji p178
Follow the pilgrim trail up Japan's most famous peak for a sunrise to beat all others, or admire views of the perfect snowcapped cone from below.

Nikkō p180
Take in the grandeur of old Edo at the spectacular shrines and temples of Nikkō, in the wooded mountains north of Tokyo.

Hakone p184
A centuries-old hot-spring resort in the mist-shrouded hills southwest of Tokyo, Hakone offers scenery straight out of a woodblock painting and plenty of onsen.

Kamakura p187
An ancient feudal capital, seaside Kamakura is packed with temples and shrines, plus the Daibutsu (Big Buddha) statue.

TOP SIGHT
MT FUJI

Catching a glimpse of Mt Fuji (富士山; 3776m), Japan's highest and most famous peak, will take your breath away. Climbing it and watching the sunrise from the summit is one of Japan's superlative experiences (though it's often cloudy). The official climbing season runs from 1 July to 31 August.

GETTING THERE

During the climbing season, **Keiō Dentet-su Bus** (☏03-5376-2222; www.highwaybus.com) runs direct buses (¥2700, 2½ hours; reservations necessary) from the Shinjuku Bus Station to Fuji Subaru Line Fifth Station (aka Kawaguchi-ko Fifth Station).

Climbing

The Japanese proverb 'He who climbs Mt Fuji once is a wise man, he who climbs it twice is a fool' remains as valid as ever. While reaching the top brings a great sense of achievement, it's a gruelling climb not known for its beautiful scenery or for being at one with nature.

The mountain is divided into 10 'stations' from base (First Station) to summit (Tenth). From the base station is the original pilgrim trail, but these days most climbers start from the halfway point at one of the four Fifth Stations. The **Kawaguchi-ko Trail** is by far and away the most popular route. It's accessed from Fuji Subaru Line Fifth Station (aka Kawaguchi-ko Fifth Station), and has the most modern facilities and is easiest to reach from Tokyo.

Allow five to six hours to reach the top (though some climb it in half the time) and about three hours to descend, plus 1½ hours for circling the crater at the top.

Know Before You Go

Mt Fuji is a serious mountain, high enough for altitude sickness, and on the summit it can go from sunny and warm to wet, windy and cold remarkably quickly. Even if conditions are fine, you can count on it being close to freezing in the morning, even in summer. Also be aware that visibility can rapidly disappear with a blanket of mist rolling in suddenly.

At a minimum, bring clothing appropriate for cold and wet weather, including a hat and gloves. Also bring at least two litres of water (you can buy more on the mountain during the climbing season), as well as a map, snacks and cash for other necessities, such as toilets (¥200). If you're climbing at night, bring a torch (flashlight) or headlamp, and spare batteries.

When to Go

To time your arrival for dawn you can either start up in the afternoon, stay overnight in a mountain hut and continue early in the morning, or climb the whole way at night. You do not want to arrive on the top too long before dawn, as it will be very cold and windy, even at the height of summer.

It's a very busy mountain during the two-month climbing season. To avoid the worst of the crush head up on a weekday, or start earlier during the day.

Authorities strongly caution against climbing outside the regular season, when the weather is highly unpredictable and first-aid stations on the mountain are closed. Outside of the climbing season, check weather conditions carefully before setting out, bring appropriate equipment, do not climb alone, and be prepared to retreat at any time. A guide will be invaluable. Once snow or ice is on the mountain, Fuji becomes a very serious and dangerous undertaking and should only be attempted by those with winter mountaineering equipment and plenty of experience. Off-season climbers should register with the local police department; fill out the form at the Kawaguchi-ko Tourist Information Centers.

Mountain Huts

Mountain huts, at each station on the Kawaguchi-ko Trail, offer spartan sleeping conditions and hot meals. Reservations are recommended and are essential on weekends.

These two on the Kawaguchi-ko Trail usually have English-speaking staff:

Taishikan (太子館; ☎0555-22-1947; www.mfi.or.jp/w3/home0/taisikan; per person incl 2 meals from ¥8500) Vegetarian or halal meals possible with advance request.

Fujisan Hotel (富士山ホテル; ☎0555-22-0237; www.fujisanhotel.com; per person excl/incl 2 meals from ¥5950/8350) One of the largest and most popular huts.

Resources

Climbing Mt Fuji (www17.plala.or.jp/climb_fujiyama) and the Official Web Site for Mt Fuji Climbing (www.fujisan-climb.jp) are good online resources. The Climbing Mt Fuji brochure is available at the **Kawaguchi-ko Tourist Information Center** (☎0555-72-6700; ⏰8.30am-5.30pm Sun-Fri, to 7pm Sat).

Tours

Discover Japan Tours (www.discover-japan-tours.com/en; 2-day Mt Fuji tours per person ¥10,000) Guided tours from Tokyo for groups of two or more, and specialising in less-frequented routes.

Fuji Mountain Guides (☎042-445-0798; www.fujimountainguides.com/; 2-day Mt Fuji tours per person ¥44,000) Excellent tours run both in and out of season by highly experienced and professional American bilingual guides.

Fuji-spotting

Outside the climbing season, you can hunt for views of Mt Fuji in the Fuji Five Lake region, where placid lakes, formed by ancient eruptions, serve as natural reflecting pools. Kawaguchi-ko, the most popular lake, has excellent views from its north side. Winter and spring are your best bet for catching a glimpse, though often the snow-capped peak is visible only in the morning before it retreats behind its cloud curtain.

On the lower eastern edge of the lake, the **Kachi Kachi Yama Ropeway** (カチカチ山ロープウェイ; www.kachikachiyama-ropeway.com; 1163-1 Azagawa; one way/return adult ¥450/800, child ¥230/400; ⏰9am-5pm) runs to the Fuji Viewing Platform at 1104m, which also offers (weather permitting) a dramatic portrait of the mountain. Several hiking trails through the foothills offer similarly rewarding vistas (with smaller crowds). Ask for a map at the Kawaguchi-ko Tourist Information Center.

Frequent buses to Kawaguchi-ko (¥1750, one hour and 45 minutes) run from Shinjuku Bus Terminal.

UP CLOSE

Buses to the Fifth Station from Kawaguchi-ko Station (one way/return ¥1540/2100, one hour) run roughly mid-April to early December, so even if you can't climb you can still get up close to the hulking volcano.

Check summit weather conditions at www.snow-forecast.com/resorts/Mount-Fuji/6day/top before planning a climb. This is a must outside the official season.

MEET UP

With helpful English-speaking staff, **K's House Mt Fuji** (☎0555-83-5556; http://kshouse.jp; 6713-108 Funatsu; dm from ¥2500, d with/without bathroom from ¥8800/7200; P ⊙ @ 🛜), in Kawaguchi-ko, is an excellent place to stay near the mountain and to meet fellow travellers/climbers. Note that it fills up fast during the climbing season.

Ashino-ko, in Hakone, is another famous Mt Fuji viewing spot. A classic photo-op is the mountain reflecting in the lake with the red *torii* (shrine gate) of Hakone-jinja rising from the water in the foreground.

Nikkō

Explore

Ancient moss clinging to a stone wall; rows of perfectly aligned stone lanterns; vermilion gates; and towering cedars: this is only a pathway in Nikkō (日光), a sanctuary that enshrines the glories of the Edo period (1600–1868). Scattered among hilly woodlands, Nikkō is one of Japan's major attractions, its key World Heritage Site temples and shrines an awesome display of wealth and power by the Tokugawa shogunate.

The Best...

➡**Sight** Tōshō-gū (p180)
➡**Place to Eat** Gyōshintei (p183)
➡**Place to Drink** Nikkō Coffee (p183)

Top Tip

In high season (summer and autumn) and at weekends Nikkō can be extremely crowded. Spending the night here allows for an early start before the crowds arrive.

Getting There & Away

Nikkō is best reached from Tokyo via the Tōbu Nikkō line from Asakusa Station. You can usually get last-minute seats on the hourly reserved *tokkyū* (limited-express) trains (¥2700, 1¾ hours). *Kaisoku* (rapid) trains (¥1360, 2½ hours, hourly from 6.20am to 5.30pm) require no reservation, but you may have to change at Shimo-imaichi. Be sure to ride in the last two cars to reach Nikkō (some cars may separate at an intermediate stop).

Getting Around

Tōbu Nikkō Station is southeast of the shrine area within a block of Nikkō's main road (Rte 119). From the station, follow this road uphill for 20 minutes to reach the shrine area, past restaurants, souvenir shops and the main tourist information centre, or take a bus to the Shin-kyō bus stop (¥200). Bus stops are announced in English.

Need to Know

➡**Area Code** ☑0288
➡**Location** 120km north of Tokyo
➡**Tourist Office** (☑0288-54-2496; www. nikko-jp.org; 591 Gokomachi; ☺9am-5pm; ☎)

◉ SIGHTS

★**TŌSHŌ-GŪ**   SHINTO SHRINE
(東照宮; www.toshogu.jp; 2301 Sannai; adult/child ¥1300/450; ☺8am-4.30pm Apr-Oct, to 3.30pm Nov-Mar) A World Heritage Site, Tōshō-gū is a brilliantly decorative shrine in a beautiful natural setting. Among its notable features is the dazzling 'Sunset Gate' Yōmei-mon.

As the shrine gears up for its 400th anniversary, a major restoration program is underway. Until at least 2018, the Yōmei-mon and Shimojinko (one of the Three Sacred Storehouses) will be obscured by scaffolding. Don't be put off visiting, as Tōshō-gū remains an impressive sight. A museum building also debuted in 2015.

The stone steps of **Omotesandō** lead past the towering stone *torii* (entrance gate), **Ishi-dorii**, and the **Gōjūnotō** (五重塔; Five Storey Pagoda), a 1819 reconstruction of the mid-17th-century original, to **Omotemon** (表門), Tōshō-gū's main gateway, protected on either side by Deva kings.

In Tōshō-gū's initial courtyard are the **Sanjinko** (三神庫; Three Sacred Storehouses); on the upper storey of the Kamijinko (upper storehouse) are relief carvings of 'imaginary elephants' by an artist who had never seen the real thing. Nearby is the **Shinkyūsha** (神厩舎; Sacred Stable), adorned with relief carvings of monkeys. The allegorical 'hear no evil, see no evil, speak no evil' simians demonstrate three principles of Tendai Buddhism.

Further into Tōshō-gū's precincts, to the left of the drum tower, is **Honji-dō** (本地堂), a hall known for the painting on its ceiling of the Nakiryū (Crying Dragon). Monks demonstrate the hall's acoustic properties by clapping two sticks together. The dragon 'roars' (a bit of a stretch) when the sticks are clapped beneath its mouth, but not elsewhere.

Once the scaffolding comes off in 2018, the **Yōmei-mon** (陽明門; Sunset Gate) will be grander than ever, its gold leaf and intricate, coloured carvings and paintings of flowers, dancing girls, mythical beasts and Chinese sages all shiny and renewed. Worrying that the gate's perfection might arouse envy in the gods, those responsible for its construction had the final supporting pillar placed upside down as a deliberate error.

Gōhonsha (御本社), the main inner courtyard, includes the **Honden** (本殿;

Nikkō

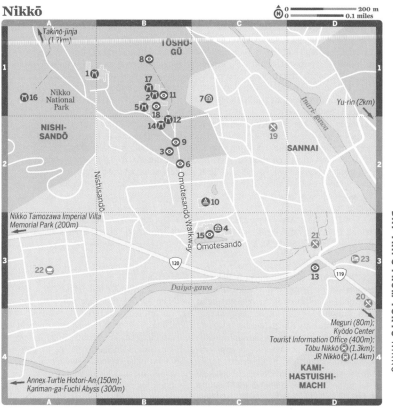

Nikkō

◉ Sights

1 Futarasan-jinja	A1
2 Gōhonsha	B1
3 Gōjūnotō	B2
4 Hōmotsu-den	C3
5 Honji-dō	B1
6 Ishi-dorii	B2
7 Nikkō Tōshō-gū Museum of Art	C1
8 Okumiya	B1
9 Omote-mon	B2
10 Rinnō-ji	C2
11 Sakashita-mon	B1
12 Sanjinko	B2
13 Shin-kyō	D3
14 Shinkyūsha	B2
15 Shōyō-en	C3
16 Taiyūin-byō	A1
17 Tōshō-gū	B1
18 Yōmei-mon	B1

✗ Eating

19 Gyōshintei	C2
20 Hippari Dako	D3
21 Hongū Cafe	D3

◕ Drinking & Nightlife

22 Nikkō Coffee	A3

◖ Sleeping

23 Nikkorisou Backpackers	D3

Main Hall) and **Haiden** (拝殿; Hall of Worship). Inside these halls are paintings of the 36 immortal poets of Kyoto, and a ceiling-painting pattern from the Momoyama period; note the 100 dragons, each different. *Fusuma* (sliding door) paintings depict a *kirin* (a mythical beast that's part giraffe and part dragon).

CHŪZEN-JI ONSEN & YUMOTO ONSEN

The highlands west of Nikkō, part of Nikkō National Park, offer travellers a chance to stretch their legs and then soak them in hot springs. The village of Chūzen-ji Onsen (中禅寺温泉), spread along the 161m-deep and fabulously blue lake Chūzenji-ko (中禅寺湖), has several, admittedly mostly fading, resort hotels that nonetheless have excellent bathhouses, which day trippers can use for ¥1000 to ¥1500.

From Chūzenji you can embark on an easy three-hour hike along the **Senjōgahara Shizen-kenkyu-rō** (戦場ヶ原自然研究路; Senjōgahara Plain Nature Trail). Take a Yumoto-bound bus and get off at **Ryūzu-no-taki** (竜頭ノ滝; ¥460, 20 minutes), a lovely waterfall overlooked by a teahouse that marks the trailhead. The hike traverses the picturesque marshland of **Senjōgahara** (mainly on wooden plank paths), alongside the 75m-high falls of **Yu-daki** (湯滝) to the lake **Yu-no-ko** (湯の湖), then around to the hot-springs village Yumoto Onsen (湯元温泉). Here seek out the humble bathhouse (with extremely hot water) at the temple **Onsen-ji** (温泉時; adult/child ¥500/300; ⊘9am-4pm); look for a row of stone lanterns near the final village bus stop that leads to the temple.

The Tōbu Nikkō Bus Free Pass (adult/child ¥3000/1500) is valid for two-days and allows unlimited rides between Nikkō, Chūzen-ji Onsen and Yumoto Onsen, including the World Heritage Site area.

To the right of the Gōhonsha is **Sakashita-mon** (坂下門), into which is carved a tiny wooden sculpture of the **Nemuri-neko** that's famous for its lifelike appearance (though admittedly the attraction is lost on some visitors). From here it's an uphill path through towering cedars to the appropriately solemn **Okumiya** (奥宮), Ieyasu's tomb.

Bypassed by nearly everyone at Tōshō-gū is the marvellous **Nikkō Tōshō-gū Museum of Art** (日光東照宮美術館; ☏0288-54-0560; www.toshogu.jp/shisetsu/bijutsu.html; 2301 Yamanouchi; adult/child ¥800/400; ⊘9am-5pm Apr-Oct, to 4pm Nov-Mar) in the old shrine offices, showcasing fine paintings on its doors, sliding screens, frames and decorative scrolls, some by masters including Yokoyama Taikan and Nakamura Gakuryo. Follow the path to the right of Omote-mon to find it.

RINNŌ-JI   BUDDHIST TEMPLE

(輪王寺; ☏0288-54-0531; http://rinnoji.or.jp; 2300 Yamanouchi; adult/child ¥400/200; ⊘8am-5pm Apr-Oct, to 4pm Nov-Mar) This Tendai-sect temple was founded 1200 years ago by Shōdō Shōnin. Rinnō-ji's **Hōmotsuden** (宝物殿, Treasure Hall; ¥300; ⊘8am-5pm, to 4pm Nov-Mar) houses some 6000 treasures associated with the temple; the separate admission ticket includes entrance to the **Shōyō-en** (逍遥園; in combination with Hōmotsu-den ¥300; ⊘8am-5pm Apr-Oct, to 4pm Nov-Mar) strolling garden.

TAIYŪIN-BYŌ   SHINTO SHRINE

(大猷院廟; adult/child ¥550/250; ⊘8am-4.30pm Apr-Oct, to 3.30pm Nov-Mar) Ieyasu's grandson Iemitsu (1604–51) is buried here, and although the shrine houses many of the same elements as Tōshō-gū (storehouses, drum tower, Chinese-style gates etc), the more intimate scale and setting in a cryptomeria forest make it very appealing.

Look for dozens of lanterns donated by *daimyō* (domain lords), and the gate Niōmon, whose guardian deities have a hand up (to welcome those with pure hearts) and a hand down (to suppress those with impure hearts).

Inside the main hall, 140 dragons painted on the ceiling are said to carry prayers to the heavens; those holding pearls are on their way up, and those without are returning to gather more prayers.

FUTARASAN-JINJA   SHINTO SHRINE

(二荒山神社; www.futarasan.jp; adult/child ¥200/100) Set among cypress trees, this very atmospheric shrine was founded by Shōdō Shōnin; the current building dates from 1619, making it Nikkō's oldest. It's the protector shrine of Nikkō itself, dedicated to Nantai-san (2484m); the mountain's consort, Nyotai-san; and their mountainous progeny, Tarō. There are other branches of the shrine on Nantai-san and by Chūzenji-ko.

NIKKŌ TAMOZAWA IMPERIAL VILLA MEMORIAL PARK
HISTORIC SITE

(日光田母沢御用邸記念公園; ☑53-6767; www.park-tochigi.com/tamozawa; 8-27 Hon-chō; adult/child ¥510/260; ⊘9am-5pm Wed-Mon, to 4.30pm Nov-Mar) About 1km west of Shin-kyō bridge, this splendidly restored imperial palace of more than 100 rooms showcases superb artisanship, with parts of the complex dating from the Edo, Meiji and Taishō eras. Apart from the construction skills involved there are brilliantly detailed screen paintings and serene garden views framed from nearly every window.

Visit in autumn to see the gardens at their most spectacular.

TAKINŌ-JINJA
SHINTO SHRINE

(滝尾神社) **FREE** About 1km north of Futarasan-jinja, close by the Shiraito Falls, is this serene, delightfully less crowded shrine that has a history stretching back to 820. The stone gate, called **Undameshi-no-torii**, dates back to 1696. Before entering, it's customary to try your luck tossing three stones through the small hole near the top.

Maps available at the tourist offices show the route to the shrine, which also passes the tomb of Shōdō Shōnin.

KANMAN-GA-FUCHI ABYSS
PARK

(憾満ガ淵) Escape the crowds along this wooded path lined with a collection of *Jizō* statues (the small stone effigies of the Buddhist protector of travellers and children). After passing the **Shin-kyō bridge** (神橋; crossing fee ¥300), follow the Daiya-gawa west for about 1km, crossing another bridge near Jyoko-ji temple en route. It's said that if you try to count the statues there and again on the way back, you'll end up with a different number, hence the nickname 'Bake-jizō' (ghost *Jizō*).

✖ EATING & DRINKING

HONGŪ CAFE
CAFE ¥

(本宮カフェ; ☑0288-54-1669; www.hongucafe. com; 2384 Sannai; espresso ¥350, dessert sets from ¥650; ⊘10am-6pm Fri-Wed) Refresh with a cup of espresso, or a traditional Japanese dessert set of *matcha* and *yomogi-mochi* (mugwort dumplings topped with sweet *azuki*-bean paste) – it tastes better than it sounds. Set in a refurbished historic house near the entrance of the national park,

this cafe is a great place to take a breather après-shrine.

HIPPARI DAKO
YAKITORI ¥

(ひっぱり凧; ☑0288-53-2933; 1011 Kamihatsu-ishimachi; meals ¥550-900; ⊘11am-8pm; ☑) An institution for more than a quarter of a century among foreign travellers, as layers of business cards tacked to the walls testify, this no-frills restaurant serves comfort food, including curry *udon, yuba* sashimi and *yaki-udon* (fried noodles).

★MEGURI
VEGAN ¥¥

(☑0288-25-3122; 909 Nakahatsuishi-machi; lunch ¥1400; ⊘11.30am-6pm Sat-Wed; ☑) A dedicated young couple dish up lovingly prepared tasty vegan Japanese meals in this former art shop with an amazing painting on its ceiling. Arrive as soon as they open if you want to secure lunch – it's a popular place and once they've run out of food, it's sweets and drinks only.

★GYŌSHINTEI
KAISEKI ¥¥¥

(尭心亭; ☑0288-53-3751; www.meiji-yakata. com/gyoushin; 2339-1 Sannai; set lunch/dinner from ¥2100/4500; ⊘11am-7pm Fri-Wed) Splash out on deluxe spreads of vegetarian *shōjin-ryōri,* featuring local bean curd and vegetables served half a dozen delectable ways, or the *kaiseki* courses which include fish. The elegant tatami dining room overlooks a carefully tended garden, which is part of the Meji-no-Yakata compound of chic restaurants close by the World Heritage Site.

★NIKKŌ COFFEE
CAFE

(日光珈琲; http://nikko-coffee.com; 3-13 Honchō; coffee ¥550, meals from ¥1000; ⊘10am-6pm Tue-Sun) A century-old rice shop has been sensitively reinvented as this retro-chic cafe with a garden, where expertly made hand-dripped coffee is served alongside cakes and snack meals such as bacon, cheese and egg galette (buckwheat pancake) or pork curry.

🛏 SLEEPING

★NIKKORISOU BACKPACKERS
HOSTEL ¥

(にっこり荘バックパッカーズ; ☑080-9449-1545; http://nikkorisou.com/eng.html; 1107 Kamihatsu-ishi-machi; dm/d with shared bathroom from ¥3000/6900; ✳🛜) The closest hostel to the World Heritage Site offers a riverside location and relaxed, friendly vibe. As it's run single-handedly by the English-speaking Hiro, guests need to be elsewhere between 10am and 4pm, but at any other hour the roomy kitchen, huge deck and cosy common area are havens for hanging out. Well-maintained hybrid mountain bikes are available for rent (¥500).

ANNEX TURTLE HOTORI-AN INN ¥¥
(アネックスーほとり庵; ☎0288-53-3663; www.turtle-nikko.com; 8-28 Takumi-chō; s/tw from ¥6700/13,000; ❀❄@☎) Only steps away from the trailhead to Kanman-ga-Fuchi Abyss, this tidy, comfortable inn offers Japanese- and Western-style rooms, plus river views from the house onsen. It's a lovely spot in a quiet neighbourhood giving way to open space.

Hakone

Explore

Offering serene onsen, world-class art museums and spectacular mountain scenery crowned by Mt Fuji, Hakone (箱根) can make for a blissful escape from Tokyo. Ashino-ko (芦ノ湖) is the lake at the centre of it all, the setting for the iconic image of Mt Fuji with the *torii* of Hakone-jinja rising from the water. Naturally, this is all quite attractive, so it can feel crammed, particularly at weekends and holidays.

The classic route goes from Hakone-Yumoto to Gōra by train, then by cable car and ropeway over Owakudani followed by a lake cruise to Moto-Hakone. This is most convenient, but can feel rather packaged – feel free to shake it up.

The Best...

➡**Sight** Hakone Open-Air Museum (p186)
➡**Onsen** Hakone Yuryō (p186)
➡**Place to Eat** Itoh Dining by Nobu (p187)

Top Tip

The Hakone Freepass (two-day pass adult/child ¥5140/1500), available at Odakyū stations, covers the return express train fare between Shinjuku and Hakone-Yumoto, unlimited use of most transport around Hakone and discounts at attractions. Freepass-holders need to pay a limited-express surcharge (¥890 each way) to ride the Romance Car.

Getting There & Away

The Odakyū line (www.odakyu.jp) from Shinjuku Station goes directly into Hakone-Yumoto, the region's transit hub. Use either the convenient Romance Car (¥2080, 90 minutes) or *kyūkō* (regular-express) service (¥1190, two hours); the latter may require a transfer at Odawara.

Getting Around

The narrow-gauge, switchback Hakone-Tōzan line runs from Odawara to Gōra (¥670, one hour) via Hakone-Yumoto, Tōnosawa, Miyanoshita, Kowakidani and Chōgoku-no-mori. From Gōra take the cable car to **Sōun-zan**, from where you can catch the Hakone Ropeway to **Ōwakudani** and **Tōgendai**. From Tōgendai, sightseeing boats criss-cross Ashino-ko to **Hakone-machi** (☎0460-83-7550; Hakonemachi-ko) and **Moto-Hakone** (one-way/return

Hakone Region

◉ Sights
1 Hakone Museum of Art C2
2 Hakone Open-Air Museum D2
3 Hakone-jinja C4
4 Okada Museum of Art C2
5 Ōwakudani B2

✗ Eating
6 Bakery & Table C4
7 Itoh Dining by Nobu C2
8 Yamagusuri D2

◉ Drinking & Nightlife
9 Amazake-chaya C4
10 Naraya Cafe D2

◉ Sports & Activities
11 Hakone Yuryō E2
12 Tenzan Tōji-kyō E3
13 Yunessun C2

◉ Transport
14 Hakone Sightseeing Cruise C4
15 Ōwakudani Station B2
16 Sōun-zan Station C2
17 Tōgendai Station A2

DAY TRIPS FROM TOKYO

Hakone Region

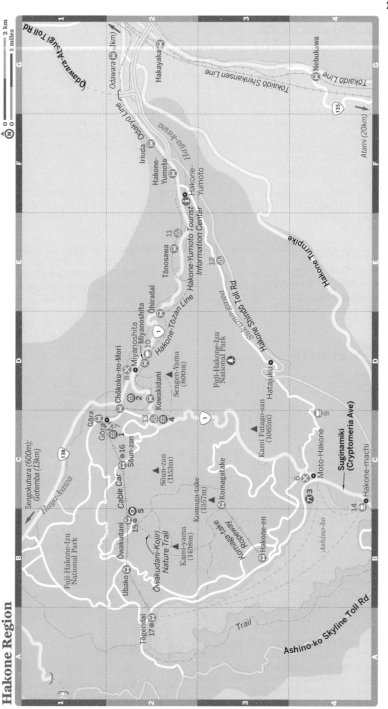

WORTH A DETOUR

OLD HAKONE HIGHWAY

Up the hill from the lakeside Moto-Hakone bus stop is the entrance to the stone-paved Old Hakone Highway (箱根旧街道), part of the Edo-era Tōkaidō Highway that connected the shogun's capital with Kyoto. You can walk back to Hakone-Yumoto via the trail through the woods, which will take about 3½ hours.

About 30 minutes in you'll pass wonderful **Amazake-chaya** (甘酒茶屋; ☑0460-83-6418; www.amasake-chaya.jp/; 395-1 Futoko-yama; amazake ¥400, snacks from ¥250; ☺7am-5.30pm), a thatched-roofed teahouse that has been serving naturally sweet *amazake* (a thick sweet drink made from the rice used to make sake; ¥400) for more than 360 years. If you happen to visit in winter, you can warm yourself around the *irori* (traditional fireplace).

¥1000/1840, 30 minutes). The Hakone-Tōzan and Izu Hakone bus companies also service the Hakone area, linking most of the sights.

Need to Know

➡ **Area Code** ☑0460

➡ **Location** 92km southwest of Tokyo

➡ **Tourist Office** (☑0460-85-8911; www.hakone.or.jp; ☺9am-5.45pm)

◎ SIGHTS

★ HAKONE OPEN-AIR MUSEUM   MUSEUM
(彫刻の森美術館; ☑0460-82-1161; www.hakone-oam.or.jp; 1121 Ninotaira; adult/child ¥1600/800; ☺9am-5pm) In a rolling, leafy hillside setting, this safari for art lovers includes an impressive selection of 19th- and 20th-century Japanese and Western sculptures (including works by Henry Moore, Rodin and Miró) as well as an excellent Picasso Pavilion with more than 300 works ranging from paintings and glass art to tapestry.

Kids will love the giant crochet artwork/playground with its Jengalike exterior walls, as well as the spiral staircase of the stained-glass Symphonic Structure. End the day by soaking your feet in the outdoor footbath. Hakone Freepass holders get ¥200 off the admission price.

★ OKADA MUSEUM OF ART   MUSEUM
(岡田美術館; ☑0460-87-3931; www.okada-museum.com; 483-1 Kowakidani; adult/student ¥2800/1800; ☺9am-5pm) Showcasing the dazzling Japanese, Chinese and Korean art treasures of industrialist Okada Kazuo, this mammoth museum should not be missed. You could spend hours marvelling at the beauty of so many pieces, including detailed screen paintings and exquisite pottery. Interactive, multilingual interpretive displays enhance the experience. The museum is opposite the Kowakien bus stop.

HAKONE MUSEUM OF ART   MUSEUM
(箱根美術館; ☑0460-82-2623; 1300 Gōra; adult/child ¥900/free; ☺9.30am-4.30pm Fri-Wed, to 4pm in winter) Sharing grounds with a lovely velvety moss garden and teahouse (¥700 *matcha* green tea and sweet), this museum has a collection of Japanese pottery dating from as far back as the Jōmon period (some 5000 years ago). The gardens are spectacular in autumn.

ŌWAKUDANI   VOLCANO
(大桶谷; www.kanagawa-park.or.jp/owakudani) **FREE** The 'Great Boiling Valley' was created 3000 years ago when Kami-yama erupted and collapsed, also forming Ashino-ko. Hydrogen sulphide steams from the ground here and the hot water is used to boil onsen *tamago*, eggs blackened in the sulphurous waters, which you can buy to eat (they're fine inside). At the time of writing, Ōwakudani was closing intermittently due to volcanic activity.

HAKONE-JINJA   SHINTO SHRINE
(箱根神社; ☺9am-4pm) A pleasant stroll around Ashino-ko follows a cedar-lined path to this shrine set in a wooded grove, in Moto-Hakone. Its signature red *torii* (gate) rises from the lake; get your camera ready for that picture-postcard shot.

🏃 ONSEN

★ HAKONE YURYŌ   ONSEN
(箱根湯寮; ☑0460-85-8411; www.hakoneyuryo.jp; 4 Tōnosawa; adult/child ¥1400/700, private

bath from ¥3900; ⏰10am-9pm Mon-Fri, to 10pm Sat & Sun) A free shuttle bus will whisk you in three minutes from Hakone-Yumoto station to this idyllic onsen complex ensconced in the forest. The *rotemburo* (outdoor onsen) are spacious and leaf shaded, and you can book private ones up to a month in advance. No tattoos allowed (but if you book a private room, no one's the wiser).

It's about a five-minute walk from Tōnosawa Station on the Hakone-Tōzan line.

TENZAN TŌJI-KYŌ ONSEN

(天山湯治郷; ☎0460-86-4126; www.tenzan.jp; 208 Yumoto-chaya; adult/child ¥1300/650; ⏰9am-10pm) Soak in *rotemburo* of varying temperatures and designs (one is constructed to resemble a natural cave) at this large, popular bath 2km southwest of town. To get here, take the 'B' course shuttle bus from the bridge outside Hakone-Yumoto Station (¥100). Tattoos are not a problem here.

YUNESSUN ONSEN

(箱根小涌園ユネッサン; www.yunessun.com; 1297 Ninotaira; Yunessun adult/child ¥2900/1600, Mori-no-Yu ¥1900/1200, both ¥4100/2100; ⏰9am-7pm Mar-Oct, to 6pm Nov-Feb) Best described as an onsen amusement park with a whole variety of outdoor water slides and baths, including wine, coffee, green-tea and sake baths...yes, for putting your body in, not the other way round. Yunessun is mixed bathing so you'll need to bring a swimsuit. The connected Mori-no-Yu complex (11am to 8pm) is traditional single-sex bathing.

Take a bus from Hakone-machi, Gōra or Hakone-Yumoto to the Kowakien bus stop. There's also a variety of accommodation here.

✖ EATING & DRINKING

BAKERY & TABLE INTERNATIONAL ¥¥

(☎0460-85-1530; www.bthjapan.com; 9-1 Moto-Hakone; mains ¥1000-2500; ⏰bakery 10am-5pm, parlour 10am-3pm, cafe 8.30am-5pm, restaurant 11am-6pm) There are options that appeal to everyone at this lakeside venue with a footbath terrace outside. The take-away bakery is on the ground floor, a cafe is one floor up, and the restaurant serving fancy open sandwiches and crêpes is above that.

YAMAGUSURI JAPANESE ¥¥

(山藥; ☎0460-82-1066; 224 Miyanoshita; meals ¥2300; ⏰7am-9pm) Yamagusuri is a popular spot for substantial, healthy meal sets featuring *tororo* (grated yam) that you pour over barley and rice. The dining room overlooks the forested gorge below.

ITOH DINING BY NOBU JAPANESE ¥¥¥

(☎0460-83-8209; www.itoh-dining.co.jp/; 1300-64 Gōra; lunch/dinner from ¥3000/7000; ⏰11.30am-3pm & 5-9.30pm; ✈) Savour some premium Japanese beef, cooked teppanyaki-style in front of you by the chef, at this elegant restaurant, a branch of the celeb chef Nobu's dining empire. It's just uphill from Koenshimo station on the funicular, one stop from Gōra.

NARAYA CAFE CAFE

(ナラヤカフェ; 404-13 Miyanoshita; coffee from ¥350; ⏰10.30am-6pm, to 5pm Dec-Feb, closed Wed & 4th Thu of the month; 🖧) Beside the station, this woodsy cafe and craft shop is a pleasant pit stop for drinks and light meals. You can also soak your toes in the footbath on the terrace looking out over the mountains.

Kamakura

••••••••••••••••••••••••••••••••••••••

Explore

The glory days of Japan's first feudal capital (from 1185 to 1333) coincided with the spread of populist Buddhism in Japan. This legacy is reflected in the area's proliferation of stunning temples. Kamakura (鎌倉) also has a laid-back, earthy vibe complete with organic restaurants, summer beach shacks and surfers – which can be added to sunrise meditation and hillside hikes as reasons to visit. Only an hour from Tokyo, it tends to get packed on weekends and holidays, so plan accordingly.

••••••••••••••••••••••••••••••••••••••

The Best...

➡ **Sight** Daibutsu (p189)

➡ **Activity** Daibutsu Hiking Course (p190)

➡ **Place to Eat** Bonzō (p190)

••••••••••••••••••••••••••••••••••••••

Top Tip

Bicycles are great for touring Kamakura's shrines and temples; **Kamakura Rent-a-Cycle** (レンタサイクル; ☎0467-24-2319; per hr/

Kamakura

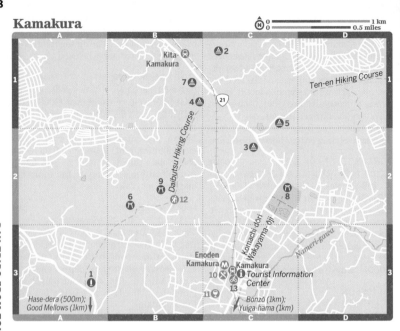

Kamakura

⊙ Sights
1 Daibutsu...A3
2 Engaku-ji...C1
3 Ennō-ji..C2
4 Jōchi-ji..B1
5 Kenchō-ji...C1
6 Sasuke-inari-jinja..................................B2
7 Tōkei-ji...B1
8 Tsurugaoka
   Hachiman-gū..C2
9 Zeniarai-benten....................................B2

⊗ Eating
10 Wander Kitchen....................................C3

⊖ Drinking & Nightlife
11 Univibe...C3

⊙ Sports & Activities
12 Daibutsu Hiking Course......................B2

⊙ Transport
13 Kamakura Rent-a-Cycle.......................C3

day ¥800/1800; ⊘8.30am-5pm) is outside the east exit of Kamakura Station.

Getting There & Away

JR Yokosuka-line trains run to Kamakura from Tokyo (¥920, 56 minutes) and Shinagawa (¥720, 46 minutes), via Yokohama (¥340, 27 minutes). Alternatively, the Shōnan Shinjuku line runs from the west side of Tokyo (Shibuya, Shinjuku and Ikebukuro, all ¥920) in about one hour, though some trains require a transfer at Ōfuna, one stop before Kita-Kamakura. The last train from Kamakura back to Tokyo Station is 11.20pm and Shinjuku 9.16pm.

Getting Around

You can walk to most temples and shrines from Kamakura or Kita-Kamakura Stations. Sites in the west, including the Daibutsu, can be reached via the Enoden line from Kamakura Station to Hase (¥200) or by bus from Kamakura Station stops 1 and 6.

Need to Know

➜ **Area Code** ☎0467
➜ **Location** 65km south of Tokyo
➜ **Tourist Office** (鎌倉市観光総合案内所; ☎0467-22-3350; ⊘9am-5pm)

SIGHTS & ACTIVITIES

★ DAIBUTSU · MONUMENT

(大仏; ☎0467-22-0703; www.kotoku-in.jp; Kōtoku-in, 4-2-28 Hase; adult/child ¥200/150; ⊙8am-5.30pm Apr-Sep, to 5pm Oct-Nov) Kamakura's most iconic sight, an 11.4m bronze statue of Amida Buddha (*amitābha* in Sanskrit), is in Kōtoku-in, a Jōdo sect temple. Completed in 1252, it's said to have been inspired by Yoritomo's visit to Nara (where Japan's biggest Daibutsu holds court) after the Minamoto clan's victory over the Taira clan. Once housed in a huge hall, today the statue sits in the open, the hall having been washed away by a tsunami in 1498.

For an extra ¥20, you can duck inside to see how the sculptors pieced the 850-tonne statue together.

Buses from stops 1 and 6 at the east exit of Kamakura Station run to the Daibutsu-mae stop (¥190). Alternatively, take the Enoden Enoshima line to Hase Station and walk north for about eight minutes. Better yet, take the Daibutsu Hiking Course (p190).

HASE-DERA · BUDDHIST TEMPLE

(長谷寺; Hase Kannon; ☎0467-22-6300; www.hasedera.jp; Hase; adult/child ¥300/100; ⊙8am-5pm Mar-Sep, to 4.30pm Oct-Feb) The focal point of this Jōdo sect temple, one of the most popular in the Kantō region, is a 9m-high carved wooden *jūichimen* (11-faced) Kannon statue. Kannon (*avalokiteshvara* in Sanskrit) is the Bodhisattva of infinite compassion and, along with Jizō, is one of Japan's most popular Buddhist deities. The temple is about 10 minutes' walk from the Daibutsu and dates back to AD 736, when the statue is said to have washed up on the shore near Kamakura.

TSURUGAOKA HACHIMAN-GŪ · SHINTO SHRINE

(鶴岡八幡宮; http://hachimangu.or.jp; 2-1-31 Yukinoshita; ⊙5am-8.30pm Apr-Sep, 6am-8.30pm Oct-Mar) FREE Kamakura's most important shrine is, naturally, dedicated to Hachiman, the god of war. Minamoto no Yoritomo himself ordered its construction in 1191 and designed the pine-flanked central promenade that leads to the coast. The sprawling grounds are ripe with historical symbolism: the Gempei Pond, bisected by bridges, is said to depict the rift between the Minamoto (Genji) and Taira (Heike) clans.

LOCAL KNOWLEDGE

GET ZEN

Kenchō-ji (p190) offers beginner-friendly, public *zazen* (seated meditation) sessions from 5pm to 6pm on Fridays and Saturdays (enter before 4.30pm). Instruction is in Japanese, but you can easily manage by watching everyone else. Check the website for the occasional session held in English.

ENGAKU-JI · BUDDHIST TEMPLE

(円覚寺; ☎0467-22-0478; www.engakuji.or.jp; 409 Yamanouchi; adult/child ¥300/100; ⊙8am-4.30pm Mar-Nov, to 4pm Dec-Feb) One of Kamakura's five major Rinzai Zen temples, Engaku-ji was founded in 1282 as a place where Zen monks might pray for soldiers who lost their lives defending Japan against Kublai Khan. All of the temple structures have been rebuilt over the centuries; the Shariden, a Song-style reliquary, is the oldest, last rebuilt in the 16th century. At the top of the long flight of stairs is the Engaku-ji bell, the largest bell in Kamakura, cast in 1301.

TŌKEI-JI · BUDDHIST TEMPLE

(東慶寺; www.tokeiji.com; 1367 Yamanouchi; adult/child ¥200/100; ⊙8.30am-5pm Mar-Oct, to 4pm Nov-Feb) Across the railway tracks from Engaku-ji, Tōkei-ji is famed as having served as a women's refuge. A woman could be officially recognised as divorced after three years as a nun in the temple precincts. Today, there are no nuns; the grave of the last abbess can be found in the cemetery, shrouded by cypress trees.

ENNŌ-JI · BUDDHIST TEMPLE

(円応寺; 1543 Yamanouchi; ¥200; ⊙9am-4pm Mar-Nov, to 3pm Dec-Feb) Ennō-ji is distinguished by its statues depicting the judges of hell. According to the Juo concept of Taoism, which was introduced to Japan from China during the Heian period (794–1185), these 10 judges decide the fate of souls, who, being neither truly good nor truly evil, must be assigned to spend eternity in either heaven or hell. Presiding over them is Emma (Yama), a Hindu deity known as the gruesome king of the infernal regions.

★KENCHŌ-JI   BUDDHIST TEMPLE

(建長寺; www.kenchoji.com; 8 Yamanouchi; adult/child ¥300/100; ☺8.30am-4.30pm) Established in 1253, Japan's oldest Zen monastery is still active today. The central Butsuden (Buddha Hall) was brought piece by piece from Tokyo in 1647. Its Jizō Bosatsu statue, unusual for a Zen temple, reflects the valley's ancient function as an execution ground – *Jizō* consoles lost souls. Other highlights include a bell cast in 1253 and a juniper grove, believed to have sprouted from seeds brought from China by Kenchō-ji's founder some seven centuries ago.

DAIBUTSU
HIKING COURSE   HIKING

This 3km wooded trail connects Kita-Kamakura with the Daibutsu (p189) in Hase (allow about 1½ hours) and passes several small, quiet temples and shrines, including **Zeniarai-benten** (銭洗弁天; 2-25-16 Sasuke; ☺8am-4.30pm) FREE, one of Kamakura's most alluring Shinto shrines.

The path begins at the steps just up the lane from pretty **Jōchi-ji** (浄智寺; 1402 Yamanouchi; adult/child ¥200/100; ☺9am-4.30pm), a few minutes from Tōkei-ji. Near Zeniarai-benten a cavelike entrance leads to a clearing where visitors come to bathe their money in natural springs, with the hope of bringing financial success. From here, continue down the paved road, turning right at the first intersection, walking along a path lined with cryptomeria and ascending through a succession of *torii* to **Sasuke-inari-jinja** (佐助稲荷神社; 2-22-10 Sasuke; ☺24hr) FREE before meeting up with the Daibutsu path once again. To hike in the opposite direction, follow the road beyond Daibutsu and the trail entrance is on the right, just before a tunnel.

 EATING

WANDER KITCHEN   INTERNATIONAL ¥

(☎0467-61-4751; http://wanderkitchen.net; 10-15 Onarimachi; sweets/lunch from ¥400/1000; ☺noon-8pm; ☏) It's worth searching out this charmingly decorated, retro-chic wooden house with a small garden out front for its cool vibe and tasty meals, cakes and drinks. It's tucked away just off the main street about five minutes' walk south of the west exit of Kamakura Station.

★BONZŌ   SOBA ¥¥

(梵蔵; ☎0467-73-7315; http://bonzokamakura. com; 3-17-33 Zaimokuza; dishes ¥300-2000, set-course menu from ¥3500; ☺11.30am-3pm & 6-9pm, closed Thu) Intimate, rustic, Michelin-star restaurant that specialises in handmade *ju-wari* (100% soba), including *kamo seiro* (cold soba in hot broth) with wild duck imported from France. The homemade sesame tofu is incredibly creamy and not to be missed. Catch bus 12, 40 or 41 to Kuhon-ji and look for the brown shopfront next to the tiny post office.

GOOD MELLOWS   CAFE ¥¥

(☎0467-24-9655; 27-39 Sakanoshita; burgers from ¥850; ☺10.30am-7pm Wed-Mon) Americana meets Japanese kitsch opposite the beach, with neatly stacked, charcoal-grilled juicy burgers of bacon, mozzarella and avocado, plus perfect fries, washed down with a Dr Pepper or a cold California microbrew. Once a month or so they stay open till 11.30pm on Saturday with DJs playing.

UNIVIBE   BAR

(☎0467-67-8458; www.univibe.jp; 2nd fl, 7-13 Onaricho; ☺11am-3pm & 6pm-late; ☏) Spacious upstairs bar kitted-out in retro vintage decor, with friendly bartenders, table football and a relaxed vibe. A five-minute walk from the Kamakura JR station.

Sleeping

Tokyo is known for being expensive; however, more attractive budget and midrange options are popping up every year. Business hotels are an economic option, while ryokan fill the need for small, character-filled sleeping spaces. The best deals are on the east side of town, in neighbourhoods such as Ueno and Asakusa. Levels of cleanliness and service are generally high everywhere.

Business Hotels

Functional and economical, 'business hotels' are geared to the lone traveller on business. The compact rooms usually have semidouble beds (140cm across; roomy for one, a bit of a squeeze for two) and tiny en-suite bathrooms. They're famous for being deeply unfashionable, though many chains have updated their rooms in recent years. Expect to pay from ¥10,000 to ¥15,000 (or ¥14,000 to ¥19,000 for double occupancy). Most accept credit cards.

Boutique Hotels

Boutique hotels have been late to catch on in Tokyo; there is only a handful. This is perhaps because the concept – intimate and with memorable decor – is too similar in the minds of some to that of a hotel with unsavoury repute: the love hotel.

Capsule Hotels

Capsule hotels offer rooms the size of a single bed, with just enough headroom for you to sit up. Think of it like a bunk bed with more privacy (and a reading light, TV and alarm clock). Most are men-only, though some have floors for women, too. Prices range from ¥3500 to ¥5000, which usually includes access to a large shared bath and sauna. Most only accept cash and do not permit guests with visible tattoos.

Hostels

In the last five years, Tokyo hostels have gone from ordinary to outstanding. Always known for being clean and well managed, they now outdo themselves to provide cultural activi-ties and social events for guests. Most have a mixture of dorms and private rooms, and cooking and laundry facilities. Expect to pay about ¥3000 for a dorm and ¥8000 for a private room (double occupancy).

Luxury Hotels

In the top-end bracket, you can expect to find the amenities of deluxe hotels anywhere in the world: satellite TV, concierge service in fluent English and enough space to properly unwind. Many of Tokyo's luxury hotels are in high-rise buildings and offer fantastic city views. They also offer direct airport access, via the Limousine Bus. Prices vary wildly, with online deals possible.

Ryokan

Ryokan (Japanese-style inns) offer a tradi-tional experience, with tatami (woven-mat floor) rooms and futons (traditional quilt-like mattresses) instead of beds. Exclusive estab-lishments can charge upwards of ¥25,000; however, there are a number of relatively inexpensive ryokan in Tokyo, starting at around ¥8000 a night (for double occupancy).

Most ryokan have 'family rooms' that can sleep four or five – an economical choice if you're travelling as a group or with kids. Some offer rooms with private baths, but one of the pleasures of staying in a traditional inn is the communal bath. These are segregated by sex, spacious, and sometimes made of cedar or stone. Most inns provide cotton robes called *yukata,* which you can wear to and from the baths. Many ryokan accept cash only.

NEED TO KNOW

Price Ranges
The following price ranges reflect the cost of one night's accommodation for double occupancy.

¥	less than ¥8000
¥¥	¥8000 to ¥25,000
¥¥¥	under ¥25,000

Taxes
Sales tax (8%) applies to hotel rates. There is also a city-wide 'accommodation tax' of ¥100 on rooms over ¥10,000 and ¥200 for rooms over ¥15,000.

Discounts
Hostels, guesthouses and ryokan have fixed rates; for hotels of all classes, rates can vary tremendously, and discounts significantly below rack rates can be found online. Many hotels offer cheaper rates if you book two weeks or a month in advance. Note that prices tend to increase on weekends.

Reservations
Advanced booking is highly recommended as popular spots fill up. Walk-ins can fluster staff at smaller inns or ryokan (or staff might not be present). Busy periods include the first week of January, 'Golden Week' (29 April to 5 May) and August.

Lonely Planet's Top Choices

Sawanoya Ryokan (p199)

Hoshinoya Tokyo (p194)

Claska (p196)

Nui (p199)

Hanare (p199)

Best by Budget

¥
Toco (p199) Hostel in a charming old wooden house near Ueno.

Kimi Ryokan (p198) Welcoming budget ryokan in northwest Tokyo.

K's House Tokyo (p200) Cosy and social backpacker fave near Asakusa.

¥¥
Shibuya Granbell Hotel (p196) Funky boutique hotel on the quieter side of Shibuya.

Hotel Mystays Premier Akasaka (p195) New Akasaka hotel with excellent rates.

Hotel S (p195) Stylish rooms down the road from Roppongi's legendary nightlife.

¥¥¥
Park Hyatt Tokyo (p198) Palatial high-rise atop a Shinjuku skyscraper.

Aman Tokyo (p194) Gorgeous new retreat with excellent views in Ōtemachi.

Palace Hotel Tokyo (p194) Elegant rooms alongside the Imperial Palace in Marunouchi.

Best Ryokan

Hōmeikan (p199) Atmospheric, 100-year-old ryokan near Ueno.

Sukeroku No Yado Sadachiyo (p200) Traditional inn with big tatami rooms and fantastic baths, in Asakusa.

Ryokan Seikō (p197) Rambling, homey inn in the western suburbs.

Best Designer Digs

Reversible Destiny Lofts (p197) Colourful (slightly disorienting) rooms in an eccentrically designed apartment complex in west Tokyo.

Andon Ryokan (p200) Minamalist modern ryokan with rooftop jacuzzi near Asakusa.

BnA Hotel (p197) Kōenji hotel decorated by artists (who share in the profit).

Best Capsule Hotels

9 Hours (p195) Futuristic pods in Narita Airport.

First Cabin (p195) Bigger-than-average berths in Akasaka.

Capsule & Sauna Century (p196) Classic capsules in the thick of Shibuya.

Best Quirky Stays

Japonica Lodge (p200) Tents and sleeping bags inside a sporting goods store.

Khaosan World (p200) Trippy hostel in a former love hotel.

Book & Bed (p197) Bunks built into bookshelves.

Where to Stay

Neighbourhood	For	Against
Marunouchi & Nihombashi	Convenient for all sights and for travel out of the city.	Area is mostly businesspeople; sky-high prices and quiet on weekends.
Ginza & Tsukiji	Ginza's shops and restaurants at your doorstep.	Congested and few inexpensive options compared to other districts.
Roppongi, Akasaka & Around	A wealth of good eating and drinking options, as well as sights.	Roppongi can be noisy at night; if you're not into the nightlife there's little reason to stay here.
Ebisu, Meguro & Around	Near major hubs but with fewer crowds; great bars and restaurants.	No major sights in the neighbourhood, and can feel removed from the city centre.
Shibuya & Shimo-Kitazawa	Convenient transport links; plenty of nightlife and a buzzing streetscape in Shibuya.	Youth-centric Shibuya has no real adult vibe; extremely crowded; possible sensory overload.
Shinjuku & Northwest Tokyo	Superb transport links, a wealth of food and nightlife options in Shinjuku; good budget options in Ikebukuro.	Very crowded around station areas; cheap options in Shinjuku are clustered around the red-light district.
West Tokyo	Slightly cheaper rates than central Tokyo; direct trains to downtown; local vibe.	Far from main sights; riding the crowded Chūō line everyday can be a drag.
Akihabara, Kaguraza-ka & Kōrakuen	Central, reasonable prices and with good transit links.	Few budget options; many areas quiet at night.
Ueno, Yanesen & Komagome	Ryokans abound; lots of greenery and museums; easy airport access.	The good ryokan here tend to be isolated in residential neighbourhoods.
Asakusa & Sumida River	Atmospheric old city feel; convenient for east Tokyo sights; great budget options and backpacker vibe.	Asakusa is quiet at night, and a good 20-minute subway ride from more central areas.
Harajuku & Aoyama	Sights, restaurants and shops galore.	Very limited sleeping options.
Odaiba & Tokyo Bay	Proximity to family-friendly attractions.	Over-priced.

SLEEPING

Useful Websites

Many smaller, independent inns and hostels offer slightly better rates if you book directly.

Jalan (www.jalan.net) Popular Japanese discount accommodation site, searchable in English.

Japanese Inn Group (www.japaneseinngroup.com) Bookings for ryokan and other small, family-run inns.

Japanican (www.japanican.com) Accommodation site for foreign travellers run by JTB, Japan's largest travel agency.

Lonely Planet (lonelyplanet.com/Japan/Tokyo/hotels) Reviews, recommendations and bookings

🛌 Marunouchi & Nihombashi

⭐ WISE OWL HOSTELS TOKYO
HOSTEL ¥

Map p266 (☎03-5541-2960; www.wiseowlhostels.com; 3-22-9 Hatchōbori, Chūō-ku; dm/d from ¥3600/9000; ⊖❄🅷🛜) This industrial-looking hostel ticks all the right boxes, starting with a super-convenient location above the subway and a relatively short walk or taxi ride from Marunouchi and Ginza. A clever configuration of wooden-cubicle bunks makes up the dorms. There's friendly service, a third-wave coffee stand in the lobby, DJ bar in the basement and attached *izakaya* for food.

GRIDS AKIHABARA
HOSTEL ¥

Map p266 (☎03-5822-6236; www.grids-hostel.com; 2-8-16 Higashi-kanda, Chiyoda-ku; dm/s/d from ¥3300/3500/7200; ⊖❄🛜; 🆂Shinjuku line to Iwamotochō, exit A4) Following what is becoming a common hostel format in Tokyo (conversions of old office buildings with a cafe-bar on the ground floor), Grids adds to the mix by throwing in four Japanese-style tatami-mat rooms (sleeping up to four; ¥20,000), as well as more private rooms with en-suite bathrooms. The dorms offer sturdy metal-frame bunks with good mattresses.

YAESU TERMINAL HOTEL
BUSINESS HOTEL ¥¥

Map p266 (八重洲ターミナルホテル; ☎03-3281-3771; www.yth.jp; 1-5-14 Yaesu, Chūō-ku; s/d ¥11,500/16,500; ❄@🛜; 🅁JR lines to Tokyo, Yaesu north exit) This sleek little business hotel on cherry-tree-lined Sakura-dōri has contemporary lines and a minimalist look. Rooms are the usual compact business-hotel size, but they're decently priced for this neighbourhood and each showcases intriguing contemporary artworks by radiographic artist Steven Meyers.

⭐ HOSHINOYA TOKYO
RYOKAN ¥¥¥

Map p266 (星のや東京; ☎050-3786-1144; http://hoshinoyatokyo.com/en; 1-9-1 Ōtemachi, Chiyoda-ku; r from ¥72,000; 🆂Marunouchi line to Ōtemachi, exit A1) In creating its brand-new contemporary ryokan in the heart of Tokyo, Hoshinoya has barely put a foot wrong. Overcoming a location boxed in by office towers, this ryokan is all about insulating yourself from the city in a building that incorporates timeless craftsmanship and the best of traditional Japanese design and service.

⭐ AMAN TOKYO
DESIGN HOTEL ¥¥¥

Map p266 (☎03-5224-3333; www.aman.com/resorts/aman-tokyo; 1-5-6 Ōtemachi, Chiyoda-ku; r from ¥90,750; ⊖❄@🛜❄; 🆂Marunouchi line to Ōtemachi, exit A5) Overlooking the Imperial Palace (p56) from atop Ōtemachi Tower, the Aman incorporates natural materials – including dark stone walls, blonde wood and white *washi* (rice paper) – into its elegant, minimalist design. Enormous rooms all have baths with stunning city views – something you also get from the giant stone bath filled with onsen water in the spa. It's outstanding.

⭐ PALACE HOTEL TOKYO
HOTEL ¥¥¥

Map p266 (パレスホテル東京; ☎03-3211-5211; www.palacehoteltokyo.com; 1-1-1 Marunouchi, Chiyoda-ku; r from ¥62,000; ⊖❄@🛜❄; 🆂Chiyoda line to Ōtemachi, exit C13b) With its prestigious address, the gorgeously renovated Palace Hotel offers the refinement and elegance that its name suggests. Sniff the botanically perfumed air as you stride its plush corridors. Request a room with a balcony – they're a bit more expensive but worth it for the chance to soak up private alfresco views of the city.

🛏 Ginza & Tsukiji

⭐ PRIME POD GINZA TOKYO
CAPSULE HOTEL ¥

Map p268 (☎03-5550-0147; http://theprimepod.jp; 13th fl, Duplex Tower 5/13 Bldg, 5-13-19 Ginza, Chūō-ku; capsules from ¥5200; 🆂Hibiya line to Higashi-Ginza, exit 3) You're unlikely to find a cheaper place to sleep in chic Ginza than this capsule hotel, which is suitably contemporary in its stylings. For a bit more headroom than in your average capsule, request one of the corner pods when you book (rates are also cheaper online).

There are separate male and female floors. The lobby is on the 13th floor next to a cafe-bar with great views of the area.

DAIWA ROYNET HOTEL GINZA
BUSINESS HOTEL ¥¥

Map p268 (ダイワロイネットホテル銀座; ☎03-5159-1380; www.daiwaroynet.jp/english/ginza; 1-13-15 Ginza, Chūō-ku; s/d & tw from ¥16,500/22,000; ⊖❄@🛜; 🆂Yūrakuchō line to Ginza-itchōme, exit A10) You can take your pick from various drinks and amenities kits at the reception of this very centrally located business hotel. Rooms are well designed, with larger than usual bathrooms for this type of set-up. There's also a women-only floor.

★MITSUI GARDEN HOTEL GINZA PREMIER HOTEL ¥¥¥

Map p268 (三井ガーデンホテル銀座プレミア; ☎03-3543-1131; www.gardenhotels.co.jp; 8-13-1 Ginza, Chūō-ku; r from ¥38,000; ⊖ ❄ @ 📶; [S] Ginza line to Shimbashi, exit 1) If you book ahead and online, rooms at this upmarket business hotel are a steal – as low as ¥17,300. It has a great location, pleasantly decorated rooms, and a high-rise lobby with killer Shiodome and Tokyo Tower (p81) views.

🛏 Roppongi, Akasaka & Around

★ZABUTTON GOOD HOSTEL HOSTEL ¥

Map p270 (☎03-6277-6499; www.zabutton.jp; 1-29-20 Higashi-Azabu, Minato-ku; dm/d & tw ¥3780/8640; ⊖ ❄ 📶; [S] Ōedo line to Akabanebashi) This combined cafe-bar and hostel on a delightful shopping street is really good. The dorms have nicely designed wooden-box bunks, there's one tatami (reed mat) room that's the double, a kitchen/common room and a roof deck with a partial view of Tokyo Tower (p81). Staff are super-friendly.

★KAISU HOSTEL ¥

Map p270 (☎03-5797-7711; www.kaisu.jp; 6-13-5 Akasaka, Minato-ku; dm/r with shared bathroom from ¥3900/10,500; ⊖ ❄ 📶; [S] Chiyoda line to Akasaka, exit 7) Occupying a former *ryōtei* (geisha house), Kaisu is a flashpacker hostel with mid-century-modern and surfer-chic stylings. Dorms offer wooden bunks with the gorgeous old building's exposed beams on show. English-speaking staff are very friendly and there's a great cafe-bar where you can mingle with locals.

FIRST CABIN AKASAKA CAPSULE HOTEL ¥

Map p270 (☎03-3583-1143; http://first-cabin.jp; 3-13-7 Akasaka, Minato-ku; capsule from ¥4500; ⊖ ❄ 📶; [S] Chiyoda line to Akasaka, exit 2) This slick and modern capsule-hotel chain offers 2.5-sq-metre cabins with decent headroom and floor space filled with a comfy mattress. Upgrade to 4.4-sq-metre 1st-class cabins for more room to stand up beside the bed and a side table. There's a large communal bath to soak in, and separate floors for men and women.

★HOTEL S BOUTIQUE HOTEL ¥¥

Map p270 (ホテル S; ☎03-5771-2469; http://hr-roppongi.jp; 1-11-6 Nishi-Azabu, Minato-ku; r from ¥17,000, apt per month from ¥216,000; ⊖ ❄ @ 📶; [S] Hibiya line to Roppongi, exit 2) The various styles of room at this boutique property capture the arty design spirit of Roppongi. Some of the more expensive duplex-type rooms have Japanese design elements such as tatami (in charcoal) and circular *hinoki* (wooden baths). The entry-level rooms are also a cut above the usual.

HOTEL MYSTAYS PREMIER AKASAKA BUSINESS HOTEL ¥¥

Map p270 (☎03-6229 3280; www.mystays.com/mystays-p-akasaka; 2-17-54 Akasaka, Minato-ku; r from ¥7500; ⊖ ❄ 📶; [S] Chiyoda line to Akasaka, exit 5a or 5b) This slick new business hotel is a superb deal if you manage to bag one of its relatively spacious rooms at their low occupancy rate. When busy, the room rates increase to ¥16,000, which is still not bad for this ritzy district. Pluses include a coin laundry and small gym.

AIRPORT ACCOMMODATIONS

For late-night arrivals and early-morning departures, sleeping at the airport is an economical option.

9 Hours (☎0476-33-5109; http://ninehours.co.jp/en/narita; Narita International Airport Terminal 2; capsule ¥4900; ⊖ ❄ 📶) This slick capsule hotel inside Narita Airport has roomy, space-age pods and separate sleeping and shower rooms for men and women. It's possible to stay for only a few hours, too (¥1500 for the first hour, plus ¥500 per additional hour).

Royal Park Hotel the Haneda (ロイヤルパークホテル ザ 羽田; ☎03-6830-1111; www.rph-the.co.jp/haneda/en; Haneda Airport International Terminal; s/d from ¥15,300/19,400; ⊖ ❄ @ 📶) Haneda Airport's transit hotel is good value if you factor in the cost of not having to take a taxi for late-night arrivals. It's relatively new; rooms have modern decor and are stocked with amenities.

🛏 Ebisu, Meguro & Around

DORMY INN EXPRESS MEGURO AOBADAI BUSINESS HOTEL ¥¥

(ドーミーインエクスプレス目黒青葉台; ☎03-6894-5489; www.hotespa.net/hotels/meguro; 3-21-8 Aobadai, Meguro-ku; s/d from ¥14,000/20,000; ⊖❄@📶; [S]Hibiya line to Naka-Meguro) If you prefer to base yourself somewhere less hectic – but no less fun – try this business hotel along the canal in hip Naka-Meguro. This chain sets itself apart with its large communal bath (the rooms have showers, too), evening ramen service and free bicycles. Rooms are fresh and modern thanks to being spruced up in 2015.

★**CLASKA** BOUTIQUE HOTEL ¥¥¥

(クラスカ; ☎03-3719-8121; www.claska.com/en/hotel; 1-3-18 Chūō-chō, Meguro-ku; s/d from ¥15,400/28,500; ⊖❄📶; 🚌No 1, 2, or 7 from Meguro Station to Shimizu, 🚆Tōkyū Tōyoko line to Gakugei Daigaku, east exit) The Claska is hands-down Tokyo's most stylish hotel, though you might not know it from the retro business-hotel facade. No two rooms are alike: some have tatami and floor cushions; others have spacious terraces and glass-walled bathrooms. Its 20 rooms fill up fast. The only drawback is the out-of-the-way location, about 2km west of Meguro Station.

🛏 Shibuya & Shimo-Kitazawa

CAPSULE & SAUNA CENTURY CAPSULE HOTEL ¥

Map p273 (カプセル&サウナセンチュリー; ☎03-3464-1777; www.century-grp.com; 1-19-14 Dōgenzaka, Shibuya-ku; capsules from ¥4500; ⊖❄📶; 🚆JR Yamanote line to Shibuya, Hachikō exit) This men-only capsule hotel perched atop Dōgenzaka hill includes large shared bathrooms, massage chairs and coin laundry machines; the 'deluxe' capsules (¥5000) are slightly bigger. It's a clean, well-run place, and major credit cards are accepted. It's also pretty popular, so it's a good idea to reserve a spot before you head out for the night. Sorry: no visible tattoos.

★**SHIBUYA GRANBELL HOTEL** BOUTIQUE HOTEL ¥¥

Map p273 (渋谷グランベルホテル; ☎03-5457-2681; www.granbellhotel.jp; 15-17 Sakuragaoka-chō, Shibuya-ku; s/d from ¥14,000/23,000; ⊖❄@📶; 🚆JR Yamanote line to Shibuya, south

ONLY-IN-TOKYO SLEEPING ALTERNATIVES

Add a cultural experience, and save a little money, by staying the night in one of these unique sleeping alternatives.

Love Hotels

At these hotels for amorous encounters – known in Japanese as *rabu hoteru* (or *rabuho*, for short) – you can stop for a short afternoon 'rest' (from ¥3000) or an overnight 'stay' (from ¥6500); you can't stay consecutive nights, though. Some love hotels have kitschy interiors (and amenities that range from costumes to video-game consoles). Pictures of the rooms are usually displayed out front. There's a cluster of love hotels on Dōgenzaka in Shibuya.

Manga Kissa

Manga kissa are nominally cafes for reading manga and surfing the internet. Since they started adding private cubicles for DVD-viewing, they've become places to sleep too. A 'night pack' (eight to nine hours) costs ¥1500 to ¥2000. Reliable chains include **GeraGera** (www.geragera.co.jp), on the cheaper end and easily identified by its green frog logo; and **Gran Cyber Cafe Bagus** (www.bagus-99.com/internet_cafe), which is pricier but has showers and blanket rentals. You'll find branches of both in neighbourhoods you're likely to be out late in, including Roppongi, Shibuya and Shinjuku.

Spas & Saunas

Many spas and saunas – **Spa LaQua** (p146) and **Ōedo Onsen Monogatari** (p173) included – have 'relaxation rooms' with mats on the floor or reclining chairs where you can stay overnight for an extra fee (about ¥1500 to ¥2000).

exit) Though priced about the same as a business hotel, the Granbell is far more stylish. Some rooms have glass-enclosed bathrooms, Simmons beds and pop-art curtains. The hotel is on the quieter side of Shibuya, towards Daikanyama; still, it's just a few minutes' walk from the station.

HOTEL METS SHIBUYA   BUSINESS HOTEL ¥¥¥

Map p273 (ホテルメッツ渋谷; ☑03-3409-0011; www.hotelmets.jp/shibuya; 3-29-17 Shibuya, Shibuya-ku; s/d incl breakfast from ¥15,500/25,000; ☢❀@☎; ⓡJR Yamanote line to Shibuya, new south exit) Super-convenient and comfortable, the Hotel Mets is part of Shibuya Station's quiet south side. For a business hotel it's fairly stylish and the double beds clock in at a roomy 160cm. Bonus: breakfast is included, either a buffet spread or toast and eggs at the in-house cafe. Reception is on the 4th floor.

🛏 Harajuku & Aoyama

DORMY INN PREMIUM
SHIBUYA JINGŪMAE   BUSINESS HOTEL ¥¥

Map p276 (ドーミーインプレミアム渋谷神宮前; ☑03-5774-5489; www.hotespa.net/hotels/shibuya; 6-24-4 Jingūmae, Shibuya-ku; s/d from ¥11,490/15,990; ☢❀☎; ⓡJR Yamanote line to Harajuku, Omote-sandō exit) Dormy is a popular chain of business hotels, thanks to its free nightly ramen service (9.30pm to 11pm) and traditional communal baths (rooms have private showers, too). Other perks include bicycle rentals and a free morning shuttle service to Shibuya Station. Rooms are typically small with double beds (140cm).

🛏 West Tokyo

★REVERSIBLE
DESTINY LOFTS   APARTMENT ¥¥

(天命反転住宅; Tenmei Hanten Jūtaku; ☑0422-26-4966; www.rdloftsmitaka.com/english; 2-2-8 Ōsawa, Mitaka-shi; s/d/q from ¥17,300/20,300/29,300; ☢❀☎🍴; ⓡJR Sōbu-Chūō line to Mitaka, south exit) This is a rare opportunity to sleep within one of Tokyo's most eccentric architectural landmarks. The two apartments – one has one bedroom, the other has two (sleeping up to two or four, respectively) – were designed for maximum wonderment, with contrasting colours and textures and oddly shaped rooms. Both have washing machines, kitch-

ens and hammocks. You need to book a minimum of four nights.

The drawback is that the units are rather out of the way. From JR Mitaka Station, take bus 51 or 52 (¥220, 15 minutes, every 10 to 15 minutes) from bus stop 2 on the station's south side and get off at Ōsawa Jūjiro (大沢十字路); you can see the building from the bus stop. Not all buses go this far, so show the driver where you want to go. Bus 1 (¥220, 25 minutes, every 10 to 15 minutes) goes here from Kichijōji Station (south exit, bus stop 3), alongside Inokashira-kōen.

★RYOKAN SEIKŌ   RYOKAN ¥¥

(旅館西郊; ☑03-3391-0606; www.ryokan.or.jp/english/yado/main/28600; 3-38-9 Ogikubo, Suginami-ku; s/d from ¥6000/12,000; ☢☎; ⓡJR Sōbu-Chūō line to Ogikubo) Maximise your Japan experience by shacking up at this rambling traditional lodge in an 80-year-old building. Rooms have tatami floors, sliding paper doors and futons; bathrooms are shared. The halls are of highly polished wood; the lobby looks like a slightly cluttered living room. The downside: curfew is 11pm (midnight at the absolute latest).

BNA HOTEL   BOUTIQUE HOTEL ¥¥

Map p278 (www.bna-hotel.com; 2-4-7 Kōenji-kita, Suginami-ku; tw from ¥20,000; ☢☎; ⓡJR Sōbu line to Kōenji, north exit) There's a lot to love about new Kōenji hotel BnA: it's in a fun neighbourhood, just a minute's walk from the train station, the rooms were decorated by two Tokyo artists and the lobby doubles as a bar and event space. There's just not a lot of space: so far just two small rooms, though there are plans to expand.

🛏 Shinjuku & Northwest Tokyo

BOOK AND BED   HOSTEL ¥

Map p280 (☑03-6914-2914; http://bookandbedtokyo.com; 7th fl, 1-17-7 Nishi-Ikebukuro, Toshima-ku; dm from ¥3780; ☢❀@☎; ⓡJR Yamanote line to Ikebukuro) Tokyo's newest headline-generating hostel invites guests to curl up in cubbyholes tucked inside a bookshelf. 'Compact' bunks have 80cm-wide beds; standard ones (¥4860) have 120cm-wide beds and lockers. Naturally, all come with reading lights. Of the 2000 or so books on display, about 200 are in English, including many travel guides.

Note that the 'bookshelf' room is also the common area (though bunks have curtains); the 'bunk' room has more privacy. The hostel is above the Kirin City pub. Staff speak English.

KIMI RYOKAN
RYOKAN ¥

Map p280 (貴美旅館; ☎03-3971-3766; www.kimi-ryokan.jp; 2-36-8 Ikebukuro, Toshima-ku; s/d from ¥4860/6590; ❄✳@◈₪; ⊠JR Yamanote line to Ikebukuro, west exit) Easily one of the best budget ryokan in Tokyo, Kimi has been welcoming overseas guests for decades. There are tatami rooms of various sizes and a Japanese-style lounge area that's conducive to meeting other travellers. Clean showers and toilets are shared, and there's a lovely Japanese cypress bath. Book well in advance.

TŌKYŪ STAY SHINJUKU
HOTEL ¥¥

Map p280 (東急ステイ新宿; ☎03-3353-0109; 3-7-1 Shinjuku, Shinjuku-ku; s/d ¥15,600/30,000; ❄✳@◈; ⓢMarunouchi line to Shinjuku-sanchōme, exit C3) This new property is nestled among the *izakaya* and bars of Shinjuku-sanchōme. Rooms are stark to the point of having zero personality, but everything is crisp and clean. All rooms have washing machines; doubles have kitchenettes and 160cm-wide beds. Smaller, cheaper 'semi-double' rooms have 140cm beds (and no kitchen; ¥22,000). Prices drop slightly if you stay a week.

KADOYA HOTEL
HOTEL ¥¥

Map p280 (かどやホテル; ☎03-3346-2561; www.kadoya-hotel.co.jp; 1-23-1 Nishi-Shinjuku, Shinjuku-ku; s/d from ¥9980/15,800; ❄✳@◈; ⊠JR Yamanote line to Shinjuku, west exit) Kadoya has been welcoming foreign tourists for decades and is above all friendly and accommodating. The standard rooms show their age, but are clean, comfortable and a steal for Nishi-Shinjuku. The more recently updated 'comfort' rooms (single/double from ¥12,200/17,800) have more space, Japanese-style bath-tubs and more stylish decor. There's also a coin laundry.

HOTEL GRACERY SHINJUKU
HOTEL ¥¥

Map p280 (ホテルグレイスリー新宿; ☎03-6833-2489; http://shinjuku.gracery.com/; 1-19-1 Kabukichō, Shinjuku-ku; s/d from ¥16,000/22,000; ❄✳@◈; ⊠JR Yamanote line to Shinjuku, east exit) The big draw of this huge (970 rooms!) new hotel in the new Todo Building complex is the enormous Godzilla statue that seems to be taking a bite out of it (you'll have no trouble finding it). Everything here is fresh and modern, though the lobby can be noisy and chaotic. Also, it's smack in the middle of Kabukichō, the red-light district.

★ PARK HYATT TOKYO
LUXURY HOTEL ¥¥¥

Map p280 (パークハイアット東京; ☎03-5322-1234; http://tokyo.park.hyatt.com; 3-7-1-2 Nishi-Shinjuku, Shinjuku-ku; d from ¥60,000; ❄✳@◈₪; ⓢŌedo line to Tochōmae, exit A4) This eyrie atop a Tange Kenzō–designed skyscraper in west Shinjuku looks no less tasteful and elegant than when it opened 20 years ago, and it remains a popular spot for visiting celebrities. The hotel starts on the 41st floor, meaning even the entry-level rooms have fantastic views; 'Park Deluxe' rooms look out towards Mt Fuji. Perks include morning yoga classes.

🛏 Akihabara, Kagurazaka & Kōrakuen

TOKYO CENTRAL YOUTH HOSTEL
HOSTEL ¥

Map p282 (東京セントラルユースホステル; ☎03-3235-1107; www.jyh.gr.jp/tcyh; 18th fl, 1-1 Kagurashashi, Shinjuku-ku; dm ¥4050, with YHA discount ¥3450; ❄✳@◈₪; ⊠JR Sōbu line to Iidabashi, west exit) Sitting right on top of well-connected Iidabashi Station, this clean, well-managed hostel has fantastic transport access. It also has luxury-hotel-worthy night views. The drawbacks: a utilitarian atmosphere and an 11pm curfew. Sleeping is on basic wooden bunks in gender-segregated four-bed dorms. There's a breakfast buffet (¥600) and laundry machines.

There's little signage out front, but it's in the big office building in front of Iidabashi Station; take the elevator to the 18th floor.

★ HOTEL NIWA TOKYO
HOTEL ¥¥

Map p283 (庭のホテル; ☎03-3293-0028; www.hotelniwatokyo.com; 1-1-6 Misaki-chō, Chiyoda-ku; s/d from ¥14,600/17,400; ✳@◈; ⊠JR Sōbu line to Suidōbashi, east exit) A traditional Japanese design with a contemporary spin in the public areas and the reasonably spacious rooms of the Niwa put it well ahead of the usual bland midrangers. We like the rock garden and bamboo grove out front and the *shōji* (traditional paper screens) across the windows in the rooms.

★**HILLTOP HOTEL** HISTORIC HOTEL ¥¥¥
Map p283 (山の上ホテル; ☎03-3293-2311; www.
yamanoue-hotel.co.jp; 1-1 Kanda-Surugadai, Chiyoda-ku; s/d from ¥20,100/28,320; ✳ @ 🛜; 🚉JR
Chūō or Sōbu lines to Ochanomizu, Ochanomizu
exit) This art-deco gem from the 1930s ex-
udes personality and charm, with antique
wooden furniture and a wood-panelled
lounge. Mishima Yukio wrote his last few
novels here. The older rooms in the main
building come with antique writing desks
and leather chairs.

🛏 Ueno, Yanesen & Komagome

★**TOCO** HOSTEL ¥
(トコ; ☎03-6458-1686; http://backpackersja-
pan.co.jp; 2-13-21 Shitaya, Taitō-ku; dm/r from
¥2800/6800; ➿ ✳ @ 🛜; Ⓢ Hibiya line to Iriya,
exit 4) A group of friends renovated this old
wooden building (which dates to 1920 and
was once frequented by geisha) and turned
it into one of Tokyo's most attractive hostels. Private tatami rooms and dorms with
wooden bunks surround a small garden.
The hostel is hidden behind a trendy bar-
lounge (open 7pm to 11.30pm) in a modern
building at the front.

★**HANARE** GUESTHOUSE ¥¥
Map p284 (☎03-5834-7301; http://hanare.
hagiso.jp; 3-10-25 Yanaka, Taitō-ku; r incl breakfast from ¥12,960; Ⓢ Chiyoda line to Sendagi,
exit 2) A project of Tokyo University of the
Arts, Hanare offers five immaculate tatami
rooms in an old dormitory house, which has
been tastefully upgraded to retain original
features such as wooden beams. There is a
shared bathroom, but you'll be given tickets
to the local *sentō* (public bath), as the concept is to use Yanaka as an extension of the
guesthouse.

Reception is based in the nearby cafe-
gallery Hagiso (p155), where you'll be
served a traditional breakfast.

★**HŌMEIKAN** RYOKAN ¥¥
(鳳明館; ☎03-3811-1181; www.homeikan.
com; 5-10-5 Hongō, Bunkyō-ku; s/d from
¥8100/14,040; ✳ 🛜 🚻; Ⓢ Ōedo line to Kasuga,
exit A6) Although it's a little out of the way
in a residential neighbourhood, this beautifully crafted wooden ryokan is an old-world
oasis in the middle of Tokyo. The main
Honkan wing dates from the Meiji era

┌─────────────────────────────────┐
APARTMENT RENTALS
Short-term rental and apartment-share
sites currently operate in a grey zone in
Tokyo. According to law, a unit may be
rented for a minimum of 30 days. Otaku (where Haneda Airport is located) is
an exception; here the minimum stay is
seven nights. This may change, as the
government plans to review legislation
pertaining to vacation rentals (called
minpaku).
└─────────────────────────────────┘

and is registered as an important cultural
property, though we prefer the annexe,
Daimachi Bekkan, with its winding corridors and garden.

★**SAWANOYA RYOKAN** RYOKAN ¥¥
Map p284 (旅館澤の屋; ☎03-3822-2251; www.
sawanoya.com; 2-3-11 Yanaka, Taitō-ku; s/d from
¥5400/10,152; ➿ ✳ @ 🛜 🚻; Ⓢ Chiyoda line to
Nezu, exit 1) Sawanoya is a gem in quiet Yanaka, run by a very friendly family and with
all the traditional hospitality you would expect of a ryokan. The shared cypress and
earthenware baths are the perfect balm after a long day (some rooms have their own
bath, too). The lobby overflows with information about travel options in Japan.

Bicycles are also available for rent, and
lion-dance performances are occasionally
held for guests.

ANNEX KATSUTARŌ RYOKAN RYOKAN ¥¥
Map p284 (アネックス勝太郎旅館; ☎03-3828-
2500; www.katsutaro.com; 3-8-4 Yanaka, Taitō-ku;
s/d from ¥6600/12,000; ➿ ✳ @ 🛜 🚻; Ⓢ Chiyoda
line to Sendagi, exit 2) More like a modern hotel than a traditional ryokan, the family-run
Annex Katsutarō has spotless, thoughtfully
arranged tatami rooms with attached bathrooms. It's ideal for exploring the old Yanaka
district. Breakfast (from ¥430) and bicycles
(a bargain ¥300 a day) are also available.

🛏 Asakusa & Sumida River

★**NUI** HOSTEL ¥
(ヌイ; ☎03-6240-9854; http://backpackersja-
pan.co.jp/nui_en; 2-14-13 Kuramae, Taitō-ku;
dm/d from ¥3000/8000; ➿ ✳ @ 🛜; Ⓢ Ōedo line
to Kuramae, exit A7) In a former warehouse,
this hostel has raised the bar for stylish

budget digs in Tokyo. High ceilings mean bunks you can comfortably sit up in and there is an enormous shared kitchen and work space. Best of all is the ground-floor cafe-bar and lounge (open 8am to 1am), with furniture made from salvaged timber; it's a popular local hang-out.

★BUNKA HOSTEL TOKYO
HOSTEL ¥

Map p286 (☎03-5806-3444; http://bunka-hostel.jp; 1-13-5 Asakusa, Taitō-ku; dm/f from ¥3000/16,800; 🚆Tsukuba Express to Asakusa, exit 4) This is one of the most stylish of the new crop of hostels popping up across town, which combine a cafe or bar open to the public in the foyer with a hostel above. Bunka offers capsule-style bunks; roomier versions where you can stand up go for ¥5000 a bed.

★ANDON RYOKAN
RYOKAN ¥

(行燈旅館; ☎03-3873-8611; www.andon.co.jp; 2-34-10 Nihonzutsumi, Taitō-ku; s/d from ¥6500/7560; 🚭❄@📶; [S]Hibiya line to Minowa, exit 3) About 2km north of Asakusa, the contemporary Andon Ryokan is fabulously designed in form and function. It has tiny but immaculate tatami rooms and a spectacular upper-floor spa with a manga-style mural, which can be used privately. Toshiko, the friendly owner, collects antiques, which are displayed around the ryokan, and will serve you breakfast on dishes worth more than your stay.

Andon also has a full program of cultural events, bike rentals and laundry facilities. It's a five-minute walk from the subway.

JAPONICA LODGE
HOSTEL ¥

Map p286 (ジャポニカロッジ; ☎03-6802-7495; www.japonica-lodge.com; 1-3-3 Hanakawado; tent from ¥2500; 🚭❄📶; [S]Ginza line to Asakusa, exit 5) This is far from a conventional hostel. Japonica Lodge is an outdoor goods shop (also selling traditional crafts and running a green-tea cafe) that allows guests to road test their tents, sleeping mats and bags for the night. The shop is open from 11.30am to 8pm, but you're allowed to slip into your tent after 6pm.

For those planning an outdoor adventure trip in Japan, this place is a dream, with a knowledgeable English-speaking owner and lots of information on hiking and climbing routes.

KHAOSAN WORLD
HOSTEL ¥

Map p286 (☎03-3843-0153; http://khaosan-tokyo.com/en/world; 3-15-1 Nishi-Asakusa, Taitō-ku; dm/d from ¥2800/9000; 🚭❄@📶👪; 🚆Tsukuba Express to Asakusa, exit A2) One of Tokyo's most oddball hostels, Khaosan World has taken over an ageing love hotel and left much of the design elements intact – things like mirrored ceilings and glittering brocade wallpaper (don't worry: it's clean). There's a wide variety of rooms to choose from, including ones with tatami floors and capsule-style bunks. There are cooking and laundry facilities, too.

TOKYO RYOKAN
RYOKAN ¥

Map p286 (東京旅館; ☎090-8879-3599; www.tokyoryokan.com; 2-4-8 Nishi-Asakusa, Taitō-ku; r from ¥7000; 🚭❄📶; [S]Ginza line to Tawaramachi, exit 3) This tidy little inn has only three small tatami rooms and no en-suite bathrooms but tons of charm. There are touches of calligraphy, attractive woodwork and sliding screens. Kenichi, the owner, is an avid traveller, speaks fluent English and is super-knowledgeable about Asakusa.

K'S HOUSE TOKYO
HOSTEL ¥

(ケイズハウス東京; ☎03-5833-0555; http://kshouse.jp; 3-20-10 Kuramae, Taitō-ku; dm/s/d/tr ¥2900/4500/7200/9900; 🚭❄@📶; [S]Ōedo line to Kuramae, exit A6) This homey, modern hostel, with comfy sofas in the living room, cooking facilities and a roof terrace, is a backpacker fave. Service is friendly. From exit A6, walk northwest along Asakusa-dōri and turn left at the first corner. K's House is the yellow building at the end of the block.

★SUKEROKU NO YADO SADACHIYO
RYOKAN ¥¥

Map p286 (助六の宿貞千代; ☎03-3842-6431; www.sadachiyo.co.jp; 2-20-1 Asakusa, Taitō-ku; d with/without half-board from ¥33,600/19,600; 🚭❄@📶; [S]Ginza line to Asakusa, exit 1) This stunning ryokan virtually transports its guests to old Edo. Gorgeously maintained tatami rooms are spacious for two people, and all come with modern, Western-style bathrooms. Splurge on an exquisite meal here, and make time for the *o-furo* (traditional Japanese baths), one made of fragrant Japanese cypress and the other of black granite. Look for the rickshaw parked outside.

Understand Tokyo

TOKYO TODAY............................. 202

The city has its sights on the 2020 Olympics and beyond. Can it pull through in uncertain times?

HISTORY 204

The amazing story of how a swampy fishing village became one of the world's leading cities, despite repeated destruction.

POP CULTURE............................213

Manga, anime, hyperfashion, futuristic design and robots: Tokyo is the go-to place for all things cutting-edge (and cute).

ART & ARCHITECTURE 218

Tokyo's rich cultural offerings include the traditional, like kabuki, and the ambitiously modern, like visionary new buildings.

ONSEN.................................. 227

Take the plunge – you just might get hooked on the deeply relaxing hot springs in and around Tokyo.

Tokyo Today

Tokyo has reinvented itself countless times in the four centuries since its founding. With the 2020 Summer Olympic Games on the horizon, it hopes to do so again, with plans for a greener, friendlier city. Following decades of economic stagnation and a soon-to-be-shrinking workforce, the stakes are high. Does Tokyo still have what it takes to pull off another reincarnation?

Best on Film

Stray Dog (Kurosawa Akira; 1949) Noir thriller set in sweltering, occupied Tokyo.
Tokyo Story (Ozu Yasujirō; 1953) Portrait of a family in rapidly changing, post-WWII Japan.
Lost in Translation (Sofia Coppola; 2003) Disorienting, captivating Tokyo through the eyes of two Americans.
Adrift in Tokyo (Satoshi Miki; 2008) Two luckless anti-heroes on a long walk through the city.
Your Name (Kimi no Na wa; Shinkai Makoto; 2016) Dreamy anime contrasting life in Tokyo with life in rural Japan.

Best in Print

The Book of Tokyo: A City in Short Fiction (eds Michael Emmerich, Jim Hinks & Masashi Matsuie; 2015) Ten stories by contemporary Japanese writers set in the capital.
Coin Locker Babies (Murakami Ryū; 1980) Coming-of-age story set in a future, literally toxic, Tokyo.
After Dark (Murakami Haruki; 2004) Colourful characters come together during a night in the life of Tokyo.
A Strange Tale from East of the River (Nagai Kafu; 1937) An unlicensed prostitute in atmospheric, prewar Tokyo.

Countdown to 2020

Since it was announced in 2013 that Tokyo would hold the 2020 Summer Olympics, the city has gone into full preparation mode, enacting its 'Tokyo Vision 2020'. To understand just how much hosting the Olympics means to the city (or at least to the city's image-makers) you have to look back to the 1964 Summer Olympics. The first Games to be held in Asia, the 1964 Olympics marked Tokyo's big comeback after the city was all but destroyed in WWII. The powers that be hope that the 2020 games will again be symbolic, reaffirming Tokyo's position in the pantheon of the world's great cities, following more than two decades of economic malaise and the faltering of its export giants (such as Sony).

Much of the city's current infrastructure dates to the manic preparations leading up to the 1964 Games. And while Tokyo sold the International Olympic Committee on a compact Games that would use many existing structures, new developments are in store. The most dramatic of these are planned to take place on and along Tokyo Bay. Already in the works is the Umi-no-Mori (Sea Forest), a vast green space on one of the bay's artificial landfill islands, overseen by architect Andō Tadao. Other positive changes to look forward to: a more accessible Tokyo for people with disabilities, better English signage and tourist information, and expanded wi-fi networks.

Political Shake-up

Tokyo ran through two governors in four years, with both pressured to resign after just two years in office, amid claims of misusing campaign funds (Inose Naoki) and government money (Masuzoe Yōichi). In 2016, with the sentiment that enough was enough running high, the city elected – by a landslide among a record turnout – its first female governor, Koike Yuriko. Once a member of the long-time ruling party, the Liberal Democratic Party (LDP), Koike ran as an independent after the party chose to nominate someone else.

A former defence minister and fluent Arabic speaker, Koike has already enacted her campaign promise to rein in spending and increase transparency: with the budget for Olympic construction projects spiralling out of control, she has sent more plans back to the discussion table – and possibly the chopping block. (Even before Koike took over, the Olympic budget had become a sore point: in 2015 the central government scrapped the plan for a stadium designed by the late Iraqi-British architect Zaha Hadid, after construction costs had soared, replacing it with a more subdued and cheaper-to-make design by Kuma Kengo.) The new governor is also responsible for the abrupt decision to halt the move of Tsukiji Market to the newly constructed facility in Toyosu – after learning that contractors cut corners in carrying out decontamination of the site (where a gas refinery once stood).

The City of the Future

The Olympics isn't the only noteworthy event slated to happen in 2020: while the population of Japan has been declining since the 2000s, it's predicted that Tokyo's population will peak in 2020 and then also begin to decline. The birth rate for the capital hovers at around 1.1, the lowest in the nation (the national average is 1.4), and the labour force is shrinking but the country as a whole remains wary of immigration. The central government has campaigned for more women to enter the workforce to bolster numbers (though conservative sentiment against this lingers) *and* for families to have more children. Tokyoites vocal on social media say they can't win: the combination of the city's high cost of living, long working hours and long waiting lists for daycare means something has to give.

Tokyo is seen as a forerunner – facing the kinds of problems that major modern cities around the world will face as their populations begin a similar tapering off. The city's Tokyo Vision 2020 also includes provisions for making Tokyo a more attractive city in which to live and work – such as job centres for senior citizens, special economic zones for foreign companies and yes, more childcare facilities. If it works, Tokyo could become a model for cities of the future. For Tokyo families any progress can't come soon enough. And the government's back-up plan? Trying to sell Tokyoites on moving to the countryside. And robots.

if Tokyo were 100 people

16 would be 0-19
62 would be 20-64
21 would be 65-89
1 would be 90 years and over

ethnicity
(% of population)

Japanese 97
Korean 1
Chinese 1
Other 1

population per sq km

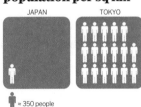

= 350 people

History

Tokyo is one of the world's great cities. It's perhaps surprising then to learn that until 450 years ago it was hardly a blip on the map. Still, while its history might be short, the city has played many roles: samurai stronghold, imperial capital and modern metropolis. Its latest identity as a city of the future – as it is portrayed in manga (Japanese comics), anime (Japanese animation) and think pieces – is just another example of Tokyo's protean nature.

Humble Beginnings

The enormous built space that is Tokyo, population 13 million, has come a long way from its origins as a collection of tidal flats at the mouth of the Sumida-gawa (Sumida River). Its first permanent inhabitants were part of a pottery-producing culture who settled here around 10,000 BC. These early Tokyoites lived as fishers, hunters and food gatherers. Some 4000 years later, wet-rice farming techniques were introduced from Korea, and the Shintō religion also began to develop.

Around AD 300, the proto-Japanese nation began to form in the Kansai area, around what is today Nara Prefecture, under the control of the Yamato clan. These forerunners of the current imperial family claimed descent from the sun goddess Amaterasu. In the 6th century, Buddhism arrived in Japan from China, which had a dramatic effect on the course of events to come. Buddhism introduced a highly evolved system of metaphysics, codes of law and the Chinese writing system, a conduit for the principles of Confucian statecraft. By the end of the 8th century, the Buddhist clerical bureaucracy had become vast, threatening the authority of the nascent imperial administration. The emperor responded by relocating the capital to Heian-kyō (modern-day Kyoto). From that point on, Kyoto generally served as the capital until the Meiji Restoration in 1868, when Tokyo became the new chief city.

All of this was happening in the west: Edo (the old name for Tokyo) was still just a sleepy fishing village, and would continue to be so for the next several hundred years.

TIMELINE	10,000 BC	AD 710	794
	Tokyo area inhabited by pottery-making people during late neolithic Jōmon period. The Kantō region around Tokyo is among the most densely settled in this era.	Japan's first permanent capital established at Nara, ending the practice of moving the capital after an emperor's death. The city is modelled on Chang'an, capital of the Tang dynasty China.	Imperial capital moved to Heian-kyō, renamed Kyoto in the 11th century. It is laid out in a grid in accordance with Chinese geomancy principles.

Rise of the Warrior Class

Throughout the Heian period (794–1185), courtly life in the capital developed into a golden age of culture and refinement. Meanwhile, lesser nobles, with little chance of improving their rank and standing, led military excursions to rein in the outer-lying provinces. They were accompanied by their loyal retainers, skilled warriors called samurai.

By the 12th century, some of the clans established by these lesser nobles had gained significant power and influence. A feud broke out between two, the Minamoto (also known as Genji) and the Taira (also known as Heike), who were backing different claimants to the imperial throne. The Minamoto were eventually the victors, in 1192, and their leader, Minamoto Yoritomo, created a new position for himself – shogun (generalissimo).

The emperor in Kyoto remained the nation's figurehead, granting authority to the shogun, though in reality it was the shogun who wielded power. Minamoto set up his *bakufu* (military government) in his eastern stronghold, a seaside cove named Kamakura – bringing the seat of power closer to Tokyo for the first time. The Kamakura *bakufu* lasted until 1333, when it was trounced by imperial forces led by the general Ashikaga Takauji. The emperor resumed power; the position of shogun was retained – awarded to Ashikaga – but removed to Kyoto, making the government once again centralised.

Over the next two centuries, the Ashikaga shoguns were increasingly unable to control the provincial warlords, called *daimyō,* who had set about consolidating considerable power. Castles and fortresses were erected around the country. One such castle was constructed in the mid-15th century by a warrior poet named Ōta Dōkan in a place called Edo.

Besides loyal samurai, Tokugawa Ieyasu stocked his capital with ninja. Their commander was Hattori Hanzō, renowned for his cunning and deadly tactics that helped Ieyasu at key moments in his career. The ninja master's legacy was enshrined in Hanzōmon, a gate that still exists today at the Imperial Palace.

Battle for Supremacy

By the time Portuguese traders and missionaries arrived in 1543, feudal warlords had carved Japan into a patchwork of fiefdoms. One of the most powerful *daimyō,* Oda Nobunaga of the Chūbu region, near present-day Nagoya, was quick to see how the Portuguese could support his ambitious plans. He viewed their Christianity as a potential weapon against the power of the Buddhist clergy and made ample use of the firearms they introduced. By the time he was assassinated in 1581, Oda had united much of central Japan. Toyotomi Hideyoshi took over the job of consolidating power, but looked less favourably on the growing Christian movement, subjecting it to systematic persecution.

Toyotomi's power was briefly contested by Tokugawa Ieyasu, son of a minor lord allied to Oda. After a brief struggle for power, Tokugawa agreed to a truce with Toyotomi; in return, Toyotomi granted him eight provinces in eastern Japan – which included Edo. While Toyotomi in-

1457	1600	1638	1657
Ōta Dōkan orders construction of the first Edo Castle. Later developed by shogun Tokugawa Ieyasu in the 17th century, it becomes the largest fortress the world has seen.	Tokugawa Ieyasu, victor in the Battle of Sekigahara, establishes his capital in Edo, beginning 250 years of peace under Tokugawa rule, known as the Edo period.	*Sakoku* national isolation policy; Japan cuts off all contact with the outside world, except for limited trade with the Dutch and Chinese off Nagasaki. The policy remains until the 1850s.	Great Meireki Fire devastates Edo, killing over 100,000 people and destroying two-thirds of the city. Reconstruction plans include the widening of streets to prevent further conflagrations.

tended this to weaken Tokugawa by separating him from his ancestral homeland Chūbu, the upstart looked upon the gift as an opportunity to strengthen his power. He set about turning Edo into a real city.

When Toyotomi Hideyoshi died in 1598, power passed to his son, Toyotomi Hideyori. However, Tokugawa Ieyasu had been busily scheming to secure the shogunate for himself and soon went to war against those loyal to Hideyori. Tokugawa's forces finally defeated Hideyori and his supporters at the legendary Battle of Sekigahara in 1600, moving him into a position of supreme power. He chose Edo as his permanent base and began 2½ centuries of Tokugawa rule.

SAMURAI: THOSE WHO SERVE

The culture of Kyoto originated in the imperial court. Osaka is still associated with its mercantile roots. Tokyo, meanwhile, is the city of the samurai.

The prime duty of a samurai, a member of the warrior class, was to give faithful service to his *daimyō* (feudal lord). In fact, the origin of the term 'samurai' is closely linked to a word meaning 'to serve'. Over the centuries, the samurai established a code of conduct that came to be known as *bushidō* (the way of the warrior), drawn from Confucianism, Shintō and Buddhism.

Confucianism required a samurai to show absolute loyalty to his lord. Towards the oppressed, a samurai was expected to show benevolence and exercise justice. Subterfuge was to be despised, as were all commercial and financial transactions. A real samurai had endless endurance and total self-control, spoke only the truth and displayed no emotion. Since his honour was his life, disgrace and shame were to be avoided above all else, and all insults were to be avenged.

From Buddhism, the samurai learnt the lesson that life is impermanent – a handy reason to face death with serenity. Shintō provided the samurai with patriotic beliefs in the divine status both of the emperor and of Japan – the abode of the gods.

Seppuku (ritual suicide), also known as hara-kiri, was an accepted means of avoiding dishonour. Seppuku required the samurai to ritually disembowel himself, watched by an aide, who then drew his own sword and lopped off the samurai's head. One reason for this ritual was the requirement that a samurai should never surrender but always go down fighting.

Not all samurai were capable of adhering to their code of conduct – samurai indulging in double-crossing or subterfuge, or displaying outright cowardice, were popular themes in Japanese theatre.

Though the samurai are long gone, there are echoes of *bushidō* in the salaryman corporate warriors of today's Japan. Under the once-prevalent lifetime employment system, employees were expected to show complete obedience to their company, and could not question its decisions if, for example, they were transferred to distant Akita-ken.

1707	1721	1853	1868
Mt Fuji erupts, spewing ash over the streets of Edo 100km to the northeast. The stratovolcano is still active today but with a low risk of eruption.	Edo's population grows to 1.1 million as people move in from rural areas, making it the world's largest city. Meanwhile, London's population is roughly 650,000.	Black ships of the US navy arrive in Japan under the command of Commodore Matthew Perry, who succeeds in forcing Japan open to US trade; international port established in Yokohama in 1859.	Meiji Restoration; Tokugawa shogunate loyalists are defeated in civil war. The imperial residence moves to Edo, which is renamed Tokyo.

Boomtown Edo

In securing a lasting peace nationwide and ruling from Edo, Tokugawa Ieyasu laid the foundation for Tokyo's ascendancy as one of the world's great cities. In 1603 the emperor appointed him shogun, and the Tokugawa family ruled from Edo Castle (Edo-jō), on the grounds of the current Imperial Palace. The castle became the largest fortress the world had ever seen, with elaborate rituals shaping the lives of its many courtiers, courtesans, samurai and attendants. Edo would also grow to become the world's largest city – topping one million people in the early 1700s and dwarfing much older London and Paris – as people from all over Japan flocked there to serve the growing military class.

This came as the result of a canny move by the Tokugawa that ensured their hegemony: they implemented a system called *sankin kōtai* that demanded that all *daimyō* in Japan spend alternate years in Edo. Their wives and children remained in Edo while the *daimyō* returned to their home provinces. This dislocating policy made it hard for ambitious *daimyō* to usurp the Tokugawas. The high costs of travelling back and forth with a large retinue also eroded their financial power.

Society was rigidly hierarchical, comprising (in descending order of importance) the nobility, who had nominal power; the *daimyō* and their samurai; the farmers; and finally the artisans and merchants. Class dress, living quarters and even manner of speech were all strictly codified, and interclass movement was prohibited.

The caste-like society imposed by Tokugawa rule divided Edo into a high city (Yamanote) and a low city (Shitamachi). The higher Yamanote (literally 'hand of the mountains') was home to the *daimyō* and their samurai, while the merchants, craftsmen and lower orders of Edo society were forced into the low-lying Shitamachi (literally 'downtown').

The typical residential neighbourhood of the Shitamachi featured squalid conditions, usually comprising flimsy wooden structures with earthen floors. These shanty towns were often swept by great conflagrations, which locals referred to as *Edo-no-hana,* or flowers of Edo; the expression's bravura sums up the spirit of Shitamachi. Under great privation, Shitamachi subsequently produced a flourishing culture that thumbed its nose at social hardships and the strictures of the shogunate. Increasingly wealthy merchants patronised the kabuki theatre, sumo tournaments and the pleasure quarters of the Yoshiwara – generally enjoying a *joie de vivre* that the dour lords of Edo castle frowned upon. Today, the best glimpses we have into that time come from *ukiyo-e* (woodblock prints).

1871	1872	1889	1914
Samurai domain system abolished, and Tokyo Prefecture (Tokyo-fu) established out of the former Musashi Province. Tokyo is initially divided into 15 wards.	Japan's first train line connects Shimbashi in Tokyo with Yokohama to the southwest; Osaka–Kōbe services are launched in 1874 and Osaka–Kyoto services in 1877.	Constitution of the Empire of Japan declared. Based on a Prussian model of constitutional monarchy, the emperor shares power with an elected parliament.	Tokyo Station opens. Designed by Tatsuno Kingo, it begins operations with four platforms. Greatly expanded over the past 100 years, it now serves more than 3000 trains per day.

The 'Eastern Capital' Is Born

Edo was divided into *machi* (towns) according to profession. It's still possible to stumble across small enclaves that specialise in particular wares. Most famous are Jimbōchō, the bookshop area; Kappabashi, with its kitchen supplies; and Akihabara, which now specialises in electronics and manga (comics).

Edo's transformation from a grand medieval city into a world-class capital required an outside nudge, or *gaiatsu* (external pressure). This came in the form of a fleet of black ships, under the command of US Navy Commodore Matthew Perry, that sailed into Edo-wan (now Tokyo Bay) in 1853. Perry's expedition demanded that Japan open itself to foreign trade after centuries of isolation.

The coming of Westerners heralded a far-reaching social revolution against which the antiquated Tokugawa regime was powerless. In 1867–68, civil war broke out between Tokugawa loyalists and a band of upstart *daimyō* from southern Kyūshū. The latter were victorious; faced with widespread antigovernment feeling and accusations that the regime had failed to prepare Japan for this threat, the last Tokugawa shogun resigned. Power reverted to Emperor Meiji in what became known as the Meiji Restoration; though in reality, the southern lords were the real decision makers. In 1868, the seat of imperial power was moved from Kyoto to Edo, and the city renamed Tokyo (Eastern Capital).

Japan's new rulers pushed the nation into a crash course in industrialisation and militarisation. A great exchange began between Japan and the West: Japanese scholars were dispatched to Europe to study everything from literature and engineering to nation building and modern warfare. Western scholars were invited to teach in Japan's nascent universities.

The new Japanese establishment learnt quickly: in 1872 the first railroad opened, connecting Tokyo with the new port of Yokohama, south along Tokyo Bay, and by 1889 the country had a Western-style constitution. In a remarkably short time, Japan achieved military victories over China (1894–95) and Russia (1904–05) and embarked on modern, Western-style empire building, with the annexation of Taiwan (1895), then Korea (1910) and Micronesia (1914).

Nationalists were also busy transforming Shintō into a jingoistic state religion. Seen as a corrupting foreign influence, Buddhism suffered badly – many valuable artefacts and temples were destroyed, and the common people were urged to place their faith in the pure religion of State Shintō.

During the Meiji period, and the following Taishō period, changes that were taking place all over Japan could be seen most prominently in the country's new capital city. Tokyo's rapid industrialisation, uniting around the nascent *zaibatsu* (huge industrial and trading conglomerates), drew job seekers from around Japan, causing the population to grow rapidly. In the 1880s electric lighting was introduced. Western-style brick buildings began to spring up in fashionable areas such as Ginza.

1923	1923	1926	1936
Great Kantō Earthquake kills more than 140,000. An estimated 300,000 houses are destroyed; a reconstruction plan is only partly realised due to money shortages.	Yamanote line completed. One of Japan's busiest lines, today the 34.5km loop around the heart of Tokyo has 29 stations. It takes trains about an hour to circle the city.	Hirohito ascends the throne to become the Shōwa emperor. Presiding over Japan's military expansion across East Asia and atrocities, he is spared trial by Allied forces after WWII.	February 26, over 1000 Imperial Japanese Army troops stage a coup d'état, killing political leaders and occupying the centre of Tokyo before surrendering to government loyalists.

The Great Kantō Earthquake

If the Meiji Restoration sounded the death knell for old Edo, there were two more events to come that were to erase most traces of the old city: the Great Kantō Earthquake and the firebombings of WWII.

According to Japanese folklore, a giant catfish living underground causes earthquakes when it stirs. At noon on 1 September 1923 the catfish really jumped: the Great Kantō Earthquake, a magnitude 7.9 quake that struck south of Tokyo in Sagami Bay, caused unimaginable devastation in Tokyo. More than the quake itself, it was the subsequent fires, lasting some 40 hours, that laid waste to the city, including some 300,000 houses. A quarter of the quake's 142,000 fatalities occurred in one savage firestorm in a clothing depot.

In true Edo style, reconstruction began almost immediately. The spirit of this rebuilding is perhaps best summed up by author Edward Seidensticker in *Tokyo Rising* (1990), which outlined how popular wisdom had it that any business that did not resume trading within three days of being burnt did not have a future. Opportunities were lost in reconstructing the city – streets might have been widened and the capital transformed into something more of a showcase – but its spirit prevailed.

Low City, High City (Edward Seidensticker; 1970) and *Tokyo Now & Then* (Paul Waley; 1984) are two classic tomes that tell the story of how Edo became Tokyo, revealing along the way traces of the old city that still remain today.

Modern Boys, Modern Girls

The devastating effects of the Great Kantō Earthquake aside, the first few decades of the 20th century were a time of optimism in Tokyo. Old feudal-era loyalties finally buckled and party politics flourished for the first time, giving rise to the term Taishō Democracy – after the era of the short-lived Taishō emperor (1912–26). In 1925 suffrage was extended to all males, not just property owners (women wouldn't be given the vote until the American occupation after WWII).

Western fashions and ideas, initially the domain of only the most elite, began to trickle down to the middle class. More and more Tokyoites began adopting Western dress (which they most likely traded for kimonos as soon as they got home). Cafes and dance halls flourished. Women began to work outside the home, in offices, department stores and factories, enjoying a new freedom and disposable income. Like women around the world in the 1920s, they cut their hair short and wore pants. These were the 'modern girls' – or *moga* for short – who walked arm in arm with their male counterparts, the *moba,* around Ginza, then the most fashionable district in the city.

1944–45	1947	1948	1951
Allied air raids during WWII destroy large swaths of the city, including the Imperial Palace; casualties of more than 100,000 are reported.	New constitution adopted, including Article 9 in which Japan renounces war and the possession of armed forces. Japan's Self-Defense Forces are built into a formidable military arsenal.	Tokyo War Crimes Tribunal concludes, resulting in the execution of six wartime Japanese leaders. In 1978, they are secretly enshrined at Yasukuni-jinja.	Japan signs San Francisco Peace Treaty, officially ending WWII, renouncing Japan's claims to overseas colonies and outlining compensation to Allied territories.

The Beginning of Shōwa & WWII

In 1904, the kimono shop Echigoya, founded in 1673, decided to reinvent itself as Japan's first Western-style department store, Mitsukoshi. The shop in Nihombashi (1914) was called the grandest building east of the Suez Canal. The retailer remains one of the most prestigious shops in Tokyo.

Following the accession of Emperor Hirohito (*Shōwa tennō* to the Japanese) and the initiation of the Shōwa period in 1926, the democratic spirit of the last two decades was replaced by a quickening tide of nationalist fervour. In 1931 the Japanese invaded Manchuria, and in 1937 embarked on full-scale hostilities with China. By 1940, a tripartite pact with Germany and Italy had been signed and a new order for all of Asia formulated: the Greater East Asia Co-Prosperity Sphere. On 7 December 1941, the Japanese attacked Pearl Harbor, bringing the US, Japan's principal rival in the Asia-Pacific region, into WWII.

Despite initial successes, the war was disastrous for Japan. On 18 April 1942, B-25 bombers carried out the first bombing and strafing raid on Tokyo, with 364 casualties. Much worse was to come. Incendiary bombing commenced in 1944, the most devastating of which took place over the nights of 9 and 10 March 1945, when some two-fifths of the city, mainly in the Shitamachi area, went up in smoke and tens of thousands of lives were lost. The same raids destroyed Asakusa's Sensō-ji, and later raids destroyed Meiji-jingū. By the time Emperor Hirohito made his famous capitulation address to the Japanese people on 15 August 1945, much of Tokyo had been decimated – sections of it were almost completely depopulated, like the charred remains of Hiroshima and Nagasaki after they were devastated by atomic bombs. Food and daily necessities were scarce, the population was exhausted by the war effort and fears of marauding US military overlords were high.

The Postwar Miracle

Black markets thrived after WWII when goods by other channels were scarce. The remains of Ueno's black market can be seen in Ameya-yokochō, which is still a lively market. Shinjuku, too, has two former black markets that are now popular places to eat and drink: Omoide-yokochō and Golden Gai.

Tokyo's phoenix-like rise from the ashes of WWII and its emergence as a major global city is something of a miracle. Still, during the US occupation in the early postwar years, Tokyo was something of a honky-tonk town. Now-respectable areas such as Yūrakuchō were the haunt of the so-called *pan-pan* girls (prostitutes).

In 1947, Japan adopted its postwar constitution, with the now-famous Article 9, which barred the use of military force in settling international disputes and maintaining a military for warfare (although the nation does maintain a self-defence force).

By 1951, with a boom in Japanese profits arising from the Korean War, Tokyo began to rapidly rebuild, especially the central business district. Once again, Tokyoites did not take the devastation as an opportunity to redesign their city (as did Nagoya, for example), but rebuilt where the old had once stood. (Extravagant plans, which included a lush greenbelt around the city, existed, but pragmatism – and financial constraints – prevailed.)

1952	1955	1958	1964
US occupation ends; Japan enters a period of high economic growth. The Korean War provides an incentive for Japanese manufacturers, who supply US forces.	Liberal Democratic Party (LDP) founded; it has a virtually uninterrupted hold on power into the 21st century despite recurring corruption scandals and deep-seated factionalism.	Tokyo Tower (333m) completed, designed for broadcasts and inspired by the Eiffel Tower. By the 1960s it is a tourist magnet and symbol of Japan's high growth.	Tokyo Olympic Games held, marking Japan's postwar reintegration into the international community and the first time the Games are hosted by a non-Western country.

During the 1960s and '70s, Tokyo re-emerged as one of the centres of growing Asian nationalism (the first phase was in the 1910s and '20s). Increasing numbers of Asian students came to Tokyo, taking home with them new ideas about Asia's role in the postwar world.

One of Tokyo's proudest moments came when it hosted the 1964 Summer Olympics. In preparation, the city embarked on a frenzy of construction unequalled in its history. Many Japanese see this time as a turning point in the nation's history, the moment when Japan finally recovered from the devastation of WWII to emerge as a fully fledged member of the modern world economy.

The Bubble Bursts

Construction and modernisation continued at a breakneck pace through the '70s, with the interruption of two Middle East oil crises, to reach a peak in the late '80s, when wildly inflated real-estate prices and stock speculation fuelled what is now known as the 'bubble economy'. When the bubble burst in 1991, the economy went into a protracted slump that was to continue, more or less, into the present.

There were other, more disturbing, troubles in Japanese society. In March 1995, members of the Aum Shinrikyō doomsday cult released sarin nerve gas on crowded Tokyo subways, killing 12 and injuring more than 5000. This, together with the devastating Kōbe earthquake of the same year, which killed more than 6000 people, signalled the end of Japan's feeling of omnipotence, born of the unlimited successes of the '80s.

21st Century

Tokyo has weathered a long hangover since the heady days of the bubble economy. Despite periods of small but hopeful growth, and declarations that 'Japan is back', the economy is still sputtering. In 2014, the administration of Prime Minister Abe Shinzō launched an ambitious stimulus plan – nicknamed 'Abenomics' – that seemed promising but ultimately couldn't pull Japan out of its slump. The raising of the consumption tax the same year, from 5% to 8%, put a squeeze on spending (it's set to increase again in 2019).

Japan is also struggling with its international role, particularly the leeway allowed by its 'Peace Constitution'. In 2004, then Prime Minister Koizumi Junichirō sent Self-Defense Force (SDF) troops to join Allied forces in Iraq. Though it was a humanitarian – not combat – mission, this marked the first deployment of Japanese troops overseas since WWII; the move was received with apprehension and even protest. The Defense Agency was promoted to a fully fledged ministry and Japanese

Based on the price paid for the most expensive real estate in the late 1980s, the land value of Tokyo exceeded that of the entire US. During the late '80s, Japanese companies also bought international icons including Pebble Beach Golf Course, the Rockefeller Center and Columbia Pictures movie studio.

1968–69	1972	1989	1995
Tokyo University students take over administrative buildings to protest the Vietnam War. No one is allowed to graduate in 1969 and entrance exams are cancelled.	Okinawa, captured and held by US forces in WWII, is returned to Japan. High concentration of lingering US military bases on the islands angers locals even today.	Death of Emperor Hirohito; Heisei era begins as Hirohito's son Akihito ascends the throne; stock market decline begins, initiating a decade-long economic slump in Japan.	Doomsday cult Aum Shinrikyō releases sarin gas on the Tokyo subway, killing 12 and injuring more than 5000. Guru Shōkō Asahara is sentenced to death for Aum-related crimes in 2004.

RISE OF THE MEGAMALLS

When **Roppongi Hills** (p78) opened in 2003, it was more than just another shopping mall: it was an ambitious prototype for the future of Tokyo. It took developer Mori Minoru (1934–2012) no fewer than 17 years to acquire the land and to construct this labyrinthine kingdom. He envisioned improving the quality of urban life by centralising home, work and leisure into a utopian microcity.

Foreign investment banks and leading IT companies quickly signed up for office space, and Roppongi was positioned as the centre of the new economy – an alternative to Marunouchi, a bastion of traditional (read: old-fashioned) business culture. The nouveau riche who lived, worked and played at Roppongi Hills were christened *Hills-zoku* (Hills tribe) by the media, and their lavish lifestyles were splashed across the tabloids.

Similar projects appeared in succession: Shiodome Shio-site (2004), **Tokyo Midtown** (p79; 2005), Akasaka Sacas (2008) and **Toranomon Hills** (Map p270; http://toranomonhills.com; 1-23 Toranomon, Minato-ku; §Ginza line to Toranomon, exit 1; 2014). While they open to much fanfare, such developments have proved polarising: conceived during the economic bubble of the late '80s and early '90s and unveiled in harder times, the luxury and exclusivity that they project seem out of step with today's lingering economic malaise. Still, Roppongi Hills at least is credited with transforming the neighbourhood of Roppongi, once synonymous with sleazy nightlife, into a cultural attraction.

military cooperation with the US escalated. In 2014, the Abe administration passed a resolution to reinterpret Article 9 (the peace clause) of the constitution to allow the SDF to come to the aid of an ally under attack. It was a decision that was not supported by the majority of citizens; demonstrations were held in the capital.

On 11 March 2011, a magnitude 9.0 earthquake rocked northeastern Japan, resulting in a record-high tsunami that killed nearly 20,000 people and sparked a meltdown at the Dai-ichi nuclear plant in Fukushima-ken. Tokyo experienced little actual damage, but was shaken nonetheless. (The capital itself is long overdue for a major earthquake and for a time the idea of decentralisation was bandied about – to mitigate the effects of a potential disaster.) Of greater concern to ordinary citizens was the risk of radioactive contamination of foodstuffs, prompting many to form organisations to petition the government for greater transparency of safety monitoring, and in more extreme cases, the abolition of nuclear power.

With the announcement in 2013 that Tokyo would hold the 2020 Summer Olympics, all talk of decentralisation evaporated. With a renewed focus on turning the city into a showpiece, Tokyo is now focusing on what it does best: building.

2009	2011	2013	2016
LDP loses control of the House of Representatives to the opposition Democratic Party of Japan (DPJ) for only the second time since 1955; by 2012 the LDP is back in power.	Magnitude 9.0 earthquake strikes off Sendai in Tōhoku, unleashing tsunami waves, killing nearly 20,000, and crippling the Fukushima Dai-ichi nuclear plant.	Tokyo is awarded the 2020 Summer Olympics; plans are set in motion to revitalise the bayfront and make the city a more international destination.	Tokyo elects its first female governor, Koike Yuriko; Emperor Akihito (b 1933) announces his wish to retire.

Pop Culture

A Studio Ghibli movie; a manga by Tezuka Osamu; day-glo accessories from cutesy pioneer 6% Dokidoki; the latest Sony PlayStation: Tokyo is a master at crafting pop-cultural products that catch the attention of the world. Here more people read manga (comics) than newspapers, street fashion is more dynamic than that on the catwalk, robots are the stars of anime (Japanese animation) as well as real-life marvels of technology, and everyone, including the police, has a *kawaii* (cute) cartoon mascot.

Manga

Walk into any Tokyo convenience store and you can pick up several phone-directory-sized weekly manga anthologies. Inside you'll find about 25 comic narratives spanning everything from gangster sagas and teen romance to bicycle racing to *shōgi* (Japanese chess), often with generous helpings of sex and violence. The more successful series are

Above: Akihabara (p136)

collected in volumes *(tankōbon)*, which occupy major sections of book-shops.

As Japan's publishing industry faces a severe decline in sales across the board, manga is the one bright hope, with sales of *tankōbon* clocking up more than 500 million volumes in 2015, and the market booming for *keitai* manga – comics read on smartphones. Top seller *One Piece* shifts more than 14 million units a year alone. Major publishers, including Kodansha and Kadokawa, are based in Tokyo and this is where many *mangaka* (manga artists) get their start in the industry.

Comiket (www.comiket.co.jp; short for 'Comic Market') is a massive twice-yearly convention for fan-produced amateur manga known as *dōjinshi*. To the untrained eye, *dōjinshi* looks like 'official' manga, but most are parodies (sometimes of a sexual nature) of famous manga titles.

Top Manga

Astro Boy

Barefoot Gen

Black Jack

Doraemon

Lone Wolf and Cub

Nausicaä of the Valley of the Wind

Rose of Versailles

Anime

Many manga have inspired anime for TV and cinema. For example, *Nausicaä of the Valley of the Wind,* a 1982 manga by Miyazaki Hayao, Japan's most revered living animator, was made into a movie in 1984. Beloved TV anime *Astro Boy* and *Kimba the White Lion* were the first successful manga for Tezuka Osamu (1928–89), an artist frequently referred to as *manga no kamisama* – the 'god of manga'.

Studio Ghibli (www.ghibli.jp) is Japan's most critically acclaimed and commercially successful producer of animated movies. Its films include classics such as the Oscar-winning *Spirited Away*, directed by Miyazaki Hayao. In 2016 Miyazaki announced he was coming out of retirement to direct a full-length version of *Kemushi no Boro (Boro the Caterpillar)*, a short movie he had previously made for the Ghibli Museum.

Miyazaki's creative partner and mentor from their time working together in the 1960s for animation studio Tōei is Takahata Isao. He is the director of anime classics including *Grave of the Fireflies* (1988), *Only Yesterday* (1991) and the Oscar-nominated *The Tale of Princess Kaguya* (2013).

Studio Ghibli's premium product is far superior to the vast majority of low-budget anime, which tends to feature saucer-eyed schoolgirls, cute fluorescent monsters and mechatronic superheroes in recycled and tweaked plots. Nevertheless, the international success of series such as *Mobile Suit Gundam* and *Pokémon* continues to tempt many fans to anime's creative source in Tokyo.

Top Anime

Akira (1988)

My Neighbor Totoro (1988)

Ghost in the Shell (1995)

Tokyo Godfathers (2003)

Mind Game (2004)

The Tale of Princess Kaguya (2013)

GODZILLA RESURGENCE

Following a major US-movie reboot in 2014, Godzilla, the legendary star of Japanese cinema, has been experiencing a revival in Tokyo. Of course, as true fans know, this pop-culture icon has never really gone away, starring in 29 movies produced by studio Toho in Japan alone. The latest, *Shin Godzilla*, directed by anime supremos Anno Hideaki and Higuchi Shinji, was a local box-office smash in 2016.

A mash-up of the Japanese words for gorilla *(gorira)* and whale *(kujira)*, Godzilla first stomped his way out of Tokyo Bay in 1954, blasting everything in his path with his atomic breath. Recreating something of that moment for a contemporary audience is an installation of the monster's head and claws on the 8th floor of the **Hotel Gracery Shinjuku** (p198). On the hour from noon to 8pm, the giant artwork comes to life with flashing red eyes and laser lights, and steam ejected from its roaring mouth. Die-hard fans can cuddle up with Godzilla in the hotel's themed room.

Other Godzilla pilgrimage locations in Tokyo include Hibiya's **Chanter Square**, where there's a 2.5m-tall statue of the monster on a plinth; and the Yamanote line platform at **Shinagawa Station**, where his silhouette appears in a floor tile marking the spot from where distances on the line are calculated.

Teens in costume, Harajuku

Leading the pack of current talented anime directors is Shinkai Makoto, hailed the 'new Miyazaki' for beautifully realised movies including 2013's *Kotonoha no Niwa (The Garden of Words)* and the 2015 smash-hit *Kimi no Na wa (Your Name)*. Also look out for movies by Hosoda Mamoru, including *Toki o Kakeru Shōjo (The Girl Who Leapt Through Time*; 2009) and *Bakemono no Ko (Boy and the Beast*; 2015).

Hyperfashion

Visitors are often in awe of Tokyo's incredible sense of style and its broad range of subcultures. It's not uncommon to see Japanese wearing kimonos for special occasions, and *yukata* (light summer kimonos) for fireworks shows and festivals in summer. Everyday wear ranges from the standard-issue salaryman suit (overwhelmingly dark blue or black) to the split-toed shoes and baggy trousers of construction workers.

Tokyo's fashion designers who have become international superstars include Issey Miyake, Yohji Yamamoto and, more recently, Rei Kawakubo of Comme des Garçons. Other designers include Fujiwara Hiroshi, a renowned streetwear fashion arbiter, who has a huge impact on what Japanese youth wear.

Fashion trends come and go in the blink of a heavily made-up eye in Tokyo. The streets of Harajuku and Shibuya remain the best places to view the latest looks such as *guro-kawaii* (somewhat grotesque cuteness). More mainstream, not to mention affordable, are Muji (p64) and Uniqlo (p75), whose inspired, practical fashions are simple without being bland; the former also offers an amazing selection of household and lifestyle goods, including furniture, stationery and food staples.

Tokyo Fashion

Tokyo Fashion (http://tokyofashion.com)

Tokyo Adorned/ Thomas C Card (www.tokyoadorned.com)

Tokyo Fashion Diaries (www.tokyofashiondiaries.com)

Amazon Fashion Week Tokyo (https://amazonfashionweektokyo.com/en)

ASIMO robot, National Museum of Emerging Science and Innovation (p173)

J-Pop

Japanese pop music, commonly shortened to J-pop, is a major driver of the country's fashion industry. An icon of the scene is Kyary Pamyu Pamyu (http://kyary.asobisystem.com/english). A runaway success since her musical debut in 2011 with PonPonPon, Kyary (whose real name is Takemura Kiriko) has been compared to Lady Gaga for her outrageous fashions and self-promotion, which includes being the Harajuku ambassador of *kawaii* (cuteness).

Avex is one of Japan's biggest recording labels and one of its brightest stars is Hamasaki Ayumi (http://avex.jp/ayu). Noted for her chameleon style and high-concept videos, Ayu – as she is known to her adoring fans – has shifted more than 50 million records since her debut in 1998.

There was consternation from fans in 2016 as SMAP, a 'boy band' who have sold 35 million-plus records over a 25-year career, announced they would be quitting the scene. However, in this multi-billion-yen industry, there is no shortage of wannabes waiting to fill their shoes.

Pop Culture Districts

Akihabara

Akihabara should be the first stop on any pop-culture Tokyo tour. With its multitude of stores selling anime and manga-related goods, not to mention maid cafes and all the electronic gizmos imaginable, Akiba (as it's known to locals) is peak geek territory.

West Tokyo

Book ahead to visit the massively popular Ghibli Museum (p120) at Mitaka, a brilliantly creative mini-theme park based around the com-

Pop Culture Events

Tokyo Game Show (http://expo.nik keibp.co.jp/tgs) September

Comiket (www. comiket.co.jp) August and December

AnimeJapan (www.anime-japan.jp/en) March

Design Festa (http://design festa.com/en) May and November

pany's movies. Die-hard anime fans will also want to schedule time in Nakano to cruise the aisles of pop-culture emporium Mandarake Complex (p124). There's also the **Suginami Animation Museum** (杉並アニメーションミュージアム; http://sam.or.jp; 3-29-5 Kami-Ogi, Suginami-ku; ⊙10am-6pm Tue-Sun; ⏺; ⏹JR Sōbu-Chūō line to Ogikubo, north exit) **FREE** at Suginami.

Northwest Tokyo

Fans of Tezuka Osamu should hop off the JR Yamanote line at Takadanobaba to view a fabulous mural homage to his characters under the railway tracks there. Further north, Ikebukuro is home to a cluster of anime and manga-related shops and businesses, including butler cafes (*cosplay* theme cafes aimed at geek gals) and the world's largest Pokemon store (p135).

Harajuku & Shinjuku

The streets of Harajuku – Takeshita-dōri, Cat St and Omotesandō – remain the best places to survey Tokyo's multiple style tribes. Among the most striking are the *gosurori* (gothic Lolita) kids posing like vampires at noon. Think Halloween meets neo-Victorian with the odd glam-rock accent and you'll get the idea. More wannabe street fashionistas strut their stuff a little further south in Tokyo's trend-Mecca, Shibuya.

Ginza & Marunouchi

Check out the Tokyo Character Street (p64) arcade of shops beneath Tokyo Station and the Hello Kitty emporium, Sanrioworld Ginza (p75).

Top pop-culture books include Hector Garcia's *A Geek in Japan* (2011), Peter Carey's *Wrong about Japan* (2006) and *Cruising the Anime City: An Otaku Guide to Neo Tokyo* (Patrick Macias & Machiyama Tomohiro; 2004).

Online

Culture Japan (www.dannychoo.com)

Tezuka in English (http://tezukainenglish.com/wp)

GhibliWiki (www.nausicaa.net/wiki/Main_Page)

TOKYO ROBOTS

The success of Shinjuku's **Robot Restaurant** (p134) is no fluke. Long before fantasy *mecha* (a manga/anime term for robot technology) caught on with the likes of Go Nagai's *Mazinger Z* (an anime featuring a flying robot) and the video series *Patlabor,* the Japanese had an affinity for robotic devices. During the Edo period (1603–1868), small mechanical dolls known as *karakuri ningyō* were used by feudal lords to serve tea and entertain guests.

Fast forward to 21st-century Tokyo and human-scale robots are still entertaining people. At **Honda Welcome Plaza Aoyama** (Hondaウエルカムプラザ青山; Map p270; ☑03-3423-4118; www.honda.co.jp/welcome-plaza; 2-1-1 Minami-Aoyama, Minato-ku; ⊙10am-6pm; ⓢGinza line to Aoyama-itchōme, exit 5) **FREE** and the **National Museum of Emerging Science & Innovation** (Miraikan; p173) in Odaiba, ASIMO, the world's most advanced humanoid robot, does brief daily demonstrations, including bowing, jogging and posing for photos. Also at Miraikan, marvel as the female android (a human-like robot), Otonaroid, answers questions from the audience and moves in an uncannily human way.

In Odaiba's Aqua City, you can ask questions of the robot concierge **ChihiraJunco** (p173), a realistic, multilingual android. Coming soon, next to Tokyo Disney Resort in nearby Chiba Prefecture, will be Japan's second **Henn-na Hotel** (www.h-n-h.jp/en), staffed by robots.

Not quite as sophisticated is **Pepper**, a 1.2m-tall robot developed by SoftBank and Aldebaran Robotics and available for a base price of ¥198,000. As you interact with Pepper, it evolves with your tastes and preferences. You'll likely spot Pepper at shops around Akihabara as well as in the lobby of the **Hotel the M Innsomnia Akasaka** (ホテル アバンシェル赤坂; Map p270; ☑03-3568-3456; www.m-innsomnia.com; 2-14-14 Akasaka, Minato-ku; ☺❄@☎; ⏹Chiyoda line to Akasaka, exit 2).

Arts & Architecture

Tokyo has an arts scene that is broad, dynamic and scattered – much like the city itself. It offers a beguiling blend of traditional and modern (and is rivalled only by Kyoto for position as Japan's centre of arts and culture). Highlights include the city's contemporary art museums and those devoted to Tokyo's signature visual art form, *ukiyo-e* (woodblock prints), its old-world kabuki stage and the fascinating creations of Japan's 20th-century architects, which line many a downtown street.

Performing Arts

Tokyo, when it was Edo (1600–1868), had a rich theatre culture. Above all, there was kabuki, captivating, occasionally outrageous and beloved by the townspeople – and still performed today at the city's dedicated kabuki theatre. Other classical forms that appear regularly on Tokyo stages include *nō*, a centuries-old dramatisation of the aesthetic quality *yūgen* (subtle, elusive beauty); and *rakugo*, a form of comedic monologue, which was a popular diversion for the working classes of Edo.

Theatre in Tokyo today doesn't have the same sway over audiences that it did in centuries past – much to the lament of those involved. The city has a baffling number of theatres, though many stage mostly Western works in translation (especially musicals) or unchallenging performances starring celebrities from film and television. There is an active fringe scene, one that has supported some compelling, introspective and daring playwrights, though this is difficult to access without some Japanese-language ability. One contemporary movement that fortunately requires no language comprehension is *butō*, a style of dance that is raw, electrifying and often unsettling.

Every November, Tokyo's month-long theatre festival, Festival/Tokyo (http://festival-tokyo.jp/en), takes place in venues around the city. In addition to new works from Japanese theatre troupes, works from around the world (and particularly Asia) are performed, sometimes with English subtitles.

Kabuki

Kabuki reached its golden age in Edo, but got its start in Kyoto. Around the year 1600, a charismatic shrine priestess led a troupe of female performers in a new type of dance people dubbed 'kabuki' – a slang expression that meant 'cool' or 'in vogue' at the time. The dancing – rather ribald and performed on a dry riverbed for gathering crowds – was also a gateway to prostitution, which eventually led the Tokugawa establishment to ban the female performers. Adolescent men took their place, though they too attracted amorous admirers (who engaged in the occasional brawl with competing suitors). Finally, in 1653, the authorities mandated that only adult men with shorn forelocks could perform kabuki, which gave rise to one of kabuki's most fascinating elements, the *onnagata* (actors who specialise in portraying women).

When kabuki arrived in Edo, it developed hand-in-hand with the increasingly affluent merchant class, whose decadent tastes translated into the breathtaking costumes, dramatic music and elaborate stagecraft that have come to characterise the art form. It is this intensely visual nature that makes kabuki accessible to foreign audiences – you don't really have to know the story to enjoy the spectacle. (Tip: if you opt for the cheap seats, bring binoculars.)

The plays draw from a repertoire of popular themes, such as famous historical accounts and stories of love-suicide. But more than by plot, kabuki is driven by its actors, who train for the profession from childhood. The leading families of modern kabuki go back many generations, as sons follow their fathers into the *yago* (kabuki acting house) in order to perpetuate an ancestor's name on stage. Thus the generations of certain families (eg Bando and Ichikawa) run into the double digits. The Japanese audience takes great interest in watching how different generations of one family perform the same part. A few actors today enjoy great social prestige, with their activities on and off the stage chronicled in the tabloids.

Though kabuki isn't as popular as it once was, it still has its devout followers. You might be surprised to hear audience members shouting during the play. This is called *kakegoe;* it usually occurs during pivotal moments such as well-known lines of dialogue or *mie* (dramatic poses held for a pause) and expresses encouragement and delight. Actors note they miss this reinforcement when performing overseas.

Ginza's Kabukiza Theatre (p69), in business since 1889, is the last of Tokyo's dedicated kabuki theatres.

Nō

Kabuki was seen as too unrefined for the military classes (though they may have secretly enjoyed it); *nō*, with its roots in indigenous Shintō rituals, was considered a better match. It developed in Kyoto between 1350 and 1450. Rather than a drama in the usual sense, *nō* seeks to express a poetic moment by symbolic and almost abstract means: glorious movements, grand and exaggerated costumes and hairstyles, sonorous chorus and music, and subtle expression. Actors frequently wear masks while they perform before a spare, unchanging set, which features a painting of a large pine tree.

Most plays centre around two principal characters: the *shi-te,* who is sometimes a living person but more often a demon or a ghost whose soul cannot rest; and the *waki,* who leads the main character towards the play's climactic moment. The elegant language used is that of the court of the 14th century. (There are exceptions, like the modern *nō* plays penned by Mishima Yukio in the 1950s.)

Some visitors find *nō* rapturous and captivating; others (including most Japanese today) find its subtlety all too subtle. The intermissions of *nō* performances are punctuated by *kyōgen* (short, lively, comic farces) – these have a more universal appeal.

ARTS EVENTS

March
Classical-music festival Haru-sai (p158) takes place in venues around Ueno. Also: **Art Fair Tokyo**.

May
Weekend-long Design Festa (p27) is the largest art event in Asia.

July
The **International Gay & Lesbian Film Festival** screens dozens of films from Japan and around the world.

September
The **Tokyo Jazz Festival** has three days of shows by international and local stars. The year's top animation, manga and digital installations go on display at the **Japan Media Arts Festival**.

October
Performances and larger-than-life installations hit the streets for Roppongi Art Night (p27). Meanwhile, Tokyo International Film Festival (p77) fills Roppongi cinema screens. Alt-art event **Trans Arts** (www.kanda-tat.com) shines a light on east Tokyo.

November
Tokyo's theatre festival **Festival/Tokyo**, the celebration of interior design that is **Tokyo Designer's Week**, and the alternative film festival Tokyo Filmex (p27) are all on this month. Also: round two for Design Festa (p27).

ARTS & ARCHITECTURE PERFORMING ARTS

Tokyo has its own public theatre dedicated to *nō*, the National Nō Theater, near Harajuku; the new Ginza Six (p74) mall also has a stage. Masks and costumes are on display at the Tokyo National Museum (p149).

Arts Online

....

Tokyo Art Beat (www.tokyoart beat.com)

....

Real Tokyo (www. realtokyo.co.jp)

....

Tokyo Stages (http:// tokyostages. wordpress.com)

....

Art Info Japan (http://enjp.blouin artinfo.com)

Rakugo

While kabuki tickets now fetch a handsome price and carry an air of sophistication, *rakugo* has held on to its down-to-earth vibe. The performer, in a kimono, sits on a square cushion on a stage; props are limited to a fan and hand towel. The audience, too, usually sits on cushions on the floor. Some comedians specialise in classic monologues, which date to the Edo and Meiji periods; others pen new ones that address issues relevant to contemporary life. A number of famous comedians, including movie director Kitano Takeshi, have studied *rakugo* as part of their development.

Rakugo is still performed regularly in Tokyo's few remaining *yose* (vaudeville theatres), such as Asakusa Engei Hall (p169). It is sometimes possible, both in Japan and abroad, to catch one of the few comedians who can perform *rakugo* in English, such as Katsuri Kaishi.

Underground & Fringe

Theatre around the world spent the 1960s redefining itself, and Tokyo was no different. The *angura* (underground) theatre movement saw productions take place in any space available: tents, basements, open spaces and street corners. Concurrent movements abroad, such as that of the Situationists, were clearly an inspiration, though so too was a desire to reconsider and re-evaluate just what a Japanese aesthetic should – and could – look like after a century of cultural influence from the West. For influential avant-garde playwright and director Kara Jūrō, for example, taking the stage outside was evocative of kabuki's formative years along the riverbed. The *angura* also gave rise to *shōgeki* (literally 'small theatre', but more like 'fringe theatre'). Many of these theatres, active for decades, are located in Shimo-Kitazawa.

Some current names to look for include Okada Toshiki and his troupe Chelfitsch, which earned critical acclaim for *Five Days in March* (*Sangatsu no Itsukukan*; 2004), a hyper-real portrayal of two *furītā* (part-time workers), holed up in a Shibuya love hotel at the start of the second Iraq War. Chelfitsch relies heavily on disjointed, hyper-colloquial language. More accessible to visitors with little or no Japanese ability are the physical, and often risqué, works of Miura Daisuke and his troupe Potudo-ru. He recently adapted his award-winning *Love's Whirlpool* (*Ai no Uzu*; 2005), set at a Roppongi swingers' party, into a film of the same name (2014).

Butō

Butō is Japan's unique and fascinating contribution to contemporary dance. It was born out of a rejection of the excessive formalisation that characterises traditional forms of Japanese dance and of an intention to return to more ancient roots. Hijikata Tatsumi (1928–86) is credited with giving the first *butō* performance in 1959; for more on Hijikata's life and work, see *Hijikata Tatsumi and Butoh* (Bruce Baird; 2012). Ōno Kazuo (1906–2010) was also a key figure.

During a performance, dancers use their naked or seminaked bodies to express the most elemental and intense human emotions. Nothing is forbidden in *butō* and performances often deal with taboo topics such as sexuality and death. For this reason, critics often describe *butō* as scandalous, and *butō* dancers delight in pushing the boundaries of what can be considered beautiful in artistic performance. It's also entirely visual, meaning both Japanese and non-Japanese spectators are on level footing.

TEA CEREMONY

Sadō (the way of tea) is a celebration of the aesthetic principle of *wabi-sabi*, reached when naturalness, spontaneity and humility come together. Many Japanese art forms, including pottery, ikebana (the art of flower arranging), calligraphy and garden design, developed in tandem with the tea ceremony. A few of Tokyo's most prestigious hotels have tearooms where ceremonies are performed in English, including the **Imperial Hotel** (帝国ホテル; Map p268; ☎03-3504-1111; www.imperialhotel.co.jp; 1-1-1 Uchisaiwai-chō, Chiyoda-ku; s/d from ¥41,580/47,350; 🚭❄@📶🏊; [S]Hibiya line to Hibiya, exit A13); reservations are necessary. You can also see pottery associated with the tea ceremony at the **Tokyo National Museum** (p149) and the **Hatakeyama Collection** (p90).

Dairakudakan (www.dairakudakan.com), which operates out of a small theatre in Kichijōji, west of Shinjuku, is one of the more active troupes today. You can also sometimes catch *butō* at the Setagaya Public Theatre (p104).

Visual Arts

Ukiyo-e

Far from the nature scenes of classical paintings, *ukiyo-e* (woodblock prints, but literally 'pictures of the floating world') were for the common people, used in advertising or in much the same way posters are used today. The subjects of these woodblock prints were images of everyday life, characters in kabuki plays and scenes from the 'floating world', a term derived from a Buddhist metaphor for life's fleeting joys.

Edo's particular 'floating world' revolved around pleasure districts such as the Yoshiwara. In this topsy-turvy kingdom, an inversion of the usual social hierarchies imposed by the Tokugawa shogunate, money meant more than rank, actors were the arbiters of style, and courtesans elevated their art to such a level that their accomplishments matched those of the women of noble families.

The vivid colours, novel composition and flowing lines of *ukiyo-e* caused great excitement when they finally arrived in the West; the French came to dub it 'Japonisme'. *Ukiyo-e* was a key influence on Impressionists and post-Impressionists (eg Toulouse-Lautrec, Manet and Degas). Yet among the Japanese, the prints were hardly given more than passing consideration – millions were produced annually in Edo, often thrown away or used as wrapping paper for pottery. For years, the Japanese were perplexed by the keen interest foreigners took in this art form.

The Ukiyo-e Ōta Memorial Museum of Art (p109) in Harajuku has fantastic collections from masters such as Hokusai, Hiroshige and Utamaro; you can also see their works at the Tokyo National Museum (p149). The new Sumida Hokusai Museum (p164) specialises, naturally, in works by Hokusai.

Don't miss Robert Indiana's *Love* and Roy Lichtenstein's *Tokyo Brushstrokes* at Shinjuku I-Land (Nishi-Shinjuku); Miyajima Tatsuo's *Counter Void* and Louise Bourgeois' *Maman* at Roppongi Hills; and Okamoto Tarō's *Myth of Tomorrow* inside Shibuya Station.

Nihonga

Japan has a rich history of painting (though one heavily influenced by China). Traditionally, paintings consisted of black ink or mineral pigments on *washi* (Japanese handmade paper) and were sometimes decorated with gold leaf. These works adorned folding screens, sliding doors and hanging scrolls; never behind glass, they were a part of daily life. Throughout the Edo period, the nobility patronised artists such as those from the Kanō school, who depicted Confucianism subjects, mythical Chinese creatures or scenes from nature.

With the Meiji Restoration (1868) – when artists and ideas were sent back and forth between Europe and Japan – painting necessarily became either a rejection or an embracement of Western influence. Two terms were coined: *yōga* for Western-style works and *nihonga* for works in the traditional Japanese style, though in reality, many *nihonga* artists incorporate shading and perspective into their works, while using techniques from all the major traditional Japanese painting schools.

The best place in Tokyo to see *nihonga* is the Yamatane Museum of Art (p89)t in Ebisu. The National Museum of Modern Art (p57) has some important works as well.

Superflat & Beyond

The '90s was a big decade for Japanese contemporary art: love him or hate him, Murakami Takashi brought Japan back into an international spotlight it hadn't enjoyed since 19th-century collectors went wild for *ukiyo-e* (woodblock prints). His work makes fantastic use of the flat planes, clear lines and decorative techniques associated with *nihonga* (Japanese-style painting), while lifting motifs from the lowbrow subculture of manga (Japanese comics).

As much an artist as a clever theorist, Murakami proclaimed in his 'Superflat' manifesto that his work picked up where Japanese artists left off after the Meiji Restoration – and might just be the future of painting, given that most of us now view the world through the portals of two-dimensional screens. Murakami inspired a whole generation of artists who worked in his 'factory', Kaikai Kiki, and presented their works at his Geisai art fairs.

Another name concurrent with Murakami is Nara Yoshitomo. Known for his paintings and sculptures of punkish tots with unsettling depth, Nara also found global success and recognition. You can see some of his works at A to Z Cafe (p113) in Aoyama.

Naturally, younger artists have had trouble defining themselves in the wake of 'Tokyo Pop' – as the highly exportable art of the '90s came to be known. Just as artists were looking to move past questions of Japanese-ness, the March 2011 earthquake, tsunami and nuclear meltdown caused another wave of soul searching about the role of art in contemporary (and contemporary Japanese) society. Some artists addressing this include conceptual artist Tanaka Koki (named Deutsche Bank's Artist of the Year in 2015) and the collection of irreverent pranksters known as ChimPom, who run a gallery space in Kōenji.

Roppongi's Mori Art Museum (p78) holds a show every three years called Roppongi Crossing, featuring up-and-coming artists, that has become an important barometer of current trends. The next one is in 2019.

Ikebana

What sets Japanese ikebana (literally 'living flowers') apart from Western forms of flower arranging is the suggestion of space and the sym-

> Check out the annual anthology of new Japanese writing *Monkey Business* (http://monkeybusiness mag.tumblr.com). For news and reviews of Japanese works translated into English, see the blog Contemporary Japanese Literature (https://japaneselit.net).

DESIGNER CITY

It may be a fully automated toilet that sings while you use it, or a smartphone that can also check for bad breath – Japanese are inimitable in their flair for tricking out ordinary gadgets with primo engineering and lots of fun, hot looks. Tokyo brims with such innovative Japanese designs; to see classics, head to the display by the Japan Design Council at the department store Matsuya (p75). Trade shows such as Tokyo Designers Week (http://tokyodesignweek.jp) draw the brightest designers and manufacturers from around Japan, as well as massive public attendance.

bolism inherent in the choice and placement of the flowers and, in some cases, bare branches. It's not as esoteric as it sounds. Tokyo's classic Ohara School of Ikebana (p117) and the more avant-garde Sōgetsu Kaikan (p80) offer classes in English.

Photography

Photography is an important medium in modern and contemporary Japanese art – perhaps no suprise, as Japan is famous for producing cameras. However, as a new medium, it was also free from the weighted history of, for example, painting and sculpture. Japan's most well-known photographers are Moriyama Daido (b 1938) and Araki Nobuyoshi (b 1940).

Moriyama is a tireless chronicler of Tokyo's underbelly. His grainy, monochrome shots of Shinjuku – usually the Kabukichō red-light district – reveal a whole other side of the city. Meanwhile Araki is known for risqué, erotic images that walk that fine line between art and pornography (though his subject is often his own wife). He takes evocative (and sometimes absurdist) photos of other things too, including the streets of his hometown, Tokyo.

Among the next generation, Honma Takashi (b 1962), a former ad man and one-time staff photographer for London magazine *I-D*, views urban life from a cool, ofttimes distant gaze. He won acclaim for his series, *Tokyo Suburbia* (1998); his latest is *The Narcissistic City* (2016).

The TOP Museum (p89) is the best place for photo exhibits; Fujifilm Square (p79) holds free exhibitions.

Literature

Much of Japan's national literature since the Edo period has been penned by authors writing in Tokyo (now and then the centre of Japan's publishing industry). Consequently, no other city in Japan has a greater hold on the national imagination and, as more and more Japanese works are translated, the global imagination.

Haiku

Poetry in Japan was historically social in nature. Groups would come together to collaborate on long *renga* (linked verse), with each new verse playing off some word or association in the one that came before. *Renga* were composed in a game-like atmosphere and were more about witty repartee than about creating works to be preserved and read. Sometime in the 17th century, however, the opening stanza of a *renga* became accepted as a standalone poem – and the haiku was born. Today, the haiku is Japan's most widely known form of poetry; at just 17 sparse syllables, it is also the shortest.

Matsuo Bashō (1644–94) is considered the master of the form, and is Japan's most famous poet. He's also the origin of the popular image of the haiku artist as a Zen-like ascetic figure. Yet before Bashō left for the wilds of northeast Japan to pen his opus, *Oku no*

JAPANESE CINEMA

ARTS & ARCHITECTURE · **LITERATURE**

1950s
The golden age of Japanese film. Watch Kurosawa Akira's *Rashōmon* (1950); Mizoguchi's *Ugetsu Monogatari* (1953).

1960s
Colour and prosperity arrive. Watch Ozu's *Sanma no Aji* (An Autumn Afternoon; 1962).

1970s
Ōshima Nagisa brings new-wave visual techniques and raw sex. Watch *Ai no Korīda* (In the Realm of the Senses; 1976).

1980s
Imamura Shōhei and Itami Jūzō earn critical success for a new generation. Watch Imamura's *Naruyama Bushiko* (The Ballad of Naruyama; 1983); Itami's *Tampopo* (1986).

1990s
Actor and comedian Takeshi Kitano emerges as a successful director, winning a Venice international Film Festival Golden Lion. Watch *Hana-bi* (Fireworks; 1997).

2000s
Anime and horror flicks are international hits. Watch Miyazaki Hayao's *Sen to Chihiro no Kamikakushi* (Spirited Away; 2001); Fukasaku Kinji's *Battle Royale* (2000).

2010s
New voices and visions. Watch Sion Sono's *Love & Peace* (2015); Hirokazu Koreeda's *Our Little Sister* (2015).

Edo-era Buildings

Kiyōmizu Kannon-dō (1631)

Kyū-Kan'ei-ji Five-Storey Pagoda (1639)

Asakusa-jinja (1649)

Tōshō-gū (1651)

Nezu-jinja (1706)

Hosomichi (*The Narrow Road to the Interior;* 1702) he lived in a little hut with a banana tree on the edge of Edo, in the neighbourhood of Fukagawa.

20th-Century Modernism

The most important writer of the modern era, Sōseki Natsume (1867–1916) was born in Tokyo in the last year that it was called Edo. One of the first generation of scholars to be sent abroad, Sōseki studied English literature in London. His ability to convey Japanese subtlety and wit through the lines of the then newly imported Western-style novel, while taking a critical look at modernising Japan and its morals, has endeared him to generations of Japanese readers.

Nobel Prize-winner Kawabata Yasunari (1899–1972) may not have been born in the capital, but he made up for it during his 20s, which he spent living in Asakusa – then Tokyo's equivalent of Paris' Montmartre. His novel *The Scarlet Gang of Asakusa* (*Asakusa Kurenaidan;* 1930), about the neighbourhood's demi-monde, was inspired by his time there.

Japan's other Nobel Laureate, Ōe Kenzaburo (b 1935), confronts modern Japan head-on, using the individual as a stand-in for society in disturbing works such as *A Personal Matter* (*Kojinteki na taiken;* 1964). Ōe grew up in rural Shikoku but has made Tokyo his home where, as a vocal pacifist and antinuclear activist, he can still be found speaking at rallies and symposiums. His latest work to be published in English, *The Changeling* (2000), is the first in a series inspired by the suicide of Japanese film director Itami Jūzō, Ōe's brother-in-law.

Japan's most controversial literary figure, Mishima Yukio (1925–70) grew up in central Tokyo, attending the elite Gakushūin (the school attended by the aristocracy). A prolific writer, Mishima wrote essays in addition to dense, psychological novels. His growing obsession with *bushidō* (the samurai code) eventually led to a bizarre, failed attempt to takeover the Tokyo headquarters of the Japanese Self-Defense Forces that ended with Mishima committing seppuku (ritual suicide). *Death in Midsummer and Other Stories* (1956) is a good introduction to his work.

Contemporary Writers

Among contemporary novelists, Murakami Haruki (b 1949) is the biggest star, both at home and internationally. His latest novel, *Colorless Tsukuru Tazaki and His Years of Pilgrimage* (2013), moved a million copies in a week – and this at a time when bestseller lists in Japan are largely filled with how-to manuals and self-help books. The English translation topped the US bestsellers list when it was released the following year. (A collection of short stories, *Men Without Women*, was

TEMPLE OR SHRINE?

Buddhist temples and Shintō shrines were historically intertwined, until they were forcibly separated by government decree in 1868. But centuries of coexistence means the two resemble each other architecturally; you'll also often find small temples within shrines and vice versa. The easiest way to tell the two apart though is to check the gate. The main entrance of a shrine is a *torii* (gate), usually composed of two upright pillars, joined at the top by two horizontal crossbars, the upper of which is normally slightly curved. *Torii* are often painted a bright vermilion. In contrast, the *mon* (main entrance gate) of a temple is often a much more substantial affair, constructed of several pillars or casements, joined at the top by a multitiered roof. Temple gates often contain guardian figures, usually *Niō* (deva kings).

recently published.) Of all his books, the one most Japanese people are likely to mention as their favourite is the one that established his reputation, *Norwegian Wood* (1987). It's a wistful story of students in 1960s Tokyo trying to find themselves and each other. Like the main character, Murakami once worked at a record store; the university in the novel is modelled after his Alma Mater, Waseda University.

The other literary Murakami, Murakami Ryū (b 1952), is known for darker, edgier works that look at Japan's urban underbelly. His signature work is *Coin Locker Babies* (1980), a coming-of-age tale of two boys left to die in coin lockers. Both survive, though the Tokyo they live to face is literally toxic. His most recent work in English translation is the short-story collection *Tokyo Decadence: 15 Stories* (2016).

Literature in Japan is not, entirely, a boys' club. Banana Yoshimoto (b 1964) – who picked her pen name because it sounded androgynous – had an international hit with *Kitchen* (1988). More recently, in 2011, her novel *The Lake* (2005) was shortlisted for the Man Asian Literary Prize. In 2003, the prestigious Akutagawa Prize for emerging writers was awarded to two young women: Wataya Risa (b 1984) for the novel *The Back You Want to Kick* (just published in English in 2015) and Kanehara Hitomi (b 1983) for the novel *Snakes and Earrings*. Wataya has gone on to have further success, winning the Kenzaburō Ōe prize in 2012 for her latest work, *Isn't It a Pity?*.

For more on the city's architecture, see *21st Century Tokyo: A Guide to Contemporary Architecture* (Julian Worrall & Erez Golani Solomon; 2010); for a discussion on cinema, see *Hundred Years of Japanese Film* (Donald Richie; 2012).

Architecture

Traditional Architecture

Until the end of the Edo period, the city's houses and shops were almost entirely constructed of wood, paper and tile, and early photos show a remarkable visual harmony in the old skyline. Unfortunately, such structures were also highly flammable and few survived the twin conflagrations of the first half of the 20th century – the Great Kantō Earthquake and WWII. However, traditional elements are still worked into contemporary structures. These include tatami (reed mat) floors and *shōji* (sliding rice-paper screen doors), which you'll encounter if you stay in a ryokan (traditional inn) or eat at a traditional restaurant. Temples and shrines, though almost all modern reconstructions, more often than not mimic their earlier incarnations.

Foreign Influences

When Japan opened its doors to Western influence following the Meiji Restoration (1868), the city's urban planners sought to remake downtown Tokyo in the image of a European city. A century-long push and pull ensued, between enthusiasts and detractors, architects who embraced the new styles and materials, and those who rejected them. Tokyo Station (p58), with its brick facade and domes looking very much like a European terminus, went up in 1914. Meanwhile, the Tokyo National Museum (p149), from 1938, was done in what was called the Imperial Style, a sturdy, modern rendering of traditional design. There was also some meeting in the middle: around the turn of the 20th century it became fashionable among the elite to build houses with both Japanese and Western-style wings; the Kyū Iwasaki-teien (p154) is one example.

A few decades later, the International Style, characterised by sleek lines, cubic forms and materials such as glass, steel and brick, arrived in Japan. Many structures in this style were put up around Marunouchi and Nihombashi; though many have since been rebuilt to add more floors, the street-floor facades of some buildings still pay homage to the original structures.

First built in 1278 and last rebuilt in 1407, the Jizō-dō in Shōfuku-ji is Tokyo's oldest building. The temple is located in the northwest suburb of Higashi-Murayama; the Jizō-dō (hall dedicated to the bodhisattva Jizō) is only open to the public on 3 November, the day of celebration for Jizō.

Modern Icons

Meiji-era Buildings

Former Ministry of Justice (1895)
....
Bank of Japan (1896)
....
Kyū Iwasaki-teien (1896)
....
Akasaka Palace (1909)

Modern Japanese architecture really came into its own in the 1960s. The best known of Japan's 20th-century builders was Tange Kenzō (1913–2005), who was influenced by traditional Japanese forms as well as the aggressively sculptural works of French architect Le Corbusier. Some of Tange's noteworthy works include St Mary's Cathedral (1964), the National Gymnasium (1964), the Tokyo Metropolitan Government Building (1991) and the Fuji Television Japan Broadcast Centre (1996).

Concurrent with Tange were the 'metabolists', Shinohara Kazuo, Kurokawa Kishō, Maki Fumihiko and Kikutake Kiyonori. The Metabolism movement promoted flexible spaces and functions at the expense of fixed forms in building. Kurokawa's Nakagin Capsule Tower (1972) is a seminal work, designed as pods that could be removed whole from a central core and replaced elsewhere.

Kikutake went on to design the Edo-Tokyo Museum (1992). This enormous structure encompasses almost 50,000 sq metres of built space and reaches 62.2m (the height of Edo Castle) at its peak. Meanwhile, Maki's Spiral Building (1985) is a favourite with Tokyo residents for its user-friendly design, gallery space, cafe and shops. Tange and Maki have both been recipients of the prestigious Pritzker Architecture Prize, in 1987 and 1993 respectively.

Next Generation Builders

Since the 1980s a new generation of Japanese architects has emerged who continue to explore both modernism and postmodernism, while incorporating a renewed interest in Japan's architectural heritage. Among the most esteemed are Itō Toyō and Andō Tadao, both winners of the prestigious Pritzker Architecture Prize. Andō's works are earthy and monumental; Itō's are lighter and more conceptual. Both architects have structures along Omote-sandō (p110).

Across the street from Andō's Omotesandō Hills is the work of one of Itō's protégées, Sejima Kazuyo, who designed the flagship boutique for Dior with her partner Nishizawa Ryūe in the firm SANAA. Sejima and Nishizawa picked up Pritzker awards in 2010; their structures often have a mutable quality, blurring the line between inside and out.

Meanwhile, Tange protégé Taniguchi Yoshio landed the commission to redesign the Museum of Modern Art (1999) in New York City. He also designed the Gallery of Hōryū-ji Treasures at the Tokyo National Museum and Tokyo Sea Life Park, both of which showcase his minimal and elegant aesthetic.

Japan's most recent Pritzker winner, Ban Shigeru, marches to the beat of his own drum entirely, purposefully using low-cost and recycled materials, building prefab houses and disaster shelters in addition to prestigious projects, mostly overseas.

Another name to know is Kengo Kuma, Tange successor in terms of impact on Tokyo, having received a number of high-profile commissions lately, including the 2020 Olympic stadium. Known for his use of wood and light, his recent works include reboots of Kabuki-za, the Nezu Museum and Suntory Museum of Art, Akagi-jinja and the Asakusa Culture Tourist Information Center.

Standing 634m tall, Tokyo Sky Tree (2012) is the world's tallest, free-standing tower. It employs an ancient construction technique used in pagodas: a *shimbashira* column (made of contemporary, reinforced concrete), structurally separate from the exterior truss. It acts as a counterweight when the tower sways, cutting vibrations by 50%.

Onsen

It's known as *hadaka no tsukiai*, meaning 'naked friendship'; communal bathing is seen in Japan as a great social leveller. With thousands of onsen (hot springs) scattered across the archipelago, the Japanese have been taking the plunge for centuries. The blissful relaxation that follows a good long soak can turn a sceptic into a convert, and is likely to make you an onsen fanatic. Even in Tokyo there are opportunities for a dip, in either onsen or *sentō* (public baths).

Healing Waters

What sets an onsen apart from an ordinary *sentō* (public bath) is the nature of the water. Onsen water comes naturally heated from a hot spring and often contains a number of minerals and gases; *sentō* water comes from the tap and is mechanically heated. Onsen are reputed to makes one's skin *sube-sube* (smooth), while the chemical composition

Above: A Japanese open-air hot spa

of particular waters are also believed to help alleviate such ailments as high blood pressure and poor circulation.

Konyoku (mixed bathing) was the norm in Japan until the Meiji Restoration, when the country sought to align itself with more 'civilised' Western ideas and outlawed the practice. Within Tokyo's central 23 wards you won't encounter it, but in the countryside and on the Izu Islands (where baths may be no more than a pool in a riverbed blocked off with stones, or a tidal basin beside crashing waves), *konyoku* is more common.

Outdoor onsen pools are called *rotemburo* (or *notemburo*). Facilities can be publicly run or attached to a ryokan (traditional Japanese inn) or *minshuku* (Japanese guesthouse).

The Japanese Spa: A Guide to Japan's Finest Ryokan & Onsen (Akihiko Seki & Elizabeth Heilman Brooke; 2005) is a lush coffee-table book covering the country's most luxurious baths. *A Guide to Japanese Hot Springs* (Anne Hotta with Yoko Ishiguro; 1986), though dated, still offers up some classic gems.

Where to Soak

You don't have to travel far outside Tokyo (or leave the city limits at all) to discover onsen. The best have a rustic charm that adds multiple layers to the experience: picture yourself sitting in a *rotemburo* on a snow-flecked riverside or watching the autumn leaves fall. With express train and bus services, it's possible to get there and back in a day, though staying in an *onsen ryokan* (traditional inn with its own baths) is certainly a treat. In addition to having longer use of the baths, a stay typically includes a multicourse dinner of seasonal delicacies and a traditional breakfast.

Many *onsen ryokan* open their baths to day trippers in the afternoon; ask any tourist information centre where there are places offering *higaeri-onsen* (bathing without accommodation).

Tokyo Onsen

Deep beneath the concrete tangle that is Tokyo, there is pure hot-spring water. The city has several large bathing complexes, where you can spend hours going from pool to pool (and even stay the night). These include Spa LaQua (p146), smack in the city centre with several floors of upmarket baths; Ōedo Onsen Monogatari (p173), in Odaiba, which bills itself as an onsen 'theme park' and includes a recreation of an old Edo downtown; and Thermae-yu (p135), a slick new multi-bath facility among the bars and clubs of Shinjuku. All of these also offer spa treatments including massage and body scrubs, if you're that way inclined.

Onsen water is also pumped into some *sentō* (public baths), including Jakotsu-yu (p170) in Asakusa and Rokuryu Kōsen (p158) in Ueno.

Hakone

Less than two hours southwest of the city is Tokyo's favorite onsen getaway, Hakone, a centuries-old resort town with several distinct hot springs set among forested peaks. Top public facilities include Hakone Yuryō (p186), Tenzan Tōji-kyo (p187) and Yunessun (p187). There are also many *onsen ryokan* (traditional hot-spring inns) here, ranging from reasonable to lavish.

Tokyo Sentō (www.1010.or.jp/index.php) is the official guide to Tokyo *sentō* from the Tokyo Sentō Association, while Sentō Guide (www.sentoguide.info) is an English blog with a searchable database for *sentō* in Tokyo and beyond.

Chūzen-ji Onsen & Yumoto Onsen

Onsen are a feature of this beautiful lakeland area 11.5km west of the old pilgrim town of Nikkō, itself around two hours northeast of Tokyo. The town of Chūzen-ji Onsen (p182), once a retreat for foreign dignitaries, has several rambling old resort hotels with excellent bathhouses, which are open to day trippers.

Beyond Chūzen-ji Onsen, and accessible via a pleasant three-hour hike across picturesque marshland (or by car or bus), is the more humble hot-spring town Yumoto Onsen (p182). Hotels here also have baths you can use, but better is the hot-spring temple Onsen-ji (p182), which

Onsen in Hakone (p184)

has a small wooden bathhouse; it's dedicated to Yakushi Nyorai, the Buddha of healing.

The waters in these parts are milky-white and rich in sulphur.

Sentō

As little as 50 years ago, many private homes in Japan did not have baths, so in the evenings people headed off to the local neighbourhood *sentō* (public bath). More than just a place to wash oneself, the *sentō* served as a kind of community meeting hall, where news and gossip were traded and social ties strengthened.

In 1968, at the peak of their popularity, Tokyo had 2687 *sentō;* now there are around 1000. Some look as though they haven't changed in decades. Others – sometimes called *super sentō* – have evolved with the times, adding saunas, jet baths, *denki-buro* (literally an 'electric bath' that's spiked with an electric current; it feels as unsettling as it sounds) and coin laundries.

A soak in a *sentō* is both a cultural experience and an ideal way to recover from a day of sightseeing. Bathhouses can be identified by their distinctive *noren* (half-length curtains over the doorway), which usually bear the hiragana (ゆ; yu) for hot water (occasionally, it may be written in kanji: 湯).

Admission to a *sentō* rarely costs more than ¥500. You're expected to bring your own towel and toiletries; however, you can show up empty handed and rent a towel and purchase soap, shampoo etc for a small price. Most bathhouses open from around 3pm to midnight.

Two *sentō* worth trying are Shimizu-yu (p117), popular with shoppers freshening up in Aoyama; and Komparu-yu (p75), a Ginza institution for more than 150 years.

Many onsen, larger bathhouses with leisure facilities (called *super sentō*) and saunas refuse entry to people with tattoos because of the association of tattoos with the *yakuza* (Japanese mafia). However, most ordinary *sentō*, which are public bathhouses for the local community, are open to all.

Accoutrements for bathing

Bathing Etiquette

Bathing isn't just a pastime, it's a ritual – one so embedded in Japanese culture that everyone knows exactly what to do. This can be intimidating to the novice, but really all you need to know to avoid causing alarm is to wash yourself before getting into the bath. It's also a good idea to memorise the characters for men (男) and women (女), which will be marked on the *noren* hanging in front of the respective baths.

Upon entering an onsen or *sentō*, the first thing you'll encounter is a row of lockers for your shoes. After you pay your admission and head to the correct changing room, you'll find either more lockers or baskets for your clothes. Take everything off here, entering the bathing room with only the small towel.

That little towel performs a variety of functions: you can use it to wash (but make sure to give it a good rinse afterwards) or to cover yourself as you walk around. It is not supposed to touch the water though, so leave it on the side of the bath or – as the locals do – folded on top of your head.

Park yourself on a stool in front of one of the taps and give yourself a thorough wash. Make sure you rinse off all the suds. When you're done, it's polite to rinse off the stool for the next person. At more humble bathhouses you might have little more than a ladle to work with; in that case, crouch low and use it to scoop out water from the bath and pour over your body – taking care not to splash water into the tub – and scrub a bit with the towel.

In the baths, keep splashing to a minimum and your head above the water. Before heading back to the changing room, wipe yourself down with the towel to avoid dripping on the floor.

Survival Guide

TRANSPORT 232

ARRIVING IN
TOKYO 232
Narita Airport 232
Haneda Airport 233
GETTING
AROUND TOKYO 234
Train & Subway 234
Taxi 236
Bicycle 236
Boat 236
Bus 236
Car & Motorcycle 237
TOURS 237
Bus Tours 237
Walking Tours 237

DIRECTORY A–Z 238

Discount Cards 238
Electricity 238
Embassies 238
Emergency 238
Gay & Lesbian
Travellers 239
Health 239
Internet Access 239
Legal Matters 239
Medical Services 240
Money 240
Opening Hours 241
Public Holidays 241
Post 241
Safe Travel 241
Taxes & Refunds 242
Telephone 242
Time 243
Toilets 243
Tourist Information 243
Travellers with
Disabilities 244
Visas 244
Volunteering 244

LANGUAGE 245

Transport

ARRIVING IN TOKYO

Tokyo has two international airports. Narita Airport, in neighbouring Chiba Prefecture, is the primary gateway to Tokyo; most budget flights end up here. Haneda Airport, closer to the city centre, is now seeing an increasing number of international flights; this is also where most domestic flights arrive. Flying into Haneda means quicker and cheaper access to central Tokyo. Both airports have smooth, hassle-free entry procedures, and are connected to the city centre by public transport.

Flights, tours and cars can be booked online at lonelyplanet.com/bookings.

Narita Airport

The excellent, modern **Narita Airport** (NRT; 成田空港; ☑0476-34-8000; www.narita-airport.jp) is inconveniently located 66km east of Tokyo. There are three terminals (the new Terminal 3 handles low-cost carriers). Note that only Terminals 1 and 2 have train stations. Free shuttle buses run between all the terminals every 15 to 30 minutes (from 7am to 9.30pm). Another free shuttle runs between Terminal 2 and Terminal 3 every five to 12 minutes (4.30am to 11.20pm); otherwise it is a 15-minute walk between the two terminals. All terminals have tourist information desks.

Bus

Purchase tickets from kiosks in the arrivals hall (no advance reservations necessary). From Tokyo, there's a ticket counter inside the **Shinjuku Bus Terminal** (バスタ新宿; Busuta Shinjuku; Map p280; ☑03-6380-4794; http://shinjuku-busterminal.co.jp; 5-24-55 Sendagaya, Shibuya-ku; ☎; ⓇJR Yamanote line to Shinjuku, new south exit).

Friendly Airport Limousine (www.limousinebus.co.jp/en) Scheduled, direct, reserved-seat buses (¥3100) depart from all Narita Airport terminals for major hotels and train stations in Tokyo. The journey takes 1½ to two hours depending on traffic. At the time of research, discount round-trip 'Welcome to Tokyo Limousine Bus Return Voucher' tickets (¥4500) were available for foreign tourists; ask at the ticket counter at the airport.

Keisei Tokyo Shuttle (www.keiseibus.co.jp) Discount buses connect all Narita Airport Terminals and Tokyo Station (¥1000, approximately 90 minutes, every 20 minutes from 6am to 11pm). There are less frequent departures from Tokyo Station for Narita Airport terminals 2 and 3 between 11pm and 6am (¥2000), which are handy for budget flights at odd hours.

CLIMATE CHANGE & TRAVEL

Every form of transport that relies on carbon-based fuel generates CO_2, the main cause of human-induced climate change. Modern travel is dependent on aeroplanes, which might use less fuel per kilometre per person than most cars but travel much greater distances. The altitude at which aircraft emit gases (including CO_2) and particles also contributes to their climate change impact. Many websites offer 'carbon calculators' that allow people to estimate the carbon emissions generated by their journey and, for those who wish to do so, to offset the impact of the greenhouse gases emitted with contributions to portfolios of climate-friendly initiatives throughout the world. Lonely Planet offsets the carbon footprint of all staff and author travel.

Train

Both Japan Railways (JR) and the independent Keisei line run between central Tokyo and Narita Airport Terminals 1 and 2. For Terminal 3, take a train to Terminal 2 and then walk or take the free shuttle bus to Terminal 3 (and budget an extra 15 minutes). Tickets can be purchased in the basement of either terminal, where the entrances to the train stations are located.

Keisei Skyliner (www.keisei. co.jp/keisei/tetudou/skyliner/ us) The quickest service into Tokyo runs nonstop to Nippori (¥2470, 36 minutes) and Ueno (¥2470, 41 minutes) stations, on the city's northeast side, where you can connect to the JR Yamanote line or the subway (Ueno Station only). Trains run twice an hour, 8am to 10pm. Foreign nationals can purchase advanced tickets online for slightly less (¥2200). The Skyliner & Tokyo Subway Ticket, which combines a one-way or round-trip ticket on the Skyliner and a one-, two- or three-day subway pass, is a good deal.

Keisei Main Line Limited-express trains (*kaisoku kyūkō*; ¥1030, 71 minutes to Ueno) follow the same route as the Skyliner but make stops. This is a good budget option. Trains run every 20 minutes during peak hours.

Narita Express (www.jreast. co.jp/e/nex) A swift and smooth option, especially if you're staying on the west side of the city, N'EX trains depart Narita approximately every half-hour from 7am and 10pm for Tokyo Station (¥3020, 53 minutes) and Shinjuku (¥3190, 80 minutes); the latter also stops at Shibuya (¥3190; 75 minutes). Additional trains run to Shinagawa (¥3190, 65 minutes) and Ikebukuro (¥3190, 85 minutes).

BAGGAGE SHIPMENT

Baggage couriers provide next-day delivery of your large luggage from Narita and Haneda airports to any address in Tokyo (around ¥2000 per large bag) or beyond, so you don't have to haul it on the trains. Look for kiosks in the arrival terminals. If you plan on taking advantage of this service, make sure to put the essentials you'll need for the next 24 hours in a small bag. Going the other way, many Tourist Information Centers can ship luggage to the airport.

At the time of research, foreign tourists could purchase return N'EX tickets for ¥4000 (valid for 14 days; ¥2000 for under 12s). Check online or enquire at the JR East Travel Service centres at Narita Airport for the latest deals. Long-haul JR passes are valid on N'EX trains, but you must obtain a seat reservation (no extra charge) from a JR ticket office.

Taxi

Fixed-fare taxis run ¥20,000 to ¥22,000 for most destinations in central Tokyo. There's a 20% surcharge between 10pm and 5am. Credit cards accepted.

Haneda Airport

Closer to central Tokyo, **Haneda Airport** (HND; 羽田空港; ✈ international terminal 03-6428-0888; www. tokyo-airport-bldg.co.jp/en) has two domestic terminals and one international terminal. Note that some international flights arrive at awkward night-time hours, between midnight and 5am, when trains, buses and the monorail to central Tokyo will not be running. Keep in mind the price of a taxi (or the hours spent camped at the airport) when you book your ticket.

There's a **Tourist Information Center** (✆03-6428-0653; ☺24hr; ☎) in the international terminal, on the 2nd floor of the arrivals lobby.

Bus

Purchase tickets at the kiosks at the arrivals hall. In Tokyo, there's a ticket counter inside the **Shinjuku Bus Terminal** (バスタ新宿; Busuta Shinjuku; Map p280; ✆03-6380-4794; http://shinjuku-busterminal.co.jp; 5-24-55 Sendagaya, Shibuya-ku; ☎; ⊠JR Yamanote line to Shinjuku, new south exit).

Friendly Airport Limousine (www.limousinebus.co.jp/en) Coaches connect Haneda with major train stations and hotels in Shibuya (¥1030), Shinjuku (¥1230), Roppongi (¥1130), Ginza (¥930) and others; fares double between midnight and 5am. Travel times vary wildly, taking anywhere from 30 to 90 minutes depending on traffic. Night buses depart for Shibuya Station at 12.15am, 12.50am and 2.20am and Shinjuku Bus Terminal at 12.20am and 1am; for Haneda, there is a bus from Shibuya Station at 3.30am and one from Shinjuku Bus Terminal at 4am. Regular service resumes at 5am.

Haneda Airport Express (http://hnd-bus.com) Though more useful for suburban destinations than downtown ones, coaches do travel to handy places such as Shibuya Station (¥1030) and Tokyo Station (¥930) in about an hour, depending on traffic, from 5am to midnight. Night buses depart for Shibuya Station (¥2600) via Roppongi Hills at 12.50am and 2.20am.

SUICA & PASMO CARDS

Prepaid re-chargeable Suica and Pasmo cards work on all city trains, subways and buses. With either (they're essentially the same), you'll be able to breeze through the ticket gates of any station without having to work out fares or transfer tickets. Fares for pass users are also slightly less (a few yen per journey) than for paper-ticket holders. The only reason not to go with a Suica or Pasmo is to take advantage of Tokyo Metro's 24-hour unlimited-ride pass (adult/child ¥600/300). Note that this is only good on the nine subway lines operated by Tokyo Metro. There are other (more expensive) passes that include rides on Toei subway and Tokyo-area JR lines, but the Tokyo Metro pass is the best deal.

Suica or Pasmo cards can be purchased from any touch-screen ticket-vending machine in Tokyo (including those at Haneda and Narita Airports). Suica (available at JR stations) requires a minimum initial charge of ¥2000 (which includes a ¥500 deposit). Pasmo (available at subway and commuter line stations) requires a minimum initial charge of ¥1000 (which includes a ¥500 deposit). The deposit (along with any remaining charge) is refunded when you return the pass to any ticket window.

Both passes can be topped-up at any touch-screen ticket-vending machine (not just, for example, at JR stations for Suica passes) in increments of ¥1000. Ticket-vending machines have an English option so all of this is actually quite easy.

Monorail

Tokyo Monorail (www.tokyo-monorail.co.jp/english) leaves approximately every 10 minutes (5am to midnight) for Hamamatsuchō Station (¥490, 15 minutes), which is a stop on the JR Yamanote line. Good for travellers staying near Ginza or Roppongi.

Train

Keikyū Airport Express (www.haneda-tokyo-access.com/en) trains depart several times an hour (5.30am to midnight) for Shinagawa (¥410, 12 minutes), where you can connect to the JR Yamanote line. From Shinagawa, some trains continue along the Asakusa subway line, which serves Higashi-Ginza, Nihombashi and Asakusa stations.

Note that the international and domestic terminals have their own stations; when traveling to the airport, the international terminal is the second to last stop.

Taxi

Fixed fares include Ginza (¥5600), Shibuya (¥6400), Shinjuku (¥6800), Ikebukuro (¥8500) and Asakusa (¥6900). There's a 20% surcharge between 10pm and 5am. Credit cards accepted.

GETTING AROUND TOKYO

Efficient, clean and virtually crime-free, Tokyo's public transport system is the envy of the world. Of most use to travellers is the train and subway system, which is easy to navigate thanks to English signage.

Train & Subway

Tokyo's extensive rail network includes JR lines, a subway system and private commuter lines that depart in every direction for the suburbs, like spokes on a wheel. Trains arrive and depart precisely on time. Journeys that require transfers between lines run by different operators cost more than journeys that use only one operator's lines. Major transit hubs include Tokyo, Shinagawa, Shibuya, Shinjuku, Ikebukuro and Ueno stations.

Japan Railways (JR) Lines

The JR network covers the whole country and includes the *shinkansen* (bullet train). In Tokyo, the above-ground Yamanote (loop) and the Chūō–Sōbu (central) lines are the most useful. Tickets start at ¥133 and go up depending on how far you travel.

Subway

Tokyo has 13 subway lines, nine of which are operated by **Tokyo Metro** (www.tokyometro.jp/en) and four by **Toei** (www.kotsu.metro.tokyo.jp/eng). The lines are colour-coded, making navigation fairly simple. Unfortunately a transfer ticket is required to change between the two; a Pasmo or Suica card makes this process seamless, but either way a journey involving more than one operator comes out costing more. Rides on Tokyo Metro cost ¥170 to ¥240 (¥90 to ¥120 for children) and on Toei ¥180 to ¥320 (¥90 to ¥160 for children), depending on how far you travel.

Private Commuter Lines

Private commuter lines service some of the hipper residential neighbourhoods. Useful trains:

Keiō Inokashira line (from Shibuya for Shimo-Kitazawa and Kichijōji)

Odakyū line (from Shinjuku for Shimo-Kitazawa)

Tōkyū-Tōyoko line (from Shibuya for Daikanyama and Naka-Meguro)

Note that the commuter lines run *tokkyū* (特急; limited-express services), *kyūkō* (急行; express) and *futsū* (普通; local) trains; when in doubt, take a local.

Tickets

➡ Purchase paper tickets or top up train passes at the touch-screen ticket-vending machines outside station ticket gates. These have an English function. (Older push-button machines do still exist in some stations and sell only paper tickets.)

➡ To purchase a paper ticket, you'll need to work out the correct fare from the chart above the machines. If you can't work it out, just buy a ticket for the cheapest fare.

➡ All ticket gates have card readers for Suica and Pasmo train passes; simply wave your card over the reader.

➡ If you're using a paper ticket or a one-day pass, you'll need to use a ticket gate with a slot for inserting a ticket. Make sure to pick it up when it pops out again.

➡ You'll need your ticket or pass to exit the station as well. If your ticket or pass does not have sufficient charge to cover your journey, insert it into one of the 'fare adjustment' machines near the exit gates.

Discount Passes

CITY PASSES

If you're planning a packed day, you might consider getting an unlimited-ride ticket. For details and information on other passes, see www.gotokyo.org/en/tourists/info/profit/index.html.

Tokyo Metro One-Day Open Ticket (adult/child ¥600/300) Unlimited rides over a 24-hour period on Tokyo Metro subway lines only. Purchase at Tokyo Metro stations.

Common One-Day Ticket for Tokyo Metro & Toei Subway Lines (adult/child ¥1000/500) Unlimited rides for one calendar day on all 13 lines operating underground in Tokyo. Purchase at Tokyo Metro or Toei stations.

Tokyo Combination Ticket (adult/child ¥1590/800) Unlimited rides for one calendar day on Tokyo Metro, Toei and JR lines operating in Tokyo. Purchase at stations serviced by any of these lines.

LONG-HAUL PASSES

The following passes are fantastic if you plan to travel outside Tokyo, however, they are only available for foreign-passport holders on a tourist visa. The latter two options can be purchased at JR East Travel Service Centers in either airport or at Tokyo Station. Tickets for children are half-price. For details and information on other passes, see www.japanrailpass.net/en.

Japan Rail Pass Covers travel on JR trains throughout the nation. A seven-day pass costs ¥29,110 and must be purchased *before* arriving in Japan; 14-day and 21-day passes are also available.

JR East Nagano & Niigata Area Pass Covers bullet trains between Tokyo, Nagano and Niigata (good for skiing, hiking and onsen) and limited-express trains to Izu and Narita Airport. Costs ¥18,000 for unlimited travel on five days of your choosing within a 14-day period.

JR Kantō Area Pass Three consecutive days of unlimited rides on all Kanto-area JR East lines, including limited-express trains and *shinkansen* (but not the Tōkaidō *shinkansen*) for ¥10,000. This is good for travellers wanting to visit the Nikkō and Mt Fuji areas.

Female Carriages

Groping male hands have long been a problem for women when trains are packed. Most Tokyo train lines have women-only carriages at peak times. The carriages are marked with

---

KEY TRAIN & SUBWAY ROUTES

Ginza subway line Shibuya to Asakusa, via Ginza and Ueno. Colour-coded orange.

Hibiya subway line Naka-Meguro to Ebisu, Roppongi, Ginza, Akihabara and Ueno. Colour-coded grey.

JR Yamanote line Loop line stopping at many sightseeing destinations, such as Shibuya, Harajuku, Shinjuku, Tokyo and Ueno. Colour-coded light green.

JR Chūō line Tokyo Station to points in west Tokyo, via Shinjuku. Colour-coded reddish-orange.

JR Sōbu line Runs across the city centre, connecting Shinjuku with Iidabashi, Ryōgoku and Akihabara. Colour-coded yellow.

Yurikamome line Elevated train running from Shimbashi to points around Tokyo Bay.

TOP TRAIN TIPS

➜ Figure out the best route to your destination with the Japan Travel app (https://navitimejapan.com); you can download routes to be used offline, too.

➜ Most train and subway stations have several different exits. Try to get your bearings and decide where to exit while still on the platform; look for the yellow signs that indicate which stairs lead to which exits.

➜ If you're not sure which exit to take, look for street maps of the area usually posted near the ticket gates, which show the locations of the exits.

signs (usually pink) in Japanese and English. Children can ride in them, too.

Lost & Found

Larger stations have dedicated lost-and-found windows (labelled in English); otherwise lost items are left with the station attendant. Items not claimed on the same day will be handed over to the operator's lost-and-found centre. Items not claimed after several days are turned over to the police.

JR East Infoline (☑ in English 050-2016-1603; ⏱ 10am-6pm)

Toei Transportation Lost & Found (☑ 03-3816-5700; ⏱ 9am-8pm)

Tokyo Metro Lost & Found (Map p282; ☑ 03-5227-5741; www.tokyometro.jp/en/support/lost/index.html; ⏱ 9am-8pm) Office located inside Iidabashi Station on the Namboku line.

Taxi

Taxis in Tokyo feature white-gloved drivers, seats covered with lace doilies and doors that magically open and close – an experience in itself. They rarely make economic sense though, unless you have a group of four.

➜ All cabs run by the meter. Fares start at ¥730 for the first 2km, then rise by ¥90 for every 280m you travel (or for every 105 seconds spent in traffic).

➜ There's a surcharge of 20% between 10pm and 5am.

➜ Drivers rarely speak English, though fortunately most taxis now have navigation systems. It's a good idea to have your destination written down in Japanese, or better yet, a business card with an address.

➜ Most (but not all) taxis take credit cards.

Hailing a Taxi

➜ Train stations and hotels have taxi stands where you are expected to queue.

➜ In the absence of a stand, you can hail a cab from the street, by standing on the curb and sticking your arm out.

➜ A red light means the taxi is free and a green light means it's taken.

Bicycle

Tokyo is by no means a bicycle-friendly city. Bike lanes are almost nonexistent and you'll see no-parking signs for bicycles everywhere (ignore these at your peril: your bike could get impounded, requiring a half-day excursion to the pound and a ¥3000 fee). Still, you'll see people cycling everywhere and it can be a really fun way to get around the city. Some hostels and ryokan have bikes to lend. See **Rentabike** (http://rentabike.jp) for places around town that rent bicycles.

Cogi Cogi (http://cogicogi.jp; 24hr ¥2400) is a bike-sharing system with a growing number of ports around the city. There are instructions in English, but it's a little complicated to use and requires that you sign up in advance online and have wi-fi connection to sync with the ports.

Boat

Tokyo Cruise (水上バス, Suijō Bus; ☑ 0120-977-311; http://suijobus.co.jp) water buses run up and down the Sumida-gawa (Sumida River), roughly twice an hour between 10am and 6pm, connecting Asakusa with Hama-rikyū Onshi-teien (¥980, 35 minutes) and Odaiba (¥1260, 70 minutes). Tickets can be purchased immediately before departure, if available, at any pier.

Tokyo Mizube Cruising Line (東京水辺ライン; ☑ 03-5608-8869; www.tokyo-park.or.jp/waterbus) water buses head down the Sumida-gawa from Asakusa to Ryōgoku (¥310), Hama-rikyū Onshi-teien (¥620) and Odaiba (¥1130), and then back up again. Schedules are seasonal, and infrequent in winter. Tickets don't have to be reserved in advance but can be purchased just before departure.

Bus

Toei (www.kotsu.metro.tokyo.jp/eng/services/bus.html) runs an extensive bus network, though in most cases it's easier to get around by subway.

➜ Fares are ¥210/110 per adult/child; there are no transfer tickets. Deposit your fare into the box as you enter the bus; there's a change machine at the front of the bus that accepts ¥1000 notes.

➜ Most buses have digital signage that switches between

Japanese and English. A recording announces the name of each stop as it is reached, so listen carefully and press the button next to your seat when your stop is announced.

Car & Motorcycle

Considering the traffic, the confusing roads and the ridiculous cost of parking, the only reason you'd want a car in Tokyo is to get out of the city.

You will need an International Driving Permit, which must be arranged in your own country before you leave. It's also wise to get a copy of *Rules of the Road* (digital/print ¥864/1404) published by the **Japan Automobile Federation** (JAF; ☎03-6833-9100, emergency roadside help 0570-00-8139; www.jaf.or.jp; 2-2-17 Shiba, Minato-ku; ⏱9am-5.30pm Mon-Fri; [S]Mita line to Shibakōen, exit A1).

Rental companies with branches around the city include **Nippon Rent-a-Car** (www.nipponrentacar.co.jp/english) and **Toyota Rent-a-Car** (https://rent.toyota.co.jp/eng/). Expect to pay ¥8000 per day for a smallish rental car.

TOURS

Bus Tours

Gray Line (☎03-3595-5948; www.jgl.co.jp/inbound/index.htm; per person ¥4000-13,000) Offers half-day and full-day tours with stops, covering key downtown sights and also day trips to Mt Fuji and Hakone. Pick-up service from major hotels is available, otherwise most tours leave from in front of the Dai-Ichi Hotel in Shimbashi (near Ginza).

Hato Bus Tours (☎03-3435-6081; www.hatobus.com; per person ¥1500-12,000; 🚆JR Yamanote line to Hamamatsuchō, south exit) Tokyo's most well-known bus-tour company offers hour-long, half-day and full-day bus tours of the city. Shorter tours cruise by the sights in an open-air double-decker bus; longer ones make stops. Tours leave from Hato Bus terminals in the annexe to the World Trade Centre in Hamamatsuchō, and Shinjuku and Tokyo stations.

SkyBus (Map p266; ☎03-3215-0008; www.skybus.jp; 2-5-2 Marunouchi, Chiyoda-ku; tours adult/child from ¥1600/700, Sky Hop Bus ¥2500/1200; ⏱ticket office 9am-6pm; 🚆JR Yamanote line to Tokyo, Marunouchi south exit) Open-top double-decker buses cruise through different neighbourhoods of the city (for roughly 50 to 80 minutes); most have English-language audio guidance aboard. The Sky Hop Bus plan allows you to hop on and off buses on any of the three routes.

Walking Tours

Haunted Tokyo Tours (www.hauntedtokyotours.com; hauntedtokyotours@hotmail.com; per person from ¥4500) Fun and friendly English-speaking guides take amblers to the scenes of some of the city's most notorious ghost haunts and urban legends. You'll never look at Tokyo the same way again.

Tokyo Metropolitan Government Tours (☎TIC 03-5321-3077; www.gotokyo.org/en/tourists/guideservice/guideservice/index.html; Tokyo Metropolitan Government Bldg No 1, 2-8-1 Nishi-Shinjuku, Shinjuku; [S]Ōedo line to Tochōmae, exit A4) The Tokyo government tourism bureau can arrange free or fairly cheap walking tours in one of seven different languages with volunteer guides. There are several routes to choose from, each lasting about three hours. Reserve online one month to three days in advance.

NAVIGATING TOKYO STREETS

Tokyo is difficult to navigate even for locals. Only the biggest streets have names, and they don't figure into addresses; instead, addresses are derived from districts, blocks and building numbers.

Like most Japanese cities, Tokyo is divided first into *ku* (wards; Tokyo has 23 of them), which in turn are divided into *chō* or *machi* (towns) and then into numbered *chōme* (pronounced cho-may), areas of just a few blocks. Subsequent numbers in an address refer to blocks within the *chōme* and buildings within each block.

It's near impossible to find your destination using the address alone. Smartphones with navigation apps have been a real boon. Many restaurants and venues have useful maps on their websites.

If you truly do get lost, police officers at *kōban* (police boxes) have maps and are always happy to help with directions (though few speak English). At the very least, you should be able to get back to the nearest train station and try again.

Directory A–Z

Discount Cards

Grutto Pass (¥2000; www.rekibun.or.jp/grutto) gives free or discounted admission to 79 attractions around town within two months. If you plan on visiting more than a few museums, it's excellent value. All participating venues sell them.

Electricity

The Japanese electricity supply is an unusual 100V AC. Appliances with a two-pin plug made for use in North America will work without an adaptor, but may be sluggish.

Type A
100V/50Hz/60Hz

Embassies

Australian Embassy (☎03-5232-4111; www.australia.or.jp/en; 2-1-14 Mita, Minato-ku; [S]Namboku line to Azabu-Jūban, exit 2)

Canadian Embassy (カナダ大使館; Map p270; ☎03-5412-6200; www.canadainternational.gc.ca/japan-japon/index.aspx?lang=eng; 7-3-38 Akasaka, Minato-ku; [S]Ginza line to Aoyama-itchōme, exit 4)

Chinese Embassy (Map p270; ☎03-3403-3388; www.china-embassy.or.jp/jpn; 3-4-33 Moto-Azabu, Minato-ku; [S]Hibya line to Hiro-o, exit 3)

French Embassy (☎03-5798-6000; www.ambafrance-jp.org; 4-11-44 Minami-Azabu, Minato-ku; [S]Hibiya line to Hiro-o, exit 1)

German Embassy (☎03-5791-7700; www.japan.diplo.de; 4-5-10 Minami-Azabu, Minato-ku; [S]Hibiya line to Hiro-o, exit 1)

Irish Embassy (☎03-3263-0695; www.irishembassy.jp; Ireland House, 2-10-7 Kōji-machi, Chiyoda-ku; [S]Hanzōmon line to Hanzōmon, exit 4)

Dutch Embassy (Map p270; ☎03-5776-5400; http://japan.nlembassy.org; 3-6-3 Shiba-kōen, Minato-ku; [S]Hibiya line to Kamiyachō, exit 1)

New Zealand Embassy (Map p273; ☎03-3467-2271; www.nzembassy.com/japan; 20-40 Kamiyama-chō, Shibuya-ku, Tokyo; 🕒9am-5.30pm; 🚆JR Yamanote line to Shibuya, Hachikō exit)

Russian Embassy (Map p270; ☎03-3583-4445; www.ruscon-sul.jp; 2-1-1 Azabudai, Minato-ku; [S]Hibiya line to Roppongi, exit 3)

South Korean Embassy (☎03-3452-7611, emergency 090-1693-5773; http://jpn-tokyo.mofa.go.kr/worldlanguage/asia/jpn-tokyo/main/; 1-2-5 Minami-Azabu, Minato-ku; [S]Namboku line to Azabu-Jūban, exit 1)

UK Embassy (☎03-5211-1100; www.gov.uk/government/world/organisations/british-embassy-tokyo; 1 Ichibanchō, Chiyoda-ku; [S]Hanzōmon line to Hanzōmon, exit 3A)

US Embassy (米国大使館; Map p270; ☎03-3224-5000; http://japan.usembassy.gov; 1-10-5 Akasaka, Minato-ku; [S]Ginza line to Tameike-sannō, exits 9, 12 or 13)

Emergency

Japan's country code is ☎81. Although most emergency operators don't speak English, they'll immediately refer you to someone who does.

Ambulance & Fire	☎119
Police	☎110
Non-Emergency Police Hotline for Foreigners (8.30am-5.15pm Mon-Fri)	☎03-3503-8484
Emergency Interpretation (Medical Info 9am-8pm)	☎03-5285-8181
Emergency Translation (5-8pm Mon-Fri, 9am-8pm Sat & Sun)	☎03-5285-8185

Gay & Lesbian Travellers

Gay and lesbian travellers are unlikely to encounter problems in Tokyo. There are no legal restraints on same-sex sexual activities in Japan apart from the usual age restrictions. Some travellers have reported being turned away or grossly overcharged when checking into love hotels with a partner of the same sex. Otherwise, discrimination is unusual. One note: Japanese people, regardless of their sexual orientation, do not typically engage in public displays of affection.

Tokyo has a small but very lively gay quarter, Shinjuku-nichōme. However, outside this and a handful of other places, the gay scene is all but invisible. For more advice on travelling in Tokyo, have a look at **Utopia Asia** (www.utopia-asia.com).

Health

Tokyo has an excellent standard of public hygiene and health (stress-related ailments notwithstanding). No vaccines are required and tap water is fine to drink.

Insurance

The only insurance accepted at Japanese hospitals is Japanese insurance. For any medical treatment you'll have to pay up front and apply for a reimbursement when you get home. Clinics that specialise in serving Tokyo's foreign community can provide claim forms in English.

Medications

Pharmacies in Japan do not carry foreign medications, so it's a good idea to bring your own. In a pinch, reasonable substitutes can be found, but the dosage may be less than what you're used to.

Stimulant drugs, which include the ADHD medication Adderall, are strictly prohibited in Japan. To bring in certain narcotics (such as codeine), you need to prepare a *yakkan shōmei* – an import certificate for pharmaceuticals. See the Ministry of Health, Labour & Welfare's website (www.mhlw.go.jp/english/policy/health-medical/pharmaceuticals/01.html) for more details about which medications are classified and how to prepare the form.

Internet Access

Free wi-fi can be found on subway platforms, on the streets of some districts and at many convenience stores, major attractions and shopping centres – though signals are often weak. Look for the sticker that says 'Japan Wi-Fi'. Download the **Japan Connected** (www.ntt-bp.net/jcfw/en.html) app to avoid having to login to individual networks; if you are unable to connect, try clearing your cache.

In addition to data-only SIM cards (for unlocked smartphones), there's the option to rent a pocket wi-fi device, which can be used by multiple devices. These can also be rented at the airport. Some services, such as **Japan Wireless** (http://japan-wireless.com), will ship to your hotel.

Most accommodation in Tokyo has, at the very least, complimentary wi-fi in the lobby.

Ubiquitous *manga kissa* (cafes for reading comic books) double as internet cafes.

Legal Matters

Japanese police have extraordinary powers compared with their Western counterparts: they have the right to detain a suspect without charging them for up to three days, after which a prosecutor can decide to extend this period for another 20 days. Police also have the authority to choose whether to allow a suspect to phone their embassy or lawyer or not, although, if you do find yourself in police custody, you should insist that you will not cooperate in any way until allowed to make such a call. Your embassy is the first place you should call if given the chance.

Police will speak almost no English; insist that a *tsuyakusha* (interpreter) be summoned; police are legally bound to provide one before proceeding with any questioning. Even if you are able

NEED HELP?

Japan Helpline English-speaking operators (☎0570-000-911) available 24 hours a day can help you negotiate tricky situations – such as dealing with a police station – or simpler ones, such as recovering a bag you left on the subway. If you don't have access to mobile service, use the contact form on the website (http://jhelp.com/english/index.html).

to speak Japanese, it is best to deny it and stay with your native language.

Note that it is a legal requirement to have your passport (or, if you are staying longer than 90 days, your resident card) on you at all times. Though checks are not common, if you are stopped by police and caught without it, you could be hauled off to a police station to wait until someone fetches it for you.

Japan takes a hard-line approach to narcotics possession, with long sentences and fines even for first-time offenders.

Medical Services

Tokyo enjoys a high level of medical services, though unfortunately, most hospitals and clinics do not have doctors and nurses who speak English. Even for those that do, getting through reception can still be challenging. Larger hospitals or clinics that specialise in serving the expat community are your best bet. Most hospitals and clinics will accept walk-in patients in the mornings (usually 8.30am to 11am); be prepared to wait.

Expect to pay about ¥3000 for a simple visit to an outpatient clinic and from around ¥20,000 and upwards for emergency care.

Clinics

Primary Care Tokyo (プライマリーケア東京; ☎03-5432-7177; http://pctclinic.com; 3rd fl, 2-1-16 Kitazawa, Setagaya-ku; ⏰9am-12.30pm Mon-Sat, 2.30-6pm Mon-Fri; 🚆Keiō Inokashira line to Shimo-Kitazawa, south exit) Fluent English-speaking, American-trained doctor who can address common health complaints.

Tokyo Medical & Surgical Clinic (東京メディカルアンドサージカルクリニック; Map p270; ☎03-3436-3028; www.tmsc.jp; 2nd fl, 32 Shiba-kōen Bldg, 3-4-30 Shiba-kōen, Minato-ku; ⏰8.30am-5pm Mon-Fri, to noon Sat; [S]Hibiya line to Kamiyachō, exit 1) Well-equipped clinic staffed with English-speaking Japanese and foreign physicians. Twenty-four-hour emergency consultation is also available. Note: these guys are pricey.

Emergency Rooms

Seibo International Catholic Hospital (聖母病院; ☎03-3951-1111; www.seibokai.or.jp; 2-5-1 Nakaochiai, Shinjuku-ku; 🚆JR Yamanote line to Mejiro, main exit) and **St Luke's International Hospital** (聖路加国際病院; Seiroka Kokusai Byōin; Map p268; ☎03-3541-5151; http://hospital.luke.ac.jp; 9-1 Akashi-chō, Chūō-ku; [S]Hibiya line to Tsukiji, exits 3 & 4) both have some English-speaking doctors.

Money

ATMs

Most Japanese bank ATMs do not accept foreign-issued cards. Even if they display Visa and MasterCard logos, most accept only Japan-issued versions of these cards.

The following have ATMs that routinely work with most cards (including Visa, MasterCard, American Express, Plus, Cirrus and Maestro; some MasterCard and Maestro with IC chips may not work). Be aware that many banks place a limit on the amount of cash you can withdraw in one day (often around US$300).

7-Eleven (セブン・イレブン; www.sevenbank.co.jp/english) The Seven Bank ATMs at 7-Eleven convenience stores have English instructions and are available 24 hours a day. Considering that 7-Eleven convenience stores are ubiquitous, this is the easiest option for getting quick cash. Withdrawal limit of ¥100,000 per transaction.

Japan Post Bank (ゆうちょ銀行; www.jp-bank.japanpost.jp/en/ias/en_ias_index.html) Post offices have Japan Post Bank ATMs with English instructions; opening hours vary depending on the size of the post office, but are usually longer than regular post-office hours. Withdrawal limit of ¥50,000 per transaction.

Cash

More and more places in Tokyo accept credit cards but it's still a good idea to

PRACTICALITIES

Newspapers *Japan Times* (www.japantimes.co.jp) is a long-running English-language daily; Japanese newspaper *Asahi Shimbun* (www.asahi.com/ajw) has English coverage on its website.

Magazines *Time Out Tokyo* (www.timeout.com/tokyo) and *Metropolis* (http://metropolisjapan.com) are two free English-language mags with city info.

Smoking Tokyo has a curious policy: smoking is banned in public spaces but allowed inside bars and restaurants (though nonsmoking bars and restaurants exist, too). Designated smoking areas are set up around train stations.

Weights & Measures The metric system is used along with some traditional Japanese measurements, especially for area (eg *jō* is the size of a tatami mat).

always keep at least several thousand yen on hand for local transport, inexpensive restaurants and shops (and even some moderately priced restaurants and shops).

The currency in Japan is the yen (¥), and banknotes and coins are easily distinguishable. There are ¥1, ¥5, ¥10, ¥50, ¥100 and ¥500 coins; and ¥1000, ¥2000, ¥5000 and ¥10,000 banknotes (the ¥2000 note is very rarely seen). The ¥1 coin is a lightweight aluminium coin; the bronze-coloured ¥5 and silver-coloured ¥50 coins both have a hole punched in the middle. Prices may be calculated using the kanji for yen (円). Prices are usually in Arabic numerals, but occasionally they are in traditional kanji.

Credit Cards

Businesses that do take credit cards will often display the logo for the cards they accept. Visa is the most widely accepted, followed by MasterCard, American Express and Diners Club. Foreign-issued cards should work fine.

Moneychangers

With a passport, you can change cash or travellers cheques at any Authorised Foreign Exchange Bank (signs are displayed in English), major post offices, some large hotels and most big department stores.

For currency other than US dollars, larger banks such as Sumitomo Mitsui (SMBC) and Tokyo-Mitsubishi UFJ (MUFG) are a better bet. They can usually change at least US, Canadian and Australian dollars, pounds sterling, euros and Swiss francs. Branches of these banks can be found near all major train stations.

MUFG also operates **World Currency Shop** (www.tokyo-card.co.jp/wcs/wcs-shop-e.php) foreign-exchange counters near major shopping centres. They will exchange a broader range of currencies, including Chinese

yuan, Korean won and Taiwan, Hong Kong, Singapore and New Zealand dollars.

Note that you receive a better exchange rate when withdrawing cash from ATMs than when exchanging cash or travellers cheques in Tokyo.

Tipping

It is not customary to tip, even in the most expensive restaurants and bars. In high-end restaurants and hotels, a 10% service fee is usually added to the bill.

Opening Hours

Note that some outdoor attractions (such as gardens) may close earlier in the winter. Standard opening hours:

Banks 9am to 3pm (some to 5pm) Monday to Friday

Bars from around 6pm to late

Boutiques noon to 8pm, irregularly closed

Cafes vary enormously; chains 7am to 10pm

Department stores 10am to 8pm

Museums 9am or 10am and close 5pm; often closed Monday

Post offices 9am to 5pm Monday to Friday; larger ones have longer hours and open Saturday

Restaurants lunch 11.30am to 2pm; dinner 6 to 10pm; last orders taken about half an hour before closing

Post

Tokyo's postal service is reliable and efficient. There are small Japan Post branches in every neighbourhood; every ward has a larger central office with extended hours. For current rates, see www.post.japanpost.jp.

Tokyo Central Post Office (東京中央郵便局; Map p266; ☑03-3217-5231; 2-7-2

Marunouchi, Chiyoda-ku; ⊙post 24hr, ATM 12.05am-11.55pm Mon-Sat, to 9pm Sun; ⊞JR lines to Tokyo Station, Marunouchi south exit)

Public Holidays

If a national holiday falls on a Monday, most museums and restaurants that normally close on Mondays will remain open and close the next day instead.

New Year's Day (Ganjitsu) 1 January

Coming-of-Age Day (Seijin-no-hi) second Monday in January

National Foundation Day (Kenkoku Kinen-bi) 11 February

Spring Equinox (Shumbun-no-hi) 20 or 21 March

Shōwa Day (Shōwa-no-hi) 29 April

Constitution Day (Kempō Kinen-bi) 3 May

Green Day (Midori-no-hi) 4 May

Children's Day (Kodomo-no-hi) 5 May

Marine Day (Umi-no-hi) third Monday in July

Mountain Day (Yama-no-hi) 11 August

Respect-for-the-Aged Day (Keirō-no-hi) third Monday in September

Autumn Equinox (Shūbun-no-hi) 23 or 24 September

Health & Sports Day (Taiiku-no-hi) second Monday in October

Culture Day (Bunka-no-hi) 3 November

Labour Thanksgiving Day (Kinrō Kansha-no-hi) 23 November

Emperor's Birthday (Tennō-no-Tanjōbi) 23 December

Safe Travel

The biggest threat to travellers in Tokyo is the city's general aura of safety. It's wise to keep up the same level of caution and common sense that you would back home. Of special note are reports that drink-spiking continues to be a problem in Roppongi (resulting in robbery, extortion and, in extreme cases, physical assault). Be wary of following touts into bars there and in Kabukichō; men are also likely to be solicited in both neighbourhoods. Women, especially those alone, walking through Kabukichō and Dōgenzaka (both are red-light districts) risk being harassed.

Twenty-four-hour staffed *kōban* (police boxes) are located near most major train stations.

Taxes & Refunds

Japan's consumption tax is 8% (with an increase to 10% planned for October 2019). A growing number of shops offer tax-free shopping (noted by a sticker in English on the window) if you spend more than ¥5000. Passport required.

Since the tax is not charged at point of sale, there is no need to collect a refund when leaving the country; however, you should hand in a form affixed to your passport to customs officials when you depart. For details, see: http://enjoy.taxfree.jp.

Telephone

Mobile Phones

Japan operates on the 3G network, so overseas phones with 3G technology should work in Tokyo.

Prepaid SIM cards that allow you to make voice calls are not available in Japan. You must sign a contract for a monthly plan (minimum six-month commitment with cancellation fees). For short-term visitors who anticipate needing to make voice calls, a rental pay-as-you-go phone is a better option. **Rentafone Japan** (www.rentafonejapan.com; email@rentafonejapan.com) offers rentals for ¥3900 a week (plus ¥300 for each additional day) and domestic calls cost a reasonable ¥35 per minute (overseas calls start at ¥45 per minute).

Data-only SIM cards for unlocked smartphones are available at kiosks at both Narita and Haneda airports and at large electronics stores (like Bic Camera, Yodobashi Camera etc). To work, they may require some fiddling with settings, so make sure you've got a connection before you leave the shop. Staff usually speak some English.

You'll also need a sense of how much data you need and how fast you need it to download, as there is a dizzying array of options (and prices). B-Mobile's **Visitor SIM** (www.bmobile.ne.jp/english/index.html), which

offers 14 days of unlimited data (the speed will be reduced for heavy users) for ¥2380, is a good choice.

Phone Codes

The country code for Japan is 81; Tokyo's area code is 03, although some outer suburbs have different area codes. Eight digits follow the area code. The area code is not used if dialling within the same area code from a landline.

Mobile phone numbers start with ☎090, ☎080 or ☎070. Calls to mobile phones are significantly more expensive than local calls. When dialling Tokyo from abroad, to either a landline or a mobile, drop the first 0; rather, dial ☎81-3 or 81-90.

Toll-free numbers begin with ☎0120, 0070, 0077, 0088 and 0800. For local directory assistance, dial ☎104 (cost ¥108). For international directory assistance in English, dial ☎0057.

Public Phones

Public phones do still exist and they work almost 100% of the time; look for them around train stations. Ordinary public phones are green; those that allow you to call abroad are grey and are usually marked 'International & Domestic Card/Coin Phone'.

Local calls cost ¥10 per minute; note that you won't get change on a ¥100 coin. The minimum charge for international calls is ¥100, which buys you a fraction of a minute – good for a quick check-in but not economical for much more. Dial ☎001 010 (KDDI), ☎0061 010 (SoftBank Telecom) or ☎0033 010 (NTT), followed by the country code, area code and local number. There's very little difference in the rates from the different providers; all offer better rates at night. Reverse-charge (collect) international calls can be made by dialling ☎0051.

UNOFFICIAL HOLIDAYS

During the New Year period, technically only New Year's Day is a holiday in Japan, but the traditional holiday period – called *Shōgatsu* – extends until at least 3 January (and often until 6 January). Expect most businesses to be closed and Tokyo to be very quiet.

Be aware that during the New Year period (29 December to 3 January), the string of national holidays called Golden Week (29 April to 5 May) and the O-Bon festival in mid-August, accommodation may be fully booked or pricier than usual as these are all major travel periods for Japanese.

If you are going to make a significant number of calls, it's worth purchasing a *terehon kādo* (telephone card). These stored-value cards are available from station kiosks and convenience stores in ¥1000 denominations and can be used in grey or green pay phones; phones display the remaining value of your card when it is inserted. Phone cards with English instructions are readily available.

JAPANESE YEARS

In addition to the typical Western calendar, Japan also counts years in terms of the reigns of its emperors – Meiji, Shōwa et al. The current era is called Heisei (pronounced hay-say) after the ceremonial name bestowed on the current emperor, Akihito, by the Imperial Household Agency. He ascended to the throne in 1989 (Heisei 1); thus 2017 is Heisei 29 (and with talk of possible retirement, a new era may soon begin).

Time

Tokyo local time is nine hours ahead of Greenwich Mean Time (GMT). Japan does not observe daylight saving time.

Toilets

➡ Toilets in Tokyo run the gamut from heated-seat thrones that wash and dry your intimate areas at the touch of a button (these are called 'washlets') to humble, porcelain squat toilets in the floor.

➡ When using squat toilets, the correct position is facing the hood, away from the door. If you just can't bear a squat toilet, look for the characters 洋式 (*yō-shiki*, Western style) on the stall door.

➡ The most common words for toilet in Japanese are トイレ (pronounced 'toire') and お手洗い ('o-te-arai'); 女 (female) and 男 (male) will also come in handy.

➡ Public toilets, free and typically clean, can be found in most train stations; convenience stores often have toilets you can use too. Toilet paper is usually present, but it's still a good idea to accept those small packets of tissue handed out on the street, a common form of advertising, just in case. Paper towels and hand dryers are often lacking, so Japanese carry a handkerchief for use after washing their hands.

➡ Separate toilet slippers are usually provided in homes and restaurants where you take off your shoes at the entrance; they are typically just inside the toilet door. These are for use in the toilet only, so remember to shuffle out of them when you leave.

Tourist Information

Tokyo Metropolitan Government Building Tourist Information Center (Map p280; ☎03-5321-3077; 1st fl, Tokyo Metropolitan Government bldg 1, 2-8-1 Nishi-Shinjuku, Shinjuku-ku; ⏰9.30am-6.30pm; [S]Ōedo line to Tochōmae, exit A4) has English-language information and publications. Additional branches in Keisei Ueno Station, Haneda Airport and Shinjuku Bus Terminal. Note that Tourist Information Centers (TICs) cannot make accommodation bookings.

Asakusa Culture Tourist Information Center (浅草文化観光センター; Map p286; ☎03-3842-5566; http://taitonavi.jp; 2-18-9 Kaminarimon, Taitō-ku; ⏰9am-8pm; 📶; [S]Ginza line to Asakusa, exit 2) This ward-run TIC has lots of info on Asakusa and Ueno, and a Pia ticket counter (for purchasing tickets to concerts and shows), near the entrance to Sensō-ji.

Japan Guide Association (☎03-3863-2895; www.jga21c.or.jp) Can put you in contact with licensed, professional tour guides.

JNTO Tourist Information Center (Map p266; ☎03-3201-3331; www.jnto.go.jp; 1st fl, Shin-Tokyo Bldg, 3-3-1 Marunouchi, Chiyoda-ku; ⏰9am-5pm; 📶; [S]Chiyoda line to Nijūbashimae, exit 1) Run by the Japan National Tourism Organisation, this TIC has information on Tokyo and beyond. There are also branches in Narita Airport terminals 1 and 2.

JR East Travel Service Center (JR東日本訪日旅行センター; Map p266; www.jreast.co.jp/e/customer_support/service_center_tokyo.html; Tokyo Station, 1-9-1 Marunouchi, Chiyoda-ku; ⏰7.30am-8.30pm; 📶; 🚆JR Yamanote line to Tokyo, Marunouchi north exit) Tourist information, money exchange, and bookings for ski and onsen getaways. There are branches in the two airports, too.

Moshi Moshi Box Harajuku Information Center (もしもしインフォメーションスペース; Map p276; 3-235 Jingūmae, Shibuya-ku; 📶; 🚆JR Yamanote line to Harajuku, Omote-sandō) Area maps, luggage forwarding and travel help in English.

Tōbu Sightseeing Service Center (Map p286; ☎03-3841-2871; www.tobu.co.jp/foreign; Tōbu Asakusa Station, 1-4-1 Hanakawado, Taitō-ku;

⏰7.20am-7pm) Sells passes for Tōbu rail transport from Asakusa to Nikkō and unlimited hop-on, hop-off bus services around Nikkō.

Tokyo Tourist Information Center (Map p266; ☎03-3287-2955; 2-4-10 Yūrakuchō, Chiyoda-ku; ⏰11am-7.30pm Mon-Fri, 10am-7pm Sat & Sun; 🛜; 🚉JR Yamanote line to Yūrakuchō, Hibiya exit) Booking counters for tours, money exchange machines, wi-fi and a shop with a range of souvenirs.

Travellers with Disabilities

Tokyo is making steps to improve universal access (called 'barrier free' here). It is a slow process, though one that is getting a boost from the 2020 Olympics preparations. Newer buildings have wheelchair access ramps, and more and more subway stations have elevators (look for signs on the platform, as not all exits have elevators). A fair number of hotels, from the higher end of midrange and above, offer a 'barrier-free' room or two (book well in advance). Larger attractions and train stations, department stores and shopping malls should have wheelchair accessible restrooms (which will have Western-style toilets).

For the blind, traffic lights have speakers playing melodies when it is safe to cross, train platforms have raised dots and lines to provide guidance and some ticket machines have Braille.

Accessible Tokyo (http://accessible.jp.org/tokyo) Describes the accessiblity of major Tokyo-area attractions, including which subway lines and exits have elevators.

Japan Accessible Tourism Centre (www.japan-accessible.com/city/tokyo.htm) A cheat-sheet for accessible sights and hotels in Tokyo.

Download Lonely Planet's free *Accessible Travel* guide from http://lptravel.to/AccessibleTravel.

Visas

Citizens of 67 countries, including Australia, Canada, Hong Kong, Korea, New Zealand, Singapore, USA, UK and almost all European nations will be automatically issued a *tanki-taizai* (temporary visitor visa) on arrival. Typically this visa is good for 90 days. For a complete list of visa-exempt countries, consult www.mofa.go.jp/j_info/visit/visa/short/novisa.html#list.

Citizens of Austria, Germany, Ireland, Lichtenstein, Mexico, Switzerland and the UK are able to extend this visa once, for another 90 days. To do so, you need to apply at the **Tokyo Regional Immigration Bureau** (東京入国管理局; Tokyo Nyūkoku Kanrikyoku; ☎03-5796-7111; www.immi-moj.go.jp; 5-5-30 Kōnan, Minato-ku; ⏰9am-noon, 1-4pm Mon-Fri; 🚉99 from Shinagawa Station, east exit to Tokyo Nyūkoku Kanrikyoku-mae, 🚉Rinkai line to Tennōzu Isle) before the initial visa expires.

Resident Card

Anyone entering Japan on a visa for longer than the standard 90 days for tourists will be issued a resident card, which must be carried at all times.

Work Visas

Arriving in Japan and looking for a job is quite a tough proposition these days, though people still do it and occasionally succeed in finding visa sponsorship. With that said, there are legal employment categories for foreigners that specify standards of experience and qualifications.

Once you find an employer in Japan who is willing to sponsor you, it is necessary to obtain a Certificate of Eligibility from your nearest Japanese immigration office. The same office can then issue your work visa, which is valid for either one or three years. This procedure can take two to three months.

Working-Holiday Visas

Citizens of Australia, Austria, Canada, Denmark, France, Germany, Ireland, Korea, New Zealand, Norway, Poland, Portugal, Slovakia, Taiwan and the UK, and residents of Hong Kong between the age of 18 and 30 (or 18 and 25 for Australians, Canadians and Koreans) can apply for a working-holiday visa. The visa is designed to enable young people to travel during their stay, and there are legal restrictions about how long and where you can work. The working-holiday visa must be obtained from a Japanese embassy or consulate abroad. Visit www.mofa.go.jp/j_info/visit/w_holiday.

Volunteering

Most meaningful volunteer work in Tokyo requires Japanese language ability; however, there are a few organisations that accept short-term, English-speaking volunteers.

Hands on Tokyo (www.handsontokyo.org) Partners with several local organisations that need volunteers to help in English classes and with outdoor activities.

Second Harvest Japan (https://2hj.org/english) Always needs volunteers to prepare food and serve at its weekly Saturday soup kitchen for the homeless; in Ueno-kōen.

Language

Japanese is spoken by more than 125 million people. While it bears some resemblance to Altaic languages such as Mongolian and Turkish and has grammatical similarities to Korean, its origins are unclear. Chinese is responsible for the existence of many Sino-Japanese words in Japanese, and for the originally Chinese kanji characters which the Japanese use in combination with the homegrown hiragana and katakana scripts.

Japanese pronunciation is easy to master for English speakers, as most of its sounds are also found in English. If you read our coloured pronunciation guides as if they were English, you'll be understood. In Japanese, it's important to make the distinction between short and long vowels, as vowel length can change the meaning of a word. The long vowels, shown in our pronunciation guides with a horizontal line on top of them (ā, ē, ī, ō, ū), should be held twice as long as the short ones. It's also important to make the distinction between single and double consonants, as this can produce a difference in meaning. Pronounce the double consonants with a slight pause between them, eg sak·ka (writer).

Note also that the vowel sound ai is pronounced as in 'aisle', air as in 'pair' and ow as in 'how'. As for the consonants, ts is pronounced as in 'hats', f sounds almost like 'fw' (with rounded lips), and r is halfway between 'r' and 'l'. All syllables in a word are pronounced fairly evenly in Japanese.

WANT MORE?

For in-depth language information and handy phrases, check out Lonely Planet's *Japanese Phrasebook*. You'll find it at **shop. lonelyplanet.com**, or you can buy Lonely Planet's iPhone phrasebooks at the Apple App Store.

BASICS

Japanese uses an array of registers of speech to reflect social and contextual hierarchy, but these can be simplified to the form most appropriate for the situation, which is what we've done in this language guide too.

Hello.	こんにちは。	kon·ni·chi·wa
Goodbye.	さようなら。	sa·yō·na·ra
Yes.	はい。	hai
No.	いいえ。	ī·e
Please. (when asking)	ください。	ku·da·sai
Please. (when offering)	どうぞ。	dō·zo
Thank you.	ありがとう。	a·ri·ga·tō
Excuse me. (to get attention)	すみません。	su·mi·ma·sen
Sorry.	ごめんなさい。	go·men·na·sai

You're welcome.
どういたしまして。 dō i·ta·shi·mash·te

How are you?
お元気ですか? o·gen·ki des ka

Fine. And you?
はい、元気です。 hai, gen·ki des
あなたは? a·na·ta wa

What's your name?
お名前は何ですか? o·na·ma·e wa nan des ka

My name is ...
私の名前は wa·ta·shi no na·ma·e wa
…です。 ... des

Do you speak English?
英語が話せますか? ē·go ga ha·na·se·mas ka

I don't understand.
わかりません。 wa·ka·ri·ma·sen

Does anyone speak English?
どなたか英語を do·na·ta ka ē·go o
話せますか? ha·na·se·mas ka

ACCOMMODATION

Where's a ...?	…はど こですか？	... wa do·ko des ka
campsite	キャンプ場	kyam·pu·jō
guesthouse	民宿	min·shu·ku
hotel	ホテル	ho·te·ru
inn	旅館	ryo·kan
youth hostel	ユース ホステル	yū·su· ho·su·te·ru

Do you have a ... room?	…ルームは ありますか？	...rū·mu wa a·ri·mas ka
single	シングル	shin·gu·ru
double	ダブル	da·bu·ru

How much is it per ...?	…いくら ですか？	... i·ku·ra des ka
night	1泊	ip·pa·ku
person	1人	hi·to·ri

air-con	エアコン	air·kon
bathroom	風呂場	fu·ro·ba
window	窓	ma·do

DIRECTIONS

Where's the ...?
…はどこですか？ ... wa do·ko des ka

Can you show me (on the map)?
(地図で) 教えて
くれませんか？ (chi·zu de) o·shi·e·te ku·re·ma·sen ka

What's the address?
住所は何ですか？ jū·sho wa nan des ka

Could you please write it down?
書いてくれませんか？ kai·te ku·re·ma·sen ka

behind ...	…の後ろ	... no u·shi·ro
in front of ...	…の前	... no ma·e
near ...	…の近く	... no chi·ka·ku
next to ...	…のとなり	... no to·na·ri
opposite ...	…の 向かい側	... no mu·kai·ga·wa
straight ahead	この先	ko·no sa·ki

Turn ...	…まがって ください。	... ma·gat·te ku·da·sai
at the corner	その角を	so·no ka·do o
at the traffic lights	その信号を	so·no shin·gō o
left	左へ	hi·da·ri e
right	右へ	mi·gi e

KEY PATTERNS

To get by in Japanese, mix and match these simple patterns with words of your choice:

When's (the next bus)?
(次のバスは)
何時ですか？ (tsu·gi no bas wa) nan·ji des ka

Where's (the station)?
(駅は) どこですか？ (e·ki wa) do·ko des ka

Do you have (a map)?
(地図)
がありますか？ (chi·zu) ga a·ri·mas ka

Is there (a toilet)?
(トイレ)
がありますか？ (toy·re) ga a·ri·mas ka

I'd like (the menu).
(メニュー)
をお願いします。 (me·nyū) o o·ne·gai shi·mas

Can I (sit here)?
(ここに座って)
もいいですか？ (ko·ko ni su·wat·te) mo ī des ka

I need (a can opener).
(缶切り)
が必要です。 (kan·ki·ri) ga hi·tsu·yō des

Do I need (a visa)?
(ビザ)
が必要ですか？ (bi·za) ga hi·tsu·yō des ka

I have (a reservation).
(予約) があります。 (yo·ya·ku) ga a·ri·mas

I'm (a teacher).
私は (教師)
です。 wa·ta·shi wa (kyō·shi) des

EATING & DRINKING

I'd like to reserve a table for (two people).
(2人) の予約を
お願いします。 (fu·ta·ri) no yo·ya·ku o o·ne·gai shi·mas

What would you recommend?
なにが
おすすめですか？ na·ni ga o·su·su·me des ka

What's in that dish?
あの料理に何
が入っていますか？ a·no ryō·ri ni na·ni ga hait·te i·mas ka

Do you have any vegetarian dishes?
ベジタリアン料理
がありますか？ be·ji·ta·ri·an ryō·ri ga a·ri·mas ka

I'm a vegetarian.
私は
ベジタリアンです。 wa·ta·shi wa be·ji·ta·ri·an des

I'm a vegan.
私は厳格な
菜食主義者
です。 wa·ta·shi wa gen·ka·ku na sai·sho·ku·shu·gi·sha des

I don't eat ... …は … wa
食べません。 ta·be·ma·sen

dairy products 乳製品 nyū·cō·hin

(red) meat （赤身の） (a·ka·mi no)
肉 ni·ku

meat or dairy products 肉や ni·ku ya
乳製品は nyū·sē·hin

pork 豚肉 bu·ta·ni·ku

seafood シーフード shī·fū·do/
海産物 kai·sam·bu·tsu

Is it cooked with pork lard or chicken stock?
これはラードか鶏の ko·re wa rā·do ka to·ri no
だしを使って da·shi o tsu·kat·te
いますか？ i·mas ka

I'm allergic to (peanuts).
私は wa·ta·shi wa
（ビーナッツ）に (pī·nat·tsu) ni
アレルギーが a·re·ru·gī ga
あります。 a·ri·mas

That was delicious!
おいしかった。 oy·shi·kat·ta

Cheers!
乾杯! kam·pai

Please bring the bill.
お勘定をください。 o·kan·jō o ku·da·sai

Key Words

appetisers 前菜 zen·sai

bottle ビン bin

bowl ボール bō·ru

breakfast 朝食 chō·sho·ku

cold 冷たい tsu·me·ta·i

dinner 夕食 yū·sho·ku

fork フォーク fō·ku

glass グラス gu·ra·su

SIGNS

入口	**Entrance**
出口	**Exit**
営業中/開館	**Open**
閉店/閉館	**Closed**
インフォメーション	**Information**
危険	**Danger**
トイレ	**Toilets**
男	**Men**
女	**Women**

grocery 食料品 sho·ku·ryō·hin

hot (warm) 熱い a·tsu·i

knife ナイフ nai fu

lunch 昼食 chū·sho·ku

market 市場 i·chi·ba

menu メニュー me·nyū

plate 皿 sa·ra

spicy スパイシー spai·shī

spoon スプーン spūn

vegetarian ベジタリアン be·ji·ta·ri·an

with いっしょに is·sho ni

without なしで na·shi de

Meat & Fish

beef 牛肉 gyū·ni·ku

chicken 鶏肉 to·ri·ni·ku

duck アヒル a·hi·ru

eel うなぎ u·na·gi

fish 魚 sa·ka·na

lamb 子羊 ko·hi·tsu·ji

lobster ロブスター ro·bus·tā

meat 肉 ni·ku

pork 豚肉 bu·ta·ni·ku

prawn エビ e·bi

salmon サケ sa·ke

seafood シーフード shī·fū·do/
海産物 kai·sam·bu·tsu

shrimp 小エビ ko·e·bi

tuna マグロ ma·gu·ro

turkey 七面鳥 shi·chi·men·chō

veal 子牛 ko·u·shi

Fruit & Vegetables

apple りんご rin·go

banana バナナ ba·na·na

beans 豆 ma·me

capsicum ピーマン pī·man

carrot ニンジン nin·jin

cherry さくらんぼ sa·ku·ram·bo

cucumber キュウリ kyū·ri

fruit 果物 ku·da·mo·no

grapes ブドウ bu·dō

lettuce レタス re·tas

nut ナッツ nat·tsu

orange オレンジ o·ren·ji

peach 桃 mo·mo

peas	豆	ma·me
pineapple	パイナップル	pai·nap·pu·ru
potato	ジャガイモ	ja·ga·i·mo
pumpkin	カボチャ	ka·bo·cha
spinach	ホウレンソウ	hō·ren·sō
strawberry	イチゴ	i·chi·go
tomato	トマト	to·ma·to
vegetables	野菜	ya·sai
watermelon	スイカ	su·i·ka

Other

bread	パン	pan
butter	バター	ba·tā
cheese	チーズ	chī·zu
chilli	唐辛子	tō·ga·ra·shi
egg	卵	ta·ma·go
honey	蜂蜜	ha·chi·mi·tsu
horseradish	わさび	wa·sa·bi
jam	ジャム	ja·mu
noodles	麺	men
pepper	コショウ	koshō
rice (cooked)	ごはん	go·han
salt	塩	shi·o
seaweed	のり	no·ri
soy sauce	しょう油	shō·yu
sugar	砂糖	sa·tō

Drinks

beer	ビール	bī·ru
coffee	コーヒー	kō·hī
(orange) juice	(オレンジ) ジュース	(o·ren·ji·) jū·su
lemonade	レモネード	re·mo·nē·do
milk	ミルク	mi·ru·ku
mineral water	ミネラル ウォーター	mi·ne·ra·ru· wō·tā

QUESTION WORDS

How?	どのように?	do·no yō ni
What?	なに?	na·ni
When?	いつ?	i·tsu
Where?	どこ?	do·ko
Which?	どちら?	do·chi·ra
Who?	だれ?	da·re
Why?	なぜ?	na·ze

red wine	赤ワイン	a·ka wain
sake	酒	sa·ke
tea	紅茶	kō·cha
water	水	mi·zu
white wine	白ワイン	shi·ro wain
yogurt	ヨーグルト	yō·gu·ru·to

EMERGENCIES

Help!
たすけて!   tas·ke·te

Go away!
離れろ!   ha·na·re·ro

I'm lost.
迷いました。   ma·yoy·mash·ta

Call the police.
警察を呼んで。   kē·sa·tsu o yon·de

Call a doctor.
医者を呼んで。   i·sha o yon·de

Where are the toilets?
トイレはどこですか?   toy·re wa do·ko des ka

I'm ill.
私は病気です。   wa·ta·shi wa byō·ki des

It hurts here.
ここが痛いです。   ko·ko ga i·tai des

I'm allergic to ...
私は…
アレルギーです。   wa·ta·shi wa ...
a·re·ru·gī des

SHOPPING & SERVICES

I'd like to buy ...
…をください。   ... o ku·da·sai

I'm just looking.
見ているだけです。   mi·te i·ru da·ke des

Can I look at it?
それを見ても
いいですか?   so·re o mi·te mo
ī des ka

How much is it?
いくらですか?   i·ku·ra des ka

That's too expensive.
高すぎます。   ta·ka·su·gi·mas

Can you give me a discount?
ディスカウント
できますか?   dis·kown·to
de·ki·mas ka

There's a mistake in the bill.
請求書に間違いが
あります。   sē·kyū·sho ni ma·chi·gai ga
a·ri·mas

ATM	ATM	ē·tī·e·mu
credit card	クレジット カード	ku·re·jit·to· kā·do
post office	郵便局	yū·bin·kyo·ku
public phone	公衆電話	kō·shū·den·wa
tourist office	観光案内所	kan·kō·an·nai·jo

TIME & DATES

What time is it?
何時ですか？　　　nan ji des ka

It's (10) o'clock.
(10)時です。　　　(jū)·ji des

Half past (10).
(10)時半です。　　(jū)·ji han des

am	午前	go·zen
pm	午後	go·go

Monday	月曜日	ge·tsu·yō·bi
Tuesday	火曜日	ka·yō·bi
Wednesday	水曜日	su·i·yō·bi
Thursday	木曜日	mo·ku·yō·bi
Friday	金曜日	kin·yō·bi
Saturday	土曜日	do·yō·bi
Sunday	日曜日	ni·chi·yō·bi

January	1月	i·chi·ga·tsu
February	2月	ni·ga·tsu
March	3月	san·ga·tsu
April	4月	shi·ga·tsu
May	5月	go·ga·tsu
June	6月	ro·ku·ga·tsu
July	7月	shi·chi·ga·tsu
August	8月	ha·chi·ga·tsu
September	9月	ku·ga·tsu
October	10月	jū·ga·tsu
November	11月	jū·i·chi·ga·tsu
December	12月	jū·ni·ga·tsu

TRANSPORT

boat	船	fu·ne
bus	バス	bas
metro	地下鉄	chi·ka·te·tsu
plane	飛行機	hi·kō·ki
train	電車	den·sha
tram	市電	shi·den

What time does it leave?
これは何時に　　　ko·re wa nan·ji ni
出ますか？　　　　de·mas ka

Does it stop at (...)?
(…)に　　　　　　(...) ni
停まりますか？　　to·ma·ri·mas ka

Please tell me when we get to (...).
(…)に着いたら　　(...) ni tsu·i·ta·ra
教えてください。　o·shi·e·te ku·da·sai

NUMBERS

1	一	i·chi
2	二	ni
3	三	san
4	四	shi/yon
5	五	go
6	六	ro·ku
7	七	shi·chi/na·na
8	八	ha·chi
9	九	ku/kyū
10	十	jū
20	二十	ni·jū
30	三十	san·jū
40	四十	yon·jū
50	五十	go·jū
60	六十	ro·ku·jū
70	七十	na·na·jū
80	八十	ha·chi·jū
90	九十	kyū·jū
100	百	hya·ku
1000	千	sen

A one-way/return ticket (to ...).
(...行きの)　　　(...yu·ki no)
片道/往復　　　　ka·ta·mi·chi/ō·fu·ku
切符。　　　　　　kip·pu

first	始発の	shi·ha·tsu no
last	最終の	sai·shū no
next	次の	tsu·gi no

aisle	通路側	tsū·ro·ga·wa
bus stop	バス停	bas·tē
cancelled	キャンセル	kyan·se·ru
delayed	遅れ	o·ku·re
ticket window	窓口	ma·do·gu·chi
timetable	時刻表	ji·ko·ku·hyō
train station	駅	e·ki
window	窓側	ma·do·ga·wa

I'd like to hire a ...	…を借りたい のですが。	... o ka·ri·tai no des ga
bicycle	自転車	ji·ten·sha
car	自動車	ji·dō·sha
motorbike	オートバイ	ō·to·bai

GLOSSARY

Amida Nyorai – Buddha of the Western Paradise

ANA – All Nippon Airways

-bashi – bridge (also *hashi*)

bashō – sumo tournament

bentō – boxed lunch or dinner, usually containing rice, vegetables and fish or meat

bosatsu – a bodhisattva, or Buddha attendant, who assists others to attain enlightenment

bugaku – dance pieces played by court orchestras in ancient Japan

bunraku – classical puppet theatre that uses life-size puppets to enact dramas similar to those of *kabuki*

chō – city area (for large cities) sized between a *ku* and *chōme*

chōme – city area of a few blocks

Daibutsu – Great Buddha

daimyō – domain lords under the *shōgun*

dōri – street

fugu – poisonous pufferfish, elevated to haute cuisine

futon – cushion-like mattress that is rolled up and stored away during the day

futsū – local train; literally 'ordinary'

gagaku – music of the imperial court

gaijin – foreigner; the contracted form of *gaikokujin* (literally, 'outside country person')

-gawa – river (also *kawa*)

geisha – a woman versed in the arts and other cultivated pursuits who entertains guests

-gū – shrine (also *-jingū* or *-jinja*)

haiden – hall of worship in a shrine

haiku – seventeen-syllable poem

hakubutsukan – museum

hanami – cherry-blossom viewing

hashi – bridge (also *-bashi*); chopsticks

higashi – east

hiragana – phonetic syllabary used to write Japanese words

honden – main building of a shrine

hondō – main building of a temple

ikebana – art of flower arrangement

irori – open hearth found in traditional Japanese homes

izakaya – Japanese pub/eatery

-ji – temple (also *tera* or *dera*)

-jingū – shrine (also *-jinja* or *-gū*)

-jinja – shrine (also *-gū* or *-jingū*)

jizō – bodhisattva who watches over children

JNTO – Japan National Tourist Organization

-jō – castle (also *shiro*)

JR – Japan Railways

kabuki – form of Japanese theatre that draws on popular tales and is characterised by elaborate costumes, stylised acting and the use of male actors for all roles

kaiseki – Buddhist-inspired, Japanese haute cuisine; called *cha-kaiseki* when served as part of a tea ceremony

kaisoku – rapid train

kaiten-sushi – conveyor-belt sushi

kamikaze – literally, 'wind of the gods'; originally the typhoon that sank Kublai Khan's 13th-century invasion fleet and the name adopted by Japanese suicide bombers in the waning days of WWII

kampai – cheers, as in a drinking toast

kanji – literally, 'Chinese writing'; Chinese ideographic script used for writing Japanese

Kannon – Buddhist goddess of mercy

karaoke – a now-famous export where revellers sing along to recorded music, minus the vocals

kawa – river

-ken – prefecture, eg Shiga-ken

kimono – traditional outer garment that is similar to a robe

kita – north

-ko – lake

kōban – local police box

kōen – park

ku – ward

kyōgen – drama performed as comic relief between *nō* plays, or as separate events

kyūkō – ordinary express train (faster than a *futsū*, only stopping at certain stations)

live house – a small concert hall where live music is performed

machi – city area (for large cities) sized between a *ku* and *chōme*

mama-san – older women who run drinking, dining and entertainment venues

maneki-neko – beckoning or welcoming cat figure frequently seen in restaurants and bars; it's supposed to attract customers and trade

matcha – powdered green tea served in tea ceremonies

matsuri – festival

midori-no-madoguchi – ticket counter in large Japan Rail stations, where you can make more complicated bookings (look for the green band across the glass)

mikoshi – portable shrine carried during festivals

minami – south

minshuku – Japanese equivalent of a B&B

mon – temple gate

mura – village

N'EX – Narita Express

Nihon – Japanese word for Japan; literally, 'source of the sun' (also known as *Nippon*)

Nippon – see *Nihon*

nishi – west

nō – classical Japanese drama performed on a bare stage

noren – door curtain for restaurants, usually labelled with the name of the establishment

NTT – Nippon Telegraph & Telephone Corporation

o- prefix used as a sign of respect (usually applied to objects)

obi – sash or belt worn with *kimono*

O-bon – mid-August festivals and ceremonies for deceased ancestors

o-furo – traditional Japanese bath

onsen – mineral hot spring with bathing areas and accommodation

o-shibori – hot towels given in restaurants

pachinko – vertical pinball game that is a Japanese craze

Raijin – god of thunder

ryokan – traditional Japanese inn

ryōri – cooking; cuisine

ryōtei – traditional-style, high-class restaurant; *kaiseki* is typical fare

sabi – a poetic ideal of finding beauty and pleasure in imperfection; often used in conjunction with *wabi*

sakura – cherry trees

salaryman – male employee of a large firm

-sama – a suffix even more respectful than *san*

samurai – Japan's traditional warrior class

-san – a respectful suffix applied to personal names, similar to Mr, Mrs or Ms but more widely used

sentō – public bath

setto – set meal; see also *teishoku*

Shaka Nyorai – Historical Buddha

shakkei – borrowed scenery; technique where features outside a garden are incorporated into its design

shamisen – three-stringed, banjo-like instrument

-shi – city (to distinguish cities with prefectures of the same name)

shinkansen – bullet train (literally, 'new trunk line')

Shintō – indigenous Japanese religion

Shitamachi – traditionally the low-lying, less-affluent parts of Tokyo

shōgun – military ruler of pre-Meiji Japan

shōjin ryōri – Buddhist vegetarian cuisine

shokudō – Japanese-style cafeteria/cheap restaurant

soba – thin brown buckwheat noodles

tatami – tightly woven floor matting on which shoes should not be worn

teishoku – set meal in a restaurant

tokkyū – limited express train

torii – entrance gate to a *Shintō* shrine

tsukemono – Japanese pickles

udon – thick, white, wheat noodles

ukiyo-e – woodblock prints; literally, 'pictures of the floating world'

wabi – a Zen-inspired aesthetic of rustic simplicity

wasabi – spicy Japanese horseradish

washi – Japanese paper

yakuza – Japanese mafia

Zen – a form of Buddhism

FOOD GLOSSARY

Rice Dishes

katsu-don (かつ丼) – rice topped with a fried pork cutlet

niku-don (牛丼) – rice topped with thin slices of cooked beef

oyako-don (親子丼) – rice topped with egg and chicken

ten-don (天丼) – rice topped with tempura shrimp and vegetables

Izakaya Fare

agedashi-dōfu (揚げだし豆腐) – deep-fried tofu in a dashi broth

jaga-batā (ジャガバター) – baked potatoes with butter

niku-jaga (肉ジャガ) – beef and potato stew

shio-yaki-zakana (塩焼魚) – a whole fish grilled with salt

poteto furai (ポテトフライ) – French fries

chiizu-age (チーズ揚げ) – deep-fried cheese

hiya-yakko (冷奴) – cold tofu with soy sauce and spring onions

tsuna sarada (ツナサラダ) – tuna salad over cabbage

Sushi & Sashimi

ama-ebi (甘海老) – shrimp

awabi (あわび) – abalone

hamachi (はまち) – yellowtail

ika (いか) – squid

ikura (イクラ) – salmon roe

kai-bashira (貝柱) – scallop

kani (かに) – crab

katsuo (かつお) – bonito

sashimi mori-awase (刺身盛り合わせ) – a selection of sliced sashimi

tai (鯛) – sea bream

toro (とろ) – the choicest cut of fatty tuna belly

uni (うに) – sea-urchin roe

Yakitori

yakitori (焼き鳥) – plain, grilled white meat

hasami/negima (はさみ/ねぎま) – pieces of white meat alternating with leek

sasami (ささみ) – skinless chicken-breast pieces

kawa (皮) – chicken skin

tsukune (つくね) – chicken meatballs

gyū-niku (牛肉) – pieces of beef

tebasaki (手羽先) – chicken wings

shiitake (しいたけ) – Japanese mushrooms

piiman (ピーマン) – small green peppers

tama-negi (玉ねぎ) – round white onions

yaki-onigiri (焼きおにぎり) – a triangle of rice grilled with *yakitori* sauce

Rāmen

rāmen (ラーメン) – soup and noodles with a sprinkling of meat and vegetables

chāshū-men (チャーシュー麺) – *rāmen* topped with slices of roasted pork

wantan-men (ワンタン麺) – *rāmen* with meat dumplings

miso-rāmen (みそラーメン) – *rāmen* with miso-flavoured broth

chānpon-men (ちゃんぽん麺) – Nagasaki-style *rāmen*

Soba & Udon

soba (そば) – thin brown buckwheat noodles

udon (うどん) – thick white wheat noodles

kake soba/udon (かけそば/うどん) – *soba/udon* noodles in broth

kata yaki-soba (固焼きそば) – crispy noodles with meat and vegetables

kitsune soba/udon (きつねそば/うどん) – *soba/udon* noodles with fried tofu

tempura soba/udon (天ぷらそば/うどん) – *soba/udon* noodles with tempura shrimp

tsukimi soba/udon (月見そば/うどん) – *soba/udon* noodles with raw egg on top

yaki-soba (焼きそば) – fried noodles with meat and vegetables

zaru soba (ざるそば) – cold noodles with seaweed strips served on a bamboo tray

Tempura

tempura moriawase (天ぷら盛り合わせ) – a selection of tempura

shōjin age (精進揚げ) – vegetarian tempura

kaki age (かき揚げ) – tempura with shredded vegetables or fish

Kushiage & Kushikatsu

ika (いか) – squid

renkon (れんこん) – lotus root

tama-negi (玉ねぎ) – white onion

gyū-niku (牛肉) – beef pieces

shiitake (しいたけ) – Japanese mushrooms

ginnan (銀杏) – ginkgo nuts

imo (いも) – potato

Okonomiyaki

mikkusu (ミックスお好み焼き) – mixed fillings of seafood, meat and vegetables

modan-yaki (モダン焼き) – *okonomiyaki* with *yaki-soba* and a fried egg

ika okonomiyaki (いかお好み焼き) – squid *okonomiyaki*

gyū okonomiyaki (牛お好み焼き) – beef *okonomiyaki*

negi okonomiyaki (ネギお好み焼き) – thin *okonomiyaki* with spring onions

Kaiseki

bentō (弁当) – boxed lunch

ume (梅) – regular course

take (竹) – special course

matsu (松) – extra-special course

Unagi

kabayaki (蒲焼き) – skewers of grilled eel without rice

unagi teishoku (うなぎ定食) – full-set *unagi* meal with rice, grilled eel, eel-liver soup and pickles

una-don (うな丼) – grilled eel over a bowl of rice

unajū (うな重) – grilled eel over a flat tray of rice

Alcoholic Drinks

nama biiru (生ビール) – draught beer

shōchū (焼酎) – distilled grain liquor

oyu-wari (お湯割り) – *shōchū* with hot water

chūhai (チューハイ) – *shōchū* with soda and lemon

whisky (ウィスキー) – whisky

mizu-wari (水割り) – whisky, ice and water

Coffee & Tea

kōhii (コーヒー) – regular coffee

burendo kōhii (ブレンドコーヒー) – blended coffee, fairly strong

american kōhii (アメリカンコーヒー) – weak coffee

kōcha (紅茶) – black, British-style tea

kafe ōre (カフェオレ) – cafe au lait, hot or cold

Japanese Tea

o-cha (お茶) – green tea

sencha (煎茶) – medium-grade green tea

matcha (抹茶) – powdered green tea used in the tea ceremony

bancha (番茶) – ordinary-grade green tea, brownish in colour

mugicha (麦茶) – roasted barley tea

Behind the Scenes

SEND US YOUR FEEDBACK

We love to hear from travellers – your comments keep us on our toes and help make our books better. Our well-travelled team reads every word on what you loved or loathed about this book. Although we cannot reply individually to your submissions, we always guarantee that your feedback goes straight to the appropriate authors, in time for the next edition. Each person who sends us information is thanked in the next edition – the most useful submissions are rewarded with a selection of digital PDF chapters.

Visit **lonelyplanet.com/contact** to submit your updates and suggestions or to ask for help. Our award-winning website also features inspirational travel stories, news and discussions.

Note: We may edit, reproduce and incorporate your comments in Lonely Planet products such as guidebooks, websites and digital products, so let us know if you don't want your comments reproduced or your name acknowledged. For a copy of our privacy policy visit lonelyplanet.com/privacy.

OUR READERS

Many thanks to the travellers who used the last edition and wrote to us with helpful hints, useful advice and interesting anecdotes:

George Farah, Jeff Rubin, Mark Breeus, Michał & Aleksandra Jankowiak, Paul Spaeth, Snir Aharon, Steven Walker, Yannick Debing

WRITER THANKS
Rebecca Milner

Much gratitude, as always, to my family and friends for their support, company (on many a research excursion) and patience (especially when deadlines loom). Thank you to Simon and Laura for being there with spot-on tips, suggestions, advice (and patience). To Tomoko, the coolest Tokyo city bureaucrat, and Will, for his input on the arts and theatre scene.

Simon Richmond

My thanks to Hollie Mantle, Will Andrews, Yoshizawa Tomoko, Toshiko, Kenichi, Chris, Giles, Steve & Emiko, and my co-author Rebecca.

ACKNOWLEDGEMENTS

Tokyo Subway Route Map, Bureau of Transportation, Tokyo Metropolitan Government, Tokyo Metro Co Ltd © 2016.3.

Illustration pp150-51 by Michael Weldon.

Cover photograph: Shibuya Crossing, Tokyo; Peter Adams/AWL.

THIS BOOK

This 11th edition of Lonely Planet's *Tokyo* guidebook was researched and written by Rebecca Milner and Simon Richmond. The previous edition was also written by Rebecca and Simon, and the 9th edition was written by Timothy N Hornyak and Rebecca. This guidebook was produced by the following:

Destination Editor Laura Crawford

Product Editor Kate Kiely

Senior Cartographer Diana Von Holdt

Book Designer Wibowo Rusli

Assisting Editors Michelle Bennett, Helen Koehne, Susan Paterson, Simon Williamson

Assisting Cartographer Alison Lyall

Cover Researcher Naomi Parker

Thanks to Naoko Akamatsu Bridget Blair, Grace Dobell, Kate James, Kathryn Rowan

See also separate subindexes for:

🍴 **EATING P258**

🍷 **DRINKING & NIGHTLIFE P259**

⭐ **ENTERTAINMENT P259**

🔒 **SHOPPING P260**

🛏 **SLEEPING P260**

🏃 **SPORTS & ACTIVITIES P261**

Index

21_21 Design Sight 79, 83, **82**

3331 Arts Chiyoda 139

A

accommodation 17, 19, 191-200
budgeting 31
language 246
websites 19

activities 24-7, see also Sports & Activities subindex, individual activities

air travel 232-4

airport
accommodation 195

Akagi-jinja 143

Akasaka, see Roppongi & Akasaka

Akihabara, see Kōrakuen & Akihabara

Akihabara Radio Center 145

Amuse Museum 163

anime 214-15

Aoyama, see Harajuku & Aoyama

apartment rental 199

Apollo 69

Archi-Depot 174

architecture 218-26, 225-6

art galleries, see museums & galleries

arts 218-26

Asakura Museum of Sculpture, Taitō 154

Asakusa & Sumida River 159-70, 199-200, **159, 286**
drinking & nightlife 160, 168
entertainment 168-9

Sights 000
Map Pages **000**
Photo Pages **000**

food 160, 165, 167-8
highlights 159-62
shopping 160, 169-70
sights 161-2, 163-5
sports & activities 170
transport 160
walks 166, **166**

ASIMO robot **216**

Atago-jinja 81

B

Bakurochō 59

bars 41

bathrooms 243

beer 42

beer gardens 113

Beer Museum Yebisu 89

bicycle travel, see cycling

boat tours 55, 176

boat travel 236

books 202

bookshops 49

boutique hotels 191

Buddhist temples 11, 22, **11**

bus travel 236-7

business hotels 191

business hours 33, 42, 47, 241

Butō 220-1

C

cafes 17, 41, 42, 43

capsule hotels 191

car travel 237

Cat Street 109-11

cell phones 18, 242

cherry blossoms 12, 24, 58, 91, **13, 93**

ChihiraJunco 173

children, travel with 28

Chūzen-ji Onsen (Nikkō) 182

cinema 45, 223

climate 19, 24, 25, 26, 27

climate change & travel 232

clothing sizes 47

clubs 41

Complex 665 79

Container 92

cooking courses 39, 75, 86

costs 18, 33, 47, 192, 242

courses 117
cooking 39, 75, 86

crafts 23, 46, 49

Crafts Gallery 57

credit cards 47, 241

culture 202-3

currency 18

cycling 64, 155, 236

D

d47 Museum 98

Daibutsu (Kamakura) 189

Daikanyama 91-3
walks 92, **92**

daimyō 205

dance 44

dangers, 84, 241-2

Design Festa 111

disabilities, travellers with 244

discount cards 238

Dōgenzaka 98

drinking & nightlife 41-3, see also Drinking & Nightlife subindex, individual neighbourhoods
budgeting 42
cafes 17, 41, 42, 43
language 246-9
local life 30
opening hours 42

E

earthquakes 209

East Sumida **287**, see also Asakusa & Sumida River

Ebisu & Meguro 87-94, 89, **274-5**
accommodation 88, 196
drinking & nightlife 88, 93-4

entertainment 94
food 88, 90-1, 93
highlights 87, **87**
shopping 94
sights 89
transport 88
walks 92, **92**

economy 211-12

Edo 207

Edo Shitamachi Traditional Crafts Museum 163

Edo-Tokyo Museum 164

Edo-Tokyo Open Air Architecture Museum 121

electricity 238

embassies 238

emergencies 238-9
language 248, 248-9

Emperor Hirohito 210

Engaku-ji (Kamakura) 189

Ennō-ji (Kamakura) 189

entertainment 44-5, see also Entertainment subindex, individual neighbourhoods

etiquette 33, 42

events 24-7, 30

F

festivals & events 24-7, 30

film 202

food 9, 32-40, **8** see also Eating subindex, individual neighbourhoods
budgeting 31
cooking courses 75, 86
costs 33
itineraries 35
language 246-8, 251-2
local life 30
opening hours 33
shopping 49
tours 39

free attractions 31

fringe theatre 220

Fuji TV Building 174
Fujifilm Square 79
Fukagawa 164
Fukagawa Fudō-dō 164-5
Fukagawa Hachiman Matsuri 26, **26**
Futarasan-jinja (Nikkō) 182

G

Gaienmae 111, 112
galleries, *see* museums & galleries
gardens 23, 56, 57, 80
Garter 121
gay travellers 239
General Nogi's Residence 79
Ghibli Museum 12, 120, **13**, **120**
Ginza & Tsukiji 65-75, 17, **268-9**
  accommodation 194-5
  drinking & nightlife 66, 71
  entertainment 71-4
  food 66, 69-70
  highlights 65, 67, **65**
  shopping 66, 74-5
  sights 67, 68-9, 70
  sports & activities 75
  transport 66
Godzilla 214
go-karting 17
Golden Gai 134
Great Kantō Earthquake 209

H

Hachikō statue 97, 103, **102**
Hakone 184-7, **185**
Hakone Museum of Art (Hakone) 186
Hakone Open-Air Museum (Hakone) 186
Hakone-jinja (Hakone) 186
Hama-rikyū Onshi-teien 68-9, 72, **73**
Hanazono-jinja 127
Haneda airport 233-4
Happō-en 89-90
Hara Museum of Contemporary Art 90
Harajuku & Aoyama 106-17, **276-7**, **10**
  accommodation 197

  drinking & nightlife 107, 113
  entertainment 113-16
  food 107, 111-112
  highlights 10, 106, 108, **106**, **10**
  shopping 107, 116-17
  sights 108, 109-11, 111
  sports & activities 117
  transport 107
  walks 110
Hara Museum of Contemporary Art 90
Harmonica-yokochō 121
Hase-dera (Kamakura) 189
Hatakeyama Collection 90
Hatsu-mōde 24
health 239
Hideyoshi, Toyotomi 205
Hie-jinja 81, 83, **83**
history 23, 204-12
holidays 241, 242
hostels 191
Hotel Mystays Premier Akasaka 195
hyperfashion 215

I

Ieyasu, Tokugawa 205-6, 207
ikebana 80, 117, 222-3
Ikebukuro 130
Ikebukuro Earthquake Hall 130
Imperial Palace 56, **56**
Imperial Palace East Garden 56
Imperial Palace Grounds 62, **62**
Inokashira Benzaiten 121
Inokashira-kōen 121
Institute for Nature Study 89
insurance
  health 239
Intermediatheque 57
internet access 239
itineraries 20-1, 35

J

Japan Folk Crafts Museum 99
Japanese calendar 243
Japanese language 245-52
Japanese Sword Museum 127
J-Pop 216
Junichirō, Koizumi 211-12

K

kabuki 15, 218-19, **15**
Kabukiza Theatre 69, 72, **73**
Kagurazaka 142-3, **142**
Kamakura 187-90, **188**
Kanda 138-9, 139, 143
Kanda Myōjin (Kanda Shrine) 138-9, **140**
Kanman-ga-Fuchi Abyss (Nikkō) 183
karaoke 41, 43
Kawaii Monster Cafe 109
Kenchō-ji (Kamakura) 189, 190
Kichijōji 121-2, 122-3, **279**
kimonos 46
Kitanomaru-kōen 57
Kite Museum 58, 61, **60-1**
KITTE 61, **60**
Kiyōmizu Kannon-dō 153
Kiyosumi 164, 167-8
Kiyosumi-teien 164
Kōenji 121, 122, **278**, *see also* West Tokyo
Kōenji Awa Odori 26
Koishikawa Kōrakuen 26, 138, **26**, **140-1**
Kōrakuen & Akihabara 136-46, **136**, **282**, **283**, **16**, **213**
  accommodation 198-9
  drinking & nightlife 137, 143-4
  entertainment 144
  food 137, 139, 143
  highlights 16, 136-7, **16**
  shopping 137, 144-6
  sights 138-9
  sports & activities 146
  transport 137
  walks 142-3, **142**
Kudanshita 138
Kuramae 17
Kuroda Memorial Hall 153
Kyū Asakura House 92
Kyū Iwasaki-teien 154

L

language 245-52
legal matters 239-40
lesbian travellers 239
LGBT travellers 43
literature 223-5
local life 29-30
love hotels 196
luggage shipment 233

M

magazines 240
Maman spider sculptures 78
manga 213-14
manga kissa 196
maple trees 26, **26**
markets 7, 23, **7**
  farmers 38, 109
  flea 47
Marunouchi & Nihombashi 54-64, **266-7**
  accommodation 194
  drinking & nightlife 55, 63
  entertainment 63
  food 55, 58-9
  highlights 54, 56, **54**
  shopping 55, 64
  sights 56, 57-8
  sports & activities 64
  transport 55
  walks 62, **62**
measures 240
medical services 240
medications 239
Mega Web 173-4
megamalls 212
Meguro, *see* Ebisu & Meguro
Meguro-gawa 91
Meiji-jingū 9, 108, **8**, **108**
Meiji-jingū Gyoen 108
Mejiro 130
Mitaka 121-2
Mitsui Memorial Museum 58
mobile phones 18, 242
Mohri Garden 78
money 18, 33, 47, 192, 240-1
  language 248
  moneychangers 241
motorcycle travel 237
Mt Fuji 178-9
Musée Tomo 81
museums & galleries 10, 22-3, 70
music 44, 45
Myōnichikan 130
Myth of Tomorrow 98

N

Nakagin Capsule Tower 68
Naka-Meguro 91-3, **93**
  walks 92, **92**
Nakano 121, 122
Nakano Broadway 121

Narita Airport 232-3
National Art Center Tokyo 79-80, **82-3**
National Museum of Emerging Science & Innovation (Miraikan) 173
National Museum of Modern Art (MOMAT) 57
National Museum of Nature & Science 153
National Museum of Western Art 153
National Shōwa Memorial Museum 138
newspapers 240
Nezu Museum 111, **114-15**
Nezu-jinja 154
nightlife 7, see also Drinking & Nightlife subindex, individual neighbourhoods
Nihombashi, see Marunouchi & Nihombashi
Nihombashi-gawa **61**
Nihonga 221-2
Nikkō 180-4, **181**
Nikkō Tamozawa Imperial Villa Memorial Park (Nikkō) 183
Nikolai Cathedral 139, **140**
Ningyōchō 59
Nishi-Shinjuku 127, 130, 132
nō 219-20
Nobunaga, Oda 205
Nogi-jinja 79
Northwest Tokyo, see Shinjuku & Northwest Tokyo
NTT Intercommunication Centre 127

O
Odaiba & Tokyo Bay 171-6, **171**, **265**, **22**
  drinking & nightlife 175
  food 172, 174-5
  highlights 171-2
  shopping 175
  sights 173-4
  sports & activities 175-6
  transport 172
Odaiba Kaihin-kōen 173
Ōedo Onsen Monogatari 16, 173, **16**
Ogikubo 122
Okada Museum of Art (Hakone) 186
Old Hakone Highway (Hakone) 186
olympics 202-3, 212

Omote-sandō architecture 110, **110**
onsen 135, 173, 227-30
Ōnsen-ji (Nikkō) 182
opening hours 33, 42, 47, 241
Origami Kaikan 138
Oshiage 163-4, 165, 167
Ōwakudani (Hakone) 186

P
packing tips 19
parks & gardens 23, 56, 57, 80
people-watching 23
Perry, Matthew 208
photography 223
Place M 127, 130
planning
  budgeting 18, 31, 33
  children, travel with 28
  festivals & events 24-7
  itineraries 20-1
  local life 29-30
  repeat visitors 17
  Tokyo basics 18-19
  Tokyo's neighbourhoods 52-3, **52**
  travel seasons 19
  websites 18
politics 202-3
pop culture 213-17
pop music 216
postal services 241
Prada Aoyama Building 115, **114**
public holidays 241

R
rakugo 220
Reversible Destiny Lofts 121-2
Rikugi-en 152, **152**
Rinnō-ji (Nikkō) 182
robots 217
Roppongi & Akasaka 76-86, **270-2**
  accommodation 195-6
  drinking & nightlife 77, 85-6
  entertainment 86
  food 77, 81-5
  highlights 76, 78, **76**
  safety 84
  shopping 77, 86
  sights 78, 79-81
  sports & activities 86
  transport 77

Roppongi Art Triangle 10
Roppongi Hills 78, **78**
Ryōgoku 164, 167-8
ryokan 191
Ryūzu-no-taki (Nikkō) 182

S
safety 84, 241-2
sake 42
sales tax 192
samurai 205, 206
Sangedatsumon 81
Sanja Matsuri 25
saunas 196
SCAI the Bathhouse 154
Science Museum, Tokyo 57
Sengaku-ji 90
Senjōgahara (Nikkō) 182
Senjōgahara Shizen-kenkyu-rō (Nikkō) 182
Sensō-ji 11, 161-2, **11**
sentō 30, 227-30
Shiba-kōen 81, 84-5
Shibuya 109, 103, 105, **102**
Shibuya & Shimo-Kitazawa 95-105, **273**, **103**
  accommodation 196-7
  drinking & nightlife 96, 99-104
  entertainment 104-5
  food 96, 98-99, 104
  highlights 14, 95, 97, **95**, **14**
  shopping 96, 105
  sights 97, 98, 99
  sports & activities 105
  transport 96
  walks 100-1, **101**
Shibuya Center-gai 97, 103, **102**
Shibuya Crossing 14, 97, **14**, **97**
Shibuya Hikarie 105
Shimo-Kitazawa 100-1, **101**, **103**, see also Shibuya & Shimo-Kitazawa
Shinjuku I-Land 127
Shinjuku & Northwest Tokyo 125-35, **125**, **280-1**, **129**
  accommodation 197-8
  drinking & nightlife 7, 126, 132-4
  entertainment 134
  food 126, 130, 132, 133
  highlights 7, 125-6, **6-7**
  shopping 126, 135
  sights 127, 130

sports & activities 135
  transport 126
  walks 131, **131**
Shinjuku-gyoen 127, **128**
Shintō shrines 9, 22, **8**
Shirakawa 167-8
Shirokane 89-90
Shitamachi 30, 166, 166
Shitamachi Museum 153-4
Shitamachi Museum Annex 154
shopping 10, 46-9, see also Shopping subindex, individual neighbourhoods
  language 248-9
  opening hours 47
smoking 42, 240
Sōgetsu Kaikan 80
Spain-zaka 98
spas 196
sports 44, 45, see also Sports & Activities subindex, individual neighbourhoods
St Mary's Cathedral Tokyo 130
State Guest House, Akasaka Palace 80
street names 237
Studio Ghibli 12, 120, **13**, **120**
Suica & Pasmo cards 234
Sumida Hokusai Museum 17, 164
Sumida River, see Asakusa & Sumida River
Sumida-gawa fireworks 25
Sumiyoshi-jinja 74
sumo 12, 44, 164, 168, **12**
Suntory Museum of Art 79
Super Dry Hall 163

T
Taiko Drum Museum 163
Taiyūin-byō (Nikkō) 182
Takanawa 89
Takeshita-dōri 109, 115, **115**
Takinō-jinja (Nikkō) 183
Taro Okamoto Memorial Museum 111
taxes 242
taxis 236
technology 222
telephone services 18, 242-3
Tennōzu Isle 17, 174
Terrada Art Complex 174
theatre 44, 45

time 18, 243
  language 249
tipping 33, 42, 241
Toguri Museum of Art 98
toilets 243
Tōkei-ji (Kamakura) 189
Tokyo Bay, see Odaiba & Tokyo Bay
Tokyo City View 78
Tokyo Garden Terrace 80
Tokyo International Forum 58, 61, **60**
Tokyo Metropolitan Government Building 127, **129**
Tokyo Metropolitan Teien Art Museum 89
Tokyo Midtown 79
Tokyo National Museum 15, 149-51, **14**, **149**
Tokyo Sky Tree 163-4
Tokyo Station 58
Tokyo Tower 81-6
Tomigaya 104
Tomioka Hachiman-gū 165
TOP Museum 89
Tōshō-gū (Nikkō) 180-1
tourist information 18, 243-4
tours 55
  food 39
  walking 75
train travel 234-6
transport
  language 249
  to/from Tokyo 19, 232-4
  within Tokyo 19, 234-7
Tsukiji, see Ginza & Tsukiji
Tsukiji Hongwan-ji 68
Tsukiji Market 7, 17, 67, 68, **7**, **67**
Tsukishima 74
Tsukuda-jima 74
Tsukudako-bashi 74
Tsurugaoka Hachiman-gū (Kamakura) 189

U

Ueno Tōshō-gū 153
Ueno & Yanesen 147-58, 199, **147**, **284-5**
  courses & activities 158
  drinking & nightlife 157
  entertainment 157-8

Sights 000
Map Pages **000**
Photo Pages **000**

food 148, 155-7
highlights 147-52
shopping 158
sights 149-54
transport 148
walks 156, **156**
Ueno Zoo 153
Ueno-kōen 153
Ukiyo-e 221
Ukiyo-e Ōta Memorial Museum of Art 109
underground theatre 220
Ura-Hara 116
US occupation 210

V

vegetarian travellers 39, 40
viewpoints 9, 23
  bars 43
visas 244
visual arts 221-2
volunteering 244

W

walking tours 75
walks
  Daikanyama & Naka-Meguro 92
  Imperial Palace Grounds 62, **62**
  Kagurazaka 142-3, **142**
  Omote-sandō architecture 110
  Shinjuku 131, **131**
  Shimo-Kitazawa 100-1, **101**
  Shitamachi 166, **166**
  Yanaka 156, **156**
Watari Museum of Contemporary Art 111
weather 19, 24, 25, 26, 27
websites 18, 19, 31, 33, 42, 45, 47, 193
weights & measures 240
West Tokyo 118-24, **118**
  accommodation 197
  drinking & nightlife 119, 123
  entertainment 124
  food 119, 122-3
  highlights 118-19, 120
  shopping 119, 124
  sights 120, 121-2
  transport 119
whisky 42
WWII 210

Y

Yamatane Museum of Art 89
Yanaka 156, 156
Yanaka Ginza 154
Yanaka-reien 154
Yanesen, see Ueno & Yanesen
Yasukuni-jinja 138
Yebisu Garden Place 89
Yoyogi-kōen 12, 109, 115, **13**, **115**
Yoyogi National Stadium 109
Yumoto Onsen (Nikkō) 182
Yūrakuchō Sanchoku Inshokugai 72, **72**
Yushima Seidō (Yushima Shrine) 139
Yushima Tenjin 154
Yūshū-kan 138

Z

Zōjō-ji 81

⚔ EATING

A

Afuri 90
Amazake-chaya (Hakone) 186
Asakusa Imahan 167
Asakusa Unagi Sansho 167

B

Baikatei 142
Bakery & Table (Hakone) 187
Bills 174
Bombay Bazar 91
Bonzō (Kamakura) 190
Botan 143

C

Camelback 104
Canal Cafe 139
Chinese Cafe 8 84
Chōchin Monaka 165
Commune 246 109

D

d47 Shokudō 98
Daikokuya 167
Daily Chiko 122
Dhaba India 58
Donjaca 132

E

Ebisu-yokochō 91
Ethiopia 139

F

Food Show 99
Fuglen Tokyo 104
Fujisan Hotel (Mt Fuji) 179

G

Gogyō 81
Gonpachi 81
Good Mellows (Kamakura) 190
Gyōshintei (Nikkō) 183
Gyūkatsu Motomura 98

H

Hagiso 155, 157
Hantei 157
Harajuku Gyōza-rō 111
Harukiya 122
Hibiki 174-5
Higashiya Man 112
Higashi-Yama 91, 93
Hippari Dako (Nikkō) 183
Hōnen Manpuku 59
Hongū Cafe (Nikkō) 183
Honmura-An 84
Hoppy-dōri 165

I

Innsyoutei 155
Ippo 91
Iriyama Sembei 165
Itoh Dining by Nobu (Hakone) 187

J

Jōmon 84

K

Kado 139
Kagari 69
Kaikaya 99
Kamachiku 155
Kanda Yabu Soba 143
Kappō Yoshiba 168
Kikanbō 139
Kikunoi 84
Kingyozaka 155
Kinokuniya International Supermarket 112
Kintame 167-8
Komagata Dozeu 165, 167
Komaki Shokudō 143

Kozue 132
Kyūbey 70
Kyūsyū Jangara 112

L

Lauderdale 84
Lumine 133

M

Maisen 111
Manboshi 123
Maru (Ginza) 70
Maru (Harajuku) 112
Matsukiya 99
Meguri (Nikkō) 183
Megutama 91
Mominoki House 112
Monja Kondō 74
Mornington Cresent 85
Mugimaru 2 142
Mylord 133

N

Nagi 130
Nagi Shokudō 99
Nagomi 157
Nakajima 130
NEWoMan 133
Nezu no Taiyaki 157
Nihonbashi Dashi Bar 59
Nikkō Coffee (Nikkō) 183
Numazukō 132

O

Odaiba Takoyaki
    Museum 174
Okajōki 122
Omoide-yokochō 130, **129**
Onigiri Yadoroku 165
Otafuku 167
Ōtaru 93
Ouca 90

R

Rokurinsha 165
Rose Bakery 69
Royal Garden Café 112
Ruby 132

S

Sagatani 98-9
Sakura-tei 111-12
Sarutahiko Coffee 94
Sasa-no-Yuki 155
Shin-chan 132
Shinjuku Asia-yokochō 132

Shinsuke 155
Sometarō 167
Sougo 84
Steak House Satou 123
Sushikuni 70

T

Ta-im 91
Taimeiken 58-9
Taishikan (Mt Fuji) 179
Takashimaya
    Times Square 133
Tensuke 122
Tetchan 122
Tofuya-Ukai 85
Tokyo Rāmen Street 59
Tonki 93
Trattoria Tsukiji
    Paradiso 70
Tsunahachi 132
TY Harbor Brewery 174

U

Uramakiya 84-5

W

Wander Kitchen
    (Kamakura) 190

Y

Yakiniku Champion 91
Yamagusuri (Hakone) 187
Yanmo 112
Yong Xiang Sheng
    Jian Guan 132
Yūrakuchō Sanchoku
    Inshokugai 70

Setagaya Public Theatre
    104-5
Shinjuku Pit Inn 134
Star Pine's Cafe 124
Suntory Hall 86
Tokyo Bunka Kaikan 157-8
Tokyo Dome 144
Tokyo Opera City Concert
    Hall 134
Tokyo Takarazuka Theatre
    71-4
Unit 94
Uplink 104
WWW 104

🍷 DRINKING & NIGHTLIFE

@Home Cafe 144
100% Chocolate Cafe 63

A

A to Z Cafe 113
Agave 85-6
Ageha 175
Aiiro Cafe 133
Arty Farty 134
Asahi Sky Room 168

B

B&B 100
Bar Goldfinger 133
Bar Martha 94
Bar Trench 93
Beat Cafe 104
BenFiddich 132-3
Bistro Marx 71
Blue Sky Coffee 123
Bousingot 157
Brewdog 85
Buri 94

C

Cafe Asan 144
Cafe de l'Ambre 71
Café Otonova 168
Cha Ginza 71
Cocktail Shobō 123
Contact 100
Craft Beer Server Land 144
Craft Beer Market
    Mitsukoshimae 63
'Cuzn Homeground 168

E

Ef 168

G

Ghetto 99
Good Beer Faucets 99-100

H

Harajuku Taproom 113

I

Imasa 143

J

Jicoo the Floating Bar 175
Jugetsudo 71

K

Kamiya Bar 168
Kagaya 71
Kayaba Coffee 157
Kōenji Gādo-shita 123

L

Little Nap Coffee Stand 113

M

Manpuku Shokudō 63
Montoak 113
Mori-no Beer Garden 113
Mother 100

N

N3331 144
Nakame Takkyū Lounge 93
Nantoka Bar 123
Naraya Cafe (Hakone) 187
Never Never Land 101
Nihombashi Toyama 63
New York Bar 133
Nonbei-yokochō 100

O

Oath 113

P

Peter: the Bar 63
Popeye 168

R

Ren 134
Rhythm Cafe 100

S

Sake Plaza 85
Samurai 133
Sekirei 113

⭐ ENTERTAINMENT

Asakusa Engei Hall 169
Club Goodman 144
Club Quattro 105
Cotton Club 63
Crocodile 116
Jingū Baseball Stadium
    113, 116
Liquid Room 94
Meiji-za 63-4
National Nō Theatre 116
National Theatre 86
Ni Man Den Atsu 124
Nippon Budōkan 63
Oiwake 169
P.A.R.M.S 144
Robot Restaurant 134
Ryōgoku Kokugikan
    168-9

Shidax Village 104
Shirube 100
SuperDeluxe 85
Suzunari 101

T
The Garden 85
These 85
Torindō 157
Town House Tokyo 71
Trouble Peach 101
Turret Coffee 71
Two Rooms 113

U
Uni Stand 123
Univibe (Kamakura) 190

W
Womb 100-4

Y
Yanagi-dōri 123
Yanaka Beer Hall 157

Z
Zoetrope 133

🛍 **SHOPPING**
2k540 Aki-Oka Artisan 144
6% Doki Doki 117

A
Acos 135
Akihabara Radio Kaikan 145
Akomeya 74
Ameya-yokochō 158
Arts & Science 117
Asagaya Pearl Centre 124
Axis Design 86

B
B&B 100
Beams 135
Bedrock 117
Bengara 170
Bingoya 135
Blue & White 86

C
Camera 169
Chabara 145
Chicago Thrift Store 117
Comme des Garçons 117
Coredo Muromachi 64

D
Daikanyama T-Site 92
Dog 116
Dover Street Market Ginza 74

E
Edokoro Allan West 158

F
Fake Tokyo 105
Fujiya 170

G
Gallery Kawano 117
Ginza Six 74

I
Isetan 135
Isetatsu 158
Itōya 74

J
Japan Traditional Crafts Aoyama Square 86
Jimbōchō Bookstores 145-6

K
Kakimori 169
Kapital 94
KiddyLand 117
Kinokuniya 135
Kita-Kore Building 124
KITTE 64
Koncent 169
Kukuli 142
Kurodaya 170

L
Laforet 116-17
Loft 105

M
mAAch ecute 145
Maito 169

Mandrake Complex (Akihabara) 145
Mandrake Complex (West Tokyo) 124
Marugoto Nippon 169
Matsuya 75
Mitsukoshi (Ginza) 75
Mitsukoshi (Nihombashi) 64
Muji 64
Musubi 116
Nakano Sun Mall 124

O
Ōedo Antique Market 64
Okura 94

P
Pigment 175
Pokemon Center Mega Tokyo 135
PukuPuku 124
Raw Tokyo 109

S
Sada 143
Sanrioworld Ginz 75
Shibuya 109 105
Shibuya Publishing Booksellers 104
Shokichi 158
Sokkyō 124
Sou-Sou 116
Souvenir from Tokyo 86
Strange Love 175

T
Takashimaya 64
Takumi 74
Tenyasu Honten 74
Tokyo Character Street 64
Tokyo Hotarudo 169
Tokyu Hands 105
Tolman Collection 86

U
Uniqlo 75

V
Vase 93

Y
Yanaka Matsunoya 158
Yodobashi Akiba 145
Yonoya Kushiho 170

🛏 **SLEEPING**
9 Hours 195

A
Aman Tokyo 194
Andon Ryokan 200
Annex Katsutarō Ryokan 199
Annex Turtle Hotori-An (Nikkō) 184

B
BnA Hotel 197
Book and Bed 197-8
Bunka Hostel Tokyo 200

C
Capsule & Sauna Century 196
Claska 196

D
Daiwa Roynet Hotel Ginza 194-5
Dormy Inn Express Meguro Aobadai 196
Dormy Inn Premium Shibuya Jingūmae 197

F
First Cabin Akasaka 195

G
Grids Akihabara 194

H
Hanare 199
Hilltop Hotel 199
Hōmeikan 199
Hoshinoya Tokyo 194
Hotel Gracery Shinjuku 198
Hotel Mets Shibuya 197
Hotel Mystays Premier Akasaka 195
Hotel Niwa Tokyo 198
Hotel S 195

J
Japonica Lodge 200

K
Kadoya Hotel 198
Kaisu 195
Khaosan World 200

Sights 000
Map Pages **000**
Photo Pages **000**

Kimi Ryokan 198
K's House Mt Fuji
    (Mt Fuji) 179
K's House Tokyo 200

M
Mitsui Garden Hotel Ginza
    Premier 195

N
Nikkorisou Backpackers
    (Nikkō) 183-4
Nui 199-200

P
Palace Hotel Tokyo 194
Park Hyatt Tokyo 198
Prime Pod Ginza Tokyo 194

R
Reversible Destiny Lofts
    197
Royal Park Hotel the
    Haneda 195
Ryokan Seikō 197

S
Sawanoya Ryokan 199
Shibuya Granbell Hotel
    196-7
Sukeroku No Yado
    Sadachiyo 200

T
Toco 199
Tokyo Central Youth Hostel
    198
Tokyo Ryokan 200
Tōkyū Stay Shinjuku 198

W
Wise Owl Hostels Tokyo
    194

Y
Yaesu Terminal Hotel 194

Z
Zabutton Good Hostel 195

**🏃 SPORTS &
ACTIVITIES**
Akiba Kart 146
Arashio Stable 164
Buddha Bellies 146
Daibutsu Hiking Course
    (Kamakura) 190
Dai-kanransha 176
Discover Japan Tours
    (Mt Fuji) 179
Fuji Mountain Guides
    (Mt Fuji) 179
Funasei 176
Hakone Yuryō
    (Hakone) 186
Hanayashiki 170
Ichigaya Fish Centre 146
Imperial Palace Cycling
    Course 64
Jakotsu-yu 170
Kachi Kachi Yama Ropeway
    (Mt Fuji) 179
Komparu-yu 75
Maricar 175-6
Mokuhankan 170
Ōedo Onsen Monogatari
    173
Ohara School of
    Ikebana 117

Purikura no Mecca 105
Rokuryu Kōsen 158
Spa LaQua 146
Super Potato
    Retro-kan 146
Shimizu-yu 117
T-Art Academy 176
Tenzan Tōji-kyō
    (Hakone) 187
Thermae-yu 135
Tokyo Cook 86
Tokyo Cooking Studio 75
Tokyo Disney Resort 176
Tokyo Dome City
    Attractions 146
Tokyo Joypolis 176
Tokyo Kitchen 170
Tokyo Sushi Academy 75
Tsukiji Market Information
    Centre 75
Tsukishima Monja
    Yakatabune 176
Ueno Free Walking Tour 158
Wanariya 170
Yanesen Tourist Informa-
    tion & Culture Center
    158
Yunessun (Hakone) 187

Tokyo Maps

Sights

- Beach
- Bird Sanctuary
- Buddhist
- Castle/Palace
- Christian
- Confucian
- Hindu
- Islamic
- Jain
- Jewish
- Monument
- Museum/Gallery/Historic Building
- Ruin
- Shinto
- Sikh
- Taoist
- Winery/Vineyard
- Zoo/Wildlife Sanctuary
- Other Sight

Activities, Courses & Tours

- Bodysurfing
- Diving
- Canoeing/Kayaking
- Course/Tour
- Sento Hot Baths/Onsen
- Skiing
- Snorkelling
- Surfing
- Swimming/Pool
- Walking
- Windsurfing
- Other Activity

Sleeping

- Sleeping
- Camping

Eating

- Eating

Drinking & Nightlife

- Drinking & Nightlife
- Cafe

Entertainment

- Entertainment

Shopping

- Shopping

Information

- Bank
- Embassy/Consulate
- Hospital/Medical
- Internet
- Police
- Post Office
- Telephone
- Toilet
- Tourist Information
- Other Information

Geographic

- Beach
- Gate
- Hut/Shelter
- Lighthouse
- Lookout
- Mountain/Volcano
- Oasis
- Park
- Pass
- Picnic Area
- Waterfall

Population

- Capital (National)
- Capital (State/Province)
- City/Large Town
- Town/Village

Transport

- Airport
- Border crossing
- Bus
- Cable car/Funicular
- Cycling
- Ferry
- Metro/MTR/MRT station
- Monorail
- Parking
- Petrol station
- Skytrain/Subway station
- Taxi
- Train station/Railway
- Tram
- Underground station
- Other Transport

Note: Not all symbols displayed above appear on the maps in this book

Routes

- Tollway
- Freeway
- Primary
- Secondary
- Tertiary
- Lane
- Unsealed road
- Road under construction
- Plaza/Mall
- Steps
- Tunnel
- Pedestrian overpass
- Walking Tour
- Walking Tour detour
- Path/Walking Trail

Boundaries

- International
- State/Province
- Disputed
- Regional/Suburb
- Marine Park
- Cliff
- Wall

Hydrography

- River, Creek
- Intermittent River
- Canal
- Water
- Dry/Salt/Intermittent Lake
- Reef

Areas

- Airport/Runway
- Beach/Desert
- Cemetery (Christian)
- Cemetery (Other)
- Glacier
- Mudflat
- Park/Forest
- Sight (Building)
- Sportsground
- Swamp/Mangrove

MAP INDEX

1 Odaiba & Tokyo Bay Area (p265)

2 Marunouchi & Nihombashi (p266)

3 Ginza & Tsukiji (p268)

4 Roppongi, Akasaka & Around (p270)

5 Shibuya & Shimo-Kitazawa (p273)

6 Ebisu & Meguro (p274)

7 Harajuku & Aoyama (p276)

8 Koenji (p278)

9 Kichijoji (p279)

10 Shinjuku & Northwest Tokyo (p280)

11 Korakuen & Around (p282)

12 Akihabara (p283)

13 Ueno & Yanesen (p284)

14 Asakusa (p286)

15 East Sumida (p287)

TOSHIMA-KU

IKEBUKURO

SHIMO-OCHIAI

NAKANO-KU

NAKAI

ARAI

NAKANO

CHŪŌ

KOENJI-KITA

8

SUGINAMI-KU

NAKAMURA

EGOTA

WAKAMIYA

NOGATA

HON-CHŌ

WADA

ŌMIYA

IZUMI

EIFUKU

SAKURA-JŌSUI

DAITA

KITAZAWA

SASAZUKA

UEHARA

KOMABA

IKEJIRI

TAISHIDŌ

SETAGAYA-KU

HATAGAYA

SHIN-ŌKUBO

TAKADANOBABA

SHINJUKU

10

SHINJUKU-KU

YOYOGI

7

HARAJUKU

SHIBUYA

5

SHIBUYA-KU

DAIKANYAMA

EBISU

6

MEGURO-KU

MITA

SHIROKANE

MEGURO-HONCHŌ

BUNKYŌ-KU

IIDABASHI

KŌRAKUEN

FUJIMI

11

CHIYODA-KU

2

JIMBŌCHŌ

AKIHABARA

12

HONGŌ

NEZU

YANAKA

UENO

TAITŌ

13

NEGISHI

SENZOKU

TAITŌ-KU

ASAKUSA

KOMAGATA

14

KURAMAE

SUMIDA-KU

OSHIAGE

RYŌGOKU

15

SHIRAKAWA

HIRANO

KIBA

FUKAGAWA

KŌTŌ-KU

CHŪŌ-KU

NIHOMBASHI

MARUNOUCHI

SHINTOMI

GINZA

SHIMBASHI

TSUKIJI

SHIODOME

3

KACHIDOKI

KONAN

SHINAGAWA-KU

MINATO-KU

KIOI-CHŌ

NAGATACHŌ

AKASAKA

ROPPONGI

4

Tokyo Bay

Tokyo Bay

Site of the new Tsukiji Market (to be renamed Toyosu Market) when it moves

ARIAKE

1

AOMI

DAIBA

Kichijoji Map (4km)

9

N

0   2 km

0   1 miles

◎ **Top Sights** (p173)

1 Ōedo Onsen Monogatari...........................B4

◎ **Sights** (p173)

2 Archi-Depot.......................................D4
3 ChihiraJunco.....................................B2
4 Fuji TV Building..................................B2
5 Mega Web..C2
6 National Museum of Emerging Science
   & Innovation (Miraikan)................B3
7 Odaiba Kaihin-kōen..............................B2
8 Statue of Liberty................................A2
9 Terrada Art Complex............................D4

⊗ **Eating** (p174)

10 Bills...B2
11 Hibiki...A2

Odaiba Takoyaki
   Museum..(see 10)
12 TY Harbor Brewery.............................D4

● **Drinking & Nightlife** (p175)

13 Jicoo the Floating Bar..........................A2

🔒 **Shopping** (p175)

14 Pigment...D4
15 Strange Love....................................B2

✦ **Sports & Activities** (p175)

16 Dai-kanransha...................................C2
17 Funasei...C3
18 Maricar..C4
   T-Art Academy..............................(see 14)
19 Tokyo Joypolis..................................B2

MARUNOUCHI & NIHOMBASHI

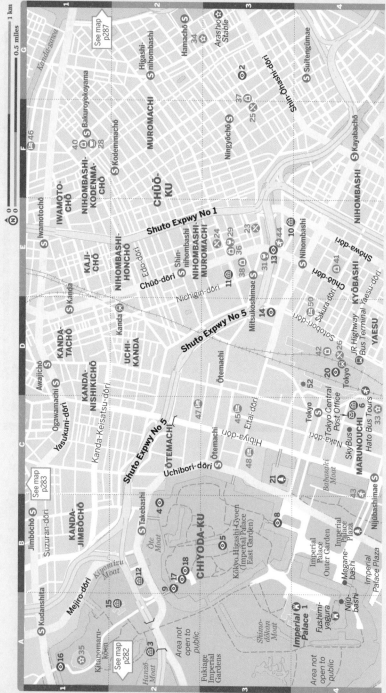

0 km 1
0 miles 0.5

See map p287

Kanda-gawa

Jimbōchō S
Suzuran-dōri

Kudanshita S

Kitanomaru-kōen

See map p283

KANDA-JIMBŌCHŌ

Awajichō S

Ogawamachi S

Yasukuni-dōri

KANDA-NISHIKICHŌ

Kanda-Keisatsu-dōri

Iwamotochō S

IWAMOTO-CHŌ

KAJI-CHŌ

KANDA-TACHŌ

Kanda S

Kanda S

UCHI-KANDA

NIHOMBASHI-KODENMA-CHŌ

NIHOMBASHI-HONCHŌ

Edo-dōri

Chūō-dōri

Shuto Expwy No 1

Kodemmachō S

CHŪŌ-KU

MUROMACHI

Higashi-nihombashi S

Hamachō S

Arashio Stable

Suitengūmae S

Shin-Ōhashi-dōri

Kayabachō S

NIHOMBASHI

Ningyōchō S

Shin-nihombashi S

NIHOMBASHI-MUROMACHI

Nichigin-dōri

Mitsukoshimae S

Nihombashi S

Showa-dōri

Chūō-dōri

KYOBASHI

Sakura-dōri

Sotobori-dōri

YAESU

Yaesu-dōri

JR Highway Bus Terminal

Tokyo S

Tokyo Central Post Office

Tokyo

SkyBus

MARUNOUCHI

Hato Bus Tours

Nijūbashimae S

Naka-dōri

Hibiya-dōri

Eitai-dōri

Ōtemachi S

ŌTEMACHI

Uchibori-dōri

Shuto Expwy No 5

Takebashi S

CHIYODA-KU

Kōkyo Higashi-Gyoen (Imperial Palace East Garden)

Ōte Moat

Kiyomizu Moat

Mejiro-dōri

See map p282

Hanzō Moat

Shimo-dōkan Moat

Fukiage Imperial Gardens

Imperial Palace 1

Fushimi-yagura

Nijū-bashi

Megane-bashi

Imperial Palace Outer Garden

Imperial Palace Plaza

Imperial Palace Plaza

Babasaki Moat

Area not open to public

Area not open to public

Top Sights (p56)

1 Imperial Palace........................A4

Sights (p57)

2 Amazake Yokochō......................G3
3 Crafts Gallery.........................A2
4 Hirakawa-mon..........................B2
5 Imperial Palace East
   Garden..............................B3
6 Intermediatheque......................C4
7 Iwaida-bashi..........................B5
8 Kikyō-mon.............................B3
9 Kitahanebashi-mon.....................B2
10 Kite Museum..........................E3
11 Mitsui Memorial Museum...............E3
12 National Museum of
   Modern Art (MOMAT)..................B2
13 Nihombashi (Nihonbashi)..............E3
14 Pasona...............................D3
15 Science Museum, Tokyo................A2
16 Tayasu-mon...........................A1
17 Tenshudai............................B2
18 Tōkagakudō Concert Hall..............B2
19 Tokyo International Forum.............C5
20 Tokyo Station........................D4
21 Wadakura Fountain Park...............C3

Eating (p58)

22 Dhaba India..........................D5
23 Hōnen Manpuku........................E3
24 Nihonbashi Dashi Bar.................E3
25 Taimeiken..........................(see 10)
26 Tamahide.............................F3
   Tokyo Ramen Street..................D4

Drinking & Nightlife (p63)

27 100% Chocolate Cafe..................D5
28 Art + Eat............................E3
29 Craft Beer Market
   Mitsukoshimae.......................D3
                                       A2

30 Manpuku Shokudō......................C5
31 Nihombashi Toyama....................E3
32 Peter: the Bar.......................C5

Entertainment (p63)

33 Cotton Club..........................C4
34 Meiji-za.............................G2
35 Nippon Budōkan.......................A1

Shopping (p64)

36 Coredo Muromachi.....................E3
37 Futaba...............................G3
   KITTE..............................(see 6)
38 Mitsukoshi...........................E3
39 Muji.................................C5
40 Ōedo Antique
   Market.............................(see 19)
   Starnet.............................F1
41 Takashimaya..........................E4
42 Tokyo Character Street...............D4

Sports & Activities (p64)

43 Imperial Palace Cycling
   Course..............................C4
44 Tokyo Bay Cruise.....................E3

Sleeping (p194)

45 Aman Tokyo...........................C3
46 Grids Akihabara......................F1
47 Hoshinoya Tokyo......................C2
48 Palace Hotel Tokyo...................C3
   Peninsula Tokyo....................(see 32)
49 Wise Owl Hostels Tokyo...............E5
50 Yaesu Terminal Hotel.................D4

Information

51 JNTO Tourist Information
   Center..............................C5
52 JR East Travel Service Center........D4
53 Tokyo Tourist Information
   Center..............................C5

GINZA & TSUKIJI

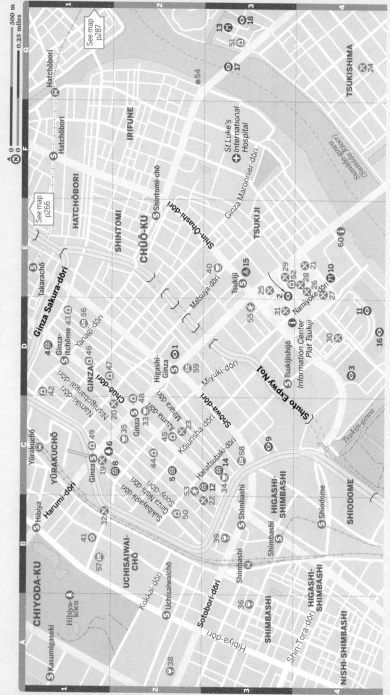

See map p287
See map p266

500 m
0.25 miles

Hatchōbori
Hatchōbori
Hatchōbori

TSUKISHIMA

IRIFUNE

St Luke's International Hospital

HATCHŌBORI

SHINTOMI

CHŪŌ-KU

Shintomi-chō

Shin-Ōhashi-dōri

Ginza Maronnier-dōri

TSUKIJI

Sumida-gawa (Sumida River)

Takarachō

Ginza Sakura-dōri

Ginza-Itchōme

Yanagi-dōri

Matsuya-dōri

Tsukiji

GINZA

Ginza-Itchōme

Higashi-Ginza

Miyuki-dōri

Tsukijishijō

Information Center Plat Tsukiji

YŪRAKUCHŌ

Namiki-dōri

Nishigobangai-dōri

Chūō-dōri

Namiyoke-dōri

Ginza

Ginza

Azuma-dōri

Minara-dōri

Shōwa-dōri

Shuto Expwy No1

Tsukiji-gawa

Yūrakuchō

Ginza

Harumi-dōri

Sukibayashi-dōri

Ginza Nishi-dōri

Sony-dōri

Kōjunsha-dōri

Hanatsubaki-dōri

HIGASHI-SHIMBASHI

SHIODOME

Hibiya

Shimbashi

Shimbashi

Shimbashi

Shiodome

CHIYODA-KU

Kasumigaseki

UCHISAIWAI-CHŌ

Uchisaiwaichō

Hibiya-kōen

Kokkai-dōri

Hibiya-dōri

Sotobori-dōri

Shin-Tora-dōri

HIGASHI-SHIMBASHI

SHIMBASHI

NISHI-SHIMBASHI

GINZA & TSUKIJI

◎ Top Sights (p67)
1 Kabukiza Theatre.....................D2
2 Tsukiji Outer Market..............E3

◎ Sights (p68)
3 Fruit & Vegetable Auctions......D4
4 Gallery Koyanagi....................D1
5 Ginza Graphic Gallery.............C2
6 Ginza Sony Park......................C1
7 Hama-rikyū Onshi-teien........C5
8 METoA Ginza..........................C2
9 Nakagin Capsule Tower...........C3
10 Namiyoke-jinja.....................E4
11 Seafood Intermediate
   Wholesalers' Area...............D4
12 Shiseido Gallery....................C3
13 Sumiyoshi-jinja.....................G3
14 Tokyo Gallery + BTAP............C3
15 Tsukiji Hongwan-ji.................E3
16 Tsukiji Market.......................D4
17 Tsukuda Ohashi.....................G3
18 Tsukudako-bashi....................G3

✕ Eating (p69)
19 Apollo.....................................C1
20 Kagari......................................C2
21 Kimagure-ya..........................E4
22 Kyūbey.....................................B3
23 Maru.......................................C2
24 Monja Kondō...........................G4
Rose Bakery.....................(see 44)
25 Sanokiya.................................E3
26 Sushikuni...............................E4
27 Trattoria Tsukiji
   Paradiso!..............................E4
28 Tsukiji Uogashi......................E4
29 Tsukugon................................E3
30 Uogashi-yokocho...................D4
31 Yamachō.................................D3
32 Yūrakuchō Sanchoku
   Inshokugai...........................B1

◐ Drinking & Nightlife (p71)
33 Bistro Marx............................D4
34 Cafe de l'Ambre....................G3
35 Cha Ginza..............................C2
Jugetsudo..........................(see 1)
36 Kagaya....................................A3
37 Nakajima no Ochaya.............C5
38 Sake Plaza..............................A2
39 Town House Tokyo.................B3
40 Turret Coffee..........................E3

◎ Entertainment (p71)
41 Tokyo Takarazuka
   Theatre.................................B1

◐ Shopping (p74)
42 Akomeya.................................D1
43 Antique Mall Ginza...............D1
44 Dover Street Market
   Ginza....................................C2
45 Ginza Six................................C2
46 Itoya......................................D1
47 Matsuya..................................D1
48 Mitsukoshi.............................C2
49 Sanrioworld Ginza.................C1

50 Takumi....................................B2
51 Tenyasu Honten.....................G3
52 Tsukiji Hitachiya....................E3
Uniqlo...............................(see 44)

◎ Sports & Activities (p75)
53 Komparu-yu............................C2
54 Tokyo Cooking Studio............G2
Tokyo Sushi Academy.....(see 55)
55 Tsukiji Market Information
   Centre...................................D3

◎ Sleeping (p194)
56 Daiwa Roynet Hotel Ginza.....D1
57 Imperial Hotel........................B1
58 Mitsui Garden Hotel Ginza
   Premier.................................C3
59 Prime Pod Ginza Tokyo..........D2

◎ Information
60 Fish Information Center..........E4

MINATO-KU
SHIBA-KŌEN
KŌTŌ-KU
KACHIDOKI
Kaigan-dōri
Harumi-dōri
Kiyosumi-dōri
Hama-rikyū Onshi-teien
Shiori-no-ike
Hato Bus Tours (300m)
Ⓢ Kachidoki
See map p270

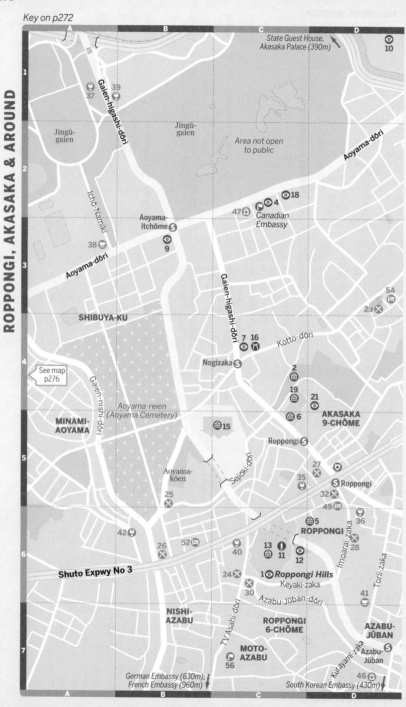

ROPPONGI, AKASAKA & AROUND

National Theatre
(100m)

See map
p266

20

Nagatachō Nagatachō

Akasaka-mitsuke

Sakurada-
boriMoat

Kokkaimae
Garden
(Western Style) Kokkai-
gijidōmae

NAGATACHŌ

National
Diet

Kokkaimae
Garden
(Japanese Style) CHIYODA-KU

8

Kasumigaseki

50

Akasaka

53

Tameike-
sannō Roppongi-dōri KASUMIGASEKI

Kokkai-dōri

See map
p268

AKASAKA

Tamachi-dōri

Sotobori-dōri

Toranomon

51

US Embassy

TORANOMON

44

ARK
HILLS

14

Atago-dōri

43 Toranomon
Hills

Shin-Tora-dōri

3

NISHI-
SHIMBASHI

Roppongi-
itchōme

Shuto Expwy No 2

Kamiyachō

57

45

Onarimon

AZABUDAI

58

SHIBA-
KŌEN

22

MINATO-KU

Hibiya-dōri

Sakurada-dōri

59

23

31

34

HIGASHI-
AZABU

33

Shiba-
kōen

17

48

Australian
Embassy (470m)

55

Japan Automobile
Federation (300m)

Hitotsugi-dōri

ROPPONGI, AKASAKA & AROUND *Map on p270*

◎ **Top Sights** **(p78)**
1 Roppongi Hills C6

◎ **Sights** **(p79)**
2 21_21 Design Sight....................................C4
3 Atago-jinja...G5
4 Canadian Embassy Stone Garden............C2
5 Complex 665 ....D6
6 Fujifilm Square..C5
7 General Nogi's Residence..........................C4
8 Hie-jinja E2
9 Honda Welcome Plaza Aoyama...............B3
10 Hotel New Ōtani Gardens D1
11 Maman Spider Sculpture...........................C6
12 Mohri Garden C6
13 Mori Art Museum......................................C6
14 Musée Tomo..F4
15 National Art Center Tokyo........................C5
16 Nogi-jinja..C4
17 Sangedatsumon..H7
18 Sōgetsu Kaikan..C2
19 Suntory Museum of Art C4
Tokyo City View ....(see 13)
20 Tokyo Garden Terrace.................................E1
21 Tokyo Midtown..D4
22 Tokyo Tower..G6
23 Zōjō-ji..G7

❌ **Eating** **(p81)**
24 Chinese Cafe 8...C6
25 Gogyō...B5
26 Gonpachi..B6
27 Honmura-An...D5
28 Jōmon...D6
29 Kikunoi...D3
30 Lauderdale..C6
31 Mornington Cresent F7
32 Sougo D5
33 Tofuya-Ukai...G7
34 Uramakiya...F7

◎ **Drinking & Nightlife** **(p85)**
35 Agave C5
36 Brewdog D6
37 Mori-no Beer Garden A1
38 Royal Garden Café A3
39 Sekirei..A1
40 SuperDeluxe..C6
41 The Garden...D6
42 These...B6
43 Toranomon Koffee.....................................G4

◎ **Entertainment** **(p86)**
44 Suntory Hall F4

🔒 **Shopping** **(p86)**
45 Axis Design.. E6
46 Blue & White..D7
47 Japan Traditional Crafts Aoyama
    Square...C2
    Souvenir from Tokyo ....(see 15)
48 Tolman Collection H7

◎ **Sports & Activities** **(p86)**
Tokyo Cook ....(see 32)

🛏 **Sleeping** **(p195)**
49 APA Hotel Roppongi..................................D5
50 First Cabin Akasaka E3
51 Hotel Mystays Premier Akasaka.............. E3
52 Hotel S...B6
53 Hotel the M Innsomnia Akasaka............... E3
54 Kaisu..D3
55 Zabutton Good Hostel...............................F7

ℹ **Information**
56 Chinese Embassy......................................C7
57 Netherlands Embassy F6
58 Russian Embassy F6
59 Tokyo Medical & Surgical Clinic..............G7

SHIBUYA & SHIMO-KITAZAWA

◎ Top Sights (p97)
1 Shibuya Crossing..........C2

◎ Sights (p98)
2 d47 Museum..................D3
3 Dōgenzaka......................B3
4 Hachikō Statue..............C3
5 Myth of Tomorrow........D3
6 Shibuya Center-gai.......C2
7 Spain-zaka....................C2
8 Toguri Museum of Art..A2

✕ Eating (p98)
d47 Shokudō..........(see 2)
9 Food Show....................C3
10 Gyūkatsu Motomura....D3
11 Kaikaya..........................A3
12 Matsukiya......................B3
13 Nagi Shokudō................C4
14 Sagatani........................B2

◻ Drinking & Nightlife (p99)
15 Beat Cafe B3
16 Contact..........................C3
17 Good Beer
     Faucets.......................B2
18 Karaoke-kan C2
19 Nonbei-yokochō............D2
20 Rhythm Cafe..................B1
21 Shidax Village C1
22 Tight..............................D2
23 Womb B3

◎ Entertainment (p104)
24 Club Quattro..................C2
25 Uplink.............................B1
26 WWW C2

◻ Shopping (p105)
27 Fake Tokyo.....................C2
28 Loft.................................C2

29 Shibuya 109...................C2
Shibuya Hikarie......(see 2)
30 Shibuya Publishing
     Booksellers................A1
31 Tokyu Hands..................C1

◎ Sports & Activities (p105)
32 Purikura no Mecca........C2

◻ Sleeping (p196)
33 Capsule & Sauna
     Century.......................B3
34 Hotel Mets Shibuya D4
35 Shibuya Granbell
     Hotel D4

◻ Information
36 New Zealand
     Embassy.....................A1

EBISU & MEGURO

See map p273

SAKURAGAOKA-CHŌ

DAIKANYAMA

Hachiman-dōri

SARUGAKU-CHŌ

26

28

Daikanyama Address

Kyū-Yamate-dōri

Daikanyama

4

EBISU-NISHI

25

2

5

29

22

14

Komazawa-dōri

Naka-Meguro

Higashi-Yama (450m);
Dormy Inn Express
Meguro Aobadai (650m)

KAMI-MEGURO

Komazawa-dōri

Yamate-dōri

NAKA-MEGURO

Komazawa-dōri

20

21

18

Ebisu

EBISU-MINAMI

27

Shibuya-gawa

Meiji-dōri

24

10

11

15

23

Ebisu

Atrè Ebisu
Mall

8

13

Komazawa-dōri

Ebisu
Prime Square
Plaza

Meiji-dōri

EBISU

19

12

Sky Walk

1

9

7

Platanus-dōri

MITA

MEGURO-KU

MEGURO

Chaya-zaka (Slope)

Yamate-dōri

Meguro-gawa

Meguro

17

KAMI-ŌSAKI

Claska
(450m)

Meguro-dōri

SHIMO-MEGURO

◉ **Sights** **(p89)**

1 Beer Museum Yebisu D4
2 Container A3
3 Institute for Nature Study F6
4 Kyū Asakura House A2
5 Meguro-gawa A3
6 Tokyo Metropolitan Teien Art Museum E5
7 TOP Museum D4
8 Yamatane Museum of Art D1
9 Yebisu Garden Place D4

✕ **Eating** **(p90)**

10 Afuri D2
   Bombay Bazar .... (see 28)
11 Ebisu-yokochō D2
12 Ippo D3
13 Megutama D1
14 Ōtaru A3
15 Ouca D2
16 Ta-im E2
17 Tonki D7
18 Yakiniku Champion C3

🍸 **Drinking & Nightlife** **(p93)**

19 Bar Martha D3
20 Bar Trench C2
21 Buri C2
22 Nakame Takkyū Lounge A3
23 Sarutahiko Coffee D2

✪ **Entertainment** **(p94)**

24 Liquid Room C2
25 Unit B3

🛍 **Shopping** **(p94)**

26 Daikanyama T-Site A2
27 Kapital C3
28 Okura A2
29 Vase A3

HARAJUKU & AOYAMA

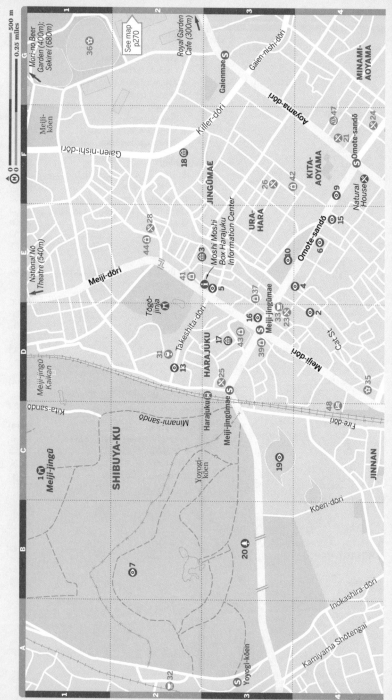

◎ Top Sights (p108)

1 Meiji-jingū C1

◎ Sights (p109)

2 Cat Street D4
3 Design Festa E2
4 Dior Omote-sandō E4
5 Kawaii Monster Cafe E3
6 Louis Vuitton Omote-sandō ... E4
7 Meiji-jingū Gyoen B2
8 Nezu Museum G5
9 Omote-sandō F4
10 Omotesandō Hills E3
11 Prada Aoyama F5
12 Spiral Building F5
13 Takeshita-dōri D2
14 Taro Okamoto Memorial
    Museum G5
15 Tod's Omote-sandō E4
16 Tōkyū Plaza D3
17 Ukiyo-e Ōta Memorial Museum
    of Art D3
18 Watari Museum of
    Contemporary Art F2
19 Yoyogi National Stadium....... C3
20 Yoyogi-kōen B3

◎ Eating (p111)

21 Commune 246 .... F4
22 Farmer's Market @UNU E5
23 Harajuku Gyōza-rō D3
24 Higashiya Man. F4
   Kinokuniya International
    Supermarket .... (see 34)
25 Kyūsyū Jangara. D3
26 Maisen. F3
27 Maru E5
28 Mominoki House. E2

Sakura-tei. .... (see 3)
29 Yanmo. F5

◎ Drinking & Nightlife (p113)

30 A to Z Cafe F5
31 Harajuku Taproom. D2
32 Little Nap Coffee
    Stand. A2
33 Montoak. D3
34 Two Rooms F5

◎ Entertainment (p113)

35 Crocodile. D4
36 Jingū Baseball
    Stadium. G1

◎ Shopping (p116)

37 6% Doki Doki. E3
38 Arts & Science. E2

Bedrock .... (see 10)
39 Chicago Thrift Store D3
40 Comme des Garçons F5
41 Dog. E2
42 Gallery Kawano F3
   KiddyLand. .... (see 33)
43 Laforet. D3
44 Musubi. E2
   On Sundays. .... (see 18)
   Raw Tokyo. .... (see 22)
45 Sou-Sou. F5

◎ Sports & Activities (p117)

46 Ohara School of Ikebana. F5
47 Shimizu-yu F4

◎ Sleeping (p197)

48 Dormy Inn Premium Shibuya
   Jingūmae. C4

SHŌTŌ

See map p273

Shibuya (130m)

Miyashita-kōen

Kottō-dōri

United Nations University

Aoyama Gakuin University

Oath (320m)

KOENJI

500 m
0.25 miles

NAKANO

NAKANO-KU

CHŪŌ

Higashi-Kōenji

Kannana-dōri

Waseda-dōri

Waseda-dōri

Kōshin-dōri

Azuma-dōri

Junjō Shōtengai

Kōenji

Kōnan-dōri

Nakano

KŌENJI-KITA

Naka-dōri

Pal Shōtengai

Etoile-dōri

KŌENJI-MINAMI

Ōkubo-dōri

Ōme-kaidō

Shin-Kōenji

Asagaya Pearl Centre (1.4km);
Ryokan Seikō (2km);
Harukiya (2.2km)

◎ Sights (p121)
1 Garter A2
2 Nakano Broadway E1
3 Nakano Sun Mall E2

✕ Eating (p122)
4 Daily Chiko E1
5 Koenji Gado-shita A2
6 Okajōki E1
7 Tensuke A2

▶ Drinking & Nightlife (p123)
8 Cocktail Shobō A2
Nantoka Bar .... (see 1)

✪ Entertainment (p124)
9 Ni Man Den Atsu C4

🛍 Shopping (p124)
Kita-Kore Building ...... (see 1)
10 Mandarake Complex E1
11 Sokkyō A2

🛏 Sleeping (p197)
12 BnA Hotel B2

◎ **Sights**	**(p121)**
1 Ghibli Museum	A4
2 Harmonica-yokochō	C2
3 Inokashira Benzaiten	B3
4 Inokashira-kōen	C3

⊗ **Eating**	**(p122)**
5 Manboshi	D4
6 Steak House Satou	C2
7 Tetchan	C2

◔ **Drinking & Nightlife**	**(p123)**
8 Blue Sky Coffee	C4
9 Uni Stand	A4

✿ **Entertainment**	**(p124)**
10 Star Pine's Cafe	D2

🛍 **Shopping**	**(p124)**
11 PukuPuku	B2

SHINJUKU & NORTHWEST TOKYO

WAKAMATSU-CHŌ

Wakamatsu-
kawada S

33

Northwest Tokyo

HIGASHI-
IKEBUKURO

Ōtome-dōri

38

31

40

Shuto Expwy No 5

Sunshine
60-dōri

TOSHIMA-KU

Minami-
Ikebukuro
Kōen

St Mary's
Cathedral
Tokyo (2km)

Meiji-dōri

200 m

0.1 miles

IKEBUKURO

Tokiwa-dōri

20

Bunka-
dōri

Ikebukuro S

Gekijo-dōri

Seibu
Ikebukuro
Metropolitan
Exit

Shinjuku
(see main map;
3km)

Sa Kashita-dōri

46

43

Azalea-dōri

Nishi-
Ikebukuro
Kōen

NISHI-
IKEBUKURO

Yasukuni-dōri

3

2

Shinjuku-
gyoenmae S

SHINJUKU-
NICHŌME

Higashi-
Shinjuku S

Meiji-dōri

Northwest Tokyo
(see inset; 3km);
Seibo International
Catholic Hospital (3.5km)

Meiji-dōri

Gyoen-dōri

21

29

23

22

ŌKUBO

Kuyakusho-dōri

42

35

1

30

8

47

Shinjuku-
sanchōme

S

Ruby (1.8km)

16

Shokuan-dōri

KABUKICHŌ

Bunka Senta-dōri

12

25

28

34

36

SHINJUKU

19

32

13

14

26

HYAKUNIN-
CHŌ

41

Kabukichō Ichiban-gai
Central Rd

17

44

Shinjuku S

Kōshū-kaidō

Seibu
Shinjuku S

15

Shinjuku S

10

11

39

48

KITA-
SHINJUKU

27

Shinjuku-
nishiguchi

S

Mode Gakuen
•Cocoon Tower

Shinjuku S

Nishi-
Shinjuku S

SHINJUKU-KU

22

24

45

NISHI-
SHINJUKU

Season Rd

5

Gijido-dōri

Tochōmae S

7

Ōme-Kaidō

Kita-dōri

Tochō-dōri

Tokyo Metropolitan
Government Building
Tourist Information Center

Kōen-dōri

Shinjuku
Chūō-
kōen

Ōme-Kaidō

Sights (p127)

1 Hanazono-jinja	E3
2 Ikebukuro Earthquake Hall	F3
3 Myōnichikan	G5
4 Place M	B3
5 Shinjuku I-Land	E5
6 Shinjuku-gyoen	A4
7 Tokyo Metropolitan Government Building	

Eating (p130)

8 Donjaca	E4
9 Kozue	A5
10 Lumine	C4
11 Mylord	C4
12 Nagi	D3
13 Nakajima	D4
14 Numazukō	D4
15 Omoide-yokochō	C3
16 Shin-chan	D1
17 Shinjuku Asia-yokochō	D2
18 Takashimaya Times Square	D5
19 Tsunahachi	D4
20 Yong Xiang Sheng Jian Guan	F2

Drinking & Nightlife (p132)

21 Aiiro Cafe	E4
22 Arty Farty	E4
23 Bar Goldfinger	E4
24 BenFiddich	B4
New York Bar	(see 9)
25 Ren	D2
26 Samurai	D4
27 Zoetrope	C2

Entertainment (p134)

28 Robot Restaurant	D3
29 Shinjuku Pit Inn	E4
30 Suehirotei	E3

Shopping (p135)

31 Acos	G2
32 Beams	D4
33 Bingoya	G1
34 Don Quijote	D3
35 Hanazono-jinja Flea Market	E3
36 Isetan	D3
37 Kinokuniya	D5
38 Mandarake Complex	G2
39 NEWoMan	C4
40 Pokemon Center Mega Tokyo	G3

Sports & Activities (p135)

41 Oslo Batting Center	D2
42 Thermae-yu	E2

Sleeping (p197)

43 Book and Bed	F2
44 Hotel Gracery Shinjuku	D2
45 Kadoya Hotel	B4
46 Kimi Ryokan	F2
Park Hyatt Tokyo	(see 9)
47 Tokyo Stay Shinjuku	E4

Transport

48 Shinjuku Bus Terminal	C4

KORAKUEN & AROUND

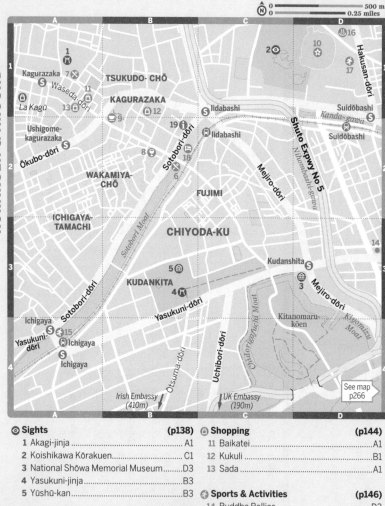

◎ **Sights** (p138)
1 Akagi-jinja A1
2 Koishikawa Kōrakuen...................... C1
3 National Shōwa Memorial Museum D3
4 Yasukuni-jinja B3
5 Yūshū-kan B3

✖ **Eating** (p139)
6 Canal Cafe B2
7 Kado A1

🍷 **Drinking & Nightlife** (p143)
8 Craft Beer Server Land B2
9 Mugimaru 2 .... B2

★ **Entertainment** (p144)
10 Tokyo Dome D1

🛍 **Shopping** (p144)
11 Baikatei A1
12 Kukuli B1
13 Sada A1

🏅 **Sports & Activities** (p146)
14 Buddha Bellies D3
15 Ichigaya Fish Centre A4
16 Spa LaQua D1
17 Tokyo Dome City
   Attractions D1

🛏 **Sleeping** (p198)
18 Tokyo Central Youth Hostel B2

ℹ **Information**
19 Tokyo Metro Lost & Found B2

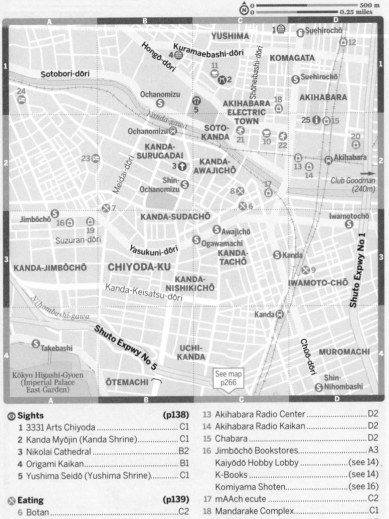

◉ **Sights** **(p138)**
1 3331 Arts Chiyoda C1
2 Kanda Myōjin (Kanda Shrine) C1
3 Nikolai Cathedral B2
4 Origami Kaikan B1
5 Yushima Seidō (Yushima Shrine) C1

⊗ **Eating** **(p139)**
6 Botan C2
7 Ethiopia B2
8 Kanda Yabu Soba C2
9 Kikanbō D3
Komaki Shokudō ....(see 15)

⊖ **Drinking & Nightlife** **(p143)**
10 @Home Cafe C2
Cafe Asan ....(see 12)
11 Imasa C1
N3331 ....(see 17)

🛍 **Shopping** **(p144)**
12 2k540 Aki-Oka Artisan D1

13 Akihabara Radio Center D2
14 Akihabara Radio Kaikan D2
15 Chabara D2
16 Jimbōchō Bookstores A3
Kaiyōdō Hobby Lobby ....(see 14)
K-Books ....(see 14)
Komiyama Shoten ....(see 16)
17 mAAch ecute C2
18 Mandarake Complex C1
19 Ohya Shobō A3
20 Yodobashi Akiba D2

⊙ **Sports & Activities** **(p146)**
21 Akiba Kart C2
22 Super Potato Retro-kan C2

🛏 **Sleeping** **(p198)**
23 Hilltop Hotel A2
24 Hotel Niwa Tokyo A1

ℹ **Information**
25 Akiba Info D2

UENO & YANESEN

0   500 m
0   0.25 miles

A   **B**   **C**   **D**

Rikugi-en (1.3km)

Nishi-Nippori

NISHI-NIPPORI

ARAKAWA-KU

Yanesen Tourist Information & Culture Center

Goten-zaka

Nippori

Ogubashi-dōri

27   20   40   2

Megurin Stop No 12

Sendagi   44   45   23

SENDAGI

Yanaka-reien

Ōtakebashi-dōri

NEGISHI

39

Sansaki-zaka

38

Sakura-dōri

21

Toco (400m)

29

31

YANAKA

42

Kototoi-dōri

Hebi-michi

Megurin Stop No 9   34

46

13   16

37

3

32

Uguisudani

Kanei-ji

33

12   28

NEZU

5

7

1 **Tokyo National Museum**

Shinobazu-dōri

26   24

Nezu   41

IKE-NO-HATA

4

8

Ueno-kōen

18

10

11   43

Megurin Stop No 2

17

19

Gojōten-jinja

35

UENO

Ueno

25

6

Tokyo University (Tokyo Daigaku)

HONGŌ

Bōto-ike

Benten-dō

Saigō Takamori Statue

Ueno

Keisei Ueno

14

Shinobazu-ike

15

9

Kyū Iwasaki-teien

Nakamachi-dōri

36

HIGASHI-UENO

Kingyozaka (300m); Hōmeikan (660m)

Yushima

Ueno-okachimachi

Nako-okachimachi

22   30

Ueno-hirokōji

Ueno-okachimachi

Okachimachi

Kasuga-dōri

UENO & YANESEN

◉ **Top Sights** (p149)
1 Tokyo National Museum........................D4

◉ **Sights** (p153)
2 Asakura Museum of Sculpture, Taitō......B2
3 Enju-ji..B4
4 Gallery of Hōryū-ji Treasures....................C4
5 Heiseikan..D4
6 Kiyōmizu Kannon-dō...........................C6
7 Kuroda Memorial Hall..........................C4
8 Kuro-mon..C4
9 Kyū Iwasaki-teien...............................B7
10 National Museum of Nature & Science...D5
11 National Museum of Western Art............D5
12 Nezu-jinja...A4
13 SCAI the Bathhouse............................B3
14 Shinobazu-ike...................................C6
15 Shitamachi Museum............................C6
16 Shitamachi Museum Annex....................C3
17 Ueno Tōshō-gū...................................C5
18 Ueno Zoo..C5
19 Ueno-kōen...C5
20 Yanaka Ginza.....................................B2
21 Yanaka-reien.....................................C3
22 Yushima Tenjin...................................B7

◉ **Eating** (p155)
23 Hagiso...B2
24 Hantei..B5
25 Innsyoutei...C6

26 Kamachiku...B4
27 Nagomi...B2
28 Nezu no Taiyaki...................................A4
29 Sasa-no-Yuki......................................D3
30 Shinsuke..B7

◉ **Drinking & Nightlife** (p157)
31 Bousingot..A3
32 Kayaba Coffee....................................B4
33 Torindō..C4
34 Yanaka Beer Hall.................................C3

◉ **Entertainment** (p157)
35 Tokyo Bunka Kaikan.............................C5

◉ **Shopping** (p158)
36 Ameya-yokochō...................................C7
37 Edokoro Allan West..............................B4
38 Isetatsu...A3
39 Shokichi..A3
40 Yanaka Matsunoya...............................B2

◉ **Sports & Activities** (p158)
41 Rokuryu Kōsen....................................B5
42 Tokyobike Rental Service.......................B3
43 Ueno Free Walking Tour.........................D5

◉ **Sleeping** (p199)
44 Annex Katsutarō Ryokan........................A2
45 Hanare..A2
46 Sawanoya Ryokan................................A4

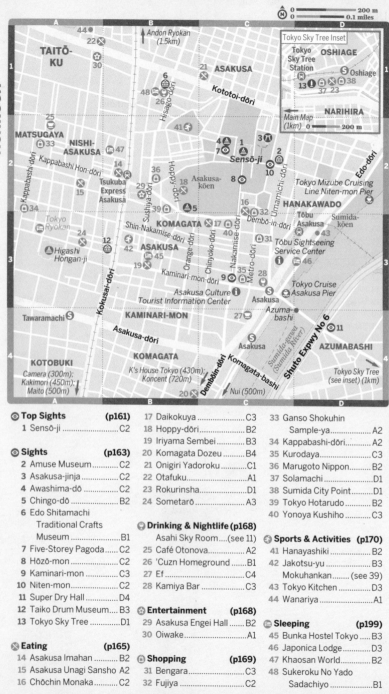

ASAKUSA

◎ Top Sights (p161)
1 Sensō-ji C2

◎ Sights (p163)
2 Amuse Museum C2
3 Asakusa-jinja C2
4 Awashima-dō C2
5 Chingo-dō B2
6 Edo Shitamachi
   Traditional Crafts
   Museum B1
7 Five-Storey Pagoda C2
8 Hōzō-mon C2
9 Kaminari-mon C3
10 Niten-mon C2
11 Super Dry Hall D4
12 Taiko Drum Museum B3
13 Tokyo Sky Tree D1

◎ Eating (p165)
14 Asakusa Imahan B2
15 Asakusa Unagi Sansho A2
16 Chōchin Monaka C2

17 Daikokuya C3
18 Hoppy-dōri B2
19 Iriyama Sembei B3
20 Komagata Dozeu B4
21 Onigiri Yadoroku C1
22 Otafuku A1
23 Rokurinsha D1
24 Sometarō A3

◎ Drinking & Nightlife (p168)
Asahi Sky Room ....(see 11)
25 Café Otonova................ A2
26 'Cuzn Homeground B1
27 Ef C4
28 Kamiya Bar C3

◎ Entertainment (p168)
29 Asakusa Engei Hall B2
30 Oiwake A1

◎ Shopping (p169)
31 Bengara C3
32 Fujiya C2

33 Ganso Shokuhin
   Sample-ya A2
34 Kappabashi-dōri A2
35 Kurodaya C3
36 Marugoto Nippon B2
37 Solamachi D1
38 Sumida City Point D1
39 Tokyo Hotarudo B2
40 Yonoya Kushiho C3

◎ Sports & Activities (p170)
41 Hanayashiki B2
42 Jakotsu-yu B3
   Mokuhankan........ (see 39)
43 Tokyo Kitchen D3
44 Wanariya....................... A1

◎ Sleeping (p199)
45 Bunka Hostel Tokyo B3
46 Japonica Lodge D3
47 Khaosan World............. B2
48 Sukeroku No Yado
   Sadachiyo B1